HUMAN RESOURCES LIBRARY
FROM WILEY LAW PUBLICATIONS

DRAFTING AND REVISING EMPLOYMENT POLICIES AND HANDBOOKS
SECOND EDITION
VOLUME 1

SUBSCRIPTION NOTICE

DRAFTING AND REVISING EMPLOYMENT POLICIES AND HANDBOOKS
SECOND EDITION
VOLUME 1

KURT H. DECKER

Partner
Stevens & Lee
Reading, Pennsylvania
Adjunct Professor
Widener University School of Law
Harrisburg, Pennsylvania
and
Graduate School of Industrial Relations
Saint Francis College
Loretto, Pennsylvania

Wiley Law Publications
JOHN WILEY & SONS, INC.
New York • Chichester • Brisbane • Toronto • Singapore

Library of Congress Cataloging-in-Publication Data

ISBN 0-471-04666-3 (v.1)
ISBN 0-471-04667-1 (v.2)
ISBN 0-471-04663-9 (set)

Printed in the United States of America

10 9 8 7 6 5 4 3 2 1

For Hilary, Christian, Allison,
and Martina with much love

K.H.D.

PREFACE

It is indisputable that today's employment relationship is becoming more complex for human resource administrators. One of the most rapidly evolving areas of employment law is individual employee rights. Prior to the 1980s, human resource administrators and employment law attorneys infrequently encountered claims concerning issues outside the collective bargaining relationship or areas regulated by federal and state fair employment practice statutes. However, as the 1990s begin, employees are asserting claims against their employers based on a variety of claims that arise out of the individual employment relationship. These employee claims relate to the erosion of at-will employment, binding commitments found in employment policies and handbooks, public policy violations, privacy intrusions, and related issues.

Individual employee rights litigation against employers is being predicated on a variety of legal theories involving tort and contractual claims. Claims are being based on defamation, invasion of privacy, false imprisonment, intentional infliction of emotional distress, negligent maintenance or disclosure of employment records, fraudulent misrepresentation, intentional interference with contractual relations, public policy, and breach of oral or written contracts, handbooks, and policies.

Because of the current focus on individual employee rights, employers, human resource administrators, and their attorneys must find new or revised alternatives for confronting problems arising out of the employment relationship. Using employment policies and handbooks is one way to delineate clearly the at-will employment relationship and to define employment terms, compensation, benefits, and other matters.

This book is designed to meet three needs: First, it brings together into one source the general legal principles for forming, drafting, and implementing employment policies and handbooks. Second, employment policies are examined in general and specialized terms, thereby providing an overall understanding of the drafting and liability issues that may potentially arise in their use. Third, because the book is intended to be theoretical as well as practical, it can be used by human resource administrators, attorneys, researchers, or students as a reference when dealing with the issues involving employment policies.

Chapter 1 serves as an overview of human resources law and the individual employee relationship. **Chapter 2** discusses human resources audits as a prelude to policy development and the pinpointing of potential legal problems. Drafting considerations for employment policy clauses, including introductory matters, compensation, benefits, leaves of absence, discipline, performance, layoffs, and general matters relating to employee data verification, records, medical concerns, information collection/distribution, outside employment, and so forth are discussed in **Chapters 3** through **13.** For each policy, examples are given and the pertinent legal principles and drafting considerations are reviewed. **Chapters 14** and **15** discuss the use of handbooks as a source for presenting employment policies to preserve the at-will employment relationship. Samples of complete handbooks for small, medium, and large employers are included in **Chapter 16.** These sample handbooks demonstrate how employment policies can be used in a given work situation. Problems relating to employee discipline and how human resource administrators should apply discipline to minimize liability are examined in **Chapter 17. Chapters 18** and **19** discuss for human resource administrators aspects of employment litigation and the liabilities that may arise along with the remedies that employees may seek.

The procedures, policies, and forms presented in this book should be used only as guidelines. Each one should be considered in relation to the particular factual situation. When compensation and benefit issues are involved, the policy should be reviewed by a tax or benefit consultant versed in these areas. This book is not intended to provide or be a substitute for any required tax or benefit evaluation.

As this book nears completion, it becomes ever more apparent that this undertaking will never be truly finished. The new challenges of the individual employment relationship have made this feeling a reality. Perhaps it was best said by the late historian, Barbara W. Tuchman, in her introduction to *The Proud Tower:*

> I realize that what follows offers no overall conclusion. . . . I also know that what follows is far from the whole picture. It is not false modesty which prompts me to say so but simply an acute awareness of what I have not included. The faces and voices of all that I have left out crowd around me as I reach the end.

This is, then not the final word on drafting employment policies. As new techniques, policies, procedures, and statutes challenge individual employee rights for human resource administrators, periodic updates will be needed to revise this book and to retain its usefulness.

Reading, Pennsylvania   KURT H. DECKER
February 1994

ACKNOWLEDGMENTS

Little in life is a solitary undertaking. Much is a culmination of other people's thoughts and efforts. The material in this book is no different. Many individuals either provided opportunities or shared their knowledge. Even though those who have made specific and concrete contributions can be named, others who have participated in shaping my understanding of employment law cannot all be recognized. However, H. Thomas Felix II, Esq. of Montgomery, McCracker, Walker & Rhoads, Philadelphia, Pennsylvania cannot be overlooked. Throughout the years he has served as a mentor, friend, and as the individual who has most encouraged my employment research, writing, and teaching interests. In addition, he served as the coauthor for two other books that we prepared, namely *Drafting and Revising Employment Contracts* (John Wiley & Sons, Inc. 1991) and *Drafting and Revising Employment Handbooks* (John Wiley & Sons, Inc. 1991). My good friend, Arbitrator John Skonier of Norristown, Pennsylvania, must also be mentioned. Throughout the years he has always been there to offer the necessary encouragement to begin or complete a project.

Among those who provided specific materials for this book are Robert B. Coulson, President of the American Arbitration Association, for kindly permitting the use and reproduction of various materials found throughout this book. James Troebliger, manager of human resources of GPU Nuclear Corp. at Three Mile Island in Middletown, Pennsylvania, who provided input regarding alcohol and drug abuse policies. Gary D. Kraft, director of corporate services for Spotts, Stevens & McCoy in Reading, Pennsylvania, and Mark R. O'Neill, former manager of personnel at Morgan Corp. in Morgantown, Pennsylvania and currently director of human resources for Bridon American in Wilkes Barre, Pennsylvania for their access to and reproduction of materials dealing with employment handbooks. Joseph E. Herman, Esq., of Seyfarth, Shaw, Fairweather & Geraldson's Los Angeles, California office permitted adaptation of his employee relations audit materials. Mary E. Pivec, Esq., of Frank, Bernstein, Conaway & Goldman in Baltimore, Maryland, permitted adaptation of her materials regarding temporary United States visas suitable for employment.

Others who should be mentioned are Dr. Robert D. Lee, Jr. in giving hope that a future existed after military service, Dr. William E. Caldwell for nurturing my interest in employment law, Professor Paul H. Sanders for instilling the recognition of conflict resolution's paramount importance in employment law, Professor Robert N. Covington who provided the initial opportunities to research individual employee rights issues while at law school, Dr. Harry Kershen for affording the first opportunity to appear in print and supporting the idea for *The Journal of*

Individual Employment Rights, Dr. Edwin M. Wagner for encouraging the sharing of knowledge through teaching, and Dean John Gedid for recognizing the importance of the developing area of individual employee rights to the law school curriculum.

Finally, I am deeply appreciative to all of the individuals at Wiley Law for supporting my projects throughout the years. Among the more significant have been Kathy Osborn and Carol Gross, who never overlooked the importance of this developing area of the law to human resource administrators and attorneys.

K.H.D.

HOW TO USE THIS BOOK

This book, with its accompanying policies and forms, synthesizes into legal principles and samples the basic principles for drafting employment policies and handbooks for human resource administrators and attorneys. After the general principles have been reviewed regarding human resources law and the individual employment relationship, **Chapters 3** through **13** should be consulted in drafting a specific employment policy or handbook. These chapters provide sample policies along with sample handbook forms. Each policy is reviewed by discussing the applicable legal principles and drafting considerations.

These sample policies and handbook forms should be considered only guidelines and should not be adopted verbatim or applied without careful evaluation. Each should be considered in light of the particular factual situation, including a required tax or benefit analysis where compensation or benefit issues are involved.

Certain aspects of employment policies relate directly to at-will employment and employee privacy concerns. Where these topics are discussed or referenced, the texts by K. Decker, *Employee Privacy Law and Practice* (John Wiley & Sons, Inc. 1987); K. Decker, *Employee Privacy Forms and Procedures* (John Wiley & Sons, Inc. 1988); and H. Perritt, Jr., *Employee Dismissal Law and Practice* (John Wiley & Sons, Inc. 3d ed. 1991), should be consulted for more information. This book is intended to be used in conjunction with these more detailed reference sources.

Because employment policies encompass a broad spectrum of legal principles, no peripheral area should be overlooked. For example, tax and benefit considerations are often relevant in drafting these policies when compensation and benefit questions are present, which should not be ignored. A qualified tax or benefit consultant should be used for further review.

As this area continues to develop, new concepts will arise. These will be discussed in this book's future supplements to maintain a current understanding of this increasingly significant employment law area.

ABOUT THE AUTHOR

Kurt H. Decker is a partner with the law firm of Stevens & Lee in Allentown, Harrisburg, Lancaster, Reading, and Valley Forge, Pennsylvania. He received a B.A. degree from Thiel College, an M.P.A. from the Pennsylvania State University, his J.D. from the School of Law at Vanderbilt University, and an L.L.M. in Labor Law from the School of Law at Temple University. He serves as an adjunct assistant professor with the Widener University School of Law in Harrisburg, Pennsylvania, and as an adjunct professor with the Graduate School of Industrial Relations at Saint Francis College in Loretto, Pennsylvania. Mr. Decker is the author of numerous books and articles on employment law, including the following books published by John Wiley & Sons, Inc.: *Employee Privacy Law and Practice* (1987), *Employee Privacy Forms and Procedures* (1988), *A Manager's Guide to Employee Privacy Law, Procedures, and Policies* (1989), *Drafting and Revising Employment Contracts* (1991) with H. Thomas Felix II, *Drafting and Revising Employment Handbooks* (1991) with H. Thomas Felix II, and *Covenants Not to Compete* (1993). He is the co-editor of the *Journal of Individual Employment Rights*. Mr. Decker is a member of the American and Pennsylvania Bar Associations and their respective labor and employment law sections.

SUMMARY CONTENTS

DETAILED CONTENTS

CHAPTER 1

INTRODUCTION TO HUMAN RESOURCES LAW

§ 1.1 Introduction

§ 1.2 Employment Relationship

§ 1.3 Human Resources Law

§ 1.1 Introduction

It is only natural for employees to desire participation in determining the wages, hours, and terms and conditions that govern their employment. Historically, many employees relied on unionization and collective bargaining to achieve these objectives.[1] Today, however, employees themselves are able to assert these matters with their employer because of internal complaint procedures and litigation challenging employer decision making.[2] Human resources law is at the center of these developments.

Handbooks and employment policies are providing a means for employees to assert these rights.[3] Statements made in handbooks and employment policies may create binding commitments entitling employees to enforce these employer promises. For this reason, employers must take particular care in drafting and revising these documents to avoid unintended commitments. In understanding

---

[1] *See* The Developing Labor Law 3-48 (I.P. Hardin 3d ed. 1992) [hereinafter Hardin]. In 1989, the proportion of United States employees belonging to a union was 16.4 percent of all wage and salary employees, according to the Bureau of Labor Statistics. *See* Analysis/News and Background Information, 133 L.R.R.M. (BNA) 209 (Feb. 19, 1990).

[2] *See generally* K. Decker, Employee Privacy Law and Practice (John Wiley & Sons, Inc. 1987) [hereinafter Decker, Privacy Law]; *see also* K. Decker, Employee Privacy Forms and Procedures (John Wiley & Sons, Inc. 1988); K. Decker & H.T. Felix II, Drafting and Revising Employment Contracts (John Wiley & Sons, Inc. 1991) [hereinafter Decker, Contracts]; K. Decker & H.T. Felix II, Drafting and Revising Employment Handbooks (John Wiley & Sons, Inc. 1991) [hereinafter Decker, Handbooks].

[3] *See generally* Decker, Handbooks.

1

handbooks and employment policies, it is important to review the employment relationship's legal regulation.

Legal regulation of the employment relationship is accomplished in a variety of ways. The most common methods involve individual employment contracts, collective bargaining agreements, and governmental regulation. This chapter introduces these general principles of the employment relationship.

§ 1.2   Employment Relationship

The relationship between employee and employer constitutes the basis of our economic and social structures and affects most people over the greater part of their lives. People increasingly depend on others to offer them the means to produce their daily income.

Employment is the means by which the goods and services that are needed and desired by society are provided. Through employment's economic rewards, individuals obtain assets for current and future gratifications. For many, the economic meaning of employment is paramount for their life. Absent employment, they could not provide the sustenance needed for themselves and their families.

Employment also serves social purposes. The workplace has always been a place to meet people, converse, and form friendships. Likewise, the type of employment undertaken may confer social status on the employee and his or her family.

Employers invest heavily in their employees. They spend considerable money selecting and training them. Employers are eager to retain good employees so they can capitalize on their skills and knowledge to operate a profitable business.

Employment loss can be a considerable hardship with disastrous consequences. The employment relationship has become so fundamental to society[4] that, outside of marriage, no other relationship preoccupies daily affairs so completely. The three great relationships in private life are:

1. Master and servant
2. Husband and wife and
3. Parent and child.[5]

---

[4] One commentator stated that:

> We have become a nation of employees. We are dependent upon others for our means of livelihood, and most of our people have become completely dependent upon wages. If they lose their jobs they lose every resource, except for the relief supplied by the various forms of social security. Such dependence of the mass of the people upon others for all of their income is something new in the world. *For our generation, the substance of life is in another man's hands.*

F. Tannenbaum, A Philosophy of Labor 9 (1951) (emphasis in original).

[5] *See* W. Blackstone, Commentaries 410 (1765).

Through multifaceted human resource functions, wage and benefit programs, and government regulation, the employment relationship has become complex. Historically, the employment relationship has not limited overall an employer's unfair, adverse, or damaging practices.[6] It generally "denies any right to the employee who is arbitrarily treated . . . without a union or a contract."[7] Absent a statutory or contractual restriction, an employee or employer can generally terminate the employment relationship at any time, for any or no reason, with or without notice, making it *at-will employment.*[8]

§ 1.3 Human Resources Law

Human resources law is a maze of federal and state common-law doctrines, statutes, contract-established rules, judicial pronouncements, and administrative agency findings affecting wages, hours, and terms and conditions of employment. Symmetry and clearly discernible legal patterns are not often recognizable. Even within a narrow area, human resources law can vary considerably, depending upon whether an administrative agency or a court is involved.[9] Statutes and court

---

[6] *See* H. Perritt, Jr., Employee Dismissal Law and Practice ch. 1 (John Wiley & Sons, 3d ed. 1992) [hereinafter Perritt, Dismissal Law].

[7] Bok, *Discussion of Current Confrontations in Labor Law,* Proceedings of the Nineteenth Annual Winter Meeting, Industrial Relations Research Association 104 (1966).

[8] Restatement (Second) of Agency § 442 (1958) refers to at-will employment as follows:

> Unless otherwise agreed, mutual promises by principal and agent to employ and to serve create obligations to employ and to serve which are terminable upon notice by either party; if neither party terminates the employment, it may terminate by lapse of time or by supervening events.

[9] For example, under the National Labor Relations Act (NLRA), the National Labor Relations Board's (NLRB's) decisions at times do not follow the courts regarding what are the applicable employment law principles. 29 U.S.C. §§ 151–169 (1988). This nonacquiescence of the NLRB with court decisions has occurred over: (1) whether the NLRB should initially defer its review procedures in unfair labor practice cases for resolution under the collective bargaining agreement's grievance arbitration procedure; and (2) who constitutes a "successor" employer. *See* Hardin at 761–850, 1008–1084; Maranville, *Nonacquiescence: Outlaw Agencies, Imperial Courts, and the Perils of Pluralism,* 39 Vand. L. Rev. 471 (1986); *see also* Bakaly, Jr. & Bryan, *Survival of the Bargaining Agreement: The Effect of Burns,* 27 Vand. L. Rev. 1 (1974); Nash, Wilder, Jr. & Banov, *The Development of the Collyer Deferral Doctrine,* 27 Vand. L. Rev. 23 (1974). Most courts have not taken kindly to the disrespect for authority reflected in an agency's refusal to follow court decisions. *See* NLRB v. Blackstone Co., 685 F.2d 102, 106 n.5 (3d Cir. 1982) ("We consider the Board's contrary instructions to its administrative law judges to be completely improper and reflective of a bureaucratic arrogance which will not be tolerated"). Similar nonacquiescence by other administrative agencies has occurred under the Occupational Safety and Health Act (OSHA) of 1970 and the Social Security Act (SSA). *See, e.g.,* Jones & Laughlin Steel Corp. v. Marshall, 626 F.2d 32 (3d Cir. 1980) (OSHA); Holden v. Heckler, 584 F. Supp. 463 (N.D. Ohio 1984) (SSA).

decisions reflect this shifting conflict balance between employee and employer,[10] making human resources law[11] one of the most political of legal areas.[12]

Laws affecting human resources provide a mechanism to deal with the conflict that is inherent in the employee/employer relationship. Conflict disputes involve not only wages, hours, and employment conditions but also power contests within and between various groups and personalities. These may include confrontations among employees, union officials, and employers. The National Labor Relations Act's (NLRA) protection of "employee rights" providing the "full freedom of association, self-organization, and designation of representatives . . . for . . . negotiating the terms and conditions of their employment or other mutual aid or protection" statutorily identifies potential conflict among employee, union, and employer.[13] However, the NLRA works toward restraining and defusing this employment conflict by transferring it from physical violence and economic coercion

---

[10] For discussion of the labor movement within the United States, *see* Hardin at 3–68. The NLRA's adoption in 1935 illustrates the shifting conflict balance between employee and employer. 29 U.S.C. §§ 151–169 (1988). Prior to the NLRA's adoption, three major themes illustrated this employee, union, and employer conflict in that:

1. The case law demonstrated that the courts were not institutionally capable of formulating or implementing a uniform, cohesive, and workable labor policy

2. The course of legislative and judicial action revealed increasing awareness that the role of organized labor presented a question of national proportions that no state was capable of answering definitively on an individual basis

3. There was the development of two mutually incompatible national policies towards organized labor: one regarding it as creating market restraints inimical to the national economy, and the other regarding it as necessary to a regime of industrial peace based upon a balanced bargaining relationship between employers wielding the combined power of incorporated capital wealth and unions wielding the power of organized labor.

Hardin at 3.

[11] The conflict development that resulted in the NLRA's adoption is similar to what is currently occurring in the at-will employment area, that is, either the employee or employer can terminate the employment relationship at any time, for any or no reason, with or without notice. *See generally* Perritt, Dismissal Law at chs. 1, 9. Courts are indicating that they are not institutionally capable of formulating or implementing a workable policy to address the needs of employees and employers involved in the at-will employment relationship. *See, e.g.,* Veno v. Meredith, 357 Pa. Super. 85, 99 n.3, 515 A.2d 571, 579 n.3 (1986); Martin v. Capital Cities Media, Inc., 354 Pa. Super. 199, 221, 511 A.2d 830, 841 (1986); Darlington v. General Elec., 350 Pa. Super. 183, 191, 504 A.2d 306, 309 (1986); *see also* Decker, *At-Will Employment in Pennsylvania after "Banas" and "Darlington": New Concerns for a Legislative Solution,* 32 Vill. L. Rev. 101 (1987); Decker, *Federal Regulation of At-Will Employment,* 61 U. Det. J. Urban L. 351 (1984); Decker, *At-Will Employment in Pennsylvania—A Proposal for its Abolition and Statutory Regulation,* 87 Dick. L. Rev. 477 (1983); Decker, *At-Will Employment: A Proposal for its Statutory Regulation,* 1 Hofstra Lab. L. F. 187 (1983).

[12] *See* Huge & McCarthy, *Collective Bargaining in the 1980s—Comments and Observations,* 1 Hofstra Lab. L. F. 23 (1983).

[13] 29 U.S.C. § 157 (1988).

into collective bargaining.[14] Employment law is concerned with "rules of the game," in which law and economics constantly confront society's ethical and moral problems. This is true in the individual employment relationship as well as in the collective bargaining agreement's negotiation and administration.

Despite employment's importance to the quality of an employee's economic existence, social being, self-worth, and lifestyle, the job security of about two out of every three employees in the United States depends almost entirely on their employer's continued goodwill.[15] These employees are more commonly known as *at-will employees.* In general, at-will employees may be terminated at their employer's discretion and the employees have the reciprocal right to leave their employment at any time.[16]

Employee and employer rights within the United States trace their beginnings to England's Statute of Labourers.[17] The Statute of Labourers was enacted in response to the labor shortages that resulted from the mid-fourteenth century's Black Plague. It provided that a "general hiring" of labor for an unfixed term was presumed to be for a year and that a "master" could not "put away his servant" except for "reasonable cause."[18] After its repeal, English courts continued to apply the statute's intent by presuming that a "general hiring" was to serve as an employment contract for one year.[19] If the employment continued for longer than one year, it could be terminated only at the end of an additional year.[20]

The American at-will employment doctrine has been viewed both as a departure from and as part of this English heritage. Early American courts adopted the English approach.[21] In the 1850s, however, American courts began developing their own version of what would become today's at-will employment. For example, when an employee agreed to perform work at daily wages, but was never

---

[14] Sanders, *Some Comments on Labor Dispute Settlement Processes,* 27 Vand. L. Rev. 5, 12–13 (1974).

[15] Note, *Protecting At-Will Employees Against Wrongful Discharge: The Duty to Terminate Only in Good Faith,* 93 Harv. L. Rev. 1816 (1980) (citing U.S. Bureau of the Census, Department of Commerce, Statistical Abstract of the United States (1979); the government's statistics show about 22 percent of employees are unionized, about 15 percent are federal or state employees, and the remaining 63 percent are hired for an indefinite time period that is generally terminable at the employer's discretion).

[16] An in-depth analysis of the at-will employment relationship and its subsequent modification is beyond this text's scope. For further information, *see generally* Decker, Privacy Law; Perritt, Dismissal Law.

[17] W. Blackstone, Commentaries 425 (1765).

[18] *Id.* at 425–26.

[19] Annot., *Duration of Contract of Hiring Which Specified No Term, but Fixes Compensation at a Certain Amount Per Day, Week, Month, or Year,* 11 A.L.R. 469 (1921); *see generally* Perritt, Dismissal Law.

[20] Beeston v. Collyer, 130 Eng. Rep. 786 (C.P. 1827).

[21] P. Selznick, Law, Society, and Industrial Justice 133 (1969); *see, e.g.,* Adams v. Fitzpatrick, 125 N.Y. 124, 26 N.E. 143 (1891); Davis v. Groton, 16 N.Y. 255 (1857); Bascom v. Shillito, 37 Ohio St. 431 (1881).

called to duty, he sued and won a jury verdict; however, on appeal the verdict was set aside because the employment's term was no longer than one day, with the court stating that:

> An infirmity in this contract is, that it fixed no time during which the plaintiff's services should be rendered to the defendant. Suppose the plaintiff had gone to Hallowell, and tendered his services, there was nothing to prevent the defendant from discharging him at the end of a single day. In such a contract there is no value.[22]

Another court ruled against a barkeeper who had been terminated and ejected from his room by noting that he was not hired for any definite period.[23] Likewise, a newspaper deliverer's contract for an indefinite period could be terminated "at pleasure" by the employer.[24]

In 1871, the Wisconsin Supreme Court ruled in a breach of contract action that "[e]ither party, however, was at liberty to terminate the service at any time, no definite period for which the service was to continue having been agreed upon."[25] An Illinois court reached the same result in 1874 when an employee was denied recovery because the contract "contain[ed] no undertaking . . . for a definite period."[26]

In 1877, H.G. Wood's treatise on the master-servant relationship articulated what became America's at-will employment doctrine when he wrote that:

> With us the rule is inflexible that a general or indefinite hiring is prima facie a hiring at will, and if the servant seeks to make it out a yearly hiring, the burden is upon him to establish it by proof. A hiring at so much a day, week, month, or year, no time being specified, is an indefinite hiring, and no presumption attaches that it was for a day even, but only at the rate fixed for whatever time the party may serve.[27]

Almost every state eventually accepted Wood's formulation of the at-will employment doctrine. The Maryland Court of Appeals termed Wood an authority of great repute when it adopted the at-will employment doctrine.[28] New York's highest court noted that the at-will doctrine was correctly stated by Mr. Wood.[29]

Wood's at-will employment analysis was simple and consistent. It settled conflict among the courts and spared courts from undertaking complicated factual

---

[22] Blaisdell v. Lewis, 32 Me. 515 (1851).

[23] De Brier v. Minturn, 1 Cal. 450 (1851).

[24] Hathaway v. Bennett, 10 N.Y. 108 (1854).

[25] Prentiss v. Ledyard, 28 Wis. 131 (1871).

[26] Orr v. Ward, 73 Ill. 318 (1874).

[27] H. Wood, Master and Servant § 134 (3d ed. 1886).

[28] McCullough Iron Co. v. Carpenter, 67 Md. 554, 11 A.2d 176 (1887).

[29] Martin v. New York Life Ins. Co., 148 N.Y. 117, 42 N.E. 416 (1895).

analyses of employment cases. Although "Wood's Rule" has today been persuasively challenged and in certain instances negated, it has become the primary basis for what remains of at-will employment in this country.[30]

American courts probably accepted Wood's analysis to facilitate economic development during the industrial revolution by promoting the prevalent ideology of laissez-faire and freedom of contract.[31] Within this economic framework, Wood's Rule seemed equitable. It provided the employer the flexibility to control the workplace through the unchallengeable power to terminate the employment relationship. In turn, the employee retained the freedom to resign for more favorable employment or if working conditions became intolerable. Even today, the at-will employment relationship remains codified in several jurisdictions.[32]

In the early part of this century, the United States Supreme Court even endorsed the at-will employment doctrine as follows:

> In the absence, however, of a valid contract between the parties controlling their conduct towards each other and fixing a period of service, it cannot be, we repeat, that an employer is under any legal obligation, against his will, to retain an employee in his personal service any more than an employee can be compelled, against his will, to remain in the personal service of another . . . [The employee] was at liberty to quit the service without assigning any reason for his leaving. And the defendant was at liberty, in his discretion, to discharge [the employee] from service without giving any reason for so doing.[33]

Perhaps the most significant legal development affecting employment relations since 1970 has been the modification of at-will employment. Courts[34] and some

---

[30] *See generally* Decker, Privacy Law; Perritt, Dismissal Law.

[31] *See* Adair v. United States, 208 U.S. 161 (1908).

[32] *See, e.g.,* Cal. Lab. Code § 2922 (West 1971 & Supp. 1990); Ga. Code Ann. § 34-7-1 (1982); *see also* Prince III, *A Modest Proposal: The Statutory "No Cause" Alternative to Wrongful Discharge in California,* 24 San Diego L. Rev. 137 (1987).

[33] Adair v. United States, 208 U.S. 161, 175–76 (1908).

[34] *See, e.g.,* Tameny v. Atlantic Richfield Co., 27 Cal. 3d 167, 610 P.2d 1330, 164 Cal. Rptr. 839 (1980); Sheets v. Teddy's Frosted Foods, Inc., 179 Conn. 471, 427 A.2d 385 (1980); Jackson v. Minidoko Irrigation, 98 Idaho 330, 563 P.2d 54 (1977); Kelsay v. Motorola, Inc., 74 Ill. 2d 172, 384 N.E.2d 353 (1978); Frampton v. Central Ind. Gas Co., 260 Ind. 249, 297 N.E.2d 425 (1973); Murphy v. City of Topeka-Shawnee County Dep't of Labor Servs., 6 Kan. App. 2d 488, 630 P.2d 186 (1981); Adler v. American Standard Corp., 290 Md. 615, 432 A.2d 464 (1981); Siles v. Travenal Laboratories, Inc., 13 Mass. App. Ct. 354, 433 N.E.2d 103 (1982); Sventko v. Kroger Co., 69 Mich. App. 644, 245 N.W.2d 151 (1976); Henderson v. St. Louis Hous. Auth., 605 S.W.2d 800 (Mo. 1979); Monge v. Beebe Rubber Co., 114 N.H. 130, 316 A.2d 549 (1974); Lally v. Copygraphics, 85 N.J. 668, 428 A.2d 1317 (1981); McCullough v. Certain Teed Prods. Corp., 70 A.D.2d 771, 417 N.Y.S.2d 353 (1979); Nees v. Hocks, 272 Or. 210, 536 P.2d 512 (1975); Reuther v. Fowler & Williams, Inc., 255 Pa. Super. 28, 386 A.2d 119 (1978); Krystad v. Lau, 65 Wash. 2d 817, 400 P.2d 72 (1965); Harless v. First Nat'l Bank, 246 S.E.2d 270 (W. Va. 1978).

state legislatures[35] have responded by developing exceptions to the at-will employment doctrine.

The circumstances under which an employer's right to terminate at-will employees has been curtailed under a tort or abuse theory generally involve the following categories:

1. *Public policy,* when the termination violates a "clear," statutorily declared policy[36]
2. *Whistleblowing,* when employees have been involved in unlawful or improper employer conduct[37]
3. *Employee refusals,* when an employee refuses to accede to the employer's improper requests or demands.[38]

The public policy exception is usually applied when employees were terminated for:

1. Refusing to violate a criminal statute
2. Exercising a statutory right

---

[35] Mont. Code Ann. §§ 39-2-901 to 39-2-914 (1988) (Montana's Wrongful Discharge from Employment Act); *see* Barnes v. Stone Container Corp., 942 F.2d 689 (9th Cir. 1991) (federal Labor Management Relations Act preempts employee who is covered by a collective bargaining agreement from filing a claim under Montana's Wrongful Discharge from Employment Act); Allmaras v. Yellowstone Basin Properties, 248 Mont. 477, 812 P.2d 770 (1991) (Montana's Wrongful Discharge from Employment Act does not violate any constitutional right to a jury trial); Johnson v. State, 238 Mont. 215, 776 P.2d 1221 (1989) (classifications created under Montana's Wrongful Discharge from Employment Act do not violate equal protection guarantees under state's constitution); Meech v. Hillhaven W., Inc., 238 Mont. 21, 776 P.2d 488 (1989) (elimination of common-law tort actions in Montana's Wrongful Discharge from Employment Act does not violate state's constitution); *see also* Perritt, Dismissal, ch. 9; Perritt, *Model Termination Act,* in H. Perritt, 1993 Wiley Employment Law Update, Ch. 6 (John Wiley & Sons, Inc. 1993); Rosemann, *Summary of Model Employment Termination Act,* in H. Perritt, 1992 Wiley Employment Law Update, Ch. 8 (John Wiley & Sons, Inc. 1992); Coulson, *Will the Model Termination Act Provide a Remedy for the Employment Discrimination Logjam,* 2 J. of Individual Employment Rts 1 (1993); Perritt, *State Wrongful Dismissal Legislation,* 1 J. of Individual Employment Rts 185 (1992); Henry, *A State-By-State Comparison of Recent Developments in Legislative Proposals on Employment Termination Law for Private Nonunionized Employees,* 1 J. of Individual Employment Rts 93 (1992); Peirce, Rosen & Schwoerer, *Reactions to the Proposed Employment Termination Act,* 1 J. of Individual Employment Rts 19 (1992).

[36] *See, e.g.,* Perks v. Firestone Tire & Rubber Co., 611 F.2d 1363 (3d Cir. 1979) (refusing to take a polygraph examination to obtain or maintain employment in a state prohibiting its administration for these purposes).

[37] *See, e.g.,* Palmateer v. International Harvester Co., 85 Ill. 2d 124, 421 N.E.2d 876 (1981), *after remand,* 140 Ill. App. 3d 857, 489 N.E.2d 474 (1986) (reporting criminal activity).

[38] *See, e.g.,* Petermann v. International Bhd. of Teamsters, 174 Cal. App. 2d 184, 344 P.2d 25 (1959) (refusing to perjure oneself).

3.   Complying with a statutory duty
4.   Observing the general public policy of the state.

Specific examples of employee terminations violating some form of recognized public policy include:

1.   Declining to commit perjury at the employer's command[39]
2.   Refusing to participate in an illegal price-fixing scheme[40]
3.   Serving on a jury[41]
4.   Filing workers' compensation claims[42]
5.   Refusing to take a polygraph examination in a state prohibiting its forcible administration to obtain or maintain employment[43]
6.   Performing unauthorized catheterizations[44]
7.   Mislabeling packaged goods[45]
8.   Avoiding payment of commissions[46]
9.   Avoiding payment of a pension.[47]

Although the public policy exception has expanded the circumstances under which an employee may challenge a termination, it is not without limits. Generally, the employee is required to demonstrate initially that the termination concerns a matter of public policy clearly affecting the rights of others at and outside the workplace. When only private interests were involved, employees have had their claims denied when terminated for:

---

[39] Ivy v. Army Times Pub. Co., 428 A.2d 831 (D.C. 1981); Petermann v. International Bhd. of Teamsters, 174 Cal. App. 2d 184, 344 P.2d 25 (1959).

[40] Tameny v. Atlantic Richfield Co., 27 Cal. 3d 167, 610 P.2d 1330, 164 Cal. Rptr. 839 (1980); see also Adler v. American Standard Corp., 290 Md. 615, 432 A.2d 464 (1981); Pierce v. Ortho Pharmaceutical Corp., 84 N.J. 58, 417 A.2d 505 (1980). Some federal courts have permitted employees fired for refusing to participate in illegal price-fixing schemes to maintain a private cause of action under the federal antitrust laws. See Ostrofe v. H.S. Crocker Co., Inc., 670 F.2d 1378 (9th Cir. 1982); Shaw v. Russell Trucking Line Inc., 542 F. Supp. 776 (W.D. Pa. 1982); but see In re Industrial Gas Antitrust Litig., 681 F.2d 514 (7th Cir. 1982).

[41] Nees v. Hocks, 272 Or. 210, 536 P.2d 512 (1975).

[42] Kelsay v. Motorola, Inc., 74 Ill. 2d 172, 384 N.E.2d 353 (1978); Frampton v. Central Ind. Gas Co., 260 Ind. 249, 297 N.E.2d 425 (1973); Lally v. Copygraphics, 85 N.J. 668, 428 A.2d 1317 (1981); contra Martin v. Tapley, 360 So. 2d 708 (Ala. 1978); Segal v. Arrow Indus. Corp., 364 So. 2d 89 (Fla. App. 1978).

[43] Perks v. Firestone Tire & Rubber Co., 611 F.2d 1363 (3d Cir. 1979).

[44] O'Sullivan v. Mallon, 160 N.J. Super. 416, 390 A.2d 149 (Law Div. 1978).

[45] Sheets v. Teddy's Frosted Foods, Inc., 179 Conn. 471, 427 A.2d 385 (1980).

[46] Fortune v. National Cash Register Co., 373 Mass. 96, 364 N.E.2d 1251 (1977).

[47] Savodnik v. Korvettes, Inc., 489 F. Supp. 1010 (E.D.N.Y. 1980).

1. Questioning an employer's internal management system[48]
2. Questioning an employer's integrity[49]
3. Threatening to sue an employer for an injury unrelated to employment[50]
4. Taking too much sick leave[51]
5. Misusing the employer's Christmas funds[52]
6. Seeking to examine an employer's books in the employee's status as a shareholder[53]
7. Attending night school[54]
8. Cohabiting with a coemployee.[55]

Related to the public policy exception are terminations involving reporting of the employer's or another employee's allegedly unlawful or improper conduct to the employer or to governmental authorities. These are essentially instances of either:

Protective whistleblowing or

Active whistleblowing.

Protective whistleblowing occurs when the employee is asked to commit a crime and refuses.[56] *Active whistleblowing* involves employees who seize the initiative and disclose their suspicions (that may or may not be well founded) to government or employer authorities regarding conduct that may violate the law, although no statute requires an employee to report it.[57]

---

[48] Keneally v. Orgain, 186 Mont. 1, 606 P.2d 127 (1980).

[49] Abrisz v. Pulley Freight Lines, Inc., 270 N.W.2d 454 (Iowa 1978).

[50] Daniel v. Magma Copper Co., 127 Ariz. 320, 620 P.2d 699 (Ct. App. 1980).

[51] Jones v. Keogh, 137 Vt. 562, 409 A.2d 581 (1979).

[52] Jackson v. Minidoka Irrigation Dist., 98 Idaho 330, 563 P.2d 54 (1977).

[53] Campbell v. Ford Indus. Inc., 274 Or. 243, 546 P.2d 141 (1976).

[54] Scroghan v. Kraftco Corp., 551 S.W.2d 811 (Ky. App. 1977).

[55] Ward v. Frito-Lay, Inc., 95 Wis. 2d 372, 290 N.W.2d 536 (1980); *but see* Rulon-Miller v. IBM, 162 Cal. App. 3d 241, 208 Cal. Rptr. 524 (1984) (privacy invaded when no legitimate conflict of interest existed in dating employer's competitor, for which the employee was terminated).

[56] *See* Tameny v. Atlantic Richfield Co., 27 Cal. 3d 167, 610 P.2d 1330, 164 Cal. Rptr. 839 (1980) (refusing to participate in an illegal scheme to fix retail gasoline prices); Petermann v. International Bhd. of Teamsters, 174 Cal. App. 2d 184, 344 P.2d 25 (1959) (refusing to perjure oneself).

[57] Palmateer v. International Harvester Co., 85 Ill. 2d 124, 421 N.E.2d 876 (1981), *after remand,* 140 Ill. App. 3d 857, 489 N.E.2d 474 (1986) (reporting criminal activity); Harless v. First Nat'l Bank, 246 S.E.2d 270 (W. Va. 1978) (termination in retaliation for bringing to employer's attention violations of state and federal consumer protection statutes).

Abusive or *retaliatory terminations* occur when the employer tries to exploit a position of power in the employment relationship. The employer then retaliates against the employee for refusing to accede to its demands.[58]

Contract theories are also involved in exceptions to the at-will employment doctrine. Express or implied guarantees of employment are concerned when employees have been told upon hiring that they would be employed so long as they did the job, or a pattern of employer conduct has developed requiring termination only for cause.[59] Commitments of this nature may occur through implied or express agreement, oral or written, especially when an employer handbook sets forth that terminations will occur "for just cause only."[60] Employer liability, however, can be minimized if no assurances or promises, oral or written, are given at any time.[61]

Some courts have indicated that there is an implied-in-law covenant of good faith and fair dealing contained in all contracts, including employment contracts.[62] This may exist when the employment relationship firmly establishes the indicia of an implied agreement that give rise to the requirement of good faith and fair dealing. Among the factors supporting this are:

1. Extraordinary length of service
2. Good employee performance verified by routinely receiving raises, bonuses, and promotions
3. Employer assurances that employment would continue

---

[58] Monge v. Beebe Rubber Co., 114 N.H. 130, 316 A.2d 549 (1974) (refusing to have a social relationship with a foreman).

[59] Pugh v. See's Candies, Inc., 116 Cal. App. 3d 311, 171 Cal. Rptr. 917 (1981) (oral promise created when employer's practice was to terminate only for just cause); Cleary v. American Airlines, Inc., 111 Cal. App. 3d 443, 168 Cal. Rptr. 722 (1980) (implied covenant of good faith and fair dealing created through longevity of service, requiring just cause for termination); Magnan v. Anaconda Indus., Inc., 37 Conn. 38, 429 A.2d 492 (1980) (implied covenant of good faith and fair dealing); Toussaint v. Blue Cross & Blue Shield, 408 Mich. 579, 292 N.W.2d 880 (1980) (oral statement and handbook "just cause" provision are binding commitments). *But see* Rowe v. Montgomery Ward, 437 Mich. 627, 473 N.W.2d 268 (1991) (applying "objective test," i.e., how would a reasonable person view an alleged oral promise as creating a binding commitment on an employer; enforcement denied to oral representation that created no binding employer commitment when viewed in conjunction with employment handbook containing no elaborate disciplinary procedure or just-cause language to overcome at-will employment presumption). See also ch. 9.

[60] *See* Toussaint v. Blue Cross & Blue Shield, 408 Mich. 579, 292 N.W.2d 880 (1980) (oral statement and handbook "just cause" provision binding commitments). See also ch. 9.

[61] *See* Novosel v. Sears, Roebuck & Co., 495 F. Supp. 344 (E.D. Mich. 1980) (application disclaimer sufficient to preserve at-will employment status). See also chs. 4, 9, 15.

[62] Cleary v. American Airlines, Inc., 111 Cal. App. 3d 443, 168 Cal. Rptr. 722 (1980) (implied covenant of good faith and fair dealing); Fortune v. National Cash Register Co., 373 Mass. 96, 364 N.E.2d 1251 (1977) (same).

4.   Employer practice of not terminating except for cause, whether based on an oral or written policy

5.   No prior warning that the employee's position was in jeopardy.[63]

Federal[64] and state[65] statutes prohibit, in certain instances, the summary termination of an at-will employee. Courts have found that an employer may terminate an employee for any reason except when statutorily prohibited.[66]

The principal goals of this federal and state legislation have been to:

1.   Promote unionization as a countervailing force against employer power and control[67]

2.   Establish a minimum level of economic entitlement for employees[68]

3.   Combat discrimination against specific groups in hiring and terminations[69]

4.   Protect employee health and safety[70]

5.   Guarantee a minimum level of security for retirement and for the survivors of wage earners.[71]

---

[63] *See* Cleary v. American Airlines, Inc., 111 Cal. App. 3d 443, 168 Cal. Rptr. 722 (1980) (implied covenant of good faith and fair dealing).

[64] United States government employees, along with various state and municipal employees, may not be terminated without a hearing. *See, e.g.,* 5 U.S.C. § 7513 (1988) (Civil Service Reform Act of 1978). In some instances, government employees cannot be terminated except for cause. *Id.* The Civil Service Reform Act of 1978 provides that a government agency may remove or otherwise discipline a covered employee only for such cause as will promote the efficiency of the Civil Service. It also provides a notice period prior to adverse action and affords the employee the right to be represented by an attorney and the right to a written decision enumerating the reasons for the action taken.

[65] In Montana, employees are protected from summary termination by state statute. Mont. Code §§ 39-2-901 to 39-2-914 (1988) (Montana's Wrongful Discharge from Employment Act).

[66] *See, e.g.,* NLRB v. Condenser Corp. of Am., 128 F.2d 67, 77 (3d Cir. 1942) (employee properly terminated for refusing to work and insisting on having increased compensation demands addressed during middle of working day although employer had agreed to discuss these issues at end of workday).

[67] *See* 29 U.S.C. §§ 151–169 (1988) (National Labor Relations Act).

[68] 26 U.S.C. §§ 3301–3331 (1988) (Federal Unemployment Tax Act); 29 U.S.C. §§ 201–219 (1988) (Fair Labor Standards Act of 1938).

[69] *See* 42 U.S.C. §§ 12101–12213 (Supp. 1992) (Americans with Disabilities Act); *see also* H. Perritt, Jr., Americans with Disabilities Handbook (John Wiley & Sons 1990); 42 U.S.C. §§ 2000e-1 to 2002-2017 (1988) (Civil Rights Act of 1964); 29 U.S.C. §§ 621–634 (1988) (Age Discrimination in Employment Act of 1967); 38 U.S.C. §§ 2021–2024 (1988) (Vietnam Era Veterans Readjustment Assistance Act); 29 U.S.C. §§ 701–796 (1988) (Vocational Rehabilitation Act of 1973).

[70] *See* 29 U.S.C. §§ 651–678 (1988) (Occupational Safety and Health Act of 1970).

[71] Employee Retirement Income Security Act of 1974, Pub. L. No. 93-406, § 2, 88 Stat. 829 (codified in scattered sections of 5, 18, 26, 29, 31, and 42 U.S.C. (1982)); Social Security Act, Pub. L. No. 271, 49 Stat. 620 (1935) (codified in scattered sections of 42 U.S.C. (1988)).

In addition, the assumption of risk doctrine as applied to employment has been effectively repealed by state workers' compensation laws.[72]

The primary federal statutes limiting an employer's right to terminate an at-will employee are the National Labor Relations Act (NLRA)[73] and the Civil Rights Act of 1964 (Title VII).[74] The NLRA prohibits termination for exercising the right to organize and select an employee representative.[75] Title VII prohibits any termination based upon discrimination involving race, color, religion, sex, or national origin.[76] Other federal legislation restricting employee terminations includes the:

1. Americans with Disabilities Act of 1990[77]
2. Age Discrimination in Employment Act of 1967 (ADEA)[78]
3. Occupational Safety and Health Act of 1970 (OSHA)[79]
4. Vietnam Era Veterans Readjustment Assistance Act[80]
5. Fair Labor Standards Act (FLSA)[81]
6. Vocational Rehabilitation Act of 1973[82]
7. Employee Retirement Income Security Act of 1974 (ERISA)[83]
8. Family and Medical Leave Act of 1993 (FMLA)[84]
9. Employee Polygraph Protection Act of 1988[85]
10. Energy Reorganization Act of 1974[86]

---

[72] *See* I.A. Larson, Workmen's Compensation §§ 5.00–20, at 33–39 (1978).

[73] 29 U.S.C. §§ 151–169 (1988).

[74] 42 U.S.C. §§ 2000e-1 to 2002-17 (1988).

[75] *See* 29 U.S.C. §§ 158(a)(1), 158(a)(3) (1988).

[76] *See* 42 U.S.C. § 2000e-2(a) (1988).

[77] 42 U.S.C. §§ 12101–12213 (Supp. 1992) (prohibiting discrimination based on disability).

[78] 29 U.S.C. §§ 621–634 (1988) (prohibiting discrimination based on age).

[79] 29 U.S.C. §§ 651–678, 660(c)(1) (1988) (prohibiting discrimination against an employee for asserting rights guaranteed under the Occupational Safety and Health Act).

[80] 38 U.S.C. §§ 2021(a)(A)(i), 2021(a)(B), 2021(b)(1), 2024 (1988) (guaranteeing the right to reemployment upon satisfactory completion of military service and prohibiting termination "without cause" within one year after reemployment).

[81] 29 U.S.C. §§ 201–219, 215(a)(3) (1988) (prohibiting employee termination for filing any complaint or instituting any proceeding under the Fair Labor Standards Act).

[82] 29 U.S.C. §§ 701–796i, 794 (1988) (requiring affirmative action to advance the employment of handicapped individuals by government contractors or subcontractors).

[83] 29 U.S.C. §§ 1140–1141 (1988) (prohibiting employee termination to prevent them from attaining vested pension rights).

[84] P.L. 103.3 (Feb. 5, 1993).

[85] 29 U.S.C. §§ 2001–2009 (1988) (prohibiting from requiring, requesting, causing, or suggesting that an employee take a polygraph examination except under very limited circumstances).

[86] 42 U.S.C. § 5851 (1988) (prohibiting termination of employees who are assisting, participating, or testifying, or are about to do the same, in any proceeding to carry out the purposes of this Act or the Atomic Energy Act of 1954).

11. Clean Air Act[87]

12. Federal Water Pollution Control Act[88]

13. Railroad Safety Act[89]

14. Consumer Credit Protection Act[90]

15. Judiciary and Judicial Procedure Act[91]

16. Migrant and Seasonal Agricultural Worker Protection Act[92]

17. Bankruptcy Code[93]

18. Motor Carrier Act[94]

19. Federal Mine Safety Act[95]

20. Surface Mining Control and Reclamation Act[96]

21. International Safe Container Act[97]

22. Toxic Substances Control Act[98]

23. Comprehensive Environmental Response, Compensation, and Liability Act (CERCLA)[99]

24. Solid Waste Disposal Act.[100]

---

[87] 42 U.S.C. § 7622 (1988) (prohibiting employee termination for commencing, causing to commence, or testifying at proceedings against an employer for the Act's violation).

[88] 33 U.S.C. § 1367 (1988) (prohibiting employee termination for instituting or testifying at a proceeding against the employer for the Act's violation).

[89] 45 U.S.C. §§ 441(a), 441(b)(1) (1988) (prohibiting railroad companies from terminating employees who file complaints, institute or cause to be instituted any proceeding under or related to enforcement of federal railroad safety laws, or testify, or are about to, at such a proceeding; or who refuse to work under conditions they reasonably believe to be dangerous).

[90] 15 U.S.C. § 1674(a) (1988) (prohibiting employee termination because of a wage garnishment for any one indebtedness).

[91] 28 U.S.C. § 1875 (1988) (prohibiting employee termination for service on grand or petit juries).

[92] 29 U.S.C. § 1855 (1988) (prohibits retaliation against covered employees and provides for administrative enforcement).

[93] 11 U.S.C. § 525(b) (1988) (prohibits discrimination or termination of employees who file for bankruptcy).

[94] 49 U.S.C. § 2305 (1988) (antidiscrimination and antiretaliation for employees who file a complaint or institute a proceeding).

[95] 30 U.S.C. § 815(c) (1988) (prohibiting discrimination or termination).

[96] 30 U.S.C. §§ 1201–1328 (1988) (antiretaliation provision).

[97] 46 U.S.C. §§ 1501–1508 (1988) (antidiscrimination and antiretaliation provision).

[98] 15 U.S.C. §§ 2601–2629 (1988) (antidiscrimination and antiretaliation provision).

[99] 42 U.S.C. § 9610 (1988) (antidiscrimination and antiretaliation provision).

[100] 42 U.S.C. § 6971 (1988) (antidiscrimination provision).

State statutes contain similar limitations restricting the employer's unilateral discretion to impose discipline or terminate employment.[101]

---

[101] Several states have statutes prohibiting terminations based upon political activity, for example, Arizona, California, and Kentucky. *See* [1993] Individual Empl. Rights Manual (BNA) (State Laws) 541. A few states prohibit termination for serving as jurors or for indicating their availability as jurors, for example, Idaho, Massachusetts, Michigan, North Dakota, and Vermont. *See id.* Other states prohibit termination for refusing to take a polygraph examination, for example, Connecticut, Hawaii, Idaho, Maryland, Michigan, New Jersey, Oregon, Pennsylvania, Rhode Island, and Washington. *See id.* Another common provision in state laws is a prohibition against retaliatory termination for filing a workers' compensation claim, for example, California, Ohio, and Texas. *See id.* At this point, only Montana's Wrongful Discharge from Employment Act provides broad protection to employees from terminations similar to the "just cause" provision contained in a collective bargaining agreement. *See id.*

CHAPTER 2

HUMAN RESOURCES AUDITS: A PRELUDE TO POLICY DEVELOPMENT

INTRODUCTION

§ 2.1   Introduction to Dealing with Human Resources Issues and Concerns

Increasingly, employers are recognizing the potential liabilities created by the growth and expansion in employment litigation arising out of individual employee rights.[1] What was once thought of as limited to disputes occurring under grievance arbitration procedures in collective bargaining agreements[2] has now changed; any adverse employment decisions of private and public sector employers can be subject to prolonged court litigation[3] and costly damage awards or settlements,[4] along with federal[5] and state[6] agency regulation.

---

[1] See K. Decker, Employee Privacy Law and Practice (John Wiley & Sons, Inc. 1987) [hereinafter Decker, Privacy Law]; A. Gross, Employee Dismissal Law: Forms and Procedures (John Wiley & Sons, Inc. 1992) [hereinafter Gross, Dismissal Forms]; H. Perritt, Jr., Employee Dismissal Law and Practice (3d ed. John Wiley & Sons, Inc. 1992) [hereinafter Perritt, Dismissal Law].

[2] See Decker, Privacy Law § 4.15; Perritt, Dismissal Law ch. 3.

[3] See, e.g., Bratt v. International Business Machs., 392 Mass. 508, 467 N.E.2d 126 (1984) (revealing confidential employee medical or personal information); see also Decker, Privacy Law chs. 3–8.

[4] See, e.g., Lewis v. Equitable Life Assurance Soc'y, 361 N.W.2d 875 (Minn. Ct. App. 1985), aff'd in pertinent part, 389 N.W.2d 876 (Minn. 1986) (group of employees defamed by employer's false and malicious termination reasons; $425,000 damage award); see also Decker, Privacy Law ch. 5.

[5] See, e.g., 15 U.S.C. §§ 1681–1681t (1988) (Fair Credit Reporting Act); see also Decker, Privacy Law §§ 2.2–2.20.

[6] See, e.g., Cal. Civ. Code §§ 1785–1786.56 (West 1985) (California's Consumer Credit Reporting Agency Act); see also Decker, Privacy Law §§ 2.21–2.40.

Failing to recognize potential employee problem areas can produce negative employer litigation implications.[7] Employer litigation exposure can be minimized by understanding potential employee liability arising out of hiring,[8] at the workplace,[9] and outside the workplace.[10]

To assess potential liability, a systematic means must be developed for defining current interrelationships between employees and their employers and for measuring changes that have occurred in these relationships. Human resources audits provide a methodology for reviewing and evaluating employer exposure and liability potential. The human resources audit includes the initial questionnaire, a review of relevant employer documents, discussions with management and supervisors, supplemental written inquiries, and an evaluation.[11]

For a human resources audit to be useful, honest and accurate employer responses must be given, even though legal concerns may be raised in identifying potential employee liability. These responses are essential for pinpointing and isolating employee problem areas so that preventive action to minimize these issues and concerns can be taken before they create employer liability. The human resources staff should coordinate the audit function.

This chapter reviews employer procedures for assessing employee liability potential. It examines the issues and concerns present,[12] human resources audit formats,[13] and human resources audit result analysis,[14] along with human resource administration responsibilities.[15]

---

[7] *See, e.g.,* Lewis v. Equitable Life Assurance Soc'y, 361 N.W.2d 875 (Minn. Ct. App. 1985), *aff'd in pertinent part,* 389 N.W.2d 876 (Minn. 1986) (group of employees defamed by employer's false and malicious termination reasons; $425,000 damage award); *see also* Decker, Privacy Law chs. 3–8.

[8] *See, e.g.,* Green v. Missouri Pac. R.R., 523 F.2d 1290 (8th Cir. 1975) (inquiring about non-job-related convictions); *see also* Decker, Privacy Law ch. 6.

[9] *See, e.g.,* Quinones v. United States, 492 F.2d 1269 (3d Cir. 1974) (release of inaccurate personnel file); *see also* Decker, Privacy Law ch. 7.

[10] *See, e.g.,* Whitney v. Greater N.Y. Corp. of Seventh-Day Adventists, 401 F. Supp. 1363 (S.D.N.Y. 1975) (termination of white person for association with blacks outside the workplace) *see also* Decker, Privacy Law ch. 8.

[11] See §§ **2.18–2.23.**

[12] See §§ **2.2–2.17.**

[13] See §§ **2.18–2.23.**

[14] See §§ **2.24–2.25.**

[15] See §§ **2.26–2.29.**

ISSUES AND CONCERNS

§ 2.2　Recognizing Human Resources
Issues and Concerns

Employment law trends regarding individual employee rights protection mandate that employers take preventive measures to minimize their litigation potential arising out of employee claims.[16] Employers must evaluate the strengths and weaknesses of their employee procedures and policies to identify problem areas. Although some of these problem areas may be apparent, other deficiencies may be overlooked. Recognizing these issues and concerns may require consultation with legal counsel and human resource professionals[17] to assure that employer procedures and policies comply with applicable federal[18] and state[19] statutes.

　　To identify employee issues and concerns, information must be collected from a variety of sources.[20] Once collected, the information can be assembled and reported on audit forms for evaluation.[21] In collecting this information, the employer must obtain an understanding about its own structure,[22] internal organization,[23] communication,[24] human resource administration,[25] recruitment,[26] work hours,[27] compensation,[28] fringe benefits,[29] promotions and transfers,[30] fair employment practices,[31] discipline, termination, and leaves of absence,[32] union

---

[16] *See, e.g.,* Lewis v. Equitable Life Assurance Soc'y, 361 N.W.2d 875 (Minn. Ct. App. 1985), *aff'd in pertinent part,* 389 N.W.2d 876 (Minn. 1986) (group of employees defamed by employer's false and malicious termination reasons; $425,000 damage award); *see also* Decker, Privacy Law ch. 9.

[17] See §§ **2.26–2.29.**

[18] *See, e.g.,* 29 U.S.C. §§ 2001–2009 (1988) (Employee Polygraph Protection Act); *see also* Decker, Privacy Law ch. 2; Perritt, Dismissal Law ch. 2.

[19] *See, e.g.,* Cal. Civ. Code § 1783 (West 1986) (California Fair Credit Reporting Act); *see also* Decker, Privacy Law ch. 2; Perritt, Dismissal Law ch. 2.

[20] *See* Decker, Privacy Law ch. 6.

[21] See §§ **2.18–2.23.**

[22] See § **2.3.**

[23] See § **2.4.**

[24] See § **2.5.**

[25] See § **2.6.**

[26] See § **2.7.**

[27] See § **2.8.**

[28] See § **2.9.**

[29] See § **2.10.**

[30] See § **2.11.**

[31] See § **2.12.**

[32] See § **2.13.**

relations,[33] health and safety,[34] training and development,[35] and manpower planning.[36]

§ 2.3   Employer Structure

To evaluate potential employer liability, the employer's overall structure should be examined. This may reveal employer philosophy and sensitivity, as well as confidentiality considerations present in developing, manufacturing, and marketing products or services. In undertaking this, the following should be considered.[37]

1. Date operations commenced
2. Acquisition and/or merger involvement that may inherit conflicting procedures and policies
3. Products[38]
4. Facility location[39]
5. Annual revenue:
    a. Current year
    b. Prior year
    c. Five years ago
6. Number of employees by job classification:
    a. Currently
    b. One year ago
    c. Two years ago

---

[33] See § **2.14.**

[34] See § **2.15.**

[35] See § **2.16.**

[36] See § **2.17.**

[37] Adapted from Littler, Mendelson, Fastiff & Tichy, *Conducting a Labor Relations Self Audit: An Outline for Examining Personnel Policies and Practices* in The 1987 Employer H-2 to H-3 (1987) [hereinafter Littler, Audit].

[38] This may involve restrictive covenants and trade secrets. *See, e.g.,* Tabs Assocs., Inc. v. Brohawn, 59 Md. App. 330, 475 A.2d 1203 (1984) (future use of trade secrets); *see also* Decker, Privacy Law § 4.13; K. Decker, Covenants Not to Compete (2d ed. John Wiley & Sons, Inc. 1993) [hereinafter Decker, Covenants].

[39] This inquiry may pinpoint problems in communicating consistent employee procedures and policies where employer operations are spread over a considerable geographic area. See § **2.5.**
    Consistency may be achieved throughout an employer's operation by using standardized handbooks and employment policies. *See* K. Decker & H. T. Felix, Drafting and Revising Employment Handbooks (John Wiley & Sons, Inc. 1991) [hereinafter Decker, Handbooks]; *see also* Decker, Privacy Law § 4.14; Gross, Dismissal Forms ch 1; Perritt, Dismissal Law ch. 8. See chs. 15, 16.

7. Private or public ownership
8. Sales to government agencies[40]
9. Competitors[41]
10. Union organization:[42]
    a. Which unions?
    b. For how long?
    If not unionized, have attempts been made to organize?
    a. Which unions?
    b. When?
    c. Results?

§ 2.4   Internal Employer Organization

To understand how employee procedures and policies are emphasized and stressed, the employer's organization becomes important. Employer organization is important for recognizing the responsibility for developing, implementing, and communicating employee procedures and policies, along with their dissemination through a human resource function.[43] The following should be considered regarding the employer's organizational structure.[44]

1. Organization chart
2. Job position descriptions:
    a. Clearness
    b. Accuracy

---

[40] This inquiry may affect affirmative action obligations under fair employment practices (FEP) statutes and directives. *See, e.g.,* Executive Order 11246 (Affirmative Action), 3 C.F.R. § 339 (1964–1965 compilation), reprinted in 42 U.S.C. § 2000e note, issued on Sept. 24, 1965, as amended. *See also* Decker, Privacy Law § 2.12; Perritt, Dismissal Law § 2.12.

[41] This inquiry may involve restrictive covenants and trade secrets. *See, e.g.,* Tabs Assocs., Inc. v. Brohawn, 59 Md. App. 330, 475 A.2d 1203 (1984) (future use of trade secrets). *See generally* Decker, Covenants; *see also* Decker, Privacy Law § 4.13.

[42] Union organization and attempts at organization may indicate the perimeters within which an employer's privacy procedures and policies are undertaken; i.e., employer unilateral development and implementation may be constrained by collective bargaining obligations. *See, e.g.,* IBEW Local 1900 v. PEPCO, 634 F. Supp. 742 (D.D.C. 1986) (duty to bargain alcohol and drug policy); *see also* Decker, Privacy Law §§ 2.6, 4.15; Perritt, Dismissal Law § 2.18. Likewise, employee associational rights may be constrained by employer restrictions on union organizational workplace activity. *See, e.g.,* David's Kosher Deli, 282 N.L.R.B. No. 107 (1987) (employee's resignation constituted unlawful constructive termination when employer threatened to expose employee's daughter's abortion if she did not cease union activities); *see also* Decker, Privacy Law §§ 2.6, 8.6; Perritt, Dismissal Law § 2.18.

[43] See **§§ 2.26–2.29.**

[44] Adapted from Littler, Audit at H-4 to H-5.

    c. Completeness

    d. Availability

    e. Development responsibility

    f. Regular updating

3. Organization structure:

    a. Appropriateness for meeting employee goals

    b. Checks and controls

    c. Overlapping authority

    d. Authority commensurate with responsibility

4. Organization function:

    a. Employee quality for administering procedures and policies

    b. Employee knowledge of procedures and policies

    c. Employee understanding of relationships

    d. Decision level at which employee procedures and policies are formulated and implemented

    e. Acceptance of employee procedures and policies throughout the organization

§ 2.5   Communication Methods

To ensure that employee procedures and policies are understood by managers, supervisors, and employees, communication is important. Through communication, employee procedures and policies are disseminated within the employer's organization. Communication assures knowledge, understanding, and consistent application of procedures and policies. The following should be considered regarding communication:[45]

1. Providing employee information

2. Support and encouragement for internal employee procedures and policies

3. Informing managers and supervisors of employee procedures and policies, along with interpretations of those procedures and policies

4. Consistent application of employee procedures and policies

5. Encouraging employees to express views and reactions to employer interpretations of procedures and policies

6. Providing a procedure for reviewing and resolving nonunion employee complaints[46]

---

[45] *See* Littler, Audit at H-5 to H-6.

[46] For a discussion of nonunion dispute resolution procedures, *see* Gross, Dismissal Forms §§ 1.21–1.27.

7. Encouraging participation by managers and supervisors in implementing employee procedures and policies
8. Effect on employee procedures and policies of:
    a. Turnover
    b. Cooperation
    c. Complaints
9. Bypassing managers and supervisors when implementing employee procedures and policies
10. In-house newsletters or similar publications to communicate employee procedures and policies
11. Letters or other written documents to communicate employee procedures and policies
12. Suggestion system to review employee concerns
13. Receptiveness to employee concerns and issues

§ 2.6 Human Resource Administration

To implement employee procedures and policies properly, responsibility for this within the employer's organization must be assigned. Administration is important for consistency in developing, implementing, applying, interpreting, and communicating procedures and policies. Generally, this responsibility rests with those individuals involved with the human resource administration function.[47] The following should be considered regarding human resource administration:[48]

1. Existence of a human resource staff or similar personnel function:
    a. Number of employees
    b. Annual budget
    c. Organization
    d. Reporting responsibility
    e. Ratio of overall employees to the human resources staff
2. Legal and/or professional organization membership for learning of employee developments[49]

---

[47] See §§ 2.26–2.29.

[48] Adapted from Littler, Audit at H-6 to H-9.

[49] This may include membership in organizations such as the American Arbitration Association, American Bar Association, American Management Association, American Society for Industrial Security, American Society of Public Administration, Industrial Relations Research Association, the International Personnel Management Association, the Society for Human Resource Management, and so forth.

3. Professional information and journals received for access to employee developments[50]

4. Legislative information reviewed for updating employee requirements[51]

5. Human resource staff assistance in solving employee issues and concerns

6. Human resource staff solicitation of needs and information from managers and supervisors before developing procedures and policies

7. The human resource staff as a pro-active or re-active employer function to employee issues and concerns

8. Existence of an employment handbook[52]

9. Existence of a personnel record for each employee regarding its:[53]

    a. Contents

    b. Impermissible identification of employees by race, color, religion, sex, national origin, ancestry, disability, age, or marital or veteran status[54]

    c. Employer maintenance of any record regarding an applicant's or employee's race, color, religion, sex, national origin, ancestry, disability, age, or marital or veteran status for use in legal reporting[55]

    d. Record changes in employee status involving promotions, leaves of absence, rates of pay, and so forth

---

[50] In-depth material regarding employment developments is regularly provided by the Bureau of National Affairs and Commerce Clearing House. These two organizations publish various looseleaf services, texts, special reports, and pamphlets for use by private and public sector human resource professionals and attorneys. For example, the Bureau of National Affairs publishes a looseleaf service devoted exclusively to individual employee rights. *See* Individual Employment Rights (BNA) (1994).

[51] *Id.*

[52] *See, e.g.,* Leikvold v. Valley View Community Hosp., 141 Ariz. 544, 688 P.2d 170 (1984) (handbooks may create binding employment commitments). *Contra,* Reynolds Mfg. Co. v. Mendoza, 644 S.W.2d 536 (Tex. 1982) (handbooks do not create binding employment commitments); *See generally* Decker, Handbooks; *see also* Decker, Privacy Law § 4.14; Gross, Dismissal Forms ch. 1; Perritt, Dismissal Law ch. 8. See chs. 15, 16.

[53] This inquiry may reveal employee interests protected under state statutes regulating employment files. *See, e.g.,* Pa. Stat. Ann. tit. 43, §§ 1321–1324 (Purdon 1991) (Pennsylvania's statute regulating personnel file inspection); *see also* Decker, Privacy Law §§ 2.30–2.31, 7.2–7.4.

[54] These inquiries may reveal employee interests protected under federal and state FEP statutes. *See, e.g.,* 42 U.S.C. §§ 2000e-1 to 2002-17 (1988) (Civil Rights Act of 1964); *see also* Decker, Privacy Law §§ 2.7–2.12, 2.25; Perritt, Dismissal Law §§ 2.2–2.16.

[55] This inquiry may be required in administering affirmative action obligations. *See, e.g.,* Executive Order 11246 (federal contractors), 3 C.F.R. § 339 (1964–1965 compilation), reprinted in 42 U.S.C. § 2000e note, issued on Sept. 24, 1965, as amended; *see also* Decker, Privacy Law § 2.12; Perritt, Dismissal Law § 2.12.

    When this information is collected, it is usually obtained on a form that can be kept separate from other information received during the hiring process to minimize problems arising under federal and state FEP statutes.

10.	Providing employees with document copies that affect their employment status[56]

11.	Employee access to personnel records[57]

12.	Employer personnel record use for:

   a.	Hiring[58]

   b.	Transfers

   c.	Promotions

   d.	Performance reviews[59]

   e.	Disciplinary action

   f.	Staff review

   g.	Employment statistic development[60]

§ 2.7   Recruitment

The recruitment process plays an important role in employee hiring considerations. When seeking employment, an individual must provide considerable personal information and allow the employer to verify it. Recruitment creates vast employment information resources through employee disclosures, medical examinations, testing, interviews, and background investigations. It affects employee interests present in beliefs, speech, information, and association.[61] Because of this, the following should be considered regarding recruitment:[62]

---

[56] This inquiry may reveal employee interests present in information access. *See, e.g.,* Pa. Stat. Ann. tit. 43, §§ 1321–1324 (Purdon 1991) (Pennsylvania's statute regulating personnel file inspection); *see also* Decker, Privacy Law §§ 2.30–2.31, 7.2–7.4.

[57] This inquiry also may reveal employee interests present in information access. *See, e.g.,* Pa. Stat. Ann. tit. 43, §§ 1321–1324 (Purdon 1991) (Pennsylvania's statute regulating personnel file inspection); *see also* Decker, Privacy Law §§ 2.30–2.31, 7.2–7.4.

[58] This inquiry may reveal employee interests present in information release. *See, e.g.,* Dunlop v. Carriage Carpet Co., 548 F.2d 139 (6th Cir. 1977) (employer violated FLSA by informing prospective employer that a former employee had filed an overtime complaint); *see also* Decker, Privacy Law §§ 2.34, 6.13.

[59] *See, e.g.,* Bulkin v. Western Kraft E., Inc., 422 F. Supp. 437 (E.D. Pa. 1976) (negligent maintenance of employment records); *see also* Decker, Privacy Law § 7.30.

[60] This inquiry may be required in administering affirmative action obligations. *See, e.g.,* Executive Order No. 11246 (federal contractors), 3 C.F.R. § 339 (1964–1965 compilation), reprinted in 42 U.S.C. § 2000e note, issued on Sept. 24, 1965, as amended; *see also* Decker, Privacy Law § 2.12; Perritt, Dismissal Law § 2.12. When this information is collected, it is usually obtained on a form that can be kept separate from other information received during the hiring process, to minimize problems arising under federal and state FEP statutes.

[61] *See* Decker, Privacy Law ch. 6.

[62] Adapted from Littler, Audit at H-9 to H-13.

1. Recruitment:
    a. Present employee considerations
    b. Recruitment programs
    c. Recruitment sources used:
        (i)   Advertising[63]
        (ii)   Internal referrals
        (iii) Employment agencies
        (iv)   Executive search
        (v)   Other sources
2. Selection
    a. Selection methods used:
        (i)   Preliminary screening
        (ii)   Interview[64] by:
                (A) Human resources staff
                (B) Supervisor
                (C) Staff psychologist
        (iii) Testing[65]
                (A) Test description
                (B) Test validation
        (iv)   Reference investigation[66]
        (v)   Credit investigation[67]
        (vi)   Arrest and criminal record investigation[68]
        (vii) Education verification
        (viii) Post-employment offer physical examination[69]

---

[63] *See, e.g.,* Willis v. Allied Insulation Co., 174 So. 2d 858 (La. 1965) (terms of advertisement may bind employer); *see also* Decker, Privacy Law § 6.3.

[64] *See, e.g.,* Smith v. Union Oil Co., 17 Fair Empl. Prac. Cases (BNA) 960 (N.D. Cal. 1977) (national origin discrimination in recruitment and hiring); *see also* Decker, Privacy Law §§ 2.7–2.12, 2.25, 6.5; Perritt, Dismissal Law §§ 2.2–2.16.

[65] *See, e.g.,* Guardians Ass'n of N.Y. City Police Dep't v. Civil Serv. Comm'n, 630 F.2d 79 (2d Cir. 1980) (testing requirements); *see also* Decker, Privacy Law §§ 6.14–6.21.

[66] *See, e.g.,* Harrison v. Arrow Metal Prods. Corp., 20 Mich. App. 570, 174 N.W.2d 875 (1970) (disclosing information extraneous to job performance); *see also* Decker, Privacy Law §§ 2.34, 6.13.

[67] *See, e.g.,* 15 U.S.C. §§ 1681–1681(t) (1988) (Fair Credit Reporting Act); *see also* Decker, Privacy Law §§ 2.5, 2.23, 6.7.

[68] *See, e.g.,* 18 Pa. Cons. Stat. Ann. § 9125 (Purdon 1983) (Pennsylvania's statute prohibiting arrest record information use); *see also* Decker, Privacy Law §§ 2.7–2.12, 2.25, 2.32, 6.8–6.9; Perritt, Dismissal Law §§ 2.2–2.13.

[69] *See, e.g.,* 42 U.S.C. §§ 12101–12213 (Supp. 1992) (Americans with Disabilities Act) Pittsburgh Plate Glass Co., 52 Lab. Arb. (BNA) 985 (1969) (Duff, Arb.) (employer's right to require physical examinations).

    b.   The selection method's appropriateness[70]

    c.   Providing applicants information about the employer, the position, and career potential

    d.   Employment applications regarding:[71]

        (i)   Providing the applicant with a copy

        (ii)   Any questions or specifications pertaining to race, color, religion, sex, national origin, ancestry, disability, age, or marital status[72]

    e.   Post-employment offer physical examinations[73]

    f.   Requiring persons to be bonded[74]

    g.   Applicant or employee photographs[75]

    h.   Applicant or employee submission to polygraph examinations, drug screening, or similar tests[76]

    i.   Employee identification badges[77]

    j.   Communicating selection determinations to candidates regarding:

        (i)   Acceptance

        (ii)   Rejection

3.   Candidate evaluation procedures involving:[78]

    a.   Initial screening

    b.   Technical skills

    c.   Psychological examination

---

[70] *See* Decker, Privacy Law ch. 6.

[71] *See* Decker, Privacy Law § 6.3.

[72] This may affect employee interests protected under federal and state FEP statutes. *See, e.g.,* 42 U.S.C. §§ 2000e-1 to 2002-17 (1988) (Civil Rights Act of 1964); *see also* Decker, Privacy Law §§ 2.7–2.12, 2.25, 6.4; Perritt, Dismissal Law §§ 2.2–2.16.

[73] *See, e.g.,* 42 U.S.C. §§ 12101–12213 (Supp. 1992) (Americans with Disabilities Act) Pittsburgh Plate Glass Co., 52 Lab. Arb. (BNA) 985 (1969) (Duff, Arb.) (employer's right to require physical examinations).

[74] This may affect employee interests protected under federal and state FEP statutes. *See, e.g.,* 42 U.S.C. §§ 2000e-1 to 2002-17 (1988) (Civil Rights Act of 1964); *see also* Decker, Privacy Law §§ 2.7–2.12, 2.25, 6.4–6.9; Perritt, Dismissal Law §§ 2.2–2.13.

[75] This may affect employee interests protected under federal and state FEP statutes. *See, e.g.,* 42 U.S.C. §§ 2000e-1 to 2002-17 (1988) (Civil Rights Act of 1964); *see also* Decker, Privacy Law §§ 2.7–2.12, 2.25, 6.11; Perritt, Dismissal Law §§ 2.2–2.13.

[76] *See, e.g.,* 29 U.S.C. §§ 2001–2009 (1988) (Employee Polygraph Protection Act) Swope v. Florida Indus. Comm'n, 159 So. 2d 653, 654 (Fla. Dist. Ct. App. 1964) ("an innocent employee taking such a test [polygraph] could be risking loss of job and reputation at odds similar to those in Russian roulette"); *see also* Decker, Privacy Law §§ 2.35, 6.14–6.21, 7.9–7.10; Perritt, Dismissal Law § 5.26.

[77] *See, e.g.,* Briggs & Stratton Corp., 77 Lab. Arb. (BNA) 233 (1981) (Mueller, Arb.) (identification badges permissible to promote legitimate business interests); *see also* Decker, Privacy Law § 7.32.

[78] *See* Decker, Privacy Law §§ 6.14–6.21.

4. Job offers regarding:

    a. Hiring decisions

    b. Offer procedures

    c. Employment offer follow-up

    d. Monitoring outstanding employment offers

5. Familiarizing new employees through:

    a. Orientation program

    b. Employee handbook[79]

6. Recruiting staff:

    a. Number

    b. Qualifications

    c. Consistency of recruiting plans with the employer's needs

§ 2.8   Work Hours

Employee intrusions may originate out of work hours. These intrusions arise through the variety of personal attributes and problems that employees bring into the workplace, which must be molded into productivity. This assimilation process must take place while preserving employee association, speech, belief, and lifestyle interests at the workplace.[80] The following should be considered regarding work hours.[81]

1. Normal workday hours

2. Normal workweek hours

3. Normal workweek days

4. Shifts operated

5. Starting times

6. Quitting times

7. Work hour recording

8. Overtime work:

    a. Assignment

    b. Overtime equalization

---

[79] *See, e.g.,* Leikvold v. Valley View Community Hosp., 141 Ariz. 544, 688 P.2d 170 (1984) (handbooks may create binding employment commitments). *Contra,* Reynolds Mfg. Co. v. Mendoza, 644 S.W.2d 536 (Tex. 1982) (handbooks do not create binding employment commitments); *see generally* Decker, Handbooks; *see also* Decker, Privacy Law § 4.14; Gross, Dismissal Forms ch. 1; Perritt, Dismissal Law §§ 4.1, 4.8, 4.14, ch. 8. See chs. 10, 11.

[80] *See* Decker, Privacy Law chs. 7–8.

[81] Adapted from Littler, Audit at H-13 to H-14.

    c.   Employer notification of assigned employees

    d.   Employee refusal to work overtime

9.   Attendance control

10.   Outside employment restrictions[82]

§ 2.9 Compensation

Employee intrusions may originate in compensation through this information's collection, maintenance, use, and disclosure. Compensation and the confidentiality surrounding it may be one of the more personal employee issues. It can affect one's associations and the perceptions that others have. Collecting, maintaining, or disclosing inaccurate compensation information is possible because each employer has its own recordkeeping system.[83] Regarding compensation, the following should be considered:[84]

1.   Deductions withheld

2.   Deduction authorization

3.   Use of itemized statements setting forth deductions

4.   Attendance records

5.   Time off for voting[85]

6.   Time off for jury or witness duty[86]

7.   Accepting employee wage assignments

8.   Procedures and policies regarding payment to employees who resign[87]

9.   Procedures and policies regarding payment to terminated employees[88]

---

[82] *See, e.g.,* Mercoid Corp., 63 Lab. Arb. (BNA) 941 (1974) (Kossoff, Arb.) (moonlighting); *see also* Decker, Privacy Law §§ 4.3, 8.8–8.9.

[83] *See, e.g.,* Quinones v. United States, 492 F.2d 1269 (3d Cir. 1974) (release of inaccurate personnel file); Bulkin v. Western Kraft E., Inc., 422 F. Supp. 437 (E.D. Pa. 1976) (negligent maintenance of employment records); *see also* Decker, Privacy Law §§ 2.30, 2.34, 2.40, 7.3, 7.23–7.24.

[84] Adapted from Littler, Audit at H-14 to H-20.

[85] *See, e.g.,* Cal. Elec. Code § 14350 (West 1977) (California's statute permitting employee time off for voting); *see also* Decker, Privacy Law §§ 2.40, 7.24.

[86] *See, e.g.,* 28 U.S.C. § 1875 (1988) (Judiciary and Judicial Procedure Act; prohibits employee termination for service on federal grand or petit juries); *see also* Decker, Privacy Law § 7.23; Perritt, Dismissal Law §§ 2.34, 5.26.

[87] For a discussion of severance payment procedures and policies, *see* Gross, Dismissal Forms §§ 1.34–1.54.

[88] *Id.*

10. Job descriptions for:
   a. Managerial
   b. Supervisory, administrative, and technical/professional
   c. Nonexempt salaried
   d. Hourly
11. Job description updating reflecting:
   a. Existing job changes
   b. New jobs
12. Job description format concerning:
   a. Responsibilities
   b. Authority
   c. Reporting relationships
   d. Titles
   e. Qualifications
13. Job description use in:
   a. Evaluating jobs[89]
   b. Recruiting
   c. Organization planning
   d. Counseling
14. Job description release[90]
15. Preparing and maintaining job description responsibility
16. Job classification base pay ranges
17. Wage range determination
18. Job evaluation
19. Job reevaluation or updating frequency
20. Wage surveys
21. Compensation program administration
22. Responsibility level at which compensation decisions occur
23. Performance reviews:[91]
   a. Employees covered
   b. Frequency
   c. Responsibility
   d. Feedback
   e. Supervisor training in reviewing performance
   f. Performance reviews in relation to pay increases

---

[89] *See* Decker, Privacy Law § 7.30.

[90] *See* Decker, Privacy Law §§ 2.30, 7.3, 7.30.

[91] *See* Decker, Privacy Law § 7.30.

g. Performance evaluation checklist or guide

h. Performance review measurement of job performance

i. Performance review criteria establishment

j. Performance criteria communication to employees

k. Formal means of relating compensation to job performance

l. Appropriate relationship between compensation and job performance

m. Wage increases based solely on merit

n. Wage rate review frequency

o. Wage increase determination

p. Receipt by employees in the same pay range of the same merit increase

q. Performance review discussion by supervisors with employees

r. Performance review data use in management development, training, and manpower planning

s. Human resource staff involvement

t. Performance review data confidentiality[92]

u. Employee wage rate data confidentiality[93]

§ 2.10   Fringe Benefits

Employee claims may arise out of fringe benefits when information communication received from use of the benefits discloses intimate facts about the employee.[94] This may occur when sensitive employee medical information is revealed, for example. Disclosure of this information may affect employee speech and associational interests. The following should be considered regarding fringe benefits:[95]

1. Life insurance

2. Hospitalization, surgical, and medical

3. Sickness and accident

4. Major medical

---

[92] *See, e.g.,* Quinones v. United States, 492 F.2d 1269 (3d Cir. 1974) (release of inaccurate personnel file); Bulkin v. Western Kraft E., Inc., 422 F. Supp. 437 (E.D. Pa. 1976) (negligent maintenance of employment records); *see also* Decker, Privacy Law §§ 2.30, 7.3, 7.30.

[93] *See, e.g.,* Quinones v. United States, 492 F.2d 1269 (3d Cir. 1974) (release of inaccurate personnel file); Bulkin v. Western Kraft E., Inc., 422 F. Supp. 437 (E.D. Pa. 1976) (negligent maintenance of employment records); *see also* Decker, Privacy Law §§ 2.30, 7.3, 7.30.

[94] *See, e.g.,* Doe v. United States Dep't of Justice, 602 F. Supp. 871 (D.D.C. 1983) (breach of EAP confidentiality may expose employer to defamation claims); *see also* Decker, Privacy Law §§ 2.30–2.31, 4.3–4.4, 7.2–7.11.

[95] Adapted from Littler, Audit at H-20 to H-23.

5. Disability[96]
6. Dental
7. Optical
8. Travel accident
9. Pension/retirement
10. Savings plan
11. Stock purchase
12. Credit union
13. Paid holidays[97]
14. Leaves of absence[98]
15. Paid vacations[99]
16. Educational reimbursement
17. Length of service
18. Other forms of fringe benefits

§ 2.11 Promotions and Transfers

Promotions and transfers may involve employee concerns that arise out of testing affecting beliefs, speech, and associations.[100] For employers, a desire exists to fill available positions with employees qualified for the tasks assigned. Tests may deny employment to minorities without evidence that the tests were related to job success.[101] Because of this, the following should be considered regarding promotions and transfers:[102]

---

[96] *See, e.g.,* 42 U.S.C. §§ 12101–12213 (Supp. 1992) (Americans with Disabilities Act).

[97] This may involve employee interests present in religious accommodation under federal and state FEP statutes.
   See, e.g., 42 U.S.C. §§ 2000e-1 to 2002-17 (1988) (Civil Rights Act of 1964); *see also* Decker, Privacy Law §§ 2.7–2.12, 2.25, 7.33; Perritt, Dismissal Law 2.2–2.16.

[98] This may involve employee interests present in religious accommodation under federal and state FEP statutes.
   See, e.g., 42 U.S.C. §§ 2000e-1 to 2002-17 (1988) (Civil Rights Act of 1964); *see also* Decker, Privacy Law §§ 2.7–2.12, 2.25, 7.33; Perritt, Dismissal Law 2.2–2.16.

[99] This may involve employee interests present in religious accommodation under federal and state FEP statutes.
   See, e.g., 42 U.S.C. §§ 2000e-1 to 2002-17 (1988) (Civil Rights Act of 1964); *see also* Decker, Privacy Law §§ 2.7–2.12, 2.25, 7.33; Perritt, Dismissal Law 2.2–2.16.

[100] *See* Decker, Privacy Law § 6.18.

[101] *See, e.g.,* United States v. South Carolina, 434 U.S. 1026 (1978) (some tests favor white, middle-class backgrounds); *see also* Decker, Privacy Law § 6.18.

[102] Adapted from Littler, Audit at H-23 to H-24.

1. Tests the employer uses to determine employee promotion eligibility[103]
2. Test validation[104]
3. Test access to all employees
4. Communication to employees of job openings and tests
5. Selection criteria for choosing between employees with equal qualifications and abilities[105]

§ 2.12   Fair Employment Practices

Various employee claims may arise out of federal[106] and state[107] fair employment practices (FEP) statutes. These statutes may become relevant when employment decisions are made and/or information is collected, maintained, or disclosed regarding race, color, sex, religion, national origin, disability, or marital status. These FEP privacy considerations may be present at hiring, in the workplace, and outside the workplace. Wrongful collection, maintenance, use, or disclosure may affect employee interests present in beliefs, speech, and association. Because of this, the following should be considered regarding FEP:[108]

1. Employer policies against discrimination because of race, color, religious creed, sex, national origin, ancestry, disability, age, or marital status in:[109]
    a. Hiring
    b. Promotions
    c. Transfers
    d. Salary increases
    e. Work assignments
    f. Other
2. Written FEP policies
3. Communication to employees

---

[103] *See* Decker, Privacy Law § 6.18.

[104] Validity involves formulating tests to actually measure what they purport to measure. *See Uniform Guidelines on Employee Selection Procedures,* 43 Fed. Reg. 38290, 29 C.F.R. § 1607.1 *et seq.* (1992).

[105] *See* Decker, Privacy Law § 6.18.

[106] *See, e.g.,* 42 U.S.C.§§ 2000e-1 to 2002-17 (1988) (Civil Rights Act of 1964); *see also* Decker, Privacy Law §§ 2.7–2.12; Perritt, Dismissal Law §§ 2.2–2.16.

[107] *See, e.g.,* Pa. Stat. Ann. tit. 43, §§ 951–963 (Purdon 1991) Pennsylvania Human Relations Act); *see also* Decker, Privacy Law § 2.25.

[108] Adapted from Littler, Audit at H-24 to H-25.

[109] *See* Decker, Privacy Law §§ 2.7–2.12, 2.25; Perritt, Dismissal Law §§ 2.2–2.13.

4. Employer commitment to demonstrating opposition to discriminatory and harassing employment practices

5. The human resource staff's and supervisors' familiarization with and action in conformity to FEP statutes

6. Advertisements,[110] applications,[111] or interviews[112] containing any specifications regarding race, color, religious creed, sex, national origin, ancestry, disability, medical condition, age, or marital status

7. FEP policy communication to employment agencies

8. Minority group employment

9. Administration responsibility

10. Government contract involvement[113]

11. Affirmative action plans and goals[114]

12. Female and minority distribution at each employer responsibility level

13. History regarding discrimination complaints, conciliations, outstanding or pending lawsuits, or other FEP actions

§ 2.13   Discipline, Termination, and Leaves of Absence

Frequently, employee claims and liability arise out of discipline, termination, or leaves of absence.[115] Many employee claims arise out of the hiring process or before an employment termination. While employed, the adversely affected employee must usually suppress objections to obtain or retain employment.

---

[110] *See, e.g.,* Pittsburgh Press Co. v. Pittsburgh Comm'n on Human Relations, 413 U.S. 376 (1973) (sex-based advertisements prohibited); *see also* Decker, Privacy Law § 6.3.

[111] *See, e.g.,* Gregory v. Litton Sys., Inc., 316 F. Supp. 401 (C.D. Cal. 1970), *aff'd with modifications not here relevant,* 472 F.2d 631 (9th Cir. 1972) (arrest record inquiries not permitted); *see also* Decker, Privacy Law § 6.14.

[112] *See, e.g.,* Phillips v. Martin Marietta Corp., 400 U.S. 542 (1971) (sex discrimination regarding preschool children); *see also* Decker, Privacy Law § 6.5.

[113] This may be required in administering affirmative action obligations. *See, e.g.,* Executive Order No. 11246 (federal contractors), 3 C.F.R. § 339 (1964–1965 compilation), reprinted in 42 U.S.C. § 2000e note, issued on Sept. 24, 1965, as amended; *see also* Decker, Privacy Law § 2.12; Perritt, Dismissal Law § 2.12.

[114] This may be required in administering affirmative action obligations. *See, e.g.,* Executive Order No. 11246 (federal contractors), 3 C.F.R. § 339 (1964–1965 compilation), reprinted in 42 U.S.C. § 2000e note, issued on Sept. 24, 1965, as amended; *see also* Decker, Privacy Law § 2.12; Perritt, Dismissal Law § 2.12.

[115] *See, e.g.,* Patton v. J.C.Penney Co., 75 Or. App. 638, 707 P.2d 1256 (1985), *aff'd in part, rev'd in part,* 301 Or. 117, 719 P.2d 894 (1986) (employee terminated for failing to discontinue relationship with co-employee); *see also* Decker, Privacy Law chs. 3–8.

Litigation usually occurs after termination, when the employee is no longer economically dependent on the employer.

Preventive procedures may minimize employer liability. Because extensive liability[116] may arise out of discipline, termination, and leaves of absence, the following should be considered:[117]

1. Discipline:[118]
    a. Written conduct rules[119] and:
        (i)   Communication to employees
        (ii)   Consistent rule interpretation and application
        (iii) Rule enforcement responsibility
    b. Employee discipline responsibility
    c. Employee discipline imposition absent written conduct rules
2. Employment separation:
    a. Separation for:
        (i)   Resignation with notice
        (ii)   Resignation without notice
        (iii) Resignation by mutual agreement
        (iv)   Termination
        (v)   Layoff
        (vi)   Retirement
        (vii) Overstaying leave of absence
        (viii) Failure to return from leave of absence
    b. Termination documentation
    c. Documentation responsibility
    d. Employee turnover record responsibility
    e. Turnover rate:
        (i)   Currently
        (ii)   One year ago
        (iii) Two years ago

---

[116] *See, e.g.,* Lewis v. Equitable Life Assurance Soc'y, 361 N.W.2d 875 (Minn. Ct. App. 1985), *aff'd in pertinent part,* 389 N.W.2d 876 (Minn. 1986) (group of employees defamed by employer's false and malicious termination reasons; $425,000 damage award); *see also* Decker, Privacy Law ch. 5.

[117] Adapted from Littler, Audit at H-25 to H-29.

[118] For an in-depth discussion of discipline procedures and policies, *see* Gross, Dismissal Forms §§ 1.5–1.20.

[119] *See* Gross, Dismissal Forms §§ 1.1–1.6.

    f.   Exit interviews conducted for terminating employees regarding:

        (i)   Conduct

        (ii)   Interview's nature

        (iii)   Result utilization

    g.   Terminated employee record retention[120]

3.   Termination procedures:

    a.   Type of termination procedure[121]

    b.   Prior to terminating employees, consideration of:[122]

        (i)   Length of service

        (ii)   Personnel file documentation

        (iii)   Wage increases

        (iv)   Promotions

        (v)   Commendations

        (vi)   Work criticism

        (vii)   Prior discipline or warnings

    c.   Responsibility for terminating employees

    d.   Review of termination decisions by higher-level management or human resources staff prior to implementation

    e.   Review by legal counsel

    f.   Procedures for adjudicating employee disputes[123]

    g.   Employer determination that a termination occurs in accordance with its procedures and policies

    h.   Employer guidelines for achieving consistent standards in employee terminations

---

[120] *See, e.g.,* Pa. Stat. Ann. tit. 43, §§ 1321–1324 (Purdon 1991) (Pennsylvania's statute regulating personnel file inspection); *see also* Decker, Privacy Law §§ 2.30, 7.3.

[121] For an in-depth discussion of discipline procedures and policies, *see* Gross, Dismissal Forms §§ 1.5–1.20.

[122] *See, e.g.,* Cleary v. American Airlines, Inc., 111 Cal. App. 3d 443, 168 Cal. Rptr. 722 (1980) (18 years' service established cause requirement for termination); *see also* Perritt, Dismissal Law § 4.9.

[123] *See* Gross, Dismissal Forms §§ 1.21–1.27.

i. Employer oral or written promises to employees regarding employment termination[124]

j. Employer notice to employees that their employment is at-will[125]

4. Layoffs:

   a. Employee selection for layoff

   b. Employee selection for recall

5. Leaves of absence:

   a. Leave types:

      (i) Personal

      (ii) Medical

      (iii) Pregnancy[126]

      (iv) Work-related disability[127]

      (v) Bereavement

      (vi) Military

      (vii) Jury duty[128]

   b. Paid leaves

   c. Treatment of employees who fail to return from leaves of absence

   d. Treatment of employees who overextend leaves of absence without permission

   e. Treatment of employees who work elsewhere during leaves of absence without authorization[129]

   f. Procedure for granting leaves

   g. Effect of employee's leave on status, seniority, benefits, and so forth

---

[124] *See, e.g.,* Leikvold v. Valley View Community Hosp., 141 Ariz. 544, 688 P.2d 170 (1984) (handbooks may create binding employment commitments). *Contra,* Reynolds Mfg. Co. v. Mendoza, 644 S.W.2d 536 (Tex. 1982) (handbooks do not create binding employment commitments). *See generally* Decker, Handbooks; *see also* Decker, Privacy Law § 4.14; Gross, Dismissal Forms ch. 1; Perritt, Dismissal Law ch. 8. See chs. 10, 11.

[125] *See, e.g.,* Novosel v. Sears, Roebuck & Co., 495 F. Supp. 344 (E.D. Mich. 1980) (at-will employment disclaimer upheld). For a discussion of at-will employment, *see generally* Perritt, Dismissal Law. Regarding more specifics pertaining to at-will employment procedures, policies, and forms, *see generally* Gross, Dismissal Forms §§ 1.28–1.33.

[126] *See, e.g.,* 42 U.S.C.§§ 2000e-1 to 2002-17 (1988) (Civil Rights Act of 1964); *see also* Decker, Privacy Law §§ 2.8, 2.25; Perritt, Dismissal Law §§ 2.2–2.5.

[127] *See, e.g.,* 29 U.S.C. §§ 701–796i (1988) (Vocational Rehabilitation Act of 1973); *see also* Decker, Privacy Law §§ 2.10, 2.25; Perritt, Dismissal Law §§ 2.14–2.16.

[128] *See, e.g.,* 28 U.S.C. § 1875 (1988) (Judiciary and Judicial Procedures Act; prohibits employee termination for service on federal grand or petit juries); *see also* Decker, Privacy Law § 7.23; Perritt, Dismissal Law §§ 2.34, 5.26.

[129] *See, e.g.,* Mercoid Corp., 63 Lab. Arb. (BNA) 941 (1974) (Kossoff, Arb.) (moonlighting); *see also* Decker, Privacy Law ch. 8.

h.   Reinstatement of employees to their previous position upon returning from leaves of absence.

§ 2.14   Union Relations

Where collective bargaining agreements exist, unions may play an important role in the development and administration of employee procedures and policies.[130] Associational rights can be impacted by restricting the employee's right to organize under private and public sector labor relations statutes.[131] Interference with union organizational or associational activities can result from employer surveillance.[132] Refusal to bargain can result from introduction of testing or surveillance devices without consultation or bargaining with an employee representative.[133] A union's right to information also may be impacted.[134] For these reasons, the following should be considered regarding union relations:[135]

1.   Number of employees:
    a.   Supervisory
    b.   Nonsupervisory
    c.   Hourly
    d.   Salaried
2.   For unionized employees:
    a.   Bargaining unit
    b.   Union's name
    c.   Relationship length
    d.   Collective bargaining agreement's expiration date
    e.   Union membership extent
    f.   Representation election certification
    g.   Relations with employees
    h.   Relations with the union
    i.   Side agreements, oral or written
    j.   Past practices between the employer and the union

---

[130] *See* Decker, Privacy Law § 4.15.

[131] *See, e.g.,* 29 U.S.C. §§ 151–169 (1988) (National Labor Relations Act); *see also* Decker, Privacy Law §§ 2.6, 2.24; Perritt, Dismissal Law § 2.18.

[132] *See* Richman-Gordman Stores, Inc., 220 N.L.R.B. 453 (1975).

[133] *See* NLRB v. Katz, 369 U.S. 736 (1962).

[134] *See, e.g.,* Salt River Valley Water Users' Ass'n v. NLRB, 769 F.2d 639 (9th Cir. 1985) (union's limited right to personnel file disclosures for grievance processing); *see also* Decker, Privacy Law §§ 2.6, 7.3.

[135] Adapted from Littler, Audit at H-29 to H-30.

    k. Employer representatives in negotiations

    l. Collective bargaining agreement settlements after a strike

    m. Step at which most grievances are settled

    n. Number of annual grievances

    o. Number of annual arbitrations for each unit

    p. Union shop clause

    q. Check-off for dues and/or initiation fees

    r. Unauthorized walk-out experience

    s. Unfair labor practice experience

3. For nonunion employees:

    a. Complaint or grievance procedure availability[136]

    b. Groups that have attempted to organize

    c. Representation election history

    d. Majority by which unionization was defeated

    e. Work stoppage experience

    f. Unfair labor practice experience

§ 2.15   Health and Safety

Employee interests may be affected by workplace health and safety.[137] A right may arise in the employee's reasonable expectation to be free from workplace hazards or not to have one's physical condition unnecessarily queried. This expectation may involve safety concerns,[138] smoking,[139] alcohol and drug abuse,[140] acquired immune deficiency syndrome (AIDS),[141] sterilization,[142] and so forth. The following should be considered regarding health and safety matters:[143]

---

[136] For procedures and policies regarding nonunion dispute resolution mechanisms, *see* Gross, Dismissal Forms §§ 1.21–1.27.

[137] *See* Decker, Privacy Law §§ 7.5–7.11.

[138] *See, e.g.,* Whirlpool Corp. v. Marshall, 455 U.S. 1 (1980) (employee protection where reasonable belief in health or safety risk exists); *see also* Decker, Privacy Law § 7.6.

[139] *See, e.g.,* Schober v. Mountain Bell Tel., 96 N.M. 376, 630 P.2d 1231 (1980) (nonsmoker protection); *see also* Decker, Privacy Law § 7.7.

[140] *See, e.g.,* Caruso v. Ward, 133 Misc. 2d 544, 506 N.Y.S.2d 789 (1986) *rev'd,* 72 N.Y.2d 432, 530 N.E.2d 850, 534 N.Y.S.2d 142 (1988) (random police drug screenings) *see also* Decker, Privacy Law § 7.9.

[141] *See, e.g.,* Shuttleworth v. Broward County, 639 F. Supp. 654 (S.D. Fla. 1986) (AIDS as a protected handicap); *see also* Decker, Privacy Law § 7.10.

[142] *See, e.g.,* Olin Corp., 73 Lab. Arb. (BNA) 291 (1979) (Knudson, Arb.) (rule prohibiting fertile females from working near hazardous materials); *see also* Decker, Privacy Law § 7.11.

[143] Adapted from Littler, Audit at H-30 to H-31.

1. Safety program[144]
2. Furnishing employees with safety equipment, such as shoes, glasses, and so forth[145]
3. Management and supervisory personnel's knowledge
4. Worker compensation claim experience
5. Providing rooms for resting
6. Retention of a physician's services
7. Use of an industrial nurse
8. Maintenance staff looking for, documenting, and repairing possible unsafe conditions before accidents occur
9. Arrangements with a medical clinic for handling emergencies[146]

§ 2.16 Training and Development

To ensure proper implementation, communication, and understanding of employee procedures and policies, training and development involving management, supervisors, and employees must occur. Training is essential to acquaint managers, supervisors, and employees with what information can be collected, maintained, used, or disclosed, as well as with what employee activities can be legitimately regulated at and outside the workplace. The following should be considered regarding training and development as they relate to procedures and policies:[147]

1. New employees:
    a. Orientation program
    b. Materials provided
2. Current employees:
    a. Continued training
    b. Apprenticeship programs

---

[144] *See* Decker, Privacy Law § 7.6.

[145] This may be required under federal and state statutes that pertain to health and safety. *See, e.g.,* 29 U.S.C. §§ 651–678 (1988) (Occupational Safety and Health Act); *see* Decker, Privacy Law § 2.13.

[146] This may impact employee privacy interests present in medical records. *See, e.g.,* United States v. Westinghouse Elec. Corp., 638 F.2d 570 (3d Cir. 1980) (recognizing employee medical record privacy); *see also* Decker, Privacy Law §§ 2.31, 7.4.

[147] Adapted from Littler, Audit at H-31 to H-33.

3. Supervisors:
   a. Training provided regarding:
      (i)   Responsibilities
      (ii)   Structure and operations
      (iii) Role
      (iv)   Supervisorial/managerial skills
      (v)   Job requirements
      (vi)   Employee relations
   b. Other in-house training
4. Management development:
   a. Training management
   b. Formal training program
   c. Program content
   d. Program instruction
   e. Determining management training needs and program content
   f. Outside program use
   g. Determining program use responsibility
   h. Evaluating training program results

§ 2.17   Manpower Planning

To ensure consistent and quality development of employee procedures and policies, manpower planning is important. This planning is important for the proper collection, maintenance, use, and disclosure of employment information. Through this planning, employer liability can be minimized or prevented. The following should be considered regarding manpower planning as it relates to procedures and policies:[148]

1. Staffing:
   a. Number of open positions
   b. Competence level
   c. Understaffing
   d. Overstaffing
   e. Backup personnel
2. Planning techniques:
   a. Employer objectives:
      (i)   Short-term
      (ii) Long-term

---

[148] Littler, Audit at H-33 to H-35.

    b. Planning criteria appropriateness for determining employer needs

    c. Workforce forecasts

    d. Planners' cooperation with department heads

    e. Plan updating frequency

3. Implementation:

    a. Planning authority

    b. Control mechanisms

    c. Planning feedback

    d. Coordination with:

        (i)   Internal placement

        (ii) External recruiting

        (iii) Management development

HUMAN RESOURCES AUDITS

§ 2.18   Introduction to Human Resources Audits

Once employee issues and concerns are recognized,[149] a human resources audit can be considered, planned, and conducted. The audit provides a written record of the issues and concerns affecting employees. To perform a human resources audit, the following forms are provided, which may be used separately or as a whole, to evaluate the employer's procedures and policies in areas involving: (1) background information;[150] (2) recruitment, hiring, and workforce composition;[151] (3) job descriptions, assignments, promotions, and transfers;[152] (4) employer communications;[153] and (5) discipline and termination.[154]

§ 2.19   —Background Information Audit Form

This audit form (**Form 2–1**) should be used in obtaining an understanding regarding the employer's philosophy, product, services, growth, and operations. It also indicates what employment information is being collected, maintained, used, and disclosed.

---

[149] See §§ **2.2–2.17.**

[150] See § **2.19.**

[151] See § **2.20.**

[152] See § **2.21.**

[153] See § **2.22.**

[154] See § **2.23.**

FORM 2–1
BACKGROUND INFORMATION AUDIT FORM[155]

1. Attach an organizational chart of the employer's operations.

2. List all employer facilities, their location, the number of supervisory employees, and the number of nonsupervisory employees employed at each facility along with describing each facility's function.

Facility/ Location	Supervisory Employees	Nonsupervisory Employees	Total Function

3. For each facility, specify the number of employees represented by a union, the union's name, and the date of the union's recognition or certification.

Facility	Employees	Union's Name	Date of Recognition or Certification

Attach copies of current collective bargaining agreements.

4. For each facility, list all departments, indicating the person responsible for supervising the department and all job classifications/titles, indicating the number of employees in each classification.

---

[155] Adapted from J. Herman, Employee Relations Audit Questionnaire 4 (Seyfarth, Shaw, Fairweather & Geraldson, Apr. 15, 1984 [hereinafter Herman, Questionnaire]. A broad-based employee relations audit is regularly conducted for employers by Seyfarth, Shaw, Fairweather & Geraldson, to pinpoint employment liability areas, out of its offices located in Los Angeles, California; San Francisco, California; Washington, D.C.; Chicago, Illinois; and New York, New York.

| | | Job | |
Department	Supervisor	Classifications	Employees
_____	_____	_____	_____
_____	_____	_____	_____
_____	_____	_____	_____
_____	_____	_____	_____

Attach any organizational charts.

5. List the name, job title, and duties of the person who has direct responsibility for employment relations procedures and policies at each facility and the length of time that position has been held.

| | | | Time   Position |
Name	Job Title	Duties	Held
_____	_____	_____	_____
_____	_____	_____	_____
_____	_____	_____	_____

6. Identify whether written employer procedures and policies are used for implementing the following:

	Yes	No
a. Fair Employment Practices (FEP)[156]	___	___
b. Fair Labor Standards Act (FLSA)[157]	___	___
c. National Labor Relations Act (NLRA)[158]	___	___
d. Age Discrimination in Employment Act (ADEA)[159]	___	___
e. Occupational Safety and Health Act (OSHA)[160]	___	___
f. Employee Retirement Insurance Security Act (ERISA)[161]	___	___

---

[156] _See, e.g.,_ 42 U.S.C.§§ 2000e-1 to 2002-17 (1988) (Civil Rights Act of 1964); _see also_ Decker, Privacy Law §§ 2.7–2.12, 2.25; Perritt, Dismissal Law §§ 2.2–2.16.

[157] _See_ 29 U.S.C. §§ 201–219 (1988) (Fair Labor Standards Act); _see also_ Perritt, Dismissal Law § 2.25.

[158] _See_ 29 U.S.C. §§ 151–169 (1988) (National Labor Relations Act); _see also_ Decker, Privacy Law § 2.6; Perritt, Dismissal Law § 2.18.

[159] _See_ 29 U.S.C. §§ 621–634 (1988) (Age Discrimination in Employment Act); _see also_ Decker, Privacy Law § 2.9; Perritt, Dismissal Law §§ 2.6–2.7.

[160] _See_ 29 U.S.C. §§ 651–678 (1988) (Occupational Safety and Health Act); _see also_ Decker, Privacy Law § 2.13; Perritt, Dismissal Law § 2.20.

[161] _See_ 29 U.S.C. §§ 1001, 1140–1141 (1988) (Employee Retirement Income Security Act); _see_ Perritt, Dismissal Law § 2.27.

	Yes	No
g. Disabled employment[162]	___	___
h. Employee privacy federal and state statutory matters[163]	___	___
i. Employment record collection, maintenance, use, and disclosure[164]	___	___

Attach copies of existing procedures and policies relating to the above.

7.   Have any facilities been reviewed or investigated by the following governmental agencies:

	Yes	No
a. The Equal Employment Opportunity Commission (EEOC)[165]	___	___
b. A state Equal Employment Opportunity Commission (EEO)[166]	___	___
c. The Department of Labor (DOL)[167]	___	___
d. A state Wage & Hour Commission	___	___
e. The National Labor Relations Board (NLRB)[168]	___	___
f. Occupational Health and Safety Administration (OSHA)[169]	___	___
g. Any other federal or state agency	___	___

---

[162] See 29 U.S.C. §§ 701–796i (1988) (Vocational Rehabilitation Act of 1973); 42 U.S.C. §§ 12101–12213 (Supp. 1992) (Americans with Disabilities Act); see also Decker, Privacy Law § 2.10; Perritt, Dismissal Law §§ 2.14–2.16.

[163] See, e.g., 5 U.S.C. § 552a (1988) (federal Privacy Act of 1974); Cal. Civ. Code § 1783 (West 1986) (state Fair Credit Reporting Act); see also Decker, Privacy Law ch. 2.

[164] See, e.g., Cal. Labor Code § 1198.5 (West 1982) (California's statute covering personnel file regulation); see also Decker, Privacy Law §§ 2.30–2.31, 7.2–7.4.

[165] See, e.g., 42 U.S.C.§§ 2000e-1 to 2002-17 (1988) (Civil Rights Act of 1964); see also Decker, Privacy Law §§ 2.7–2.12, 2.25; Perritt, Dismissal Law §§ 2.2–2.16.

[166] See, e.g., Pa. Stat. Ann. tit. 43, §§ 951–963 (Purdon 1991) (Pennsylvania Human Relations Act); see also Decker, Privacy Law § 2.25.

[167] See, e.g., 29 U.S.C. §§ 201–219 (1988) (Fair Labor Standards Act); see also Perritt, Dismissal Law § 2.25.

[168] See 29 U.S.C. §§ 151–169 (1988) (National Labor Relations Act); see also Decker, Privacy Law § 2.6; Perritt, Dismissal Law § 2.18.

[169] See 29 U.S.C. §§ 651–678 (1988) (Occupational Safety and Health Act); see also Decker, Privacy Law § 2.13; Perritt, Dismissal Law § 2.20.

If the answer is yes to any of the above, set forth the following:

Date   *Agency and Subject*   *Result*

_____   _____   _____

_____   _____   _____

_____   _____   _____

8. Has any facility ever been subject to a conciliation or settlement agreement with:

                                                                      Yes   No

a. The Equal Employment Opportunity Commission (EEOC)[170]   ___   ___

b. A state Equal Employment Opportunity (EEO) Commission[171]   ___   ___

c. Department of Labor (DOL)[172]   ___   ___

d. A state Wage & Hour Commission   ___   ___

e. The National Labor Relations Board (NLRB)[173]   ___   ___

f. Other federal or state agency   ___   ___

9. Has any facility ever been a party to a court decree in a matter involving adverse employment practices?

    ____ Yes   ____ No

    If yes, attach a copy of any decree.

10. Is the following information collected and retained for each employee:[174]

---

[170] *See, e.g.,* 42 U.S.C. §§ 2000e-1 to 2002-17 (1988) (Civil Rights Act of 1964); *see also* Decker, Privacy Law §§ 2.7–2.12, 2.25; Perritt, Dismissal Law §§ 2.2–2.16.

[171] *See, e.g.,* Pa. Stat. Ann. tit. 43, §§ 951–963 (Purdon 1991) (Pennsylvania Human Relations Act); *see also* Decker, Privacy Law § 2.25.

[172] *See, e.g.,* 29 U.S.C. §§ 201–219 (1988) (Fair Labor Standards Act); *see also* Perritt, Dismissal Law § 2.25.

[173] *See, e.g.,* 29 U.S.C. §§ 151–169 (1988) (National Labor Relations Act); *see also* Decker, Privacy Law § 2.6; Perritt, Dismissal Law § 2.18.

[174] A variety of federal and state statutes regulate the types of employment information that may be collected, maintained, used, and disclosed. On the federal level, this is regulated by, *e.g.,* the following federal statutes:

5 U.S.C. § 552a (1988) (Privacy Act of 1974)

15 U.S.C. §§ 1681–1681t (1988) (Fair Credit Reporting Act)

29 U.S.C. §§ 621–634 (1988) (Age Discrimination in Employment Act)

29 U.S.C. §§ 651–678 (1988) (Occupational Safety and Health Act)

		Yes	No	Time Retained
a.	Employee's full name	___	___	_____
b.	Employee's address, including zip code	___	___	_____
c.	Employee's birth date	___	___	_____
d.	Source of the employee's job opening knowledge	___	___	_____
e.	Employee's employment application	___	___	_____
f.	Employee's hiring date	___	___	_____
g.	Employee's race	___	___	_____
h.	Employee's sex	___	___	_____
i.	Employee's occupation or job classification	___	___	_____
j.	Time and day when the employee's workweek begins	___	___	_____
k.	Employee's regular rate of pay such as "per hour," "per week," "piecework," and so forth	___	___	_____
l.	Hours worked by the employee each work day	___	___	_____
m.	Total hours worked by the employee each workweek	___	___	_____
n.	Employee's daily or weekly straight time wages	___	___	_____
o.	Employee's total overtime compensation for the workweek	___	___	_____
p.	Total additions or deductions from wages paid to the employee each pay period	___	___	_____
q.	Total wages paid the employee each pay period	___	___	_____
r.	Date of payment and the pay period covered by the payment	___	___	_____
s.	Date and amount of promotion or demotion received by the employee	___	___	_____

42 U.S.C. §§ 12101–12213 (Supp. 1992) (Americans with Disabilities Act)

42 U.S.C. §§ 2000e-1 to 2002-17 (1988) (Civil Rights Act of 1964)

This is also regulated on the state level. *See, e.g.,* Cal. Civ. Code § 1783 (West 1986) (California's Fair Credit Reporting Act); Cal. Labor Code §§ 1050, 1053, 1054 (West 1971) (California's statute covering employment references); Cal. Labor Code § 1198.5 (West 1982) (California's statute covering personnel file regulation). *See also* Decker, Privacy Law ch. 2; Perritt, Dismissal Law ch. 2.

		Yes	No	*Time* *Retained*
t.	Date of any disciplinary action, including termination, taken against the employee	____	____	_____
u.	Date and description of any employee work-related accidents	____	____	_____
v.	Contact for the employee in case of emergency	____	____	_____
w.	Social Security Number	____	____	_____
x.	Other employee information	____	____	_____
	Describe:			

_____

_____

_____

11. Is the following information disclosed internally or to outside third parties for each employee:[175]

		Yes	No	*If* *Disclosed,* *Explain*
a.	Employee's full name	____	____	_____
b.	Employee's address, including zip code	____	____	_____
c.	Employee's birth date	____	____	_____
d.	Source of the employee's job opening knowledge	____	____	_____
e.	Employee's employment application	____	____	_____
f.	Employee's hiring date	____	____	_____
g.	Employee's race	____	____	_____
h.	Employee' sex	____	____	_____
i.	Employee's occupation or job classification	____	____	_____
j.	Time and day when the employee's workweek begins	____	____	_____
k.	Employee's regular rate of pay such as "per hour," "per week," "piecework," and so forth	____	____	_____
l.	Hours worked by the employee each work day	____	____	_____

---

[175] *See* Decker, Privacy Law chs. 2, 6–8.

		Yes	No	If Disclosed, Explain
m.	Total hours worked by the employee each workweek	___	___	_____
n.	Employee's daily or weekly straight time wages	___	___	_____
o.	Employee's total overtime compensation for the workweek	___	___	_____
p.	Total additions or deductions from wages paid to the employee each pay period	___	___	_____
q.	Total wages paid the employee each pay period	___	___	_____
r.	Date of payment and the pay period covered by the payment	___	___	_____
s.	Date and amount of promotion or demotion received by the employee	___	___	_____
t.	Date of any disciplinary action, including termination, taken against the employee	___	___	_____
u.	Date and description of any employee work-related accidents	___	___	_____
v.	Contact for the employee in case of emergency	___	___	_____
w.	Social Security Number	___	___	_____
x.	Other employee information	___	___	_____

Describe:

_____

_____

_____

12. Is the information set forth at questions 10 and 11 maintained on a computer system?

    ____ Yes   ____ No

13. Are employees provided with the records set forth at questions 10 and 11 on request?

    ____ Yes   ____ No

14. Who has access to personnel files?

_____

15. Describe procedure for updating employee addresses.

_____

16. Are notices relating to the following statutes or subjects posted in conspicuous places in each facility?[176]

		Yes	No
a.	The Civil Rights Act of 1964 (Title VII)[177]	___	___
b.	The Fair Labor Standards Act (FLSA)[178]	___	___
c.	The Age Discrimination in Employment Act (ADEA)[179]	___	___
d.	The Americans with Disabilities Act[180]	___	___
e.	The Employee Polygraph Protection Act[181]	___	___
f.	The Family and Medical Leave Act[182]	___	___
g.	The Occupational Safety and Health Act (OSHA)[183]	___	___
h.	Applicable state wage and hour laws	___	___
i.	Workers' Compensation carrier's name	___	___
j.	Unemployment benefits	___	___
k.	Other required federal and state statute notice postings	___	___

Describe

_____

_____

If yes, where are these notices posted? _____

17. Are employees provided with each wage payment an itemization of all deductions, dates of period compensated, employer's name, employee's name/Social Security number?

____ Yes ____ No

---

[176] For a discussion of these statutory posting requirements, see ch. 3.

[177] 42 U.S.C. §§ 2000e-1 to 2002-17 (1988).

[178] 29 U.S.C. §§ 201–219 (1988).

[179] 29 U.S.C. §§ 621–634 (1988).

[180] 42 U.S.C. §§ 12101–12213 (Supp. 1992).

[181] 29 U.S.C. §§ 2001–2009 (1988).

[182] P.L. 103.3 (Feb. 5, 1993).

[183] 29 U.S.C. §§ 657–678 (1988).

18.   Are EEO-1 reports filed annually?[184]

_____ Yes   _____ No

19.   Does a written affirmative action program (AAP) exist for each facility?[185]

_____ Yes   _____ No

20.   If there is a written fair employment practice policy, attach a copy and indicate whether the written policy is:[186]

		Yes	No
a.	Included in an employee handbook	___	___
b.	Posted on employee bulletin boards	___	___
c.	Published in a newsletter, annual report, and so forth	___	___
d.	Communicated to all recruiting sources	___	___
e.	Included on all purchase orders, leases, and contracts	___	___
f.	Communicated at regularly scheduled employee meetings	___	___
g.	Communicated to manager and supervisor trainees	___	___
h.	Communicated to managers and supervisors	___	___
i.	List other places where the statement is published:		

_____

_____

_____

_____

_____

---

[184] *See, e.g.,* Executive Order No. 11246 (federal contractors), 3 C.F.R. § 339 (1964–1965 compilation), reprinted in 42 U.S.C. § 2000e note, issued on Sept. 24, 1965, as amended; *see also* Decker, Privacy Law § 2.12; Perritt, Dismissal Law § 2.12.

[185] *See, e.g.,* Executive Order No. 11246 (federal contractors), 3 C.F.R. § 339 (1964–1965 compilation), reprinted in 42 U.S.C. § 2000e note, issued on Sept. 24, 1965, as amended; *see also* Decker, Privacy Law § 2.12; Perritt, Dismissal Law § 2.12.

[186] *See, e.g.,* Executive Order No. 11246 (federal contractors), 3 C.F.R. § 339 (1964–1965 compilation), reprinted in 42 U.S.C. § 2000e note, issued on Sept. 24, 1965, as amended; *see also* Decker, Privacy Law § 2.12; Perritt, Dismissal Law § 2.12.

§ 2.20   —Recruitment, Hiring, and Workforce Composition Audit Form

This audit form (**Form 2–2**) identifies the employee interests that may be infringed upon during recruitment, hiring, and after hiring as they affect employee benefits, associations, speech, and information.[187]

FORM 2–2
RECRUITMENT, HIRING, AND WORKFORCE COMPOSITION AUDIT FORM[188]

1. List all oral and written sources in which each facility advertises for employees.[189] Attach a copy of any advertisement used within the last year.

    _____

    _____

    _____

2. Do the advertisements indicate any preference, limitation, or specification based on race, color, religion, age, sex, national origin, or disability?[190]

    _____ Yes _____ No

3. Does the oral or written advertising source used by any facility segregate advertising by sex?[191]

    _____ Yes _____ No

4. Do the advertisements indicate a preference for young applicants or place a limit on the years of experience which the applicant may have?

    _____ Yes _____ No

5. Do the advertisements indicate that the employer is an "Equal Opportunity Employer?"[192]

    _____ Yes _____ No

---

[187] *See* Decker, Privacy Law chs. 6–7.

[188] Adapted from Herman, Questionnaire at 11.

[189] *See, e.g.,* Pittsburgh Press Co. v. Pittsburgh Comm'n on Human Relations, 413 U.S. 376 (1973) (sex-based advertisements prohibited); *see also* Decker, Privacy Law § 6.3.

[190] *See, e.g.,* Pittsburgh Press Co. v. Pittsburgh Comm'n on Human Relations, 413 U.S. 376 (1973) (sex-based advertisements prohibited); *see also* Decker, Privacy Law § 6.3.

[191] *See, e.g.,* Pittsburgh Press Co. v. Pittsburgh Comm'n on Human Relations, 413 U.S. 376 (1973) (sex-based advertisements prohibited); *see also* Decker, Privacy Law § 6.3.

[192] *See, e.g.,* Pittsburgh Press Co. v. Pittsburgh Comm'n on Human Relations, 413 U.S. 376 (1973) (sex-based advertisements prohibited); *see also* Decker, Privacy Law § 6.3.

6. List any high schools, trade schools, or colleges at which each facility recruits

    _____

    _____

    _____

7. Does any facility recruit at organizations/institutions comprised solely of one sex?

    ____ Yes   ____ No

8. During the application process, are inquiries made about an applicant's:[193]

		Yes	No
a.	Credit rating	____	____
b.	Marital status	____	____
c.	Garnishment record	____	____
d.	Prior arrest record	____	____
e.	Prior conviction record	____	____
f.	Ability to be bonded	____	____
g.	Bankruptcy record	____	____
h.	Charges or complaints filed with any governmental agency	____	____
i.	Workers' compensation claims	____	____
j.	Number of children	____	____
k.	Union affiliations	____	____
l.	Ability to speak/write a foreign language	____	____
m.	Marital status	____	____
n.	Disabilities	____	____
o.	Prior addresses	____	____
p.	Religion	____	____

9. Does any facility employ an outside investigator/agency to verify applicant information?[194]

    ____ Yes   ____ No

---

[193] *See, e.g.,* Gregory v. Litton Sys., Inc., 316 F. Supp. 401 (C.D. Cal. 1970), *aff'd with modifications not here relevant,* 472 F.2d 631 (9th Cir. 1972) (arrest record inquiries not permitted); *see also* Decker, Privacy Law § 6.5.

[194] *See, e.g.,* 15 U.S.C. §§ 1681–1681t (1988) (Fair Credit Reporting Act); *see also* Decker, Privacy Law §§ 2.5, 2.23, 6.7.

10.   Are investigative or consumer reports used during the hiring process?[195]

    ____ Yes ____ No

    If yes, specify source:

    _____

    _____

    _____

11.   Are applicants notified that investigative/consumer reports will be used?[196]

    ____ Yes ____ No

12.   Are qualifications for job positions in writing prior to being advertised?

    ____ Yes ____ No

13.   Do the hiring criteria for any job include a limitation on an applicant's:[197]

		Yes	No
a.	Race	___	___
b.	Sex	___	___
c.	National origin	___	___
d.	Religion	___	___
e.	Age	___	___
f.	Height	___	___
g.	Weight	___	___
h.	Education	___	___
i.	Marital status	___	___
j.	Place of residence	___	___
k.	Sexual persuasion; i.e., homosexuality, lesbianism, transvestitism	___	___
l.	Disability	___	___
m.	Pregnancy	___	___

---

[195] *See, e.g.,* 15 U.S.C. §§ 1681–1681t (1988) (Fair Credit Reporting Act); *see also* Decker, Privacy Law §§ 2.5, 2.23, 6.7.

[196] *See, e.g.,* 15 U.S.C. §§ 1681–1681t (1988) (Fair Credit Reporting Act); *see also* Decker, Privacy Law §§ 2.5, 2.23, 6.7.

[197] *See, e.g.,* 42 U.S.C. §§ 2000e-1 to 2002-17 (1988) (Civil Rights Act of 1964); *see also* Decker, Privacy Law §§ 2.7–2.12, 2.25, 6.4–6.5.

	Yes	No
n. Military service	___	___
o. Organizations, activities	___	___
p. Filing a charge with any governmental agency	___	___
q. Ability to speak English	___	___

14. Is any preference given to applicants who are:

	Yes	No
a. Related to present or former rank-and-file employees[198]	___	___
b. Related to present or former managers or supervisors[199]	___	___
c. Referred by present or former employees[200]	___	___

15. Describe the employer's policy regarding hiring present employee relatives.[201]

_____

_____

_____

16. Describe the steps used in processing job applicants.

_____

_____

_____

17. List all individuals responsible for hiring employees.

_____

_____

_____

---

[198] *See, e.g.,* Sprogis v. United Air Lines, Inc., 444 F.2d 1194 (7th Cir.), *cert. denied,* 404 U.S. 991 (1971), *on remand,* 56 F.R.D. 420 (1972) (spousal policies); *see also* Decker, Privacy Law §§ 7.27–7.28.

[199] *See, e.g.,* Sprogis v. United Air Lines, Inc., 444 F.2d 1194 (7th Cir.), *cert. denied,* 404 U.S. 991 (1971), *on remand,* 56 F.R.D. 420 (1972) (spousal policies); *see also* Decker, Privacy Law §§ 7.27–7.28.

[200] *See, e.g.,* Sprogis v. United Air Lines, Inc., 444 F.2d 1194 (7th Cir.), *cert. denied,* 404 U.S. 991 (1971), *on remand,* 56 F.R.D. 420 (1972) (spousal policies); *see also* Decker, Privacy Law §§ 7.27–7.28.

[201] *See, e.g.,* Sprogis v. United Air Lines, Inc., 444 F.2d 1194 (7th Cir.), *cert. denied,* 404 U.S. 991 (1971), *on remand,* 56 F.R.D. 420 (1972) (spousal policies); *see also* Decker, Privacy Law §§ 7.27–7.28.

18. Are any physical, manual, written, verbal, or other tests used in the applicant selection process?[202]

_____ Yes   _____ No

If yes, attach a copy or description of each test used.

19. Are written job applications used?[203]

_____ Yes   _____ No

If yes, attach copies of the applications used.

20. Are employees required to sign applications?[204]

_____ Yes   _____ No

21. Are applicants required to take a polygraph, honesty, or similar test?[205]

_____ Yes   _____ No

22. Are applicants required to provide a photograph prior to an interview?[206]

_____ Yes   _____ No

23. Are applicants advised of the full range of job openings?

_____ Yes   _____ No

24. For any job position, is there a preference for a particular sex?[207]

_____ Yes   _____ No

25. Are any employment limitations imposed on persons with young children?

_____ Yes   _____ No

Describe if limitations:

_____

---

[202] *See, e.g.,* United States v. South Carolina, 434 U.S. 1026 (1978) (some tests favor white, middle-class backgrounds); *see also* Decker, Privacy Law §§ 6.14–6.21.

[203] For information regarding applications and their contents, see ch. 3; *see also* Decker, Privacy Law § 6.4.

[204] For information regarding applications and their contents, see ch. 3; *see also* Decker, Privacy Law § 6.4.

[205] *See, e.g.,* Leibowitz v. H.A. Winston Co., 342 Pa. Super. 111, 493 A.2d 111 (1985) (employer violation of polygraph statute); *see also* Decker, Privacy Law §§ 2.35, 6.19–6.20.

[206] *See, e.g.,* EEOC Decision (Jan. 4, 1966); Opinion Letter of EEOC's General Counsel No. 193-65 (Jan. 24, 1965) (photographing applicants prohibited under FEP statutes); *see also* Decker, Privacy Law § 6.11.

[207] *See, e.g.,* 42 U.S.C. §§ 2000e-1 to 2002-17 (1988) (Civil Rights Act of 1964); *see also* Decker, Privacy Law §§ 2.8, 2.25; Perritt, Dismissal Law §§ 2.3–2.5.

26. Is there a preferred age range for any job?[208]

_____ Yes _____ No

If yes, specify classifications and qualifications:

_____

_____

27. What is each facility's policy regarding hiring pregnant applicants?[209]

_____

_____

_____

28. Are physical examinations required only after an employment offer is made?[210]

_____ Yes _____ No

If this examination is not required for all employees, specify for which categories:

_____

_____

29. Is the examining physician provided with a description of the job to be performed by the employee?[211]

_____ Yes _____ No

30. Does each facility have the power:

		Yes	No
a.	To recruit its own applicants?	_____	_____
b.	To hire new employees?	_____	_____

---

[208] *See, e.g.,* 29 U.S.C. §§ 621–634 (1988) (Age Discrimination in Employment Act); *see also* Decker, Privacy Law §§ 2.9, 2.25; Perritt, Dismissal Law §§ 2.6–2.7.

[209] *See, e.g.,* 42 U.S.C. §§ 2000e-1 to 2002-17 (1988) (Civil Rights Act of 1964); *see also* Decker, Privacy Law §§ 2.8, 2.25; Perritt, Dismissal Law §§ 2.3–2.5.

[210] *See, e.g.,* 29 U.S.C. §§ 701–796i (1988) (Vocational Rehabilitation Act of 1973); 42 U.S.C. §§ 12101–12213 (Supp. 1992) (Americans with Disabilities Act); *see also* Decker, Privacy Law §§ 2.10, 2.25; Perritt, Dismissal Law §§ 2.14–2.16.

[211] *See, e.g.,* 29 U.S.C. §§ 701–796i (1988) (Vocational Rehabilitation Act of 1973); 42 U.S.C. §§ 12101–12213 (Supp. 1992) (Americans with Disabilities Act); *see also* Decker, Privacy Law §§ 2.10, 2.25; Perritt, Dismissal Law §§ 2.14–2.16.

Specify individuals who have the right to hire and their location:

Person	Title	Location

31. Does any policy exist regarding applicants proving legal residency?[212]

    ____ Yes   ____ No

    If yes, describe policy: _____

    _____

32. How is legal residency verified?[213]

    _____

33. How are applicants informed that they will not be offered a position?

    _____

    _____

34. Define the geographic area from which applicants come.

    _____

35. For each facility, provide the following information, if it is readily available:[214]

    a. Estimated minority population in the immediate labor area.

    _____

    b. Estimated minority percentage of the workforce in the immediate labor area.

    _____

---

[212] *See, e.g.,* McCarthy v. Philadelphia Civil Serv. Comm'n, 424 U.S. 645 (1976) (residency requirements necessary to serve legitimate employer interests are valid); *see also* Decker, Privacy Law § 8.13.

[213] *See, e.g.,* Immigration Reform and Control Act of 1986, Pub. L. No. 99-603 (Nov. 6, 1986), 100 Stat. 3359 (codified in scattered sections of 7 U.S.C. § 2025; 8 U.S.C. §§ 1101, 1152–53, 1160–61, 1184, 1186–87, 1252, 1254–55a, 1258–59, 1321, 1324–24b, 1357, 1364–65; 18 U.S.C. § 1546; 20 U.S.C. §§ 1091, 1096; 29 U.S.C. §§ 1802, 1813, 1816, 1851; 42 U.S.C. §§ 303, 502, 602–03, 672–73, 1203, 1320b-7, 1353, 1396b, 1436a, 1437r). *See also* Decker, Privacy Law §§ 2.20, 6.12.

[214] This may be required under federal and state FEP statutes. *See, e.g.,* 42 U.S.C. §§ 2000e-1 to 2002-17 (1988) (Civil Rights Act of 1964); *see also* Decker, Privacy Law §§ 2.7–2.12, 2.25; Perritt, Dismissal Law §§ 2.2–2.16.

c. Estimated size of the minority unemployment force in the immediate labor area.

_____

d. Explain what labor area is used for this data.

_____

_____

_____

36. Are employees required to sign restrictive covenants, nondisclosure of trade secrets, or noncompetition agreements?[215]

____ Yes ____ No

If so, attach a copy of this agreement(s).

§ 2.21 —Job Descriptions, Assignments, Promotions, and Transfers Audit Form

This audit form (**Form 2–3**) assists in identifying workplace employee intrusions arising out of job descriptions, assignment, promotions, and transfers.[216]

FORM 2–3
JOB DESCRIPTIONS, ASSIGNMENTS, PROMOTIONS, AND
TRANSFERS AUDIT FORM[217]

1. Are written job descriptions maintained?

____ Yes ____ No

If yes, attach copies.

If no, explain how employees are informed of their specific responsibilities.

_____

2. Are there any job classifications which contain criteria relating to a person's physical attributes; i.e., weight, height, appearance, and so forth?[218]

____ Yes ____ No

---

[215] *See, e.g.,* Tabs Assocs., Inc. v. Brohawn, 59 Md. App. 330, 475 A.2d 1203 (1984) (future use of trade secrets); *see generally* Decker, Covenants; *see also* Decker, Privacy Law §§ 4.13, 8.8–8.9.

[216] *See* Decker, Privacy Law ch. 7.

[217] Adapted from Herman, Questionnaire at 19.

[218] *See, e.g.,* 42 U.S.C. §§ 2000e-1 to 2002-17 (1988) (Civil Rights Act of 1964); *see also* Decker, Privacy Law §§ 2.7–2.12, 2.25, 6.4–6.5; Perritt, Dismissal Law §§ 2.2–2.16.

3. Are females excluded from any job categories because of state protective legis-
    lation regarding hours worked, work type, or weight-lifting restrictions?[219]

    _____ Yes   _____ No

    If yes, list categories:

    _____

    _____

    _____

    _____

4. Describe the employer's policy for accommodating employees who cannot
    work specified days of the week or hours of the day.[220]

    _____

    _____

5. Are there any jobs which employees over age 40 are unable to perform?[221]

    _____ Yes   _____ No

    If yes, list these jobs and explain why employees over age 40 cannot perform
    them.

    _____

    _____

    _____

6. Is there a minimum age for employment?

    _____ Yes   _____ No

    If yes, what is that age? _____

    _____

7. What benefits are given nonunion employees on the basis of their seniority?

    _____

    _____

---

[219] *See, e.g.,* 42 U.S.C. §§ 2000e-1 to 2002-17 (1988) (Civil Rights Act of 1964); *see also* Decker,
Privacy Law §§ 2.7–2.12, 2.25, 6.4–6.5; Perritt, Dismissal Law §§ 2.2–2.16.

[220] *See, e.g.,* 42 U.S.C. §§ 2000e-1 to 2002-17 (1988) (Civil Rights Act of 1964); *see also* Decker,
Privacy Law §§ 2.7–2.12, 2.24, 7.33; Perritt, Dismissal Law §§ 2.2–2.16.

[221] *See, e.g.,* 29 U.S.C. §§ 621–634 (1988) (Age Discrimination in Employment Act); *see also*
Decker, Privacy Law §§ 2.9, 2.25; Perritt, Dismissal Law §§ 2.6–2.7.

8. How is seniority determined?

    _____

    Is age or sex used in determining seniority?[222]

    _____ Yes   _____ No

    If yes, explain use.

    _____

    _____

9. When determining job assignments and transfers, are the following factors considered?

                                                           Yes   *No*

    a. Age[223]   _____   _____

    b. Sex[224]   _____   _____

    c. Race/Ethnic origin[225]   _____   _____

    d. Disability[226]   _____   _____

    e. Union membership[227]   _____   _____

    If yes to any factor, explain its use.

    _____

    _____

    Are records made of this?

    _____ Yes   _____ No

    If yes, where are they kept?

    _____

---

[222] *See, e.g.,* 29 U.S.C. §§ 621–634 (1988) (Age Discrimination in Employment Act); 42 U.S.C. §§ 2000e-1 to 2002-17 (1988) (Civil Rights Act of 1964); *see also* Decker, Privacy Law §§ 2.8–2.9, 2.25; Perritt, Dismissal Law §§ 2.3–2.7.

[223] *See, e.g.,* 29 U.S.C. §§ 621–634 (1988) (Age Discrimination in Employment Act); *see also* Decker, Privacy Law § 2.9, 2.25; Perritt, Dismissal Law §§ 2.6–2.7.

[224] *See, e.g.,* 42 U.S.C. §§ 2000e-1 to 2002-17 (1988) (Civil Rights Act of 1964); *see also* Decker, Privacy Law § 2.8, 2.25; Perritt, Dismissal Law §§ 2.3–2.5.

[225] *See, e.g.,* 42 U.S.C. §§ 2000e-1 to 2002-17 (1988) (Civil Rights Act of 1964); *see also* Decker, Privacy Law § 2.8, 2.25; Perritt, Dismissal Law §§ 2.3–2.5.

[226] *See, e.g.,* 29 U.S.C. §§ 701–796i (1988) (Vocational Rehabilitation Act of 1973); 42 U.S.C. §§ 12101–12213 (Supp. 1992) (Americans with Disabilities Act); *see also* Decker, Privacy Law §§ 2.10, 225; Perritt, Dismissal Law §§ 2.14–2.16.

[227] *See, e.g.,* 29 U.S.C. §§ 151–169 (1982) (National Labor Relations Act); *see also* Decker, Privacy Law §§ 2.6, 2.24, 8.6; Perritt, Dismissal Law § 2.18.

10. Has employment in any job, lines of progression, or departments been based on:

	Yes	No
a. Race[228]	⎯⎯	⎯⎯
b. Sex[229]	⎯⎯	⎯⎯
c. Age[230]	⎯⎯	⎯⎯
d. Disability[231]	⎯⎯	⎯⎯

11. Is a seniority system presently maintained which is based on service during the period when certain jobs, lines of progression, or departments were so segregated?

    ⎯⎯ Yes ⎯⎯ No

12. Are employees permitted to transfer into jobs in lines of progression or departments from which they were formerly excluded?

    ⎯⎯ Yes ⎯⎯ No

13. Are vacant job positions advertised or announced to current employees?

    ⎯⎯ Yes ⎯⎯ No

    If yes, are records maintained of who applies for these jobs?

    ⎯⎯ Yes ⎯⎯ No

14. Are records maintained reflecting the reasons for denying or awarding a job to a current employee?

    ⎯⎯ Yes ⎯⎯ No

    If yes, describe:

    _____

    _____

    _____

---

[228] *See, e.g.,* 42 U.S.C. §§ 2000e-1 to 2002-17 (1988) (Civil Rights Act of 1964); *see also* Decker, Privacy Law §§ 2.8, 2.25; Perritt, Dismissal Law §§ 2.3–2.5.

[229] *See, e.g.,* 42 U.S.C. §§ 2000e-1 to 2002-17 (1988) (Civil Rights Act of 1964); *see also* Decker, Privacy Law §§ 2.8, 2.25; Perritt, Dismissal Law §§ 2.3–2.5.

[230] *See, e.g.,* 29 U.S.C. §§ 621–634 (1988) (Age Discrimination in Employment Act); *see also* Decker, Privacy Law §§ 2.9, 2.25; Perritt, Dismissal Law §§ 2.6–2.7.

[231] *See, e.g.,* 29 U.S.C. §§ 701–796i (1988) (Vocational Rehabilitation Act of 1973); 42 U.S.C. §§ 12101–12213 (Supp. 1992) (Americans with Disabilities Act); *see also* Decker, Privacy Law §§ 2.10, 2.25; Perritt, Dismissal Law §§ 2.14–2.16.

15. How does the employer determine whether an employee should be permitted to move into another position?

     _____

     _____

     _____

16. Are any of the following factors used in determining whether an employee will move to another job?

                                                                    Yes   No

     a. Race[232]   ____ ____

     b. Sex[233]   ____ ____

     c. Age[234]   ____ ____

     d. Disability[235]   ____ ____

     If yes to any factor, explain its use.

     _____

     _____

17. Are any jobs, lines of progression, or departments limited to persons of one sex?[236]

     ____ Yes   ____ No

18. Are supervisory personnel required to submit written decisions and reasons when employees are passed over for promotions?

     ____ Yes   ____ No

19. Are employees promoted or transferred between facilities?

     ____ Yes   ____ No

---

[232] *See, e.g.,* 42 U.S.C. §§ 2000e-1 to 2002-17 (1988) (Civil Rights Act of 1964); *see also* Decker, Privacy Law §§ 2.8, 2.25; Perritt, Dismissal Law §§ 2.3–2.5.

[233] *See, e.g.,* 42 U.S.C. §§ 2000e-1 to 2002-17 (1988) (Civil Rights Act of 1964); *see also* Decker, Privacy Law §§ 2.8, 2.25; Perritt, Dismissal Law §§ 2.3–2.5.

[234] *See, e.g.,* 29 U.S.C. §§ 621–634 (1988) (Age Discrimination in Employment Act); *see also* Decker, Privacy Law §§ 2.9, 2.25; Perritt, Dismissal Law §§ 2.6–2.7.

[235] *See, e.g.,* 29 U.S.C. §§ 701–796i (1988) (Vocational Rehabilitation Act of 1973); 42 U.S.C. 12101–12213 (Supp. 1992) (Americans with Disabilities Act); *see also* Decker, Privacy Law §§ 2.10, 2.25; Perritt, Dismissal Law §§ 2.14–2.16.

[236] *See, e.g.,* 42 U.S.C. §§ 2000e-1 to 2002-17 (1988) (Civil Rights Act of 1964); *see also* Decker, Privacy Law §§ 2.8, 2.25; Perritt, Dismissal Law §§ 2.3–2.5.

If yes, how often does this occur? _____

_____

20. For each job classification, describe the training programs used, indicating any
     employee participation prerequisites.

                                                              Participation
     Training Program   *Prerequisites*

     _____   _____

     _____   _____

     _____   _____

21. Describe procedures for evaluating employee performance.[237]

     _____

     _____

     If a form is used, attach.

22. How frequently are performance evaluations conducted?[238]

     _____

     _____

23. Are performance evaluations reviewed by anyone other than the person who
     prepared the evaluation?[239]

     _____ Yes   _____ No

24. Describe procedures for reviewing performance evaluations with employees.[240]

     _____

25. Describe the training that supervisors receive regarding employee perfor-
     mance evaluations.[241]

     _____

     _____

     _____

---

[237] *See* Decker, Privacy Law § 7.30.

[238] *See* Decker, Privacy Law § 7.30.

[239] *See* Decker, Privacy Law § 7.30.

[240] *See* Decker, Privacy Law § 7.30.

[241] *See* Decker, Privacy Law § 7.30.

§ 2.22 —Employer Communications Audit Form

This audit form (**Form 2–4**) identifies how the employer communicates employee workplace procedures and policies.[242]

FORM 2–4
EMPLOYER COMMUNICATIONS AUDIT FORM[243]

1. Does the employer have an orientation program for acquainting new employees with procedures and policies?

    ____ Yes   ____ No

    If yes, list the subjects discussed and the documents presented to a new employee. Attach copies of booklets or other documents which are given to new employees.

    _____

    _____

2. If there is an orientation program, list the persons responsible for or who participate in the program.

    _____

    _____

3. Are employees required to sign a document acknowledging receipt of an employee handbook or similar document?[244]

    ____ Yes   ____ No

    If so, attach copy of acknowledgment.

4. When was the employee handbook last revised?[245]

    _____

---

[242] *See generally* Decker, Handbooks; *see also* Decker, Privacy Law § 4.14, ch. 7.

[243] Adapted from Herman, Questionnaire at 33.

[244] *See, e.g.,* Leikvold v. Valley View Community Hosp., 141 Ariz. 544, 688 P.2d 170 (1984) (handbooks may create binding employment commitments). *Contra,* Reynolds Mfg. Co. v. Mendoza, 644 S.W.2d 536 (Tex. 1982) (handbooks do not create binding employment commitments). *See generally* Decker, Handbooks; *see also* Decker, Privacy Law § 4.14; Gross, Dismissal Forms ch. 1; Perritt, Dismissal Law ch. 8. See chs. 10, 11.

[245] *See, e.g.,* Leikvold v. Valley View Community Hosp., 141 Ariz. 544, 688 P.2d 170 (1984) (handbooks may create binding employment commitments). *Contra,* Reynolds Mfg. Co. v. Mendoza, 644 S.W.2d 536 (Tex. 1982) (handbooks do not create binding employment commitments). *See generally* Decker, Handbooks; *see also* Decker, Privacy Law § 4.14; Gross, Dismissal Forms ch. 1; Perritt, Dismissal Law ch. 8. See chs. 10, 11.

By whom was the handbook revised?

_____

5. Is there an employer/facility newsletter?

 _____ Yes _____ No

 If so, attach copies for past year.

6. What is the employer's policy regarding employee bulletin board use?

 _____

 _____

7. Has the employer conducted surveys among employees during the past five years?

 _____ Yes _____ No

 If yes, when was the last survey conducted? Who conducted the survey? Attach a copy of the questionnaire and the responses.

 _____

 _____

8. Are there any committees composed entirely or partially of employees?

 _____ Yes _____ No

 If so, describe the committee's composition and purpose.

 _____

 _____

 _____

9. Are there any regularly scheduled meetings between employees and supervisors?

 _____ Yes _____ No

10. How do employees bring their complaints or concerns to the attention of managers and supervisors?[246]

 _____

 _____

 _____

---

[246] For a discussion of nonunion employee complaint resolution procedures, *see* Gross, Dismissal Forms §§ 1.21–1.27.

11.   What procedures are used by managers and supervisors for responding to employee concerns or complaints?[247]

_____

_____

12.   Are there any procedures by which an employee may appeal decisions of supervisors?[248]

_____ Yes _____ No

§ 2.23   —Discipline and Termination Audit Form

This audit form (**Form 2–5**) identifies the procedures and policies for resolving employee disputes that may arise at hiring, at the workplace, and outside the workplace regarding discipline and termination, with a view towards limiting employer liability.[249]

FORM 2–5
DISCIPLINE AND TERMINATION AUDIT FORM[250]

1.   Are there any written rules of conduct?[251]

_____ Yes _____ No

2.   When and how are employees informed of employer rules?

_____

3.   Who is responsible for enforcing employer rules?

_____

4.   Do persons responsible for enforcing rules have any discretion in determining the disciplinary penalty to be imposed once it is determined that an offense has occurred?

_____ Yes _____ No

---

[247] *Id.*

[248] *Id.*

[249] *See* Decker, Privacy Law chs. 6–8.

[250] Adapted from Herman, Questionnaire at 40.

[251] *See, e.g.,* Leikvold v. Valley View Community Hosp., 141 Ariz. 544, 688 P.2d 170 (1984) (handbooks may create binding employment commitments). *Contra,* Reynolds Mfg. Co. v. Mendoza, 644 S.W.2d 536 (Tex. 1982) (handbooks do not create binding employment commitments). *See generally* Decker, Handbooks; *see also* Decker, Privacy Law § 4.14, Gross, Dismissal Forms §§ 1.1–1.15, Perritt, Dismissal Law ch. 8. See chs. 10, 11.

5. Is there any procedure for progressive discipline?[252]

   _____ Yes   _____ No

6. How are managers and supervisors informed of the employer's disciplinary procedure?

   _____

7. How and when are employees made aware of the disciplinary procedure?

   _____

8. Are disciplinary decisions made by supervisors reviewed?

   _____ Yes   _____ No

9. How and when are employees informed of a decision to discipline them?

   _____

10. Prior to being disciplined, is an employee given an opportunity to present his or her explanation?[253]

    _____ Yes   _____ No

11. Are employees given the opportunity to discuss the reasons for disciplinary actions against them?[254]

    _____ Yes   _____ No

    If yes, please explain.

    _____

12. Are employees allowed to appeal disciplinary actions; i.e., to a higher-level manager or panel of officials?[255]

    _____ Yes   _____ No

    If yes, please explain the appeal procedure.

    _____

---

[252] "Progressive discipline" is generally considered an escalating set of steps, imposing more severe discipline for each succeeding employer rule violation by an employee, that eventually culminates in termination. These disciplinary steps may consist of an oral warning, written warning, suspension, and termination. For a discussion of progressive discipline procedures, *see* Gross, Dismissal Forms § 1.10.

[253] *Id.* §§ 1.21–1.27.

[254] *Id.*

[255] *Id.*

13. Is an employee who is being investigated to determine whether discipline is appropriate, or who is being notified of a disciplinary decision, permitted to have a person of his or her choice present at the investigation or negotiation meeting?[256]

_____ Yes _____ No

If yes and there are exceptions, explain exceptions.

_____

_____

14. If an employee receives one or more warnings or negative evaluations, are any of the following measures taken to remedy the problem:

		Yes	*No*
a.	Upward or downward vertical transfer to place the employee in a position more closely suited to his or her abilities?	____	____
b.	Lateral transfer to alleviate possible personality conflicts between the employee and immediate supervisor or between the employee and fellow workers?	____	____
c.	Additional employee job training?	____	____
d.	Other?	____	____

15. Who is responsible for terminating employees?

_____

16. Describe the procedure for documenting disciplinary decisions and the reasons for the decision.[257]

_____

17. Is age or race ever used as a factor in a decision to terminate employees?[258]

_____ Yes _____ No

If yes to any of the above factors, explain its use.

_____

---

[256] *See, e.g.,* NLRB v. J. Weingarten, Inc., 420 U.S. 251 (1975) (acknowledging private sector employee's right to union representation when an employer's investigation may reasonably result in disciplinary action); *see also* Decker, Privacy Law § 7.29.

[257] *See* Gross, Dismissal Forms § 1.15.

[258] *See, e.g.,* 42 U.S.C. §§ 2000e-1 to 2002-17 (1988) (Civil Rights Act of 1964); *see also* Decker, Privacy Law §§ 2.7–2.12, 2.25; Perritt, Dismissal Law §§ 2.2–2.16.

18. Is sex ever used as a factor in a decision to terminate employees?[259]

    _____ Yes _____ No

    If yes, explain when and how sex is used as a factor.

    _____

19. Is a terminated employee allowed to appeal to a higher-level manager or panel of officials?[260]

    _____ Yes _____ No

    If yes, please explain the appeal procedure.

    _____

20. Are employees provided with a written termination notice?[261]

    _____ Yes _____ No

21. When are terminated employees given a final paycheck?

    _____

22. Are terminated employees eligible for severance pay?

    _____ Yes _____ No

23. Are exit interviews conducted?

    _____ Yes _____ No

    By whom? _____

24. Are records maintained of all disciplinary actions, including termination?[262]

    _____ Yes _____ No

25. If yes, describe what records are maintained and where they are maintained.[263]

    _____

    _____

---

[259] *See, e.g.,* 42 U.S.C. §§ 2000e-1 to 2002-17 (1988) (Civil Rights Act of 1964); *see also* Decker, Privacy Law §§ 2.7–2.12, 2.25; Perritt, Dismissal Law §§ 2.2–2.16.

[260] For a discussion of nonunion employee complaint resolution procedures, *see* Gross, Dismissal Forms §§ 1.21–1.27.

[261] *Id.*

[262] *See, e.g.,* Pa. Stat. Ann. tit. 43, §§ 1321–1324 (Purdon 1991) (Pennsylvania's statute regulating personnel file inspection); *see also* Decker, Privacy Law §§ 2.30, 7.3.

[263] *See, e.g.,* Pa. Stat. Ann. tit. 43, §§ 1321–1324 (Purdon 1991) (Pennsylvania's statute regulating personnel file inspection); *see also* Decker, Privacy Law §§ 2.30, 7.3.

26. Are copies of warnings and terminations placed in the employee's personnel file?[264]

　　 ____ Yes ____ No

27. Do warnings contain the following:

	Yes	No
a. Offense	____	____
b. Action necessary for improvement	____	____
c. Consequences of failure to improve	____	____

HUMAN RESOURCES AUDIT RESULTS

§ 2.24 Implementing Audit Changes

After the human resources audit has been completed, the following should be considered in compiling results for further employer action. This will enable the employer to remedy procedure and policy deficiencies as follows:

1. The human resources audit report should:
   a. Identify employee priorities
   b. Distinguish facts versus opinions
   c. Evaluate employee alternatives
   d. Assess employee vulnerabilities
   e. Identify confidentiality problems
2. Implementing employee changes by:
   a. Avoiding overreaction
   b. Considering gradual versus immediate changes
   c. Publicizing changes
   d. Using employee committees
   e. Union involvement where collective bargaining agreements are involved
   f. Coordination
   g. Overall versus specific changes
   h. Reviewing the effects
   i. New contract provisions where collective bargaining agreements are involved

---

[264] *See, e.g.,* Pa. Stat. Ann. tit. 43, §§ 1321–1324 (Purdon 1991) (Pennsylvania's statute regulating personnel file inspection); *see also* Decker, Privacy Law §§ 2.30, 7.3.

3. Establishing employee monitoring systems regarding:

    a. FEP statutory compliance

    b. Union activities

    c. Health and safety

    d. Reporting and recordkeeping

    e. Management responsiveness

    f. Employee development

    g. Disclosure restrictions

§ 2.25   Overall Guidelines

The goal of any human resources audit should be the development of overall employer procedures and policies. These general guidelines should be used to prevent or minimize employer liability. Overall guidelines should include:

1. Consistently applying and following procedures and policies
2. Knowing employee rights under applicable federal and state statutes[265]
3. Making certain that management and supervisory personnel know the applicable law, as well as employer procedures and policies involving employees[266]
4. Making it a policy for employers to refrain from commenting on or disclosing information that could affect employee interests involving hair style, religion, politics, spouse, sexual habits, or other sensitive areas[267]
5. Respecting employee rights to privacy and confidentiality[268]
6. Reviewing employee privacy procedures and policies annually to ensure that they are consistent, conform to applicable statutes, and reflect the employer's philosophy[269]
7. Avoiding spontaneous action or action taken in anger
8. Providing employees with some form of due process[270] prior to implementing adverse employment actions by:

    a. Taking no adverse employment action without evidence

    b. Giving the employee an opportunity to present counter-evidence prior to a final adverse employment action

---

[265] *See generally* Decker, Privacy Law ch. 2.

[266] For a discussion of due process considerations in disciplining employees, *see* Decker, Privacy Law § 7.29; Gross, Dismissal Forms §§ 1.1–1.15.

[267] *See generally* Decker, Privacy Law.

[268] *Id.*

[269] *Id.*

[270] *Id.*

    c. Treating all adverse employment actions consistently

    d. Establishing an appeal method for adverse employment actions through internal or external procedures

    e. Giving the employee an opportunity to review, comment on, and copy any written performance evaluations or personnel file memoranda pertinent to the adverse employment action

    f. Telling the employee why the adverse employment action is being taken

    g. Making certain that appeal procedures for adverse employment actions are known and available to all employees

Employers should be aware that employee issues and concerns can confront even the most careful, ethical, and innocent employer.[271] Potential employee claims can be anticipated by periodically updating procedures and policies to reflect the employer's operation and current statutory requirements. At a minimum, updating will safeguard employers against incurring damaging liability that may curtail the employer's business prospects.[272]

HUMAN RESOURCE ADMINISTRATION

§ 2.26   Human Resource Administration of Privacy Responsibilities

Regarding employee privacy procedures and policies, the human resources staff should have the following responsibilities:

1. Preparing procedure and policy recommendations
2. Coordinating and facilitating planning by and among management and supervisors that is necessary for the orderly accomplishment of privacy procedure and policy objectives
3. Continuously reviewing the employer's progress in achieving privacy procedure and policy goals

---

[271] *Id.*

[272] *See, e.g.,* Lewis v. Equitable Life Assurance Soc'y, 361 N.W.2d 875 (Minn. Ct. App. 1985), *aff'd in pertinent part,* 389 N.W.2d 876 (Minn. 1986) (group of employees defamed by employer's false and malicious termination reasons; $425,000 damage award); *see also* Decker, Privacy Law ch. 5.

4. Consulting with employees, supervisors, and managers in determining the feasibility of any privacy procedures and policies

5. Conducting and coordinating research as may be necessary and desirable to develop and implement effective and efficient privacy procedures and policies

6. Conducting studies and analyses of the actual or potential short- and long-term effects regarding present or proposed privacy procedures and policies

7. Assisting in reviewing federal and state actions affecting privacy procedures and policies

8. Serving as the central source to collect and disseminate ideas and information bearing on privacy procedures and policies

9. Exercising all other functions as may be necessary to accomplish its duties regarding privacy procedures and policies

In addition, the human resources staff, in carrying out its employee privacy responsibilities, should:

1. Have access to records, reports, audits, reviews, documents, papers, recommendations, or other material

2. Make investigations and reports relating to procedure and policy administration of the applicable employer facility as necessary or desirable

3. Request information or assistance as may be necessary for carrying out privacy procedure and policy responsibilities

4. Require by written notice the production of information, documents, reports, answers, records, accounts, papers, and other necessary data and documentary evidence, not otherwise restricted

5. Have direct and prompt access to the company's president or chief operating officer when necessary for the performance of privacy functions and responsibilities

6. Select, appoint, and employ the persons necessary for carrying out privacy procedures and policies

§ 2.27   Handling Personnel Information

To limit potential employer liability for mishandling information in its collection, maintenance, use, or disclosure, the following should be considered:

1. Deal with employees truthfully

2. Employee conduct should not be characterized as more favorable or worse than it really is

3. Communications in and out of the workplace should be job-related and disclosed only to those who need to know[273]

4. In dealing with applicants, employers have a duty to find out as much job-related information as possible as part of the hiring process[274]

5. When asked for references, obtain or have ready a release from the former employee permitting job-related information disclosure[275]

6. In the absence of a release, disclose only truthful, verifiable information that falls within the former employer's business interests who is disclosing the information and the prospective employer who is seeking the information[276]

7. Conduct exit interviews when an employee leaves to obtain an agreement regarding how future reference inquiries should be handled[277]

8. To avoid liability for invasion of privacy, clearly notify employees of testing policies to remove any privacy expectation[278]

9. Employee adverse actions should be properly documented because this is often the employer's best litigation defense[279]

§ 2.28 Employee Complaints

In resolving employee complaints, the human resource staff should:

1. Receive and investigate complaints or information from an employee concerning violations of law, rules, or regulations along with mismanagement, gross waste of funds, abuse of authority, or a substantial and specific danger to health and safety

2. Not take, direct others to take, recommend, or approve a personnel action against any employee as a reprisal for making a complaint or disclosing information to the human resources staff, unless the complaint was made or the information disclosed with the knowledge that it was false or with willful disregard for its truth or falsity

---

[273] *See, e.g.,* Carney v. Memorial Hosp., 64 N.Y.2d 770, 475 N.E.2d 451, 485 N.Y.S.2d 984 (1985) (unfavorable employment reference); *see also* Decker, Privacy Law §§ 2.34, 4.4, 6.13.

[274] *See, e.g.,* Pruitt v. Pavelin, 141 Ariz. 195, 685 P.2d 1347 (1984) (negligent hiring in employment of known forger); *see also* Decker, Privacy Law § 6.22.

[275] See ch. 9.

[276] *Id.*

[277] *Id.*

[278] See ch. 9.

[279] *See* Schneider, *Employers Can Protect Themselves from the Growing Number of Lawsuits Involving Personnel Information,* 154 Hum. Resources Mgmt, Ideas & Trends (CCH) 167 (Oct. 16, 1987); *see also* Decker, Privacy Law chs. 3–8.

§ 2.29   Employee Complaint Form

Set forth below is **Form 2–6** for use in becoming aware of and resolving employee complaints:

FORM 2–6
EMPLOYEE COMPLAINT

NAME _____ DATE _____

DEPARTMENT _____ TITLE _____ SUPERVISOR _____

DATE COMPLAINT AROSE: _____

FACTS OF COMPLAINT: _____

_____

_____

_____

_____

_____

_____

_____

HOW SHOULD THIS BE RESOLVED? _____

_____

_____

_____

_____

_____

_____

_____

SIGNED _____

CHAPTER 3

PRE-EMPLOYMENT POLICIES

INTRODUCTION

§ 3.1 Introduction to Initial Employment Policies

Hiring is the human resource function that develops qualified applicants, and it interfaces with employee selection. Considerable personal information must be disclosed in seeking employment. Initial employment contacts create vast information resources for immediate and subsequent employee privacy intrusions.[1] Often the employer must verify information provided by applicants.

During initial employment contacts, the applicant must determine what and how much information should be revealed. Typically, newspaper advertisements include some job details that cause interested individuals to evaluate their qualifications. Many individuals decide not to apply after this self-analysis. Those individuals who apply generally reveal only the information necessary to obtain employment and not jeopardize their opportunities.

All information disclosed may be subject to employer verification. In verifying information, other data may be revealed that may or may not be employment-related. The additional data may be obtained with or without employee knowledge. After the employee is hired, the information may again be expanded through attendance records, compensation data, medical reviews, benefit reports, performance evaluations, disciplinary notices, and so forth.

The employer's concern is to collect information that is relevant to the evaluation of the applicant for the job to be filled. This information may result from advertisements,[2] applications,[3] interviews,[4] and hiring procedures.[5] Procuring this employee information immediately raises privacy concerns. The human resource principles, procedures, and policies applicable to initial employment contacts are reviewed by this chapter.

---

[1] *See* K. Decker, Employee Privacy Law and Practice ch. 6 (John Wiley & Sons, Inc. 1987) [hereinafter Decker, Privacy Law].

[2] See §§ **3.2–3.5;** *see also* Decker, Privacy Law § 6.3.

[3] See §§ **3.6–3.15;** *see also* Decker, Privacy Law § 6.4.

[4] See §§ **3.16–3.21;** *see also* Decker, Privacy Law § 6.5.

[5] See §§ **3.22–3.29;** *see also* Decker, Privacy Law §§ 6.3–6.5.

ADVERTISEMENTS

§ 3.2   Advertisements

Newspaper advertisements in the help-wanted section are a common employer recruitment method. Some employers use advertisements to publicize their products, services, or distinctive features. Advertising may motivate applicant interest by educating readers about unique employer characteristics involving philosophy, product technology, or career opportunities.

Many applicants make their first employer contact through newspaper advertisements.[6] Depending upon the advertisement's content, the applicant may inquire further or may refrain from making an inquiry. When someone does not apply for employment because he or she believes that it would be futile, employee privacy interests are affected by impacting speech, beliefs, association, or lifestyle.[7] The applicant cannot properly determine whether to exercise the "right to be let alone."[8]

Inability to exercise an employee interest is no different from an actual physical intrusion.[9] These employee interests may be enforced under federal[10] and state[11] FEP statutes or through contractual theories.[12]

§ 3.3   —Preparation

Preparing an effective employment advertisement is more involved than it appears.[13] Several preliminary considerations can ensure an advertisement's success by:

1.   Checking the job description and job specifications to be sure they are correct

---

[6] *See* Decker, Privacy Law § 6.3.

[7] *See* Teamsters v. United States, 431 U.S. 324 (1977) (not applying for employment because of belief that it would be futile).

[8] *See* Public Utils. Comm'r v. Pollack, 393 U.S. 451, 467 (1952).

[9] *See* Pearson v. Furnco Constr. Corp., 563 F.2d 815 (7th Cir. 1977) (not applying for employment because of belief that it would be futile).

[10] *See, e.g.,* 42 U.S.C.§§ 2000e-1 to 2002-17 (1988) (Civil Rights Act of 1964); *see also* Decker, Privacy Law §§ 2.7–2.12.

[11] *See, e.g.,* Pa. Stat. Ann. tit. 43, §§ 951–963 (Purdon 1991) (Pennsylvania Human Relations Act); *see also* Decker, Privacy Law § 2.25.

[12] *See, e.g.,* Willis v. Allied Insulation Co., 174 So. 2d 858 (La. 1965) (advertisement's terms created binding employer contractual commitments); *see also* Decker, Privacy Law § 6.3.

[13] *See* Decker, Privacy Law § 6.3.

2. Conducting a job analysis if there is doubt about a job description's or job specification's accuracy[14]

3. Writing the advertisement so that it can be easily read, omitting technical language

4. Selling the job to prospective applicants by writing advertisements to be appealing in structure and content, considering:

    a. Printing style

    b. Borders

    c. Layout

    d. Factual statements that highlight the job's major features[15]

§ 3.4   —Minimizing Litigation Risks

To minimize employer litigation risks, the following should be considered:[16]

1. Advertisements specifying sex, race, religion, age, national origin, disability, or relating to these areas may invite employee privacy challenges under federal and state FEP statutes[17]

2. Employers are prohibited from using help-wanted advertisements under "male" and "female" headings unless sex is a bona fide occupational qualification[18]

3. Advertisements should be worded to avoid creating contractual commitments[19] by not suggesting:

    a. Long-term employment

    b. Guaranteed job security

---

[14] Incorrect job descriptions or job specifications may inadvertently result in an adverse impact by improperly eliminating applicants who do not meet the advertised specifications but nevertheless could perform the job tasks. *See* Pearson v. Furnco Constr. Corp., 563 F.2d 815 (7th Cir. 1977) (permitting plaintiffs the opportunity to demonstrate entitlement to jobs for which employer concealed opportunities); *see also* Decker, Privacy Law § 6.3.

[15] Myers at 288–90 (1986).

[16] *See* Decker, Privacy Law § 6.3.

[17] *See, e.g.,* Hailes v. United Air Lines, 464 F.2d 1006 (5th Cir. 1972) (sex discrimination for airline stewardesses).

[18] *See, e.g.,* Pittsburgh Press Co., v. Pittsburgh Comm'n on Human Relations, 413 U.S. 376 (1973) (sex-based and sex-designated help wanted columns illegal).

[19] *See, e.g.,* Willis v. Allied Insulation Co., 174 So. 2d 858 (La. 1965) (advertisement's terms created binding employer contractual commitments).

    c. Guaranteed wages or salary

    d. Career security

4. To ensure consistency, the employer should centralize responsibility for advertisement development, writing, and placement with one group, namely the human resources staff, to minimize employee privacy problems

§ 3.5   —Advertisement Forms

The following employment advertisements should be considered as a guide:

FORM 3.5(1)
ADVERTISEMENT

HAMPTON INN

• Porter

• Secretary

• Host/Hostess

Apply in person at 1800 Paper Mill Road, Wyomissing, Pennsylvania

Equal Opportunity Employer

FORM 3.5(2)
ADVERTISEMENT

RADIOLOGY TECHS

REGISTERED AND NEW GRADS

Opportunity to work at Hazleton General Hospital. The working environment is caring, dynamic, and team-oriented.

Competitive salary and comprehensive benefits.

Interested applicants should call or write:

HUMAN RESOURCE DEPARTMENT
HAZLETON GENERAL HOSPITAL
700 E. Broad Street
Hazleton, Penna. 18201
(717) 545-4357

Equal Opportunity Employer

FORM 3.5(3)
ADVERTISEMENT

MAINTENANCE MECHANIC

PIPEFITTER & PLUMBER

1st shift. $11.49/hr. Applicant must have journeyman's license.

Minimum 3–4 yrs. industrial experience

Contact Mr. Noll at 373-4111

GLIDDEN COMPANY
3rd & Bern St.
Reading, PA 19601

Equal Opportunity Employer

FORM 3.5(4)
ADVERTISEMENT

PERSONNEL SECRETARY

An international MONTGOMERY COUNTY based company seeks individual
to assist in Human Resources Dept. Responsibilities will include processing
medical insurance, maintenance of employee files, Workers' Comp claims,
reports, typing and clerical work plus other independent projects.

For consideration, send your resume to:

J-28, P.O. Box 2066
Philadelphia, Pa. 19103

Equal Opportunity Employer

APPLICATIONS

§ 3.6   Applications

The application's purpose is to elicit job-related information from an applicant to
enable the employer to make an informed hiring decision. Applications affect
how much information an employer can collect regarding an applicant's personal
life and experiences.[20]

---

[20] *See* Decker, Privacy Law § 6.4.

At one time, the employer could inquire into almost any area. Today, constraints through federal[21] and state[22] FEP statutory protections apply to many traditional areas of employer inquiry involving age, marital status, pregnancy, disability, and so forth.[23]

Permissible employer inquiries begin with the application and extend throughout, and even beyond, the employment relationship. These information collection concerns do not merely limit the employment information that can be solicited, but require that, once this information is collected, the employer use it properly and protect it from unwarranted disclosures. The employer has a responsibility to make certain that employee personal matters in its records remain confidential and protected. Unauthorized employment information reading may be a privacy invasion imposing employer responsibility.[24]

Applications generally impact employee interests through federal[25] and state[26] FEP statutes. These concerns relate to race, color, sex, national origin, disability, and age. By inquiring into non-job-related areas, the employer may obtain information that is not job-related and eliminate certain individuals from consideration based on this information. In subsequent litigation, the employer may be required to defend the use of the information requested or to explain why the information was collected but not used.

§ 3.7   —Advantages

Despite federal[27] and state[28] FEP statutory restrictions prohibiting employer inquiries into certain areas, the application remains an important document because:

---

[21] *See, e.g.,* 42 U.S.C.§§ 2000e-1 to 2002-17 (1988) (Civil Rights Act of 1964); *see also* Decker, Privacy Law §§ 2.7–2.12.

[22] *See, e.g.,* Pa. Stat. Ann. tit. 43, §§ 951–963 (Purdon 1991) (Pennsylvania Human Relations Act); *see also* Decker, Privacy Law § 2.25.

[23] Examples of these inquiry prohibitions are set forth at §§ **3.10, 3.21.**

[24] *See* Board of Trustees v. Leach, 258 Cal. App. 2d 281, 65 Cal. Rptr. 588 (1968) (unauthorized reading of an employee's personnel file imposed employer responsibility); *see also* Decker, Privacy Law § 7.3.

[25] *See, e.g.,* 42 U.S.C.§§ 2000e-1 to 2002-17 (1988) (Civil Rights Act of 1964); *see also* Decker, Privacy Law §§ 2.7–2.12.

[26] *See, e.g.,* Pa. Stat. Ann. tit. 43, §§ 951–963 (Purdon 1991) (Pennsylvania Human Relations Act); *see also* Decker, Privacy Law § 2.25.

[27] *See, e.g.,* 42 U.S.C.§§ 2000e-1 to 2002-17 (1988) (Civil Rights Act of 1964); *see also* Decker, Privacy Law §§ 2.7–2.12.

[28] *See, e.g.,* Pa. Stat. Ann. tit. 43, §§ 951–963 (Purdon 1991) (Pennsylvania Human Relations Act); *see also* Decker, Privacy Law § 2.25.

1. It can assist the employer in limiting wrongful termination liability[29]
2. It provides an initial means of consenting to employer procedures and policies. Especially if the employer desires to conduct applicant drug screening, the application could include consent language to minimize litigation exposure[30]
3. It may provide a basis for terminating an employee who has falsified or omitted information requested on the application[31]

§ 3.8 —Preparation

Initially, the employer must determine what information is needed to determine which applicant is best suited for a position. This may involve inquiries into education, professional licenses or certifications, previous work experience, special skills, talents, fluency in a foreign language, and so forth. The employer's special needs for the position may warrant that certain additional information be elicited.

After determining what job-related and general background information should be collected from the applicant, the remainder of the application should be drafted to preserve applicant privacy and limit employer liability by:

1. Informing the applicant that the employment is at-will[32]
2. Providing an applicant's acknowledgement that any information falsification or omission may result in termination
3. Requiring the applicant's representation that the information provided is complete and accurate
4. Including a release protecting the employer and those persons the employer contacts regarding references
5. Inquiring only whether the applicant has any physical condition or limitations that would disqualify him or her from performing the job; however, this may require that the applicant's physical condition be examined to

---

[29] *See, e.g.,* Novosel v. Sears, Roebuck & Co., 495 F. Supp. 344 (E.D. Mich. 1980) (application disclaimer enforceable to preserve at-will employment relationship).

[30] *See* Decker, Privacy Law § 7.9.

[31] *See, e.g.,* Dart Indus., Inc., 56 Lab. Arb. (BNA) 799 (1971) (Greene, Arb.) (termination for application falsification).

[32] See **§ 3.14.** *See also* Decker, Privacy Law § 4.14.

determine if reasonable accommodations under federal[33] and state[34] FEP statutes could be made for the applicant to perform the job

6. Not inquiring regarding the applicant's filing for and/or receiving of benefits related to work-related illnesses or injuries, because this may be considered retaliation for these benefits' receipt[35]

§ 3.9 —Privacy Considerations

The following should be considered regarding application privacy:[36]

1. Collecting only information that is relevant to specific employment decisions

2. Telling applicants, employees, and former employees what use will be made of the collected information

3. Letting applicants know what kinds of information will be maintained

4. Adopting reasonable procedures to ensure that application information is accurate, timely, and complete

5. Limiting application disclosure internally and externally[37]

§ 3.10 —Prohibited Inquiries

Applicants are typically requested to furnish basic information involving name, address, job being applied for, experience, and education. The application form can yield information needed to compare adequately an applicant's qualifications to the job specifications. However, an improperly structured application can cause an employer problems. Employers should consider using this standard in determining whether an inquiry should be made: "How does this inquiry ensure

---

[33] *See, e.g.,* 29 U.S.C. §§ 701–796i (1988) (Vocational Rehabilitation Act of 1973); 42 U.S.C. §§ 12101–12213 (Supp. 1992) (Americans with Disabilities Act); *see also* Decker, Privacy Law § 2.10.

[34] *See, e.g.,* Pa. Stat. Ann. tit. 43, §§ 951–963 (Purdon 1991) (Pennsylvania Human Relations Act); *see also* Decker, Privacy Law § 2.25.

[35] *See, e.g.,* Darnell v. Impact Indus., 105 Ill. 2d 158, 473 N.E.2d 935 (1984) (termination for filing workers' compensation claim prohibited).

[36] Privacy Protection Study Commission, Personal Privacy in an Information Society app. 3 (Employment Records) (1977); *see also* Decker, Privacy Law ch. 9.

[37] *See* Board of Trustees v. Leach, 258 Cal. App. 2d 281, 65 Cal. Rptr. 588 (1968) (unauthorized reading of an employee's personnel file imposes employer responsibility); *see also* Decker, Privacy Law § 7.3.

a job-related selection?" Inquiries should not be made where they are not job-related.

Some employers ask potentially improper questions on applications involving an applicant's age, birth date, and so forth. Some application inquiries that may be difficult for employers to justify, and could encourage FEP complaints, include:

1. Arrests
2. Availability for Saturday and Sunday work
3. Bonding refusal
4. Children under 18
5. Citizenship of a country other than the United States
6. Credit record
7. Eye color
8. Garnishment record
9. Hair color
10. Height
11. Marital status
12. Number of children
13. Personal financial information
14. Sex
15. Spouse's employment status
16. Spouse's name
17. Weight[38]

Some of this information is sought in conjunction with affirmative action reporting requirements. When that is the purpose, it is advisable to use a tear-off sheet attached to the application to minimize improper information, use, or disclosure.[39]

§ 3.11 —Application Policies

The employer should prepare its application with the objectives of gathering the information necessary to make job-related hiring decisions and providing a foundation for defending against employment litigation that may arise if hiring does not result or if termination subsequently occurs. Employer preparation in carefully drafting applications will minimize litigation exposure. The following forms should be used in developing an application that minimizes employee intrusions.

---

[38] For a more detailed discussion of prohibited inquiries under FEP statutes, see **§ 3.21.**

[39] For a copy of this form, see **§ 3.13.**

§ 3.12   —Application Forms

The following application was designed with federal and state FEP considerations in mind:[40]

FORM 3.12(1)
APPLICATION

PLEASE PRINT

*Date: _____

Name: _____

Street: _____

City: _____

State: _____ Zip Code: _____

Area code: _____ Business telephone: _____

Area code: _____ Home telephone: _____

How were you referred?   ____ Newspaper   ____ School

                                ____ On my own   ____ Co. employee

                                ____ Agency   ____ Other

Name of referral source

_____

TYPE OF WORK DESIRED

Indicate the position for which you are applying: _____

_____

What is your minimum weekly salary requirement? _____

Date available for work: _____

Do you have any commitments to another employer that might affect your employment with us? _____

_____

---

[40] *See* Fair Empl. Prac. Manual (BNA) 443:221 (1993).

* This application will be considered only for employment purposes by the employer for a period of ninety (90) calendar days from this application's date, after which a new application must be completed and filed.

EDUCATIONAL DATA

School	Print Name, Number and Street, City, State, and Zip Code for Each School Listing	Type of Course or Major	Graduated?
High school:			
College:			
Graduate school:			
Trade, Bus., Night, or Corres.:			
Other:			

MILITARY EXPERIENCE

Were you in U.S. Armed Forces?   _____ Yes   _____ No

If yes, what branch? _____

Rank at separation: _____

Briefly describe your duties: _____

_____

EMPLOYMENT HISTORY

List present employer or most recent employer first (use other side of this application if necessary). May we contact these employers?   _____ Yes _____ No

_____

Employer:	Length of time employed:	Supervisor's name:

Address:

_____

Telephone: _____ Your job title: _____

Salary: _____

Duties: _____

_____

_____

Reason for leaving: _____

Employer: Length of time employed: Supervisor's name:

_____   _____   _____

Address:

_____

Telephone: _____ Your job title: _____

Salary: _____

Duties: _____

_____

_____

Reason for leaving: _____

Employer: Length of time employed: Supervisor's name:

_____   _____   _____

Address:

_____

Telephone: _____ Your job title: _____

Salary: _____

Duties: _____

_____

_____

Reason for leaving: _____

Employer: Length of time employed: Supervisor's name:

_____   _____   _____

Address:

_____

Telephone: _____ Your job title: _____

Salary: _____

Duties: _____

_____

_____

_____

Reason for leaving: _____

GENERAL INFORMATION

Have you previously applied for employment at this Company?

____ Yes   ____ No

If yes, when? _____

Have you previously been employed at the Company or its subsidiaries?

____ Yes   ____ No

If yes, when? _____

Are any of your relatives employed by the Company?

____ Yes   ____ No

If yes, please list name and department: _____

_____

Please include any other information you think would be helpful in considering you for employment, including additional work experience, articles/books published, activities, accomplishments, and so forth. Exclude all information indicative of age, sex, race, religion, color, national origin, and disability.

_____

_____

_____

_____

_____

_____

_____

APPLICANT'S REPRESENTATIONS FOR EMPLOYMENT

Should I be employed by the Company, I agree to conform to the Company's rules and regulations, and agree that as an at-will employee my employment and compensation can be terminated, at any time, for any or no reason, with or without notice, at the option of either the Company or myself.

I certify that the information provided on this application is true and complete to the best of my knowledge and agree that falsified information or significant omissions may disqualify me from further consideration for employment and may be considered justification for termination if discovered at a later date.

I authorize persons, schools, current employer and previous employers, and organizations named in this application to provide the Company with any relevant information that may be required. I further release all parties providing information from any and all liability or claims for damages whatsoever that may result from this information's release, disclosure, maintenance, or use.

This application has been read by me in its entirety.

_____   _____
Signature   Date

The following application was designed to solicit as little information as possible by the employer, but to place the information disclosure burden entirely on the applicant to make the choices regarding what information to reveal:

FORM 3.12(2)
APPLICATION

Please send one copy of this form along with a resume outlining your qualifications to ___*(Employer's name and address)*___.

_____

_____

Name: _____ Date: _____

Street: _____

City: _____ State: _____ Zip code: _____

Current position: _____

Currently employed at: _____

How long? _____

Ultimate employment goal? _____

_____

Next employment step? _____

_____

Why? _____

_____

_____

Are you willing to relocate? _____

Where? _____

_____ Why? _____

_____

Signature

§ 3.13 —Application: Affirmative Action Information

To allow collection of certain information required by federal[41] and state[42] FEP statutes to meet affirmative action and other statistical information, the following information should be included on the application in an area where it can be separated from the application to avoid use of prohibited[43] inquiries during the hiring process:

FORM 3.13(1)
APPLICATION: AFFIRMATIVE ACTION INFORMATION

To aid in the Company's commitment to equal employment opportunity, applicants are asked to voluntarily provide the following information. This section will be separated from the application immediately upon filing.

____ Male

____ Female

Your Age Group

1.	Under 21 ____	5.	50–59 ____
2.	21-29 ____	6.	60–69 ____
3.	30–39 ____	7.	70 and over ____
4.	40–49 ____		

Please check the one which best describes your race/ethnicity:

A. Mexican, Mexican-American, Chicano ____   B. Puerto Rican ____

---

[41] *See, e.g.,* 42 U.S.C.§§ 2000e-1 to 2002-17 (1988) (Civil Rights Act of 1964); *see also* Decker, Privacy Law §§ 2.7–2.12.

[42] *See, e.g.,* Pa. Stat. Ann. tit. 43, §§ 951–963 (Purdon 1991) (Pennsylvania Human Relations Act); *see also* Decker, Privacy Law § 2.25.

[43] See §§ **3.10, 3.21.**

C. Cuban ____   K. Eskimo ____

D. Any other Spanish/Hispanic ____   L. Aleut ____

If not Hispanic, check: M. Hawaiian ____

E. White ____   N. Samoan ____

F. Black ____   O. Japanese ____

G. Filipino ____   P. Chinese ____

H. American Indian ____   Q. Korean ____
   (Specify tribe)   R. Guamanian/Chamorro ____
   _____   X. Other, not listed _____

I. Vietnamese ____

J. Asian Indian ____

Check any major disability you have a record of which may have impeded your se-curing, retaining, or advancing in employment:

1. Hearing ____   5. Developmental ____

2. Sight ____   6. Other disability
                                          Specify: _____
3. Speech ____
                                       7. No disability ____
4. Physical Orthopedic/
   amputations ____

Are you a veteran, spouse of a 100% disabled veteran, or a widow or widower of a veteran?

____ Yes   ____ No

Only applicants who check "Yes" will be verified for veterans preference points in examinations which allow the addition of these points.

§ 3.14   —Application Employment Contract
Disclaimer Forms

To preserve the at-will employment relationship, an employer should consider placing a disclaimer within the application that covers the following:

FORM 3.14(1)
APPLICATION EMPLOYMENT CONTRACT DISCLAIMER

In consideration of my employment, I agree to conform to the Company's rules and regulations, and agree that my employment and compensation can be termi-nated, with or without cause, and with or without notice, at any time, at the option of either the Company or myself. I understand that no manager or representative, other than the Chief Executive Officer or (Name), has any authority to enter into any agreement for employment for any specified time period, or to make any agreement contrary to this. Any agreement for employment for any specified time period must be in writing and signed.[44]

FORM 3.14(2)
APPLICATION EMPLOYMENT CONTRACT DISCLAIMER

I certify that the information contained in this application is correct to the best of my knowledge and understanding and that information falsification is grounds for termination. I authorize the references listed above to provide any and all information concerning my previous employment and any pertinent information they may have, personal or otherwise, and release all parties from liability for any damage that may result from furnishing this information. In consideration of my employment, I agree to conform to the Company's rules and regulations, and my employment and compensation can be terminated, with or without cause, and with or without notice, at any time by either the Company or myself. I understand that no Company manager or representative, other than the Company's President or Vice-President, has any authority to enter into any agreement for employment for any specified time period, or to make any agreement contrary to the foregoing.[45]

§ 3.15 —Application Information Release Form

To protect the employer in securing applicant references or other applicant information, the following form should be considered as part of the application:

FORM 3.15(1)
APPLICATION INFORMATION RELEASE FORM

I authorize schools, references, prior employers, and physicians or other medical practitioners to provide my record, reason for leaving employment, and all other information they may have concerning me to the Company and I release all parties providing information from any and all liability or claims for damages whatsoever that may result from this information's release, disclosure, and use.

---

[44] *See, e.g.,* Novosel v. Sears, Roebuck & Co., 495 F. Supp. 344 (E.D. Mich. 1980) (application disclaimer enforceable to preserve at-will employment relationship); *see* Decker, Privacy Law § 4.14; L. Lorber, J. Kirk, K. Kirschner & C. Handorf, Fear of Firing (1984); Decker, *Handbooks and Employment Policies as Express or Implied Guarantees of Employment—Employer Beware!,* 5 U. Pitt. J.L. & Com. 207 (1984). See also chs. 4, 15.

[45] *See, e.g.,* Novosel v. Sears, Roebuck & Co., 495 F. Supp. 344 (E.D. Mich. 1980) (application disclaimer enforceable to preserve at-will employment relationship); *see* Decker, Privacy Law § 4.14; L. Lorber, J. Kirk, K. Kirschner & C. Handorf, Fear of Firing (1984); Decker, *Handbooks and Employment Policies as Express or Implied Guarantees of Employment—Employer Beware!,* 5 U. Pitt. J.L. & Com. 207 (1984). See also chs. 4, 15.

INTERVIEWS

§ 3.16   Interviews

Unlike the application's written inquiry, the interview is primarily oral, although a written record may be created.[46] After the initial interview, others may be conducted prior to the final hiring decision. At every interview, employee interests may be affected, because each employer decisionmaking level attempts to refine the information initially requested and to determine final selection by obtaining additional information to set the applicants apart.

Because of the prohibitions contained in federal[47] and state[48] FEP statutes, employers must take special care in applicant interviews. The employer may not use an applicant's race, color, sex, age, national origin, religion, marital status, or disability as a basis for an employment decision, unless the employer is hiring pursuant to goals and timetables contained in its affirmative action plan.[49] Similarly, an interviewer may not ask an applicant impermissible questions related to these areas, nor may a former employer be asked these questions during a written or telephone reference check.

§ 3.17   —Interview Process

Employer success depends upon applicant quality. Quality applicant recruitment is based upon the employer's reputation with its employees, the general public, customers, and the competition. The interview process should:[50]

1. Be used to:
    a. Gather additional information about an applicant not disclosed in the application
    b. Judge demeanor and presence

---

[46] *See* Decker, Privacy Law § 6.5.

[47] *See, e.g.,* 42 U.S.C.§§ 2000e-1 to 2002-17 (1988) (Civil Rights Act of 1964); *see also* Decker, Privacy Law §§ 2.7–2.12.

[48] *See, e.g.,* Pa. Stat. Ann. tit. 43, §§ 951–963 (Purdon 1991) (Pennsylvania Human Relations Act); *see also* Decker, Privacy Law § 2.25.

[49] *See* Executive Order No. 11246 (Affirmative Action), 3 C.F.R. § 339 (1964–1965 Compilation), reprinted in 42 U.S.C. § 2000e note, issued on Sept. 24, 1965, as amended; *see also* Decker, Privacy Law §§ 2.7–2.12, 2.25, 6.5.

[50] *See* American Hospital Association, The Wrongful Discharge of Employees in the Health Care Industry 20 (1987) [hereinafter American Hospital Association, Wrongful Discharge].

2. Permit the employer to:

    a. Expand on topics concerning educational background, the reasons for leaving prior employers, prior experience, training, and so forth

    b. Explain unaccounted-for time periods between schools or previous jobs, as these time gaps may indicate relevant information which the applicant might not disclose

    c. Resolve any conflicting information obtained through a reference check

§ 3.18 —Minimizing Litigation Risks

To maximize the benefits that can be derived from interviews, and to prevent statements during an interview that may lead to liability, the employer should use:[51]

1. Well-informed and well-prepared interviewers who:

    a. Become well-informed sufficiently prior to the interview by reviewing:

        (i) Applications

        (ii) Resumes

        (iii) Other pertinent information

    b. Know what further job-related information should be obtained from the applicant during the interview

    c. Know what information to convey about the employer

    d. Know what information to convey about the particular job for which the applicant has applied

2. Interviewers who are not only knowledgeable about the employer's advantages and benefits, but are aware that certain statements should not be made to "sell" applicants on the employer involving:

    a. Overemphasizing the employer's virtues to avoid creating enforceable employee rights against the employer if the employee is later terminated

    b. Becoming specific and promising definite employment terms and conditions greater than or different from the employer's oral or written policies, to avoid binding commitments[52]

    c. Asking questions that could be considered discriminatory; i.e., only job-related inquiries should be used[53]

---

[51] *See* American Hospital Association, Wrongful Discharge at 20–21.

[52] *See, e.g.,* Toussaint v. Blue Cross & Blue Shield of Mich., 408 Mich. 579, 292 N.W.2d 880 (1980) (employer liability for interviewer's statement that the employee would be employed as long as he did his job); *see also* Decker, Privacy Law § 4.14.

[53] See § **3.21.**

§ 3.19   —Interview Methods

The following types of interview methods should be considered:

1. Nondirective interview:
    a. Interviewer structures questions in response to the unique needs and qualifications of the interviewee
    b. Interviewee is permitted to talk freely
    c. The interview topics are determined by the interviewer but the interviewee is allowed to develop his or her individual responses
    d. Uses a set of specific questions prepared in advance of the interview[54]
2. Patterned interview:
    a. Uses a set of specific questions prepared in advance of the interview
    b. Attempts to limit interviewee responses to specific information
    c. Provides information to the interviewee that is planned beforehand
    d. Interviewer summarizes both interviewee responses and the progress of the interview[55]
3. Structural interview:
    a. In structured interviewing, the responsibility shifts almost entirely to the interviewer
    b. It is the interviewer's role to understand the position's scope, including the job specifications, duties, pay, benefits, and tasks by:
        (i)   Structuring questions and information items to adequately inform interviewees about the position and to elicit information about their qualifications for it
        (ii) Comparing the interviewee's responses to the position's needs and determining if the person matches the position[56]
4. Group interview:
    a. Involves two or more interviewers
    b. A simultaneous interview of an applicant occurs in the same setting where each interviewer asks the applicant at least one question[57]
5. Stress interview: Involves the purposeful introduction of stress into an interview, in order to gauge an interviewee's ability to function under stress[58]

---

[54] D. Myers, Human Resources Management: Principles and Practice 207 (2d ed. 1992) [hereafter Myers, Human Resources].

[55] *Id.*

[56] Myers, Human Resources at 208.

[57] *Id.* at 209.

[58] *Id.* at 210.

6. Depth interview:

    a. This is a structured interview

    b. Questions thoroughly measure an interviewee's qualifications within a specific area[59]

§ 3.20   —Interview Evaluation

The following form (**Form 3.20(1)**) is intended to be used by the interviewer in evaluating the applicant for a position opening.

FORM 3.20(1)
INTERVIEWER'S EVALUATION

Applicant's Name: _____ Interview Date: _____

Interviewer's Name: _____

Position Applied For _____

Job-Related Tasks: *Applicant Knowledge:*

_____ _____

_____ _____

_____ _____

_____ _____

_____ _____

_____ _____

_____ _____

_____ _____

_____ _____

_____ _____

_____ _____

_____ _____

_____ _____

_____ _____

---

[59] *Id.*

Job Knowledge Strengths: _____

_____

_____

_____

_____

_____

_____

_____

_____

_____

_____

_____

Job Knowledge Weaknesses: _____

_____

_____

_____

_____

_____

_____

_____

_____

_____

_____

_____

_____

_____

Overall appraisal of the applicant: Match the applicant's qualifications with the job position's requirements and circle the overall applicant rating.

Excellent   *Above Average*   *Average*   *Below Average*   *Poor*

_____
Signature

§ 3.21   —Interview Policies

The following interview policy (**Form 3.21(2)**) is intended to acquaint interviewers with what questions can and cannot be asked to protect employee privacy interests and minimize employer liability for improper information collection, maintenance, use, or disclosure:[60]

FORM 3.21(2)
INTERVIEW INQUIRY POLICY

Instructions to Interviewers: The following are examples of impermissible interview inquiries and their acceptable counterparts:

Unacceptable	*Acceptable*

Age[61]

Unacceptable	*Acceptable*
1. What is your age?	1. Statement that hire is subject to verification that applicant meets legal age requirements
2. When were you born?	
3. Dates of attendance or completion of elementary or high school	2. If hired can you show proof of age?
	3. Are you over eighteen years of age?
	4. If under eighteen, can you, after employment, submit a work permit?

Arrest, Criminal Record[62]

Unacceptable	*Acceptable*
1. Arrest record[63]	1. Have you ever been convicted of a felony, or, within two years, a misdemeanor which resulted in imprisonment? This question should be accompanied by a statement that a conviction will not necessarily disqualify the applicant from the job requested[65]
2. Have you ever been arrested?[64]	

---

[60] These interview principles are also applicable for applications; see **§§ 3.6–3.15.**

[61] *See, e.g.,* Goodyear Tire and Rubber Co., 22 Fair Empl. Prac. Cas. (BNA) 755 (W.D. Tenn. 1979) (age discrimination in that maximum applicant age of 40 for tire builders not a valid BFOQ); *see also* Decker, Privacy Law § 6.5.

[62] See ch. 9. *See, e.g.,* Gregory v. Litton Sys., Inc., 316 F. Supp. 401 (C.D. Cal. 1970), *aff'd with modification not here relevant,* 472 F.2d 631 (9th Cir. 1972) (race discrimination against black employee); *see also* Decker, Privacy Law §§ 2.32, 6.5, 6.8–6.9.

[63] See ch. 9.

[64] *Id.*

[65] *Id.*

Unacceptable	*Acceptable*

Birthplace, Citizenship[66]

1. Birthplace of applicant, applicant's spouse, or relatives 2. Are you a U.S. citizen?	1. Can you, prior to employment, submit verification of your legal right to work in the United States?[67] 2. Statement that this proof may be required after employment[68] 3. Requirements that applicant produce naturalization, first papers, or alien card prior to employment[69]

Bonding[70]

1. Questions regarding refusal or cancellation of bonding[71]	1. Statement that bonding is a condition of hire based on the position[72]

Military Service[73]

1. General questions regarding military service that pertain to date, type of discharge, and so forth[74] 2. Questions regarding service in a foreign military[75]	1. Questions regarding relevant skills acquired during applicant's United States military service

Name[76]

1. Maiden name	1. Have you ever used another name? 2. Is any additional information regarding a name change, assumed name use, or nickname necessary to check on your work or education record? If yes, please explain

---

[66] See ch. 9. *See, e.g.,* Smith v. Union Oil Co., 17 Fair Empl. Prac. Cas. (BNA) 960 (N.D. Cal. 1977) (national origin discrimination); *see also* Decker, Privacy Law § 6.5.

[67] See ch. 9.

[68] *Id.*

[69] *Id.*

[70] See ch. 9. *See, e.g.,* United States v. Chicago, 459 F.2d 415 (7th Cir. 1977) (disqualifying applicants based on credit checks); *see also* Decker, Privacy Law §§ 2.5, 2.15, 2.23, 6.5, 6.7, 8.5.

[71] See ch. 9.

[72] *Id.*

[73] *See, e.g.,* EEOC Dec. No. 74-25, 10 Fair Empl. Prac. Cas. (BNA) 260 (1973) (4.2% of whites and 7.5% of blacks receive general discharges; 2.6% of whites and 5.2% of blacks receive undesirable discharges); *see also* Decker, Privacy Law § 6.5.

[74] This may reveal the applicant's age.

[75] This may reveal the applicant's nationality.

[76] *See, e.g.,* Allen v. Lovejoy, 553 F.2d 522 (6th Cir. 1977) (sex discrimination in requiring married women, but not married men, to change their surnames to that of their spouses on personnel forms); *see also* Decker, Privacy Law § 6.5.

Unacceptable	*Acceptable*

National Origin[77]

1. Questions regarding nationality, lineage, ancestry, national origin, descent, or parentage of applicant, applicant's parents, or spouse 2. What is your mother tongue? 3. Language commonly used by applicant 4. How applicant acquired ability to read, write, or speak a foreign language	1. Language applicant reads, speaks, or writes for job-related purposes

Notice in Case of Emergency[78]

1. Name and address of relative to be notified in case of accident or emergency	1. Name and address of person to be notified in case of accident or emergency

Organizations/Activities[79]

1. List all organizations, clubs, societies, and lodges to which you belong.	1. List job-related organizations, clubs, professional societies, or other associations to which you belong. Omit those indicating or referring to your race, religious creed, color, national origin, ancestry, sex, or age

Physical Condition/Disability[80]

1. Questions regarding applicant's general condition, state of health, or illness	1. Statement by employer that offer may be made contingent on applicant passing a job-related physical examination[81]

---

[77] *See, e.g.,* Rogers v. EEOC, 454 F.2d 234 (5th Cir. 1971), *cert. denied,* 406 U.S. 957 (1972) (denying employee services to minorities based on language); *see also* Decker, Privacy Law §§ 6.5, 7.35.

[78] Prior to hiring, this information may constitute sex discrimination (by revealing marital status) or national origin discrimination (by revealing an ethnic name where the person is unmarried and parents must be notified). However, this information can be obtained after hiring. *See* Decker, Privacy Law §§ 6.4–6.5.

[79] *See, e.g.,* Abrams v. Baylor College of Medicine, 581 F. Supp. 1570 (S.D. Tex. 1984) (religious discrimination in denying positions in Saudi Arabia because applicant was Jewish); *see also* Decker, Privacy Law § 6.5.

[80] See ch. 9. *See, e.g.,* 42 U.S.C. §§ 12101–12213 (Supp. 1992) (Americans with Disabilities Act); Bentivegna v. Department of Labor, 694 F.2d 619 (9th Cir. 1982) (handicap discrimination in disqualifying all uncontrolled diabetics for construction positions could not be justified by an alleged risk of injury); *see also* Decker, Privacy Law § 6.5.

[81] See ch. 9.

Unacceptable	*Acceptable*
2. Questions regarding receipt of workers' compensation	2. Do you have any physical condition or handicap that may limit your ability to perform the job requested? If yes, what can be done to accommodate your limitation?
3. Do you have any physical disabilities or handicaps?	

Race, Color[82]

1. Questions regarding applicant's race or color	1. Statement that photograph may be required after employment[83]
2. Questions regarding applicant's complexion or color of skin, eyes, or hair	
3. Requirement that applicant affix a photograph to application[84]	
4. Requesting applicant, at his or her option, to submit a photograph[85]	
5. Requiring a photograph after interview but before employment[86]	

References[87]

1. Questions of applicant's former employers or acquaintances which elicit information specifying the applicant's race, color, religious creed, national origin, ancestry, physical handicap, medical condition, marital status, age, or sex[89]	1. By whom were you referred for a position?
	2. Names of persons willing to provide professional and/or character references for the applicant[88]

---

[82] See ch. 4. *See, e.g.,* Cal. Labor Code § 1051 (West 1971) (California's statute prohibiting employer from requesting a photograph as an employment condition); *see also* Decker, Privacy Law §§ 6.5, 6.11.

[83] See ch. 4.

[84] *Id.*

[85] *Id.*

[86] *Id.*

[87] See ch. 4. *See, e.g.,* Smith v. Union Oil Co., 17 Fair Empl. Prac. Cas. (BNA) 960 (N.D. Cal. 1977) (national origin discrimination in recruitment and hiring); *see also* Decker, Privacy Law § 6.5.

[88] See ch. 4.

[89] *Id.*

Unacceptable	*Acceptable*

Religion[90]

Unacceptable	Acceptable
1. Questions regarding applicant's religion 2. Religious days observed 3. Does your religion prevent you from working weekends or holidays?	1. Statement by employer of regular days, hours, or shifts to be worked

Sex, Marital Status, Family[91]

Unacceptable	Acceptable
1. Questions indicating applicant's sex 2. Questions indicating applicant's marital status 3. Number and/or ages of children or dependents 4. Questions regarding pregnancy, childbearing, or birth control 5. Name(s) of spouse or children of applicant 6. Questions regarding child care	1. Name and address of parent or guardian if applicant is a minor 2. Statement of employer policy regarding work assignment of related employees[92] 3. Do you have any relatives already employed? If so, give names and positions held[93]

HIRING PROCEDURE

§ 3.22 Hiring

To limit employer liability, an overall hiring procedure should be developed that considers advertisements, applications, and interviews.[94] The overall hiring procedure should ensure that only relevant or job-related information necessary for employment decisions is collected, maintained, and used. Likewise, this information's sensitivity should be preserved through confidentiality procedures in effect prior to, during, and after employment termination. This should be done

---

[90] See ch. 4. *See, e.g.,* Compston v. Borden, Inc., 424 F. Supp. 157 (S.D. Ohio 1977) (religious discrimination where plaintiff was victim of supervisor's anti-Jewish slurs); *see also* Decker, Privacy Law §§ 6.5, 7.33.

[91] *See, e.g.,* Phillips v. Martin Marietta Corp., 400 U.S. 542 (1971) (sex discrimination regarding preschool children); *see also* Decker, Privacy Law § 6.5.

[92] See ch. 9.

[93] *Id.*

[94] See §§ **3.2–3.21.** *See also* Decker, Privacy Law §§ 6.2–6.13.

to minimize employee claims that may arise out of federal[95] or state[96] FEP statutory violations as well as those arising from tort[97] or contractual[98] litigation.

§ 3.23   —General Considerations

In developing an overall hiring procedure, the following should be considered:[99]

1. Determine who should be the interviewer
2. Determine who should review records
3. Obtain information from verifiable sources[100]
4. Obtain information by permissible methods[101]
5. Use only reliable consumer reporting agencies[102]
6. Maintain information confidentiality
7. Use only permissible reference checking procedures[103]
8. Inform applicants what information will be maintained[104]
9. Inform applicants of the uses to be made of collected information[105]
10. Adopt procedures to assure the information's accuracy, timeliness, and completeness[106]
11. Permit review, copying, correction, or amendment of this information[107]

[95.]*See, e.g.,* 42 U.S.C.§§ 2000e-1 to 2002-17 (1988) (Civil Rights Act of 1964); *see also* Decker, Privacy Law §§ 2.7–2.12, 6.2–6.5.

[96] *See, e.g.,* Pa. Stat. Ann. tit. 43, §§ 951–965 (Purdon 1991) (Pennsylvania Human Relations Act); *see also* Decker, Privacy Law § 2.25, 6.2–6.5.

[97] *See, e.g.,* Slohoda v. United Parcel Serv., 193 N.J. Super. 586, 475 A.2d 618 (App. Div. 1984), *rev'd on other grounds,* 207 N.J. Super. 145, 504 A.2d 53 (1986) (inquiry by employer into extramarital sexual activities could rise to tort liability if the employee were terminated for that reason); *see also* Decker, Privacy Law §§ 4.2–4.10, 6.2–6.5.

[98] *See, e.g.,* Toussaint v. Blue Cross & Blue Shield of Mich., 408 Mich. 579, 292 N.W.2d 880 (1980) (employer liability for interviewer's statement that the employee would be employed as long as he did his job); *see also* Decker, Privacy Law §§ 4.11–4.15, 6.2–6.5.

[99] *See* Privacy Protection Study Commission, Personal Privacy in an Information Society 231–38 (1977).

[100] See ch. 9.

[101] *Id.*

[102] *Id.*

[103] *Id.*

[104] *Id.*

[105] *Id.*

[106] *Id.*

[107] *Id.*

12. Limit internal use[108]

13. Limit external disclosures, including disclosures made without authorization, to specific inquiries or requests to verify information[109]

14. Provide for a regular internal compliance review of hiring procedures[110]

§ 3.24   —Special Considerations

In developing an overall hiring procedure, the following special considerations should be noted:

1. The time required to fill vacant positions varies substantially depending upon what position is being filled

2. Employers use a wide variety of recruiting resources to find their applicants, including:

    a. Internal promotions

    b. Employee referrals

    c. Newspaper advertisements

    d. Walk-in applicants

    e. Employment agencies

3. Interviewers should be given special training

4. Employers check a wide variety of applicant information, including:

    a. Employment dates

    b. Reason for leaving a prior position

    c. Employment history

5. Employers confirm a wide variety of information by contacting:

    a. Personal and professional references

    b. Prior employers

    c. Educational institutions

    d. Medical information sources.

§ 3.25   —Recruiting Sources

The following sources may be used by employers to locate applicants for position openings:

---

[108] *Id.*

[109] *Id.*

[110] *Id.*

1. Internal sources
    a. Promotion from within
    b. Employee referrals
    c. Walk-in applicants
2. Advertising
    a. Newspapers
    b. Journals/magazines
    c. Direct mail
    d. Radio/television
3. Outside referral sources
    a. Colleges/universities
    b. Technical/vocational schools
    c. Professional societies
    d. Community agencies
    e. Unions
4. Employment services
    a. State employment service
    b. Private employment agencies
    c. Search firms
    d. United States Employment Service
    e. Employee leasing firms
    f. Computerized resume service
    g. Video interviewing service
5. Special events
    a. Career conferences/job fairs
    b. Open houses.

§ 3.26   —Hiring and Dealing with Disabled Employees

Because all employers compete for skilled employees, it is important to not over-look any sources of talent. Recruiting should extend to nontraditional sources, including those who may be physically and/or mentally challenged. Assistance in reaching this talent pool is available from rehabilitative, social service, and educational agencies that counsel individuals with disabilities for careers that could coincide with an employer's needs. A list of some of these agencies, including the services and programs they provide, can be obtained from the following:[111]

---

[111] *See* The President's Committee on Employment of People with Disabilities, *Ready, Willing, and Available: A Business Guide for Hiring People with Disabilities* Appendix B (1989) [hereinafter President's Committee, People with Disabilities].

1. The President's Committee on Employment of People with Disabilities, 1111 20th Street, N.W., Washington, D.C. 20036 or by telephoning:

    (202) 653-5044 (Voice)

    (202) 653-5050 (TDD)

    (202) 653-7386 (FAX)

2. Department of Veterans Affairs
3. Local vocational, technical, and general high schools
4. Special education schools and programs
5. Local offices of federal and state employment services
6. National organizations or their local affiliates of:

    a. Disabled American Veterans

    b. Epilepsy Foundation

    c. National Association for Retarded Citizens

    d. Easter Seal Society

    e. Goodwill Industries

    f. United Cerebral Palsy

    g. Multiple Sclerosis Society

    h. Arthritis Foundation

7. Blind centers
8. Bureaus of services for people who are blind
9. Projects with industry
10. Labor unions
11. State agencies for vocational rehabilitation
12. State departments of human services
13. State committees for people who are developmentally disabled
14. Disabilities and aging information and referral services
15. Rehabilitation/sheltered workshops
16. Community colleges
17. Welfare employment centers
18. Private industry councils.

Many of the above sources are listed in local telephone directories for easier access.

When contacting a referral source, the employer should inquire regarding the level of services it provides by asking:[112]

1. Does the agency evaluate their clients' employment potential? If so, how?
2. Does the agency provide skills training? If so, what?

---

[112] *Id.* at 6.

3. Are financial incentives available for hiring the persons that the agency represents (for instance, targeted jobs tax credits, wage subsidies, training grants, and so forth)?

4. Does the agency provide on-the-job training, coaching, counseling, follow-up, and so forth?

5. Does the agency offer awareness training to supervisors and managers?

6. What is the agency's placement record, including the number of placements in specific jobs, retention rates, and so forth?

Once a relationship is established with one agency, other agencies with similar services will probably contact the employer. One successful placement will open other avenues of opportunity.

Meeting and Evaluating Candidates

You have a job to fill and a person with a disability applies. The person is like any other applicant except for a physical, mental, or learning disability. If the person did not believe that he or she was qualified, no application would have been filed. It is the employer's responsibility to determine if the disabled person is qualified. This assessment must be done in the same manner as for any other applicant.

This is where the employer's own feelings about individuals with disabilities appear. Set forth below are some suggestions for dealing with disabled applicants.

Greeting the Applicant.   When in doubt as to whether to help an individual around the limitations caused by their disability, the following questions should break the ice and allow the applicant to tell what, if anything, is needed:

1. May I be of assistance?
2. Is there anything I can do to make your visit more pleasant?

The following should be considered when dealing with certain applicant limitations:

1. If the applicant has a visual limitation or is blind, identify yourself, shake hands, and offer the applicant the option of taking your arm for direction if you need to go to another location. Let the applicant feel the back of the chair where he or she is to sit. If a guide dog accompanies the applicant, let it do its job.

2. If the applicant has a hearing limitation and you have no experience in sign language, look at the individual, speak in your regular tone of voice, and be prepared to exchange information in writing. Have a couple of note pads and pencils handy.

3. If the applicant is accompanied by an interpreter, speak to the applicant. The interpreter will ask to sit next to you to better handle the interview.

4. If the applicant has mental limitations, there is no need to "talk down." Greet him or her as you would any other applicant and use the vocabulary common to the job. In a few minutes, you will have a good understanding of the level at which the individual can communicate.

Remember the following:

1. *Wrong perspective.* "If I were in your shoes, I don't know how I could possibly do this job."
2. *Right perspective.* "This person is applying for the job of (name of job). He or she does have a disability. If I became disabled, but was capable of performing this job, would I not wish to be treated like any other applicant without a disability? Let's see about the applicant's experience, training, and education; then we'll deal with the possibility that the disability might require an accommodation for the individual to do the job's functions."

Handling the Application. Follow the employer's regular procedures. If the applicant's disability prevents him or her from filling out an application, offer assistance or allow it to be taken home, stating a specific time for its return. This action is a reasonable accommodation to the employer's application procedures.

Testing the Applicant. If the employer requires any type of test and the applicant's disability does not interfere, the test should be administered in the same manner as for any other applicant. Blindness, motor impairment affecting the use of hands or eye/hand coordination, and learning disabilities can prevent an applicant from passing some tests even though he or she might have the ability to do the job. Rely instead on the applicant's work experience, training, and education. Remember, when the applicant's impairment makes it impractical to complete a test, particularly one which is timed, the results may reflect the testing of the individual's impairment-related limitations instead of predicting the applicant's abilities and potential job success. The following should be considered in dealing with certain disabilities and how they might affect test performance:

1. Under some circumstances, a test should be read to an applicant who has a visual impairment. For example, many individuals with visual impairments successfully hold typing positions. To test a person with a visual impairment, typing tests are put on a dictating machine and then scored in the same way as for any other applicant. If an applicant has a hearing impairment, ask some questions that will indicate whether or not the applicant understands the instructions.
2. If the applicant has a learning disability, success or failure on the test could depend solely on its instructions. Try to modify the instructions to accommodate the applicant's disability.

3. Persons who have recovered from mental illness might not be able to sustain test pressure. Honest and open discussion regarding this will help in deciding if the test is really needed.

Discussing Reasonable Accommodation. The issue of accommodation should be raised only after the individual is determined to be qualified as a potential job candidate. If the applicant is not qualified, tell him or her why; that is, explain the training and experience that other persons who perform the job possess, which he or she lacks or must obtain to become a successful applicant. In this way, the applicant will understand that his or her rejection was truly based on a lack of qualification rather than on a disability. The interview of a potentially successful candidate should end with a visit to the worksite. At that time, a better understanding of the tasks to be performed can be obtained. If a reasonable accommodation is needed, the degree of accommodation can be discussed.

Working with Agencies. If the applicant has been referred by or trained by a rehabilitation agency, the employer will have access to additional information. While it is always preferable to interview an applicant alone, the nature of the disability might require the presence of the agency counselor. This will help open the door.

Closing the Interview. If the applicant is qualified and the employer is not prepared to make a hiring offer, the usual reasons given to applicants who are not hired immediately apply, such as, "Thank you for applying, we will notify you in the future regarding any openings."[113]

Deciding What the Job Is

Job analysis is the process of breaking down a particular job into its component parts. This is a useful tool in interviewing, selecting, training, and promoting employees as well as for determining compensation. It is especially helpful when dealing with disabled applicants or employees.

The first step in a job analysis is to prepare a list of the required tasks. Next, the following questions should be asked about each task:[114]

1. How is the task performed; that is, what methods, techniques, and tools are used?
2. How often is the task performed; that is, are the tasks performed less frequently as important to success as those done more frequently?
3. How much time is allotted to perform the task? Is the pace consistent?

---

[113] *Id.* at 7–10.
[114] *Id.* at 11–12.

4. Why is the task performed?
5. Where is the task performed?
6. How is success measured?
7. What happens if the task is done incorrectly?
8. What aptitudes are necessary; that is, what is the potential to learn and accomplish a skill?
9. What knowledge is necessary; that is, the level of general or technical information?
10. What skills are necessary?
11. How much physical exertion is required, such as lifting, standing, bending, reaching, twisting, crawling, and so forth?

Supplement the above with knowledge from other sources, including:

1. Interviewing employees and supervisors
2. Observing the job
3. Using employee task logs and questionnaires.

Job analysis is particularly useful when hiring the disabled. A careful match of the individual's aptitudes and abilities with the particular job enhances the probability of success. The job analysis also helps in determining if a job accommodation is necessary. Accommodation can include:

1. Additional assistance to the individual with a disability
2. A physical change to the worksite
3. A restructuring of tasks.

Restructuring of tasks is particularly helpful with employees who have mental or emotional disabilities. For example, employees who are recovering from a mental illness may need task assignments that are basically routine. Eventually, these assignments become boring as the employee's health improves. As a means of preparing the employee for more significant assignments, tasks can be gradually added or redesigned so that they become more interesting. A job analysis will help in defining or redefining the necessary skill level for the position. Finally, a job analysis helps reassure supervisors about the real capability of a person with a disability.

Accommodating Employees with Disabilities

Employers have many resources available to assist in modifying, adapting, and providing accessibility to their buildings and facilities for the newly hired or newly disabled employee. Some of these are provided at no cost. State vocational rehabilitation agencies are a good source for this assistance. Another resource is the Job Accommodation Network (JAN), which offers toll-free telephone consultation (1-800-526-7234).

In addition to job modification, structural changes may need to be made. Structural changes may be minimal, involving only ramping, doorway widening, and making restrooms accessible. In most cases, the cost of increasing accessibility may be relatively small. Tax incentives to employers that make their facilities and vehicles accessible to disabled or elderly persons should be reviewed under federal and state tax statutes.[115]

Often accommodation involves no more than taking a common-sense approach that need not be expensive to be effective. Many situations can be handled with little or no expense. The person with the disability is usually the best person with whom to start. He or she may have already solved the problem or be able to offer constructive advice on what needs to be done.

Wheelchair users need space for their chairs when entering and leaving as well as in work areas. Local building codes state the amount of space required. Often, simply raising an ordinary desk or worktable on blocks will allow the user to draw his or her chair up to the work area and work comfortably. Specially designed workstations, as well as those that can be raised and lowered mechanically, are available. The employer should also consider limitations in the range of reach for wheelchair users and others with upper body strength and extension problems. Moving equipment and/or devices from one side of a workstation to the other may be all that is needed to allow an individual to function productively. When necessary items are out of reach and cannot be moved, a variety of devices are available to extend an individual's reach and grasp.

Helping accommodate hearing-impaired individuals may be no more complicated than turning a receptionist's desk to face the door. A variety of devices are available for telephones to amplify hearing and speech. Devices that flash lights instead of ring bells can be provided for emergency alarms as well as telephones. Some hearing-impaired persons cannot use regular telephones even if the phones are adapted with amplifying devices. Instead, individuals with severe hearing loss use telecommunication devices for the hearing-impaired (TDDs). TDDs make the telephone accessible and productive to people who would otherwise not be able to use it. For greatest efficiency, the "sender" and "receiver" should each have a TDD.

Individuals with limited or no vision can be accommodated in various ways. Examples include raised lettering or Braille symbols on signs and elevator buttons. A variety of magnification devices exist. Devices that produce Braille symbols or synthesized speech can assist those with severely limited or no vision to read printed material and access computers. While these devices may be expensive initially, they often pay for themselves in increased productivity.

---

[115] *See, e.g.,* 26 U.S.C. § 190 (1988) ($35,000 tax incentive under the Internal Revenue Code).

Individuals with severe strength and motion limitations, such as that caused by quadriplegia, can also be accommodated. Switches that can be operated with the mouth or a head stick can be connected to telephones, computers, and manufacturing equipment, as can floor strips that are triggered when a wheelchair rolls across.

Special equipment to accommodate individuals who are mentally retarded or those who have recovered from some form of mental illness may not be required. Speak with the individual about it. Providing extra training and guidance to the individual, or breaking a complex task down into simpler components, may be all that is needed to ensure understanding and productivity. Working closely with the person's rehabilitation counselor should also be considered. Avoid giving too many instructions at once, and try to limit the number of individuals giving instructions. Multiple instructors often can confuse a situation as much as multiple instructions.[116]

Obtaining Supervisor Support

Gaining supervisor support and commitment requires planning, education, support, and feedback. The supervisor is the key to the success of the employee with a disability.

Supervisors can be prepared for the specific limitations and needs of individual employees by providing them with written information, contacts with community resources, and coaching from those who have successfully supervised employees with disabilities. Depending upon the employer's size, it might be best to develop a training program for all supervisors, using knowledgeable individuals who can lead discussions about the supervisor's role. This will create an internal network and increase awareness throughout the organization. Use accurate facts and data to help the supervisor enter the relationship with a realistic, positive attitude.

Knowledge of an individual's performance expectations, reliability, and special needs is essential. For example, knowing that most employees with disabilities are extremely dependable and responsible will aid the supervisor to view the individual as an asset. However, apprehension may not totally disappear until the supervisor has experienced some degree of success in dealing with employees who have disabilities.

Ongoing support from others in the employer's organization is required, particularly from top-level management. Management must be clear about its commitment, providing consistent goals to the supervisor and the employee. This should include bonuses for supervisors who successfully manage employees with disabilities. The employer should also listen to the supervisor's concerns, provide

---

[116] *See* President's Committee, People with Disabilities at 14–16.

feedback, praise his or her successes, and encourage efforts that will make the supervisor a role model for others.

Begin by involving the supervisor in the employment process, including recruitment, interviewing, and job modification. The supervisor will know what is expected of him or her, and will become aware of the independence that most employees with disabilities attempt to attain. The supervisor's goal should be *to treat the employee with a disability the same as other employees.* Being overly cautious or protective will have a negative effect on the employee's career mobility, self-esteem, and relationships with co-employees.

The supervisor may be unsure of his or her own abilities and thus require extra assistance and support. Increasing understanding and ability to supervise employees with disabilities needs to become an integral part of the supervisor's responsibilities. Success of the supervisor can be ensured by:[117]

1. Carefully planning a process for gaining support
2. Involving the supervisor in the employment process
3. Providing education and resources
4. Providing assistance and feedback
5. Rewarding results
6. Publicizing the employer's commitment and actions so that everyone becomes part of the process.

Integrating Employees with Disabilities

Integrating employees with disabilities into the employer's organization can be achieved through the STEP process:

S Safety

T Training

E Efficiency

P Privacy

Safety. Because physical examinations tend to screen out qualified individuals with disabilities, they must be used in a manner consistent with business necessity and safe performance of the job, and be administered when all applicants are required to take them. Co-employees do not need to know detailed medical history, but may, for example, be informed of any medical alert or emergency situations involving diabetic shock reaction, the possibility of seizures, inability to hear fire alarms, and so forth. General rules of safety should be explained to all

---

[117] *Id.* at 17–18.

employees. Adaptations to safety procedures for individuals with disabilities should be outlined. Establishing a "buddy" system may help, especially during emergency situations. Emergency preparation should be planned, communicated, and conducted.

Training.   Any employee's success depends on orientation and training. This is especially true when an employee has a disability. In some cases, a veteran employee should take charge of the new employee and teach work rules and procedures, under the supervisor's direction. Review job duties along with testing accommodations and adaptations. Rework the duties if necessary, but remember it is important that co-employees recognize that the individual who has a disability can perform the essential tasks. Do not forget the basics. The most detailed job training and orientation can be undermined if more fundamental needs of getting around or finding the restrooms are not addressed adequately. Co-employees should be encouraged to be part of assisting new employees to adapt.

Efficiency.   Introduce the new employee to the organization and the job by outlining the duties and procedures. When accommodations are made, the supervisor should explain to co-employees what alterations and/or adaptations will be made to duties or procedures. It is important and essential that the supervisor dispel any myths or unspoken concerns that co-employees may have about an employee with a disability. After a reasonable orientation period, the supervisor must treat employees with disabilities consistently with their nondisabled counterparts. If job performance problems occur, they should be addressed immediately. Early identification of the employee with a behavioral or medical problem should be based entirely on evidence of unsatisfactory work performance and related factors. Supervisors should not be diagnosticians, psychologists, or medical experts, but must notice changes in behavior and recognize when people are not working safely and effectively. Inform the employee immediately of performance deficiencies. Outline specific actions for improvement, preferably in writing. Allow the employee to help identify corrective action, involving medical and rehabilitation specialists as necessary. Remember to praise and recognize good performance. Avoid patronizing employees with disabilities. Encourage team spirit whenever possible. All members of the team have unique talents and skills which contribute.

Privacy.   Only that information necessary for safe job performance should be shared in the workplace. The supervisor must have the necessary medical information to evaluate job assignments, risks, and functional characteristics of the employee. However, the employee's privacy of medical records and history must be preserved to the maximum extent possible. The detailed history and exact medical diagnosis are generally not shared in the workplace with those who do not have a need to know this information in a job-related performance situation. Information necessary for emergency procedures, health, and safety reasons should be secured and maintained by the supervisor with the proper confidentiality and job-related considerations.[118]

Career Accessibility

Individuals with disabilities are just like other employees. They want to do a good job, they appreciate constructive supervision, and they want to get ahead. The myth that individuals with disabilities are grateful just to work and are happy to stay in entry-level positions is precisely that: a myth! Some individuals need or want a steady routine, but most enjoy new challenges. Individuals with disabilities are no exception. The following can be helpful in providing career accessibility to individuals with disabilities:[119]

1. *Goal setting.* Recognize that individuals with disabilities have career goals. Sit down with these employees and discuss these goals. If the goals seem unreasonable, ask the employees what they think it would take for them to achieve the goals. See if a consensus can be reached. If the goals are unreasonable for business reasons, indicate that they are. Do not automatically assume that the employee's disability will be a barrier. The biggest barrier may be the employer's lack of understanding.

2. *Team building.* It is easy to isolate employees with disabilities from others. Make sure these employees have opportunities not only to work with others on group projects but, when appropriate, to assume leadership roles.

3. *Networking.* Bring employees with disabilities not only into formal work groups but also into informal employee gatherings. Do not assume that, just because an employee uses a wheelchair, he or she would not be interested in joining the ski club, or that an employee who is deaf would not like to attend the company dance. People with disabilities enjoy all sorts of social and athletic activities. Very often, important business is discussed at these events. All employees should be given the opportunity to participate. Events should be scheduled at facilities accessible to individuals with disabilities.

4. *The mentor system.* Anyone can benefit from the guidance of a more experienced employee. Encourage employees with disabilities to find mentors, disabled or not. When these employees become more experienced, encourage them to be mentors to other new employees, who may or may not be disabled.

5. *Performance evaluations.* Every employer differs in how it evaluates employees. Some procedures are formal, written documents. Others are less formal and oral. Whatever procedure is followed, treat employees with disabilities like all other employees. If jobs have been restructured to

---

[118] *Id.* at 19–21.
[119] *Id.* at 22–24.

accommodate disabilities, employees should only be evaluated on those tasks that they are expected to perform. Apply the same performance criteria to those employees that would be applied to all other employees. Trying to "give a break" does not encourage employees with disabilities to perform up to standards, and may cause resentment among other employees.

6. *Training.* Give employees with disabilities similar opportunities for training. If there are formal classes, make sure that they are held in accessible facilities. Materials may have to be made available in large print for individuals who are visually impaired. Interpreters should be considered for participants who are hearing impaired. If one of the employees with a disability happens to be an expert in a skill or topic to be taught, consider having that person be the trainer for the course.

§ 3.27 —Minimizing Litigation Risks

Due to litigation's high cost and the at-will employment doctrine's changing character, employers should attempt to structure their hiring procedures and policies to minimize their litigation risk by:[120]

1. Ensuring that interviewers do not make improper or exaggerated promises

2. Examining the employer's personnel policies, handbooks, and manuals to make certain that they contain no promises the employer is unable or unwilling to keep, by removing any language that might imply that employment is other than at-will by:[121]

   a. Avoiding terms like "permanent employee"

   b. Changing "probationary period" to "initial review period"

   c. Considering including in each employee handbook a statement:

   (i) That "These policies are subject to unilateral change without notice"

   (ii) Preserving the at-will nature of the employment relationship by disclaiming the creation of any employment contract

   d. If the publication contains work rules or a list of termination causes, it should state that the rules/list is not all inclusive

3. Having every applicant sign a written acknowledgement that any employment with the employer is at-will.[122] This acknowledgment should be:

---

[120] *See* American Hospital Association, Wrongful Discharge at 13–84.

[121] See § **3.14.**

[122] *Id.*

a. Included as part of the actual application[123]

b. A statement that the application has been read in its entirety.

§ 3.28 —Checklist before Employment

This form (**Form 3.28(1)**) should be used as a record to ensure that the employer's procedures and policies are adequately explained to employees, in order to obtain a consistent understanding and enforcement:

FORM 3.28(1)
CHECKLIST BEFORE EMPLOYMENT

The Company asks that you complete the following checklist before reporting for employment. It is important that the Company orient you to its procedures and policies. By signing in the appropriate place, you are acknowledging that the corresponding topic has been fully explained and that any questions you may have have been answered to your satisfaction.

TOPIC   EMPLOYEE SIGNATURE

1. Employment date.   _____

2. Rate of pay/compensation.   _____

3. I understand I may be requested to perform
    various unrelated tasks from time to time.   _____

4. I understand that my supervisor will introduce
    me to my fellow employees and personnel in
    other departments I may have contact with at
    various times.   _____

5. I have answered all questions accurately and
    completely on my Employee's State Withholding
    (W4) Allowance Certificate.   _____

6. I have answered all questions accurately and
    completely on my IRS Employee's Withholding
    (Federal W-4) Allowance Certificate.   _____

7. I have answered all questions accurately and
    completely on my Employment Eligibility
    Verification (Form I-9).   _____

---

[123] *Id.*

8.   I have completed my Employee Information Sheet.   _____

9.   I have received and read a copy of the Employee
     Handbook—Book number _____.   _____

10. I have received and read a copy of the Group
     Insurance Benefits Booklet. I also received and
     completed an enrollment card for these benefits.   _____

11. I have received and read a copy of the
     Company-paid, weekly income insurance plan.

12. I have received and read a copy of the plan
     summary for the profit-sharing program and
     understand when I am eligible to participate and
     the benefits I can derive through participation
     in the plan.   _____

_____
Date

_____
Employee Signature

_____
Supervisor Signature

§ 3.29   —Hiring Policies

The following sets forth an overall employer hiring policy:

POLICY 3.29(1)
HIRING POLICY

The following are to be applied in all employment decisions and actions:

1.   Select, retain, and promote employees based on individual ability, performance, and experience, avoiding actions influenced by personal relationships and discriminatory practices.

2.   Respect collective bargaining agreements.

3.   Recognize employees as individuals with different abilities, needs, and motivations, and encourage individual initiative, creativity, and thought in accomplishing job assignments.

4.   Maintain a working environment that provides opportunities for personal growth and advancement and that permits maximum individual progress consistent with ability and performance.

5. Promote from within whenever there is a current employee whose ability, experience, motivation, education, and performance demonstrate position qualification.

6. Use internal and external developmental activities, including normal and special job assignments, to assist employees in preparing themselves for advancement.

7. Evaluate employee performance on a regular basis and provide the evaluation's results to employees on a timely basis to assist them in their development.

8. Provide communication systems that encourage self-expression and open dialogue throughout the Company to help ensure constructive, prompt, and fair work-related problem resolution.

9. Recognize the value of a stable work force and give consideration to length of satisfactory service as well as performance in employee reduction and restoration.

10. Maintain a structure of employee benefits that provides reasonable protection against economic hazards caused by illness, disability, or death, and for income after retirement that is applied equitably to all employees in accordance with overall Company guidelines.

11. Establish compensation programs that attract and retain quality employees, motivate employee initiative, and reward superior performance.

12. Comply with all laws and regulations affecting employee relations.

POLICY 3.29(2)
HIRING POLICY

Section 1. Purpose.   It is the Company's policy always to hire a qualified employee. This selection will be based on qualifications, skill, training, personality, and ambition displayed by the applicant. It is the Company's commitment to comply with this hiring policy.

Job openings not filled from within will be filled by referrals, walk-ins, or advertisement respondents. Active files for applicants are maintained by the Human Resources Department for six (6) months. These may be used and should be reviewed when seeking new employees. The Plant Manager or Manager requesting additional employees should submit in writing a request identifying the job, position, and need to the Human Resources Department.

Section 2. General Procedures.   Prior to employing an individual, certain preliminary steps must be taken to ensure uniformity of personnel practices and compliance with federal and state employment statutes. The following procedures are to be used:

a. Applicant reception;

b. Preliminary interview and screening by the Human Resources Department;

c. Application completion;

d. Testing;

e. Interview with the prospective supervisor;

f. Reference checks;

g. Preliminary selection by the Human Resources Department after consultation with the prospective supervisor;

h. Final selection by the Plant Manager, supervisor, and Human Resources Department; and

i. Applicant hiring.

Section 3. Reception.   The applicant will be met in the Human Resources Department's lobby where literature and information concerning the Company will be made available. All referred applicants, walk-ins, or advertisement respondents report to this area first. It is the Company's policy to treat each of these applicants with the same consideration as a customer. All applicants, whether hired or not, can spread good will for the Company or give it a bad name, based on the treatment they receive. The Company's policy is to maintain a good image for attracting qualified applicants.

Section 4. Preliminary Interview and Screening by the Human Resources Department.   A short preliminary interview by the Human Resources Department's staff will be held with the applicant to identify the most promising applicants and those who are not qualified.

Section 5. Application.   After the preliminary interview, all applicants are given an application to complete. The questions used on this application are in compliance with federal and state FEP statutes and regulations. The application also includes clauses covering falsification of records and an agreement to submit to medical testing, which are also signed by the applicant. The applicant is also asked at this time for information under the Immigration Reform and Control Act (IRCA) of 1986. If the applicant cannot comply with this Act, he or she will not be considered for employment. Once obtained, IRCA information will be kept separate from the application.

Section 6. Testing.   All applicants who are approved as possible candidates, whether they are referred by employees, walk-ins, or advertisement respondents, will not be tested until job requests are given to the Human Resources Department. An outside agency will do the testing to ensure that the Company adheres to federal and state FEP statutes which require that the overall selection process show no evidence of adverse impact on minority groups.

Section 7. Interview with Prospective Supervisor.   If the applicant's testing proves positive, an interview with the prospective supervisor takes place. The times for the interviews are set up to be mutually convenient for both the supervisor and the applicant. This interview is set up to: (a) assess the applicant; (b) describe the job and working conditions to the applicant by touring the area in which he or she would work; and (c) create goodwill for the Company, whether or not the applicant is hired. To accomplish these objectives, the supervisor must be alert, perceptive, able to keep accurate records, free from prejudice, and even-tempered. Supervisors must also avoid any questioning or conduct that violates federal and state FEP statutes. After the interview, the applicant will be told that he or she will be contacted by the Human Resources Department. The supervisor does not offer the job to the employee. A checklist will be given to the supervisor to make sure that certain points are covered during the interview. The supervisor will return the application with the completed interview checklist to the Human Resources Department for determination as to whether to continue the hiring procedure.

Section 8. Reference Checking.   If the interview proves positive, the Human Resources Department will check references with former employers, schools attended, and so forth. The applicant must sign a consent form to be sent to certain employers who might not otherwise be willing to forward information on the applicant.

Section 9. Preliminary Selection by the Human Resources Department after Consultation with Prospective Supervisor.   A preliminary selection will be made by the Human Resources Department and the supervisor after they are satisfied that qualified applicants are available. If no qualified applicants are available, other applicants will be sought.

Section 10. Final Selection by the Plant Manager, Prospective Supervisor, and the Human Resources Department.   A final selection will be made by the Plant Manager, the prospective supervisor, and the Human Resources Department after all are satisfied that a qualified selection is available. All must agree on wages, terms, and conditions for the new employee. A checklist will be used to cover these points and all will sign this Selection Form.

Section 11. Placement—Hiring of Applicant.   The Human Resources Department will contact the selected applicant and offer employment. Details of the wages, terms, and employment conditions will be discussed. If the applicant accepts, the Human Resources Department will set up a time for the employee to sign in and begin the Company's orientation program.

Section 12. Rejected Applicants.   In most circumstances, a number of applicants will be interviewed for a particular position. It is conceivable that at times more than one applicant will progress through the interview procedure, but only one will be chosen. If other applicants would have been eligible for the position, these approved applicants will be retained in a special referral file for up to six (6) months to be considered for additional openings that might occur either in the same department or in other departments or shifts. As openings develop, these applicants will be referred to supervisors for consideration, along with additional new applicants, as required by the supervisor to make a quality selection.

Section 13. Applicability. Anyone being hired as a full-time employee is subject to this hiring procedure. Employees hired on a temporary basis through outside temporary services are subject to this hiring policy.

CHAPTER 4

INTRODUCTORY
EMPLOYMENT POLICIES

§ 4.1 Introduction

Employers may be tempted to avoid preparation of employment policies because, as some may mistakenly believe, "My employees know what my policies are."[1] In an age of emerging individual employment rights litigation, this is a dangerous employer attitude. A well-written, comprehensive employment policy's importance should not be underestimated. At the very least, it can help avoid confusion, abuse, and misinterpretation of employer procedures and policies.

Policies are an important communications tool for employers because employees are expected to become familiar with a variety of workplace procedures, policies, and safety regulations along with rules relating to compensation and

---

[1] Connors, *Employee Policy Handbook: Who Needs It? A Checklist for Employers,* 45 Dynamic Bus. 10 (Mar. 1990).

benefits. They establish a closer relationship between employees and employers, in addition to advancing unity and helping ensure uniform employee treatment.[2]

A well-designed handbook incorporating policies can be used as a reference guide in a single source.[3] The handbook gives an employer the opportunity to inform employees about its background, products, and place in the community, thus helping to create a commitment to the employer and its goals.

No two handbooks should be exactly alike.[4] The handbook should reflect each employer's management and operational style. Handbooks that suggest that they were prepared by an impersonal third party will not achieve their desired effect of creating closer and understandable communications.[5] Most handbooks:

1. Document employer procedures, policies, and work rules to serve as a behavioral guide for employees by clarifying the employer's position on these matters

2. Serve as an information source for new and current employees about the employer, its organizational structure, and overall philosophy

3. Provide employees with their own up-to-date, easy-to-understand reference guide on the range and comprehensiveness of the employer's compensation and benefits program.[6]

A handbook's contents may be affected by whether separate booklets covering individual subjects involving pension rights, health care benefits, and so forth are made available by the employer.[7] Should these separate documents be used, they must be consistent and coordinated with similar handbook provisions to avoid misunderstandings or unwanted liability.[8]

No set list of topics exists that must be covered in a handbook.[9] Some employers prefer to devote their handbook to uncomplicated matters covering their background, time-off policies, and disciplinary rules; other employers cover more complex issues involving pensions, profit sharing, medical benefits, and so forth.

---

[2] *Id.*

[3] See chs. 10–11.

[4] See ch. 11.

[5] *See* C. Bakaly, Jr. & J. Grossman, The Modern Law of Employment Relationships, app. B at 379 (2d ed. 1989).

[6] Research Institute of America, Employment Coordinator ¶ PM-11,051.2 (1989) [hereinafter RIA, Employment Coordinator].

[7] *Id.* at ¶ PM-11,051.4.

[8] *See, e.g.,* Berry v. Playboy Enter., Inc., 195 N.J. 520, 480 A.2d 941 (1984) (negligent misrepresentations to an employee by an employer regarding health and other supplemental benefits upon hiring when compared with internal employer documents).

[9] See ch. 10. When determining a handbook's contents, other employers' handbooks should be reviewed for possible suggestions. See also ch. 16.

A good policy should be comprehensive and precise. No matter how much care is taken in compiling the policies that comprise the handbook, a handbook that is overly technical, formal, or simply unclear will not achieve its communication purpose[10] and can also create unnecessary legal problems.[11]

Policies must be drafted with care and caution because of their potential legal implications.[12] They must reflect the current law in the particular jurisdiction in which they are to be used.[13] Statutes regarding compensation, vacations, and voting time off may also vary.[14] Policies must be carefully reviewed for compliance with these statutes. Likewise, some states have found that policies may create binding commitments, while other states have not.[15] The current law of the particular state must be consulted before the policy's final issuance, and there must be periodic subsequent reviews to determine any changes.

Introductory policies generally set forth preliminary matters outlining the information that will follow, along with the employer's position on the at-will employment relationship and what, if any, binding commitments are represented. This chapter reviews disclaimers,[16] equal employment opportunity,[17] employee definitions,[18] and so forth.

§ 4.2 Introductory Matter/Disclaimer

The introduction policy communicates the tone for the employment related information that will follow. Introduction policies may contain a letter from the company's president, a statement about the company's overall philosophy, goals, or place in the community, and a position statement on what, if any, binding commitments the policy may create. The introduction policy's main purpose should be to:

---

[10] RIA, Employment Coordinator at ¶ PM-11,051.4.

[11] See ch. 15. Damage awards against employers in these cases can be substantial. *See, e.g.,* Washington Welfare Ass'n, Inc. v. Poindexter, 479 A.2d 313 (D.C. 1984) ($42,000 damage award).

[12] See ch. 15.

[13] *Id.*

[14] *See, e.g.,* Cal. Elec. Code § 14350 (West 1977) (voting time); *see also* K. Decker, Employee Privacy Law and Practice § 2.40 (John Wiley & Sons, Inc. 1987) [hereinafter Decker, Privacy Law].

[15] *See, e.g.,* Woolley v. Hoffmann-LaRoche, Inc., 99 N.J. 284, 491 A.2d 1257, *modified,* 101 N.J. 10, 499 A.2d 515 (1985) (binding commitment); *but see* Williams v. Delta Haven, Inc., 416 So. 2d 637 (La. App. 1982) (nonbinding commitment). See also ch. 15.

[16] See §§ **3.3–3.5.**

[17] See §§ **3.6–3.8.**

[18] See §§ **3.9–3.11.**

1. Welcome employees
2. Put employees at ease about their new surroundings
3. Promote positive employee communications and relations
4. Reassure employees that they have joined a quality organization
5. Explain the policy's purposes
6. Set forth what, if any, binding or nonbinding commitments the policies may contain and emphasize that the employment relationship remains at-will by means of a disclaimer, if this is desired.[19]

An employer may wish to ensure, to the maximum extent possible, that its policies are not legally enforceable because they create no reasonable expectation that they are binding to preserve the at-will employment relationship. To maintain this nonenforceability of employer commitments, a disclaimer within the introduction may be appropriate.[20]

Considerable litigation is developing over the circumstances under which these disclaimers will be enforced.[21] It is no longer certain that a disclaimer will always defeat an at-will employee's claim.[22] Today, extreme care must be exercised in drafting the disclaimer. Likewise, it must be regularly reviewed to ensure continued effectiveness in preserving the at-will employment relationship. Disclaimers are being regularly challenged on the basis of their failure to be prominently set forth, inconsistency, lack of consideration, and dissemination.

For varying employee relations reasons, an employer may be unwilling to state clearly that its employment policies and rules are unenforceable. A disclaimer undermines the morale-boosting effect of any statement that termination will be only for cause. Equally important, if an employer has promulgated carefully developed written policies preserving the at-will employment relationship, the employer should preclude the possibility that informal communication by a recruiter or supervisor constitutes an enforceable promise outside the scope of written policies.[23]

---

[19] See ch. 15.

[20] *See* Toussaint v. Blue Cross/Blue Shield, 408 Mich. 579, 292 N.W.2d 880 (1980) (suggesting that this employer strategy of using disclaimers may be appropriate to preserve at-will employment relationship).

[21] *See, e.g.,* McDonald v. Mobil Coal Producing, Inc., 820 P.2d 986 (Wyo. 1991) (summary judgment should not have been granted for employer when material issue of fact existed regarding whether employee could reasonably rely on handbook establishing fair treatment and disciplinary procedures, even though contract disclaimer was also included).

[22] *See, e.g.,* Durtsche v. American Colloid Co., 928 F.2d 1007 (10th Cir. 1992) (employer's attempt to amend handbook invalid because disclaimer that had been added not sufficiently conspicuous to place employees on notice of change); Long v. Tazewell/Pelkin Communication Center, 211 Ill. App.3d 134, 158 Ill. Dec. 798, 574 N.E.2d 1191 (1991) (inconspicuous disclaimer not enforceable).

[23] H. Perritt, Employee Dismissal Law and Practice § 8.8 (John Wiley & Sons, Inc. 3d ed. 1993) [hereinafter Perritt, Employee Dismissal].

When drafted with care, disclaimers will be enforced by the courts.[24] Not all disclaimers, however, can defeat an employee's claim. The legal effect of disclaimers depends on their negating the reasonableness of employee reliance on subsequent employer statements or conduct that might otherwise support an inference of an employment security promise.[25]

A disclaimer does not create the at-will employment relationship as a matter of law.[26] In many cases, the dispute over the legal effect to be given a disclaimer is basically factual.[27]

For example, a handbook indicating that its purpose is to explain the employer's policies may create binding commitments despite a disclaimer.[28] Having announced this policy, presumably with a view to obtaining improved employee attitudes and behavior along with better work performance, the employer may not be able to treat its policies as illusory by using a disclaimer, in that the disclaimer is inconsistent with everything else that appears in the handbook; that is, the employer cannot have it both ways—binding for some purposes and not for others. The employee may be entitled to enforce these policy representations, despite a disclaimer's presence, if it can be demonstrated that:

1. The employer should have reasonably expected the employee to consider the representation as a binding employer commitment
2. The employee reasonably relied upon the representation
3. Injustice can be avoided only by the representation's enforcement.[29]

---

[24] *See, e.g.,* Doe v. First National Bank, 865 F.2d 864, 872–73 (7th Cir. 1989) (prominent disclaimer in employment handbook precluded any promise element of implied contract); Slemmer v. Bi-Lo, Inc., 7 I.E.R. Cas. (BNA) 505 (S.C. Ct. of Common Pleas, Florence Cty. 1992) (former employee failed to state claim against employer when conspicuous disclaimer on handbook's inside cover stated that neither its policies, procedures, nor guidelines were intended to be a contract or otherwise legally binding on the employee or employer); Suter v. Harsco Corp., 184 W. Va. 734, 403 S.E.2d 751 (1991) (employer may protect itself from being bound by statements in handbook by including clear and prominent disclaimer).

[25] Perritt, Employee Dismissal § 8.8.

[26] *See, e.g.,* Jones v. Central Peninsula General Hospital, 779 P.2d 783 (Alaska 1989) (single sentence in employment handbook stating that handbook was informational only, not employment contract, was too ambiguous and inconspicuous to be immediately effective).

[27] *See, e.g.,* Uebelacker v. Cincom Systems, Inc., 48 Ohio App.3d 268, 549 N.E.2d 1210, 1216–17 (1988) (disclaimer in handbook prevented contract status for handbook, but subsequent oral assurances entitled employee to trial on promissory estoppel theory).

[28] *See, e.g.,* McDonald v. Mobil Coal Producing, Inc., 820 P.2d 986 (Wyo. 1991) (summary judgment should not have been granted when material issue of fact existed regarding whether employee could reasonably rely on employment handbook establishing fair treatment and disciplinary procedures, even though contract disclaimer was also included).

[29] *See* Cronk v. Intermountain Rural Electric Association, 765 P.2d 619, 624 (Colo. Ct. App. 1988).

The wording and placement of the disclaimer is becoming increasingly important to preserve the at-will employment relationship. For example, an employee had signed three separate employment agreements, each containing a provision stating that "the Employee's employment with the Company may be terminated by either party at any time."[30] Despite written acknowledgment of the employment condition, the provision was silent regarding whether "good cause" was necessary for termination. The statement could not be interpreted as creating an agreement that the employee could be terminated for merely any reason.

Limiting modifications of employment policies to writings may not preclude an inference that a written modification has occurred through publication of a handbook or other written personnel policies.[31] A disclaimer, no matter what its terms or clarity, however, may not be able to extinguish the covenant of good faith and fair dealing in a jurisdiction recognizing this doctrine.[32]

Prominence

To be enforceable in preserving the at-will employment relationship, courts are increasingly finding that the disclaimer must be prominently displayed or conspicuous to the employee reading the employment handbook.[33] The question of whether a disclaimer is prominently displayed or conspicuous to the employee is a question of law to be determined by the court.

This concept was reviewed in *Arellano v. AMAX Coal Co.,*[34] where the disclaimer was located in the middle of a letter from the general manager of operations, which welcomed new employees. It was neither underlined, highlighted, nor set off, and its typeface was the same size as all other print preceding it.[35] Based on these deficiencies, the court found that the employer could not make representations to employees that their employment would be governed by certain terms to procure employment, force loyalty, discourage unionization, or for whatever other reason, yet surreptitiously reserve for the employer the right to capriciously depart from those same terms. Employees may read the disclaimer in conjunction with all other handbook provisions, but unless the disclaimer is

---

[30] Morris v. Chem-Lawn Corp., 541 F. Supp. 749 (E.D. Mich. 1982).

[31] *See, e.g.,* Butzer v. Camelot Hall Convalescent Center, Inc., 183 Mich. App. 194, 454 N.W.2d 122 (1989) (jury question presented as to whether handbook was writing within terms of disclaimer proviso limiting authority to modify at-will employment relationship).

[32] *See, e.g.,* Stark v. Circle K Corp., 751 P.2d 162 (Mont. 1988) (affirming jury verdict of $270,000 for employee terminated for refusing to sign dispute probation notice; reservation in application of right to terminate at-will could not override covenant of good faith and fair dealing, which exists as matter of law and policy).

[33] *See, e.g.,* Jimenez v. Colorado Interstate Gas Co., 690 F. Supp. 977 (D. Wyo. 1988) (to be effective, disclaimer must be conspicuously displayed).

[34] Arellano v. AMAX Coal Co., 6 I.E.R. Cas. (BNA) 1399 (D. Wyo. 1991).

[35] *Id.* at 1402.

made so prominent or conspicuous that the employee reading it knows (or should know) that the representations made in the handbook may be deviated from by the employer at any time without notice, the disclaimer will not be enforced.[36]

A similar result was reached in *McDonald v. Mobil Coal Producing, Inc.*[37] Disclaimers were included in the application and handbook; however, in neither document were they set off by bolder, larger print or capitalization. Additionally, the disclaimers were unclear regarding their effect on the employment relationship. The attempted disclaimers in the application and handbook were insufficiently conspicuous to bind the employee.[38] However, if a disclaimer is prominently placed in the handbook on the first or last page, signed, detached, and understood by the employee, it will be enforced.[39]

Inconsistency

Inconsistencies negating the disclaimer's ability to preserve the at-will employment relationship may arise out of what is or is not contained in different documents, within the same document, or in oral representations, whether implied or explicit. For example, in *McClain v. Great American Insurance*,[40] a disclaimer's effectiveness on an application was reviewed where no similar disclaimer existed in the employment handbook. The employee testified that he signed a few lines below the application's disclaimer, but had not read it and that no one from the employer ever pointed it out or discussed it with him. The handbook contained no disclaimer. Because the application did not contain an integration clause, the disclaimer was not effective where parol evidence proved the existence of a just-cause termination standard in the handbook and through the employer's termination practices.[41]

Clarity in the disclaimer's language is likewise important in avoiding inconsistencies. It would be unfair to allow an employer to distribute a policy that leads employees to believe that certain promises have been made and then permit the employer to renege on these promises. If the employer does not want policies to

---

[36] *Id.*

[37] McDonald v. Mobil Coal Producing, Inc., 820 P.2d 986 (Wyo. 1991).

[38] *Id.*

[39] *See, e.g.,* Habighurst v. Edlong Corp., 209 Ill. App.3d 426, 568 N.E.2d 226 (1991) (disclaimer prominently placed on employment handbook's final page, signed, detached, and understood by employee negated any handbook commitments and preserved at-will employment relationship).

[40] McClain v. Great American Insurance, 208 Cal. App.3d 1476, 256 Cal. Rptr. 863 (1969).

[41] *Id., see also* Harden v. Maybelline Sales Corp., 230 Cal. App.3d 1550, 282 Cal. Rptr. 96 (1991) (at-will employment clause in standardized preprinted application cannot be sole basis for determining whether just cause termination standard exists when application is only solicitation of employment offer, not employment contract, and cannot be partially integrated to preclude consideration of contemporaneous oral agreements under parol evidence doctrine).

be capable of being construed as a binding commitment, the employer can include in a very prominent position an appropriate statement

> that there is no promise of any kind by the employer contained in the manual; that regardless of what the manual says or provides, the employer promises nothing and remains free to change wage and all other working conditions without having to consult anyone and without anyone's agreement; and that the employer continues to have the absolute power to fire anyone with or without good cause.[42]

To be consistent with this statement, the handbook must avoid any contrary implied or specific reference to a cause, good cause, reasonable cause, just cause, fair discipline, or similar discipline or termination standard. Job security references pertaining to regular, permanent, or life employment should also be removed.

Consideration

The concept of consideration becomes important when an employment handbook is modified to include a disclaimer to reestablish the at-will employment relationship, if previous binding commitments existed. For the disclaimer to be enforceable, additional consideration must be provided.[43] The rationale for imposing the additional consideration requirement is similar to that used when restrictive covenant obligations are imposed upon a current employee.[44]

To be enforceable, a restrictive covenant must be given in exchange for something, either some benefit to the employee or some detriment to the employer's interest, and cannot impose undue hardship on the employee. Some form of consideration must be present. When supported by consideration ancillary to a legitimate employment contract, as well as reasonable and consistent with the public interest, restrictive covenants are enforceable.

---

[42] Woolley v. Hoffmann-LaRoche, Inc., 99 N.J. 284, 309, 491 A.2d 1257, 1271 (1989), *modified,* 101 N.J. 10, 499 A.2d 515 (1985); *see also* Martin v. Capital Cities Media, Inc., 354 Pa. Super. 199, 511 A.2d 830 (1986) (suggesting use of disclaimers by employers to preserve at-will employment relationship).

[43] *See, e.g.,* Thompson v. Kings Entertainment Co., 653 F. Supp. 871 (E.D. Va. 1987) (employer who has bargained away right to terminate employees without just cause, through an employment handbook, cannot unilaterally convert employee's status to at-will employment relationship by merely issuing a second handbook; employer must comply with contract modification requirements before doing so to ensure that employee has assented to and received additional consideration for status change); *see also* Swanson v. Liquid Air Corp., 118 Wash.2d 512, 826 P.2d 664 (1992) (determination by factfinder of whether Memorandum of Working Conditions listing specific misconduct deemed sufficient for termination and providing for at least one warning for other misconduct is part of employment contract).

[44] *See* K. Decker & H.T. Felix, Drafting and Revising Employment Contracts § 3.56 (John Wiley & Sons, Inc. 1991).

Employment may not be sufficient consideration if the employee can be terminated at will.[45] The right to be employed may be illusory consideration because the employer can terminate at any time, for any or no reason, with or without notice. Employment contracts based on illusory consideration will not support a restrictive covenant.[46] Nominal consideration, that is, the payment of one dollar, will not support a restrictive covenant.[47]

Continued employment presents other consideration problems. The employer's continued agreement to employ an employee can constitute valid consideration for a restrictive covenant when the employee cannot be terminated at will and the issue arises at the time of hiring.[48]

Continued employment, however, cannot be the sole consideration given in exchange for a restrictive covenant if the employee is already employed and the covenant is sought to be imposed.[49] Because the employee is already employed, simply continuing employment does not provide anything new. For valid consideration to exist, the employer must give the employee something new in addition to the continued employment, for example, more money, another fringe benefit, greater responsibility, or a new position.[50] If the consideration is to be something additional, it must be new, although even new consideration may be insufficient.[51] When an employee has an existing right to receive a benefit, the employer cannot condition that right on an employee's willingness to sign a restrictive covenant.[52] For example, when the employer required the employee to sign the restrictive covenant to receive a lump sum profit-sharing benefit to which the employee was already entitled, it was not enforced.[53]

---

[45] See Super Maid Cook-Ware Corp. v. Hamil, 50 F.2d 830 (5th Cir.), cert. denied, 284 U.S. 677 (1931) (restrictive covenant not enforced when no employment term was specified or other consideration present).

[46] See Markson Bros. v. Redick, 164 Pa. Super. 499, 66 A.2d 218 (1949) (week-to-week employment not sufficient consideration to support restrictive covenant).

[47] See George W. Kistler, Inc. v. O'Brien, 464 Pa. 475, 347 A.2d 311 (1975) (one dollar, along with nominal consideration, not sufficient to support restrictive covenant).

[48] See Tasty Box Lunch Co. v. Kennedy, 121 So.2d 52 (Fla. Dist. Ct. App. 1960) (continuing employment and commitment to pay commissions were sufficient consideration for restrictive covenant).

[49] See Kadis v. Britt, 224 N.C. 154, 29 S.E.2d 543 (1944) (restrictive covenant not enforced when entered into several years after original employment commenced, absent any additional consideration outside of continued employment).

[50] See, e.g., Jacobson & Co. v. International Environment Corp., 427 Pa. 439, 235 A.2d 612 (1967) (profit-sharing plan and continued employment sufficient to enforce restrictive covenant).

[51] See, e.g., Capital Bakers, Inc. v. Townsend, 426 Pa. 188, 231 A.2d 292 (1967) (change of status from house bakery salesman to supervisor not sufficient consideration to enforce subsequent restrictive covenant not ancillary to taking of employment).

[52] See Markson Bros. v. Redick, 164 Pa. Super. 499, 66 A.2d 218 (1949) (week-to-week employment not sufficient consideration to support restrictive covenant).

[53] See, e.g., Mason Corp. v. Kennedy, 286 Ala. 639, 244 So.2d 585 (1971) (no additional consideration received by employee for enforcement of restrictive covenant).

These analogous principles for determining the enforceability of restrictive covenants on current employees were applied to a disclaimer in *Thompson v. Kings Entertainment Co.*[54] In *Thompson,* the required additional consideration was lacking in enforcement of a new disclaimer that attempted to reestablish the at-will employment relationship for current employees.[55] Two handbooks were involved. The handbook under which the employee began working defined a *dismissal* as a "separation . . . for cause."[56] Subsequently, a new handbook was placed into effect providing that either the employee or the employer "may terminate [the] employment at any time with or without cause and with or without notice."[57] An analysis of the subsequent handbook within the contractual framework of restrictive covenants found it consonant with the public policy behind handbook commitment enforceability. In holding handbooks to be contracts, it was pointed out that courts have been receptive to the argument that employers should be bound by their expressed policies to preclude their offering "with one hand what [they] take away with the other."[58]

In *Thompson,* it was assumed that the employer bargained away its right to terminate the employee without just cause. To permit the employer to unilaterally convert the employee's status to an at-will employment relationship merely by issuing a second handbook to that effect would violate this policy. Requiring the elements of contract modification to be met would ensure that the employee had assented to and received consideration in exchange for the status change.

Dissemination

To enforce a disclaimer that preserves that at-will employment relationship, it is becoming increasingly important that the employer physically disseminate, distribute, and communicate the employment handbook's disclaimer to the employee and have a written record of these actions. For example, in *Rynar v. Ciba-Geigy Corp.,*[59] undistributed personnel policies were found to create no binding employer commitments. Prior to employment, the employee was not informed or given a copy of the employer's policy regarding termination, but later received a copy of the policy solely to implement it in connection with a plant closing. Because no dissemination occurred, the policy had not become part of any employ-

---

[54] Thompson v. Kings Entertainment Co., 693 F. Supp. 871 (E.D. Va. 1987).
[55] *Id.*
[56] *Id.* at 872.
[57] *Id.*
[58] *Id.* at 875.
[59] Rynar v. Ciba-Geigy Corp., 560 F. Supp. 619 (N.D. Ill. 1983).

ment agreement.[60] This rationale comports with the growing requirement that disclaimers be prominently and conspicuously displayed in the handbook.[61]

§ 4.3 —Drafting

In drafting introduction policies, the following should be considered:

1. Advise employees that the handbook does not set forth a binding commitment of any kind and that what is contained in the handbook is for guidance and illustration only

2. Advise employees that the handbook reflects current procedures and policies that the employer may change at any time for any or no reason with or without advance notice

3. Advise employees that the handbook sets forth the employer's procedures and policies in their entirety that can only be altered by an authorized written employer amendment

4. Advise employees that the handbook does not constitute an employment contract and that employment is at-will in that it can be terminated at any time for any or no reason with or without notice by the employee or employer.[62]

§ 4.4 —Sample Policies

The following examples should be considered in drafting the handbook's introduction policies:

---

[60] *Id., see also* Durtsche v. American Colloid Co., 958 F.2d 1007 (10th Cir. 1992) (employer's handbook amendments did not alter employment terms requiring cause for employee termination when reasonable notice of changes was not provided to employees and cover letter attached to amendments did not mention revision of handbook to provide for at-will employment); Suter v. Harsco Corp., 184 W. Va. 734, 403 S.E.2d 751 (1991) (employer may protect itself from being bound by statements made in handbook by having each employee acknowledge on application that employment is for no definite period).

[61] *See, e.g.,* Jimenez v. Colorado Interstate Gas Co., 690 F. Supp. 977 (D. Wyo. 1988) (to be effective, disclaimer must be conspicuously displayed).

[62] See ch. 15.

CLAUSE 4.4(1)
INTRODUCTION—COMPANY WELCOME
WITH LETTER AND DISCLAIMER

Welcome!

One of the main reasons for the Company's success is its personal concern for not only its customers but also its employees. You are a very important part of the Company! When you enjoy your work and get along with your fellow employees, it shows. The Company is committed to helping you achieve these goals.

You are naturally expected to give your best in your work. In return, you are not only compensated, but also receive a package of benefits for you and your family.

This Handbook attempts to explain what you should know in a clear, concise, and easily readable style.

Best Wishes,

President

This Handbook sets forth the Company's employment procedures and policies. **None of this Handbook's procedures or policies can be amended or changed in any way by oral statements. They can be changed only by the written amendment of an authorized Company official.**

The Company's Handbook is not intended as an express or an implied employment contract between the Company and any of its employees. Every employee has an at-will relationship with the Company. All employees are free to resign or leave employment at any time for any or no reason. Likewise, the Company is free to discontinue your employment at any time for any reason or no reason with or without notice.

CLAUSE 4.4(2)
INTRODUCTION—COMPANY WELCOME WITHOUT LETTER
BUT INCLUDING DISCLAIMER

This Handbook brings together in one source what you should know about the procedures, policies, compensation, and benefits affecting you as an employee. The Company is proud of the procedures and policies that it has developed over the years. It is the Company's hope that you will find this Handbook interesting, useful, and informative. However, if you have any questions about any of these procedures and policies, do not hesitate to ask your immediate superior. Whether you are just joining the Company or are a current employee, the Company looks forward to working with you.

None of the procedures, policies, or benefits in this Handbook are intended by reason of their publication to confer any rights or privileges upon you, or to entitle

you to be or remain employed by the Company. This Handbook's contents are presented as a matter of information only. While the Company believes in the procedures and policies described herein, they are not binding employment conditions.[63]

Any employee may voluntarily leave employment and may be terminated by the Company at any time for any or no reason with or without notice. Any oral or written statements or promises to the contrary are expressly disavowed and should not be relied upon by a prospective or current employee. This Handbook's contents are subject to change at any time with or without notice at the Company's sole discretion.[64]

CLAUSE 4.4(3)
INTRODUCTION—DISCLAIMER ONLY

These procedures and policies are not a binding employment contract but offer a set of guidelines for the implementation of these procedures and policies. They are subject to change from time to time and do not confer any obligation on the Company or right to employment. The Company explicitly reserves the right to modify any of the provisions of these procedures and policies at any time and without notice. Notwithstanding any of the provisions of these procedures and policies, employment may be terminated at any time for any or no reason with or without notice either by the employee or by the Company.[65]

CLAUSE 4.4(4)
INTRODUCTION—DISCLAIMER ONLY

In consideration of my employment, I agree to conform to the Company's rules and regulations. I understand that my employment, compensation, and benefits can be terminated, with or without cause, and with or without notice, at any time, for any or no reason, at the option of either the Company or myself. No Company manager or representative other than the Company's president or vice-president has any authority to enter into any employment agreement for any specified time period, or to make any oral or written agreement contrary to the foregoing.[66]

---

[63] Kari v. General Motors Corp., 79 Mich. App. 93, 261 N.W.2d 222 (1977), *rev'd and remanded without opinion*, 402 Mich. 926, 282 N.W.2d 925 (1978) (discussing disclaimer's use to avoid binding commitments).

[64] *See* L. Lorber, J. Kirk, K. Kirschner, & C. Handorf, Fear of Firing 22 (1984).

[65] *See* J. Kauff & M. McClain (Co-ch.), Unjust Dismissal 1984—Evaluating, Litigating, Settling, and Avoiding Claims 777–78 (1984).

[66] *See* Batchelor v. Sears, Roebuck & Co., 574 F. Supp. 1480 (E.D. Mich. 1983) (disclaimer can avoid binding commitments); *see also* Reid v. Sears, Roebuck & Co., 790 F.2d 453 (6th Cir. 1986) (same).

CLAUSE 4.5(5)
INTRODUCTION—DISCLAIMER ONLY

A job is an important benefit which an employer can provide its employees, and this is a major concern of the Company. On the other hand, each individual must contribute, in whatever degree and manner, to the success of the Company. In addition, all employees as a group must serve customers, for in the long run they are the only ones who can guarantee jobs. The Company has adopted the following procedures and policies. **Employees and the employer have the right to terminate employment at any time for any circumstance, and for any reasons or no reasons that are attributed by the employer or employee.**

§ 4.5   Equal Employment Opportunity

Employers should consider an equal employment opportunity policy to set forth their commitment for complying with federal[67] and state[68] FEP statutes. A binding employer commitment to remedy discrimination may be inferred from these clauses.[69] Equal employment opportunity, however, should not be confused with affirmative action.

Unlike equal employment opportunity, which is a statement of policy not necessitating immediate action, affirmative action generally commits the employer to take definitive or positive actions to ensure that applicants are employed and that employees are treated during employment without regard to their race, color, religion, sex, national origin, disability, or veteran's status, whether or not discrimination has occurred in the past. Affirmative action requirements may arise through employer voluntary action,[70] a consent decree,[71] federal mandate,[72] or state requirements.[73] Employer affirmative action includes, but is not limited to:

---

[67] *See, e.g.,* 42 U.S.C. §§ 2000e-1 to 2002-2017 (1988) (Civil Rights Act of 1964); 42 U.S.C. §§ 12101–12213 (Supp. 1992) (Americans with Disabilities Act); *see also* Decker, Privacy Law §§ 2.7–2.12; H. Perritt, Jr., Americans with Disabilities Act Handbook § 7.19 (John Wiley & Sons, Inc. 1990) [hereinafter Perritt, ADA Handbook].

[68] *See, e.g.,* Pa. Stat. Ann. tit. 43, §§ 951–63 (Purdon 1991) (Pennsylvania Human Relations Act); *see also* Decker, Privacy Law § 2.25.

[69] *See* Tuttle v. ANR Freight System, 797 P.2d 825 (Colo. Ct. App. 1990).

[70] *See* Tangren v. Wackenhut Servs., Inc., 658 F.2d 705 (9th Cir. 1981) (a voluntary affirmative action plan is not made involuntary by an employer's use of economic pressure in the collective bargaining process to persuade a union to agree to affirmative action affecting seniority rights).

[71] *See* Kirkland v. New York State Dep't of Correctional Servs., 711 F.2d 1117 (2d Cir.), *cert. denied,* 465 U.S. 1005 (1983) (the Constitution does not bar an affirmative action remedy in a court-approved compromise of litigation involving the Civil Rights Act of 1964 (Title VII)).

[72] *See, e.g.,* Exec. Order 11,246, 3 C.F.R. § 339 (1989), *reprinted in* 42 U.S.C. § 2000e note, issued on Sept. 24, 1965, as amended.

[73] *See, e.g.,* Minn. Stat. Ann. § 363.073 (West 1983) (no state department or agency can accept a bid or proposal for a contract or services in excess of $50,000 from any business having more

1. Recruitment
2. Recruitment advertising
3. Employment
4. Pay rates or other compensation forms
5. Selection for training, including apprenticeship
6. Layoff
7. Termination.

Employers may institute voluntary affirmative action for societal and economic reasons. Affirmative action may be considered a part of an employer's social commitment in that equal employment opportunity is a societal goal that it has a responsibility to achieve. It can be important to harmonious employment relations and be used in maintaining and increasing a local labor pool skilled in required occupations. Voluntary affirmative action is sometimes considered a means of creating and maintaining associations with all local community segments in order to increase marketplaces and profits along with enhancing business-community relations.[74]

Executive Order 11246[75] requires that every nonexempt federal government contract contain provisions that contractors and subcontractors not discriminate against employees or applicants because of race, color, religion, sex, or national origin and that they take affirmative action to ensure that applicants and employees are employed without regard to these factors.[76] The Executive Order also applies to federal and federally assisted construction contracts. Its principal

---

than 20 full-time employees unless the employer has an affirmative action program approved by the state's human rights commissioner).

[74] *See* RIA, Employment Coordinator ¶ EP-27,212.

[75] 3 C.F.R. (1964–1965 compilation), *reprinted in* 42 U.S.C. § 2000e note, issued on Sept. 24, 1965, as amended. Sex was added by Exec. Order No. 11,375, 3 C.F.R. 684 (1966–1970), 32 Fed. Reg. 14303 (1967). A nondiscrimination clause of some type has been required in government contracts since 1941, when President Roosevelt issued an order mandating nondiscrimination in employment by defense contractors. Exec. Order No. 8,802, 3 C.F.R. 957 (1938–1943). The history of succeeding executive orders is detailed in Contractors Ass'n v. Secretary of Labor, 442 F.2d 159 (3d Cir.), *cert. denied,* 404 U.S. 854 (1971).

[76] Exec. Order No. 11,246, 3 C.F.R. § 202(1). Regulations provide that a *government contract* is "any agreement . . . between any contracting agency and any person for the furnishing of supplies or services or for the use of real or personal property, including lease arrangements." 41 C.F.R. § 60-1.3 (1989). A *subcontract* is any agreement between a government contractor and any person either

(1) [f]or the furnishing of supplies or services for the use of real or personal property, including lease arrangements, which, in whole or in part, is necessary to the performance of any one or more contracts; or

(2) [u]nder which any portion of the contractor's obligation under any one or more contracts is performed, undertaken, or assumed.

exemption is for contracts or subcontracts which do not exceed $10,000.[77] Other federal Executive Orders cover affirmative action requirements for age discrimination,[78] the handicapped,[79] and Vietnam-era veterans.[80] There are also state requirements that should be consulted.[81]

§ 4.6   —Drafting

In drafting equal employment opportunity policies, the following should be considered:

1. It should set forth the employer's commitment to equal employment opportunity without regard to race, color, religion, sex, age, national origin, or disability

2. It should state that it is the employer's policy to comply with all federal[82] and state[83] FEP statutes along with their regulations

3. It should include an affirmative action statement that the employer desires to implement voluntary procedures or is a covered federal[84] or state[85] contractor

4. It should consider and encourage employees to report incidents of racial, sexual, and other discrimination

---

[77] 41 C.F.R. § 60-1.5(a)(1). This jurisdictional amount, which establishes coverage under Exec. Order No. 11,246 should not be confused with the additional prerequisite that a contractor or subcontractor have 50 or more employees and a contract or subcontract of $50,000 or more before it is required to have a written affirmative action plan pursuant to 41 C.F.R. § 60-2. Financial institutions that serve as depositories of government funds in any amount or as issuing and redeeming agents for U.S. savings bonds in any amount are covered contractors. *Id.* § 60-1.5(a)(1). Contracts for indefinite quantities must include the equal opportunity clause unless the purchaser has reason to believe the amount to be ordered in any one year will not exceed $10,000. *Id.*

[78] Exec. Order No. 11,141, 3 C.F.R. 179 (1964–1965), *reprinted in* 5 U.S.C. § 3301, issued in 1964.

[79] Exec. Order No. 11,758, 3 C.F.R. 841 (1971–1975), *reprinted in* 29 U.S.C. § 701, issued in 1974.

[80] Exec. Order No. 11,701, 3 C.F.R. 752 (1971–1975), *reprinted in* 38 U.S.C. § 2012, issued in 1973.

[81] *See, e.g.,* Minn. Stat. Ann. § 363.073 (West 1983).

[82] *See, e.g.,* 42 U.S.C. §§ 2000e-1 to 2002-2017 (1982) (Civil Rights Act of 1964); 42 U.S.C. §§ 12101–12213 (Supp. 1992) (Americans with Disabilities Act); *see also* Decker, Privacy Law §§ 2.7–2.12; Perritt, ADA Handbook § 7.19.

[83] *See, e.g.,* Pa. Stat. Ann. tit. 43, §§ 951–63 (Purdon 1991) (Pennsylvania Human Relation Act); *see also* Decker, Privacy Law § 2.25.

[84] *See, e.g.,* Exec. Order 11,246, 3 C.F.R. § 339 (1988), *reprinted in* 42 U.S.C. § 2000, issued on Sept. 24, 1965, as amended.

[85] *See, e.g.,* Minn. Stat. Ann. § 363.073 (West 1983).

5.   It should outline the employer's internal procedure for reporting equal employment violations, including the employer official to contact if the violator is in the employee's direct supervision line.

§ 4.7   —Sample Policies

The following examples should be considered when drafting equal employment opportunity policies:

CLAUSE 4.7(1)
EQUAL OPPORTUNITY CLAUSE WITH
AFFIRMATIVE ACTION COMMITMENT

Section 1. Applicants.   All employment applicants will be considered on the basis of individual qualifications with emphasis on selecting "the best qualified person for the job." Selection decisions will consider date of application, previous work record, special training and skills, work experience, attitude, physical fitness, and any other qualification that clearly is job related.

Section 2. Affirmative Action.   The Company maintains an equal employment opportunity and nondiscrimination program for all employees, to employ affirmative action for all protected classes, and to recruit and develop the best qualified persons available regardless of age, race, color, religion, sex, national origin, or disability. The Company also recruits, develops, and provides opportunities for qualified disabled persons and veterans, with particular emphasis on those who served our country during the Vietnam era.

Section 3. Selections.   All selections will continue to be based solely on job-related qualifications. The Company will ensure equal opportunity for everyone in all employment and personnel practices, Company-sponsored educational and training programs and social/recreational activities. It will make periodic reviews of personnel records to ensure that all protected classes continue to receive equal consideration as opportunities for transfer, advancement, or promotion occur.

Section 4. Responsibility.   The Director of Human Resources has overall responsibility for implementing the Company's affirmative action plan. The Equal Employment Opportunity Coordinator, with other appropriate staff and operating personnel, monitors the plan to determine if it is meeting objectives. Appropriate and affirmative actions will be taken to correct discovered deficiencies.

Section 5. Violations.   All employees are required to observe these policies and to act affirmatively to ensure full and equal participation in all opportunities available. Violations of this policy should be reported to the employee's immediate superior. If the employee's immediate supervisor is involved in this policy's violation, it should be reported directly to the Human Resources Department.

Section 6. Conflict.   If this policy is in conflict with federal Executive Orders 11246 and 11375, as amended, the Civil Rights Act of 1964 (Title VII), or any statements and regulations relating to the Company's Affirmative Action program, the provisions of the aforementioned Orders, statutes, and regulations shall prevail.

CLAUSE 4.7(2)
EQUAL OPPORTUNITY CLAUSE WITH
AFFIRMATIVE ACTION COMMITMENT

Section 1. Purpose.   [Employer's Name] is an equal employment opportunity employer and does not discriminate against employees or job applicants on the basis of race, religion, color, sex, age, national origin, disability, veteran status, or any other status or condition protected by applicable federal or state statutes, except where a bona fide occupational qualification applies.

Section 2. Affirmative Action.   The Company will:

a. Recruit, hire, train, and promote persons in all job titles without regard to race, religion, color, sex, age, national origin, disability, veteran status, or any other status or condition protected by applicable state law, except where a bona fide occupational qualification applies.

b. Ensure that all personnel actions affecting compensation, benefits, transfers, layoffs, return from layoff, company-sponsored training, education, tuition assistance, and social and recreation programs will be administered without regard to race, religion, color, sex, age, national origin, disability, veteran status, or any condition protected by applicable state law, except where a bona fide occupational qualification applies.

Section 3. Reporting.   If any employee has a suggestion, problem, or complaint with regard to equal employment, he or she should contact the Director of Human Resources.[86]

CLAUSE 4.7(3)
EQUAL OPPORTUNITY CLAUSE WITHOUT
AFFIRMATIVE ACTION COMMITMENT

The Company will not discriminate against any employee on the basis of race, creed, color, ancestry, sex, marital status, age, national origin, or disability.

---

[86] RIA, Employment Coordinator § PM-11,058.

CLAUSE 4.7(4)
EQUAL OPPORTUNITY CLAUSE WITHOUT AFFIRMATIVE
ACTION COMMITMENT (ALTERNATE)

It is the Company's policy to provide equal opportunity to all applicants for employment and to administer ongoing employment matters in a manner which does not discriminate on the basis of race, color, religion, ancestry, national origin, sex, age, marital status, or disability.

CLAUSE 4.7(5)
EQUAL OPPORTUNITY CLAUSE WITHOUT
AFFIRMATIVE ACTION COMMITMENT

The Company is an equal opportunity employer. It does not discriminate against persons because of their age, sex, race, color, religious creed, ancestry, national origin, or disability in determining suitability for employment, compensation, promotion, transfers, training, education, social and recreational programs, or termination.

§ 4.8   Employee Definition

Employee definitions can affect employment type, compensation, benefits, and career expectations. Definitions must be clearly and unambiguously stated to avoid unwanted employment right expectations.[87] Definitions are commonly provided for full-time, part-time, regular, temporary, exempt, nonexempt, and commissioned employees.

A definition that has been used in collective bargaining agreements or under public sector civil service statutes is not necessarily suitable for an employment policy, especially when an at-will employment relationship is desired to be preserved.[88] The use of these definitions may depend upon the legal implications desired.

Employers should not utilize a "permanent" employee definition because it is inconsistent with maintaining an at-will employment relationship. It may create a

---

[87] *See, e.g.,* Woolley v. Hoffmann-La Roche, Inc., 99 N.J. 284, 491 A.2d 1257, *modified,* 101 N.J. 10, 499 A.2d 515 (1985) (to the employer's argument that enforcing job security provisions will open the floodgate to litigation by disgruntled employees, the court responded: "As we view it, however, if the employer has in fact agreed to provide job security, plaintiffs in lawsuits to enforce that agreement should not be regarded as disgruntled employees, but rather as employees pursuing what is rightfully theirs.").

[88] *See* Aberman v. Malden Mills Indus., Inc., 414 N.W.2d 769 (Minn. App. 1987) (terms "permanent employment," "life employment," and "as long as the employee chooses" indicate only an at-will employment relationship absent additional express or implied stipulation evidencing employment duration).

"just cause" rather than an at-will termination standard.[89] Likewise, a "probationary" employee definition may have similar consequences,[90] possibly granting a probationary employee similar job protection.[91]

§ 4.9 —Drafting

In drafting employee definition policies, the following should be considered:

1. Preserve the at-will employment relationship unless a contrary result is definitely intended

2. Specify what employees are included or excluded

3. Use only the employee definitions needed

4. Probationary periods should be termed "initial evaluation periods" to limit any interpretation that permanent employment is intended at a later date. In addition:

    a. Set forth calendar days and not work days to retain better flexibility should the employee be unable to work during the evaluation period

    b. Reserve the employer's right to undertake additional performance evaluations

    c. Preserve the right to terminate at will

    d. Set forth benefits for which the employee is not eligible until a later date

---

[89] *See, e.g.,* Sabatowski v. Fisher Price Toys, 763 F.Supp. 705 (W.D.N.Y. 1991) (employee terminated after removing two one-dollar toys from one assembly line with intent to put them on another as joke failed to state claim for breach of express contract; neither employment application, handbook reference to "permanent hire" in context unrelated to termination, nor grant of benefits limited employer's right to terminate at will); Walker v. Northern San Diego County Hosp. Dist., 135 Cal. App. 3d 896, 185 Cal. Rptr. 617 (1982) (words "permanent employee status" in a handbook can form binding employer commitments); Arie v. Intertherm, Inc., 648 S.W.2d 142 (Mo. App. 1983) (jury's finding that employee was a permanent employee under the employer's handbook was supported by the evidence); *but see* Aberman v. Malden Mills Indus., Inc., 414 N.W.2d 769 (Minn. App. 1987) (terms "permanent employment," "life employment," and "as long as the employee chooses" indicate only an at-will employment relationship absent additional express or implied stipulation evidencing employment duration).

[90] *See, e.g.,* Royce v. Delta Int'l Indus., 187 Misc. 732, 63 N.Y.S.2d 369 (Sup. Ct.), *aff'd,* 271 A.D. 785, 65 N.Y.S. 2d 566 (1946) (the term "probationary period," as used in an employment contract, could not be construed to mean that employment was at-will); Stone v. Mission Bay Mfg. Co., 99 Nev. 802, 672 P.2d 629, 630 (1983) (court observed that the phrase "probationary period" does not "necessarily mean that the employee may be terminated without cause at any time during the probationary period").

[91] Parker v. United Airlines, 32 Wash. App. 722, 649 P.2d 181 (1982) (neither provision for probationary period nor for grievance procedure in employment handbook implies a limitation of just cause for termination of post-probationary employee).

5. Regular employees may be full-time or part-time employees:

    a. Full-time employees should be based on the total hours the employee is regularly scheduled to work

    b. Part-time employees may include those employees who work less than full-time or who work a minimum number of hours per week

    c. Participation by full-time and part-time employees in benefits should be clarified

6. Temporary employees, whether working full-time or part-time, may be eligible for all or most benefits depending upon the total hours they are scheduled to work and what benefit threshold is used.

§ 4.10   —Sample Policies

The following examples should be considered in drafting employee definition policies:

CLAUSE 4.10(1)
EMPLOYEE DEFINITION—HOURLY EMPLOYEE

Hourly Employee. As an hourly employee, your rate of pay is established on an hourly basis. Premium rates are paid for working overtime and on Sundays and holidays.

CLAUSE 4.10(2)
EMPLOYEE DEFINITION—INITIAL EVALUATION

Initial Evaluation. New employees and those hired after a break in continuous service will be evaluated during their first 520 hours of actual work and will receive no continuous service credit during this period. New employees may be transferred, laid off, or terminated at the Company's exclusive discretion. Employees who continue with the Company after the first 520 hours of actual work will receive full, continuous service credit from the date of original hiring or date of last rehiring. After completing the 520 hours of actual work, employees will be covered under the Company's benefit program.

CLAUSE 4.10(3)
EMPLOYEE DEFINITION—INITIAL EVALUATION (ALTERNATE)

Initial Evaluation. New hourly employees are hired for a thirty-calendar-day trial period. If your performance is not satisfactory during this period, you will be terminated. Within that period you will be reviewed by your department head. After the trial period you may be considered for regular employment, either full-time or part-time. All regular full-time employees will then be entitled to the benefits of employment as described in other sections of this booklet. You will be given a written description of your job so that you are fully aware of your responsibilities. After the completion of 90 calendar days and satisfactory evaluation, you will be eligible for an incremental pay increase (90 day rate).

CLAUSE 4.10(4)
EMPLOYEE DEFINITION—PART-TIME

Part-time Employee. Persons employed by the Company who are regularly scheduled to work less than [number of hours] per calendar month.

CLAUSE 4.10(5)
EMPLOYEE DEFINITION—PART-TIME (ALTERNATE)

Part-time Employee. You are a part-time employee if your regular work schedule is less than 37-½ hours a week.

CLAUSE 4.10(6)
EMPLOYEE DEFINITION—TEMPORARY

Temporary Employee. Persons hired by the Company to work for a period not to exceed [number of hours] of actual work in a calendar year.

CLAUSE 4.10(7)
EMPLOYEE DEFINITION—TEMPORARY (ALTERNATE)

Temporary Employee. You are a temporary employee if you have been employed to perform a specific function for a specified period of time. As a temporary employee you are entitled only to wage benefits.

CLAUSE 4.10(8)
EMPLOYEE DEFINITION—REGULAR EMPLOYEE

Regular Employee. Persons hired by the Company who are regularly scheduled to work more than [number of hours] per week.

CLAUSE 4.10(9)
EMPLOYEE DEFINITION—REGULAR (ALTERNATE)

Regular Employee. You are a regular employee after you have successfully completed thirty calendar days of employment.

CLAUSE 4.10(10)
EMPLOYEE DEFINITION—FULL-TIME EMPLOYEE

Full-time Employee. You are a full-time employee if your regular work schedule is at least 37½ hours a week.

§ 4.11   Employee Acknowledgment/Receipt

To further preserve the at-will employment relationship the employer should use an acknowledgment/receipt form. This form's function is similar to the disclaimer contained in the introduction clause.[92] It further emphasizes that the employee and employer are bound by the at-will employment relationship and that no contractual commitments are created by the employment policies.

§ 4.12   —Drafting

In drafting the acknowledgment/receipt form, the following should be considered:

1. At-will employment statement
2. No contractual commitments
3. Employee agreement
4. Date
5. Employee signature.[93]

§ 4.13   —Sample Forms

The following examples should be considered in drafting the handbook's acknowledgment/receipt clause:

CLAUSE 4.13(1)
EMPLOYEE RECEIPT—AT-WILL EMPLOYMENT PRESERVED

This handbook's contents reflect a general description of the policies, procedures, rules, services, and benefits of employment. It is intended that this be an informational booklet only.

---

[92] *See, e.g.*, Suter v. Harsco Corp., 184 W.Va. 734, 403 S.E.2d 751 (1991) (employer may protect itself by having employee acknowledge that employment is at will). See §§ **4.2–4.4.**

[93] *See* Suter v. Harsco Corp., 184 W.Va. 734, 403 S.E.2d 751 (1991) (employer may protect itself by having employee acknowledge in application that employment is at-will).

Nothing herein shall be deemed a contractual right or an employment condition. The Company reserves the right to change any of its policies, services, or benefits at any time with or without notice.

I acknowledge receipt of a copy of this handbook. I agree to familiarize myself with these policies, procedures, and rules and to comply with their provisions at all times. I also understand and agree that this is not an employment contract.

[* * *]
Employee's Signature

[* * *]
Employee's Name

[* * *]
Date

CLAUSE 4.13(2)
ACKNOWLEDGMENT—AT-WILL EMPLOYMENT PRESERVED

I have received my copy of the Employment Handbook and understand my responsibility to read it and to understand it. If I have questions about its interpretation, I shall seek the answers from my supervisor or the Human Resources Department. **I further acknowledge that this Handbook is provided as an informational guide only and is not to be considered a contract between myself and the Company and that either I or the Company can terminate employment at any time for any or no reason with or without notice.**

[* * *]
Date

[* * *]
Employee's Signature

CHAPTER 5

COMPENSATION POLICIES

§ 5.1   Introduction

Compensation policies generally discuss the pay that employees will receive in exchange for their work efforts. Because compensation is of paramount concern to employees and employers, disputes may arise concerning interpretation. Careful drafting can minimize and maximize dispute resolution to be consistent with the employer's intent. This chapter reviews compensation issues involving overtime,[1] timekeeping,[2] work schedules,[3] meal and rest periods,[4] payday,[5] reporting time pay,[6] holiday pay,[7] pay differentials,[8] training programs,[9] payroll deductions,[10] severance pay,[11] and so forth.

§ 5.2   Overtime

Employers must determine whether certain employees are exempt from federal[12] and state[13] overtime pay requirements. Exemptions for paying overtime generally exist for qualified executive, administrative, or professional employees, along with some commissioned salespersons and others.[14] Employment policies should set forth any differences in procedures or policies for overtime for exempt and nonexempt employees. Where policies are distributed as employment handbooks,

---

[1] See §§ 5.2–5.4.

[2] See §§ 5.5–5.7.

[3] See §§ 5.8–5.10.

[4] See §§ 5.11–5.13.

[5] See §§ 5.14–5.16.

[6] See §§ 5.17–5.19.

[7] See §§ 5.20–5.22.

[8] See §§ 5.23–5.25.

[9] See §§ 5.26–5.28.

[10] See §§ 5.29–5.31.

[11] See §§ 5.32–5.34.

[12] 29 U.S.C. §§ 201–219 (1988) (Fair Labor Standards Act).

[13] See, e.g., Pa. Stat. Ann. tit. 43, §§ 333.101–333.115 (Purdon 1991) (Pennsylvania Minimum Wage Act).

[14] 29 U.S.C. §§ 201–219 (1988) (Fair Labor Standards Act).

separate handbooks should be considered for exempt and nonexempt employees to limit problems.

The circumstances that require overtime payments and the overtime's amount vary. Overtime is statutorily required for hours worked beyond 40 in a regular work schedule.[15] However, overtime may be voluntarily paid by an employer for all hours actually worked in excess of eight hours in a day.[16]

Overtime may also be paid for hours worked on Saturdays, Sundays, and holidays.[17] Employees working Saturdays and Sundays as part of their regular schedules should be excluded automatically from overtime payments. It should be specified that overtime should only be paid for the sixth and seventh days of actual work in the regular work schedule, or over 40 hours. This will avoid situations in which employees may attempt to qualify for overtime when they are specifically paid for Saturday or Sunday work.

Employers must pay overtime if they knew or had reason to believe that eligible employees were working the requisite hours to receive overtime.[18] Overtime should be authorized in advance, and the policy must be consistently enforced. Policies should also indicate that time off for any reason, including holidays, sickness, and vacations, will not be considered hours worked for overtime eligibility.

§ 5.3   —Drafting

In drafting the overtime policy, the following should be considered:

1. Applicable federal[19] and state[20] wage and hour statutes
2. Overtime should not be permitted unless properly authorized
3. Overtime calculation should be based on hours actually worked over 40 in a workweek or on daily hours actually worked over 8
4. Only hours actually worked should be considered for overtime calculations
5. Overtime should be paid for hours worked on the sixth or seventh consecutive workday
6. Overtime payment should be evaluated for hours worked on a Saturday or a Sunday

---

[15] *Id.*

[16] *See* 29 U.S.C. § 207(e)(1) (1988); *see* Bay Ridge Operating Co. v. Aaron, 334 U.S. 446 (1948) (payment of overtime over eight hours permitted).

[17] *See* International Longshoremen's Ass'n v. National Terminals Corp., 50 F. Supp. 26 (D. Wis.), *aff'd,* 139 F.2d 853 (1943) (Sunday premium rate payable).

[18] *See* Davis v. Food Lion, Inc., 792 F.2d 1274 (4th Cir. 1986) (overtime claim denied); *but see* Clark v. J.M. Benson Co., Inc., 789 F.2d 282 (4th Cir. 1986) (overtime claim approved).

[19] 29 U.S.C. §§ 201–219 (1982) (Fair Labor Standards Act).

[20] *See, e.g.,* Pa. Stat. Ann. tit. 43, §§ 333.101–333.115 (Purdon 1991) (Pennsylvania Minimum Wage Act).

7. In determining eligibility, overtime should not be paid or considered for hours not actually worked but for which compensation is received, such as sick days, vacation, holidays, and other paid leaves of absence

8. There should be overtime equalization among employees.

§ 5.4 —Sample Policies

The following examples should be considered in drafting overtime policies:

CLAUSE 5.4(1)
OVERTIME—BASIC

Section 1. Purpose.   The Company provides a liberal overtime policy for its employees. The Company's overtime policy follows the Fair Labor Standard Act's regulations.

Section 2. Authorization and Assignment.   Overtime must be authorized by your supervisor and is paid at the rate of one and one-half (11/2) times your normal hourly rate. As an employment condition, employees are expected to work overtime when requested. The Company reserves the right to require employees to participate in overtime work. Employees will be given as much notice as reasonably possible. Overtime will be divided equally among employees qualified to do the work.

Section 3. Calculation.   The Company calculates overtime based on two methods. These two methods are:

a. Overtime is the greater of "time worked" in excess of daily standard hours (usually 8 hours a day) or weekly standard hours (usually 40 hours a week). This method is called 8 and 40.

b. Overtime is the greater of "time worked" in excess of daily standard hours (usually 8 hours a day) or bi-weekly standard hours (usually 80 hours during a two-week period). This method is called 8 and 80.

CLAUSE 5.4(2)
OVERTIME—COMPREHENSIVE

Section 1.   One and one-half of the employee's regular hourly rate of pay exclusive of any premium (double overtime rate) or shift differential pay shall be paid for work under the following conditions:

a. For any work performed in excess of 8 hours in any workday and in excess of 40 hours in any workweek; and

b. There shall be no duplication of premium pay for the same hours worked under the provisions of subsection (a) of this section.

Section 2.   The following items will be regarded as hours worked for the purpose of computing overtime hours:

a. Hours worked, excluding standby time

b. Rest period

c. Holidays, except when compensation is paid for a holiday which occurs on an employee's day off

d. Annual leave

e. Compensatory leave; to be included in the period of occurrence for the purpose of computing overtime

f. Personal day leave

g. Sick leave.

Section 3.   Double the employee's regular hourly rate of pay shall be paid as the premium rate for work under the following conditions:

a. Employees on a five-day per week schedule shall be paid double time for the seventh consecutive day worked; and

b. For fifteen-minute rest periods, in the event employees are required to work through their rest period, while receiving the premium rate.

Section 4.   The Company will attempt to equalize overtime between or among the employees within the same job classification at the site where work is being performed. The Company shall seek to obtain volunteers for the performance of overtime work. In the event that sufficient volunteers are not available, the Company shall have the right to assign such work on a nonvolunteer basis.

If there are not sufficient volunteers, assignments on a nonvolunteer basis shall commence in the inverse order of seniority. Those persons declining to work overtime shall be credited with the amount of overtime work performed by the assigned nonvolunteers for the purpose of equalization.

Assignments of overtime shall be made from the seniority list on a rotating basis. A person declining such assignment shall be credited for the purpose of equalization with the overtime worked by the person performing the declined work. Employees on the list may be passed over to comport with the equalization requirements.

Lists showing accumulations of overtime should be posted every six months.

Section 5.   Employees who are required to remain on duty during meal periods shall be compensated for these periods at the appropriate rate of pay. Employees who are required to remain on duty during rest periods shall have that time counted as time worked in addition to that which is provided for in Section 2.

Section 6.   Payment for overtime is to be made on the payday of the first pay period following the pay period in which the overtime is worked. For the purpose of this section, and in the determination of this time, pay periods will be considered as after-the-fact.

Section 7.   There shall be no duplication or pyramiding of any premium pay for the same hours worked.

CLAUSE 5.4(3)
OVERTIME—OVERTIME ASSIGNMENT

Section 1. Assignment.   Every attempt is made fulfill production requirements with minimum overtime. When additional work is available, qualified employees will be scheduled to perform the job on a nonovertime basis rather than scheduling employees for overtime. If production requirements cannot be met at straight time, the employee may be required to work overtime. Employees must remain on their job until their replacements report for duty. The Company will make reasonable efforts to obtain a replacement for any employee who has no desire to work overtime. Refusal to work emergency or scheduled overtime is a violation of Company rules.

Section 2. Distribution.   Based on operating requirements, each department has written policies which outline overtime distribution, and overtime work opportunity is divided as equitably as practicable. Only overtime worked, or offered and declined, within employees' departments is charged to overtime records. There will be no payment of overtime that is not worked due to assignment error. The employee will be offered the next overtime opportunity.

CLAUSE 5.4(4)
OVERTIME—OVERTIME AND HOLIDAY PREMIUM PAYMENT

Section 1. Definitions.

a. The payroll week consists of seven consecutive days, beginning at 12:01 a.m. Sunday or the turn-changing nearest to this time.

b. The workday for purposes of computation is the 24-hour period beginning with the time the employee begins work, except that if the employee is tardy, the workday will begin when it would have begun had the employee not been tardy.

c. The regular rate of pay, as the term is used in the calculation of overtime rates, will mean the hourly rate, which is determined by dividing the total of regular, incentive, and shift earnings for the week in which the overtime occurred by the total hours worked that week.

Section 2. Payment.   Overtime will be paid under the following conditions:

a. Overtime, at the rate of one and one-half times the regular rate of pay, will be paid for:

   (1) Hours worked in excess of eight hours on all workdays except Sunday;

   (2) Hours worked in excess of forty hours in a payroll week;

(3) Hours worked on the sixth or seventh workday in a payroll week, during which work was performed on five other working days;

(4) Hours worked on the sixth or seventh workday of a seven-consecutive-day period during which the first five days were worked. This applies whether or not all of the days fall within the same payroll week, except when worked pursuant to normal schedules in the employee's work assignment. However, no overtime will be due under these circumstances unless the employee notifies the employee's foreman of a claim for overtime within one week after such sixth or seventh day's work. If the employee fails to do so, the employee must initiate a complaint claiming overtime within 30 days after the day is worked. Furthermore, on shift changes, the seven-consecutive-day period of 168 hours may become 152 consecutive hours, depending upon the change in the shift. The provisions of this paragraph will not apply when a delay in starting the workweek occurs due to a holiday or the annual plant shutdown.

(5) Hours worked on the sixth or seventh workday in the schedule, when changes were made in the schedule so that the employee was laid off on any day within the five schedule days. However, no overtime will be due if the schedule changes were made on Thursday of the week preceding the calendar week in which the changes are to be effective. Furthermore, after Thursday, changes can be made in schedules without the requirement for overtime under this paragraph if the change results from breakdowns or other matters beyond the control of management.

(6) Hours worked on a second reporting within the same workday when the employee has been recalled or required to report to the plant after working less than eight hours on the employee's first shift. However, the employee's failure to work eight hours on the first reporting must not have been caused by the employee's request, by the employee's refusal to accept an assignment or reassignment within the first four hours, or when management gave reasonable notice of a change in scheduled reporting time or that the employee need not report.

b. For all hours worked on any of the holidays specified, overtime will be paid at the overtime rate of two and one-half times the regular rate of pay. The holiday will be the 24-hour period beginning at the turn-changing hour nearest to 12:01 a.m. of the holiday. If the calendar holiday is on Sunday, the holiday will be the following Monday.

Section 3. Pay for Holidays Not Worked.

a. If an employee does not work on an above-listed holiday, the employee will be paid eight times the average straight-time hourly rate of earnings, including applicable incentive earnings but excluding shift differential and Sunday and overtime premiums, during the payroll period preceding the one in which the holiday occurs. However, if the employee is scheduled to work on the holiday and does not report or perform scheduled assigned work, the employee will become ineligible for pay for the unworked holiday—unless the employee did not report or perform work because of sickness or death in the immediate family (mother, father (including current in-laws), children, brother, sister, husband, wife, and grandparents) or similar good cause. The holiday period will be used when no work was performed in the payroll period preceding the holiday pay period. Holiday allowance will be adjusted by an amount per hour to reflect any general increase in effect on the holiday, but not in effect in the period used for calculating holiday allowance.

b. If eligible employees perform work on a holiday but work less than eight hours, they shall be entitled to the benefits mentioned above to the extent that the number of hours worked by them on the holiday is less than eight. This applies in addition to provisions of reporting allowance where applicable.

§ 5.5   Timekeeping Requirements

Employers must keep accurate records of hours worked by nonexempt employees in compliance with applicable federal[21] and state[22] wage and hour statutes. Policies should set forth the employee's timekeeping requirements and the consequences for falsification, destruction, modification or removal of time records, late or early time recording, or recording another employee's time records. The appropriate method of recording by time card, time clock, or other method should also be specified.[23]

§ 5.6   —Drafting

In drafting timekeeping policies, the following should be considered:

1. Review applicable federal[24] and state[25] wage and hour statutes
2. Specify employees who must record their time
3. The time recording method should be indicated; that is, time cards, time clocks, time sheets, and so forth
4. Time recording period should be specified; that is, daily or weekly

---

[21] 29 U.S.C. §§ 201–219 (1988) (Fair Labor Standards Act).

[22] *See, e.g.,* Pa. Stat. Ann. tit. 43, §§ 333.101–333.115 (Purdon 1991) (Pennsylvania Minimum Wage Act).

[23] *See* Anderson v. Mt. Clemens Pottery Co., 328 U.S. 680, *reh'g denied,* 329 U.S. 822 (1946) (time clock records do not conclusively establish actual time worked if the employee is required to be on the premises or on duty at a time different from that shown by these records, or if the payroll records or other facts indicate that work starts at an earlier or later time than that recorded by the time clock).

[24] 29 U.S.C. §§ 201–219 (1988) (Fair Labor Standards Act).

[25] *See, e.g.,* Pa. Stat. Ann. tit. 43, §§ 333.101–333.115 (Purdon 1991) (Pennsylvania Minimum Wage Act).

5.   Specify consequences for time falsification, destruction, modification, tampering, removal of time records, late or early time recording, or recording another employee's time

6.   Procedures should be consistently applied and enforced.

§ 5.7   —Sample Policies

The following examples should be considered in drafting the handbook's timekeeping policies:

CLAUSE 5.7(1)
TIMEKEEPING REQUIREMENTS—TIME CARDS

A time card with the employee's number is placed in a rack at the time clock close to the work area. Time cards are official records of hours worked. All employees must punch in and out upon reporting and leaving work. A blank time card should be punched if the regular card is not available. Missing or incorrectly punched time cards should be reported immediately to the employee's supervisor. Deliberately punching someone else's time card or having someone else punch the employee's card is cause for discipline, up to and including termination. If another employee's time card is punched in error, it should be reported immediately to the employee's supervisor.

CLAUSE 5.7(2)
TIMEKEEPING REQUIREMENTS—TIME CLOCKS

There are [number] time clock locations. The time clocks are located as follows:

[Identify Time Clock Locations]

[* * *]

[* * *]

The time clock is to be punched after the employee reports for duty. Punching another person's time card is cause for discipline up to and including termination. Further information about the use of the time clock will be provided by the employee's supervisor.

§ 5.8   Work Schedules

Policies should specify normal work hours. Because federal[26] and state[27] wage and hour statutes require most employees to receive overtime pay for all hours worked

---

[26] 29 U.S.C. §§ 201–219 (1988) (Fair Labor Standards Act).

[27] *See, e.g.,* Pa. Stat. Ann. tit. 43, §§ 333.101–333.115 (Purdon 1991) (Pennsylvania Minimum Wage Act).

in excess of 40 in a workweek and require the employer to set a fixed workweek, which cannot vary from week to week, a workweek consisting of seven consecutive calendar days has become the standard. Daily and weekly scheduling is generally the employer's prerogative. When applicable, different shifts should also be discussed.

The workday may need to be defined if the employer compensates employees at an overtime rate if they work in excess of eight hours in a day. It should be defined as a period that encompasses 24 consecutive hours beginning at the same hour on one day and ending the same hour on the following workday. The definition of the workday establishes the number of hours of work that will normally be scheduled for an employee during a workday and it may impose restrictions on hour scheduling. It does not preclude an employer from scheduling more hours on any particular day or days, but if more hours are scheduled they may result in overtime liability.

§ 5.9 —Drafting

In drafting work schedule policies, the following should be considered:

1. Applicable federal[28] and state[29] wage and hour statutes
2. Beginning time
3. Ending time
4. Workday length
5. Other shifts
6. Activities that may or may not be considered work hours, including:
    a. Travel time at the beginning and end of the workday
    b. Travel time
    c. Breaks other than short break periods
    d. Meal time

§ 5.10 —Sample Policies

The following examples should be considered in drafting the handbook's work schedule policies:

---

[28] 29 U.S.C. §§ 201–219 (1988) (Fair Labor Standards Act).

[29] *See, e.g.,* Pa. Stat. Ann. tit. 43, §§ 333.101–333.115 (Purdon 1991) (Pennsylvania Minimum Wage Act).

CLAUSE 5.10(1)
WORK SCHEDULES—WORKING HOURS

Section 1. Shift Schedule.   Under normal conditions, there are three rotating shifts scheduled. Normally, day shift hours are from 7 a.m. to 3 p.m.; the afternoon shift hours are from 3 p.m. to 11 p.m.; and the night shift hours are from 11 p.m. to 7 a.m. The nature of the work in certain departments may require a slightly different schedule.

Section 2. Lunch and Breaks.   On noncontinuous operations, normally a 20-minute paid lunch break and 10-minute paid break are scheduled, based on the operations of individual departments. On continuous operations and maintenance, workbreaks are taken when convenient to the schedule.

Section 3. Work Schedule Posting.   A work schedule will be posted in each department by Thursday notifying employees of weekend work hours and tentatively outlining the following week's work schedule.

All employees are expected to be in their departments and ready to start work at the time designated for the start of their shifts. On continuous operations, the employee must work until relieved by another employee.

CLAUSE 5.10(2)
WORK SCHEDULES—WORKING HOURS (ALTERNATE)

Section 1.   The work week shall consist of five consecutive work days in a pre-established work schedule, except for employees in seven-day operations.

Section 2.   The workday shall consist of any 24 hours in a pre-established work schedule.

Section 3.   The work shift shall consist of 7-$\frac{1}{2}$ or 8 work hours within a pre-established work schedule.

Section 4.   The regular hours of work for any shift shall be consecutive except that they may be interrupted by a meal period.

Section 5.   Work schedules showing the employees' shifts, workdays, and hours shall be posted on applicable departmental bulletin boards. Except for emergencies, changes will be posted two weeks in advance.

Section 6.   Employees engaged in seven-day operations are defined as those employees working in an activity for which there is regularly scheduled employment for seven days a week. The workweek for seven-day operations shall consist of any five days within a consecutive seven-calendar-day period, except for hospital employees and correction officers (excluding maintenance and clerical employees), the work schedule shall consist of any ten days within a consecutive 14-calendar-day period.

Section 7.   In the event of a change in shift from a pre-established work schedule, employees must be off regularly scheduled work for a minimum of three shifts or their equivalent unless a scheduled day or days off intervene between such shift change.

§ 5.11   Meal and Rest Periods

Meal and rest periods are regulated by federal[30] and state[31] wage and hour statutes. Policies should briefly describe applicable meal and rest periods, including compensation arrangements.

Absent the employer's specific commitment that meal periods are compensable, bona fide meal periods need not be compensated.[32] To be considered a bona fide meal period, the period must generally last 30 minutes or more.[33] However, employers that place unnecessary restrictions on the use of a meal period that does not completely relieve employees from work may be required to compensate them for these periods.[34]

Employees are generally paid for rest periods running from five minutes to about 20 minutes. Rest periods are considered to promote the employee's efficiency;[35] however, employers may impose greater restrictions on their use.[36]

§ 5.12   —Drafting

In drafting meal and rest period policies, the following should be considered:

1.   Applicable federal[37] and state[38] wage and hour statutes
2.   Length of period

---

[30] 29 U.S.C. §§ 201–219 (1988) (Fair Labor Standards Act).

[31] *See, e.g.,* Pa. Stat. Ann. tit. 43, §§ 333.101–333.115 (Purdon Supp. 1990) (Pennsylvania Minimum Wage Act).

[32] *See* Armour & Co. v. Wantock, 323 U.S. 126, *reh'g denied,* 323 U.S. 818 (1944) (meal periods when no work is performed need not be compensated); *see also* 29 C.F.R. § 785.19(a) (1993).

[33] *But see* Blain v. General Elec. Co., 371 F. Supp. 857 (D. Ky. 1971) (18-minute meal period acceptable when employees expressed preference for this time limit).

[34] *See, e.g.,* F.W. Stock & Sons, Inc. v. Thompson, 194 F.2d 493 (6th Cir. 1952) (employees required to remain at their machines while eating).

[35] *See* 29 C.F.R. § 785.18 (1989) (rest period, coffee break, or similar idle time as work time or as hours worked).

[36] *See* Mitchell v. Greinetz, 235 F.2d 621 (10th Cir. 1956) (each case must be decided on its own facts and circumstances).

[37] 29 U.S.C. §§ 201–219 (1988) (Fair Labor Standards Act).

[38] *See, e.g.,* Pa. Stat. Ann. tit. 43, §§ 333.101–333.115 (Purdon 1991) (Pennsylvania Minimum Wage Act).

3. Scheduling
4. Compensated or not compensated
5. Restrictions

§ 5.13   —Sample Policies

The following examples should be considered in drafting meal and rest period policies:

CLAUSE 5.13(1)
MEAL PERIODS

Section 1. During Regular Working Hours. All employees shall be granted a meal period, which period shall fall within the third to fifth hours of their work day, unless emergencies require a variance. Present practices relating to meal periods for part-time employees shall remain in effect.

Section 2. Additional Meal Periods. The employee will be allowed a meal period for each four hours worked beyond his regular quitting time. If an employee works four or more hours after his or her scheduled quitting time and has not had notice of the work requirement at least four hours before commencement of his or her regular shift, the Company shall furnish a meal or compensate the employees for a meal in an amount prescribed by the appropriate expense regulations.

CLAUSE 5.13(2)
MEAL AND REST PERIODS

The Employee Dining Room is available for the convenience of all employees and will provide lunch at a reduced price. Time permitted for lunch will vary due to job requirements, and the employee's lunch schedule will be arranged by the supervisor according to the needs of each department. If the employee wishes to bring a packed lunch, the supervisor will provide information regarding designated dining areas.

Two 15-minute breaks are given each workday to employees who work an eight-hour day, at the discretion of the department head. Departmental needs will, on occasion, eliminate a break. This occurrence will be infrequent but the needs of the residents are the first consideration of the Company.

CLAUSE 5.13(3)
MEAL AND REST PERIODS

Meal periods are scheduled according to production and departmental requirements. The employee's supervisor will advise employees of their meal period. Employees are required to punch out and back in during a 30-minute lunch period.

Employees will also be advised when to take their two ten-minute break periods each day: one in each half shift. Since production must keep moving it is necessary at times to stagger these breaks. It is against Company regulations to interfere with other employees on their job during a break.

CLAUSE 5.13(4)
REST PERIODS

Section 1. During Regular Working Hours.   All employees' work schedules shall provide for a 15-minute paid rest period during each one-half work shift. The rest period shall be scheduled whenever possible at the middle of such one-half shift. The Company, however, shall be able to vary the scheduling of the period when, in its opinion, the demands of work require a variance.

Section 2. Beyond Regular Shifts.   Employees who work, without interruption, beyond their regular shifts for at least one hour shall receive a 15-minute paid rest period and shall thereafter receive a 15-minute paid rest period for each additional two hours of work unless at the end of the two-hour period work is completed. If the employee takes a meal period at the expiration of his or her normal work day, then he or she shall be given a 15-minute rest period for each additional two hours of such work unless at the end of a two-hour period work is completed.

Section 3. Part-time Employees.   Part-time employees shall be granted a 15-minute rest period during each 3¾ hour work period.

§ 5.14   Payday

Policies should specify employee payday and pay periods. Although minimum wage and overtime calculations must be made on a weekly basis under federal[39] and state[40] wage and hour statutes, there is no requirement that wages be paid on a weekly basis.[41] Wages must be paid in the course of employment and not accumulated beyond the regular payday.[42] This applies to payment of overtime premiums and compensatory time off in lieu of overtime. Minimum wages and overtime are expected to be paid promptly.[43]

---

[39] 29 U.S.C. §§ 201–219 (1988) (Fair Labor Standards Act).

[40] *See, e.g.*, Pa. Stat. Ann. tit. 43, §§ 333.101–333.115 (Purdon 1991) (Pennsylvania Minimum Wage Act).

[41] *See* Marshall v. Allen-Russell Ford, Inc., 488 F. Supp. 615, 618 (E.D. Tenn. 1980) (no set standard for a pay period).

[42] *See* United States v. Klinghoffer Bros. Realty Corp., 285 F.2d 487, 491 (2d Cir. 1960) (prompt wage payments required); Durkin v. Lov-Knit Mfg. Co., 208 F.2d 665 (5th Cir. 1953) (same).

[43] *See* Luther Z. Wilson, Inc., 528 F. Supp. 1166 (S.D. Ohio 1981) (to be paid promptly after pay period ends).

§ 5.15   —Drafting

In drafting payday policies, the following should be considered:

1. Applicable federal[44] or state[45] wage and hour statutes
2. Payday date
3. Payday frequency
4. Method of payment
   a. Mailed
   b. Direct deposit
   c. Workplace distribution

§ 5.16   —Sample Policies

The following examples should be considered in drafting the payday policies:

CLAUSE 5.16(1)
PAYDAY—COMPREHENSIVE

Section 1. Normal Paycheck Distribution.   Employees will be regularly paid, each Thursday, for time on the job from the preceding pay period. Checks will be distributed during the employee's shift. Second and third shift employees, however, will have the opportunity to pick up their checks between 10:00 a.m. and 12:00 noon, and again between 2:00 p.m. and 4:00 p.m. in the Human Resources Department. Employees receiving their check in this manner and who fail to report to work on that day will not be given their check early for a period of four (4) weeks, unless the absence can be proven to be of an extreme nature. Checks will be issued only to employees or to their representative with a written authorization.

Section 2. Holiday Paycheck Distribution.   In the event a holiday occurs on either Monday, Tuesday, or Wednesday, paychecks will not be available until after 2:00 P.M. on Thursday. Weeks that happen to have two holiday days that fall on Monday, Tuesday, or Wednesday will result in paychecks not being issued until Friday.

Section 3. Lost Paychecks.   The weekly paycheck should be treated as a valuable document. Failure to promptly cash it may lead to the check's being lost, destroyed, stolen, and so forth. Lost checks must be reported immediately to the employee's supervisor for proper action to be taken. Because of the cost involved in

---

[44] 29 U.S.C. §§ 201–219 (1988) (Fair Labor Standards Act).

[45] *See, e.g.,* Pa. Stat. Ann. tit. 43, §§ 333.101–333.115 (Purdon 1991) (Pennsylvania Minimum Wage Act).

reissuing a check, the Company urges all employees to act responsibly when their paycheck is received.

CLAUSE 5.16(2)
PAYDAYS

Nonexempt salaried employees will be paid on the 15th and the last day of each month for the preceding two-week pay period. Exempt employees will be paid on the last day of each month for that month. Should any payday fall on a holiday, Saturday, or Sunday, payday will be on the preceding workday. No salary advances will be given.

CLAUSE 5.16(3)
PAYDAYS (ALTERNATE)

Employees will be paid by check every two weeks. The biweekly pay period is from Sunday through Saturday. The employee's time card or time sheet must be turned in on Monday, and a check is issued every other Wednesday after 11:00 a.m. If a holiday falls on Wednesday, paychecks will be distributed on Tuesday. No advancement of wages is permitted under any circumstances.

CLAUSE 5.16(4)
PAYDAYS (ALTERNATE)

Paydays shall be every other Friday. The law requires the Company to deduct from the employee's pay federal income tax, Social Security tax, state income tax, local income tax, and occupational privilege tax, which payments shall be turned over by the Company to the appropriate governmental agencies. Wage increases shall not be automatic, but shall be granted as a result of the employer's review. All work-related expenses must have the prior approval of the employee's supervisor. Routine travel costs to and from work are not reimbursable. Reimbursement will be made for mileage, tolls, parking, and so forth, while on Company business, at the then-current Company-approved rate.

CLAUSE 5.16(5)
PAYDAYS (ALTERNATE)

Employees are paid weekly on ___(Day of Week)___ , other than the second shift, which is paid _(Day of Week)_ evening. The pay received on _(Day of Week)_ is for work performed the preceding week. If absent on a payday, the Company requires anyone other than the employee requesting a paycheck to produce a note from the employee which includes the employee's name, Social Security number, signature, and the name of the person authorized to collect the paycheck. If a paycheck cannot be delivered, or if the employee is unable to claim a check within a reasonable time, it will be mailed to the employee's home. Any errors in the employee's check should be immediately reported to the Human Resources Department.

CLAUSE 5.16(6)
PAYDAY—PAYCHECK

Employee paychecks are for a two-week period, payable on Thursday of the second week after the end of the payroll period. The reason for this delay is to allow the Payroll Department to properly calculate pay. Paychecks will be mailed to the employee's home or deposited directly into the employee's bank account upon written request.

§ 5.17   Reporting Time Pay

Reporting time or call-back clauses guarantee employees a minimum number of paid hours if they report for extra work as requested by the employer, even if the employer is unable to provide work on the day they report.[46] These clauses should set forth exceptions if the employer is unable to provide work.

§ 5.18   —Drafting

In drafting reporting time pay policies, the following should be considered:

1. Applicable federal[47] or state[48] wage and hour statutes
2. Minimum pay entitlement for reporting
3. Number of hours for reporting
4. Pay rate
5. Duties upon reporting
6. Release after reporting
7. Exceptions for not paying:
   a. Snowstorms
   b. Hurricanes
   c. Acts of God
   d. Notification prior to reporting

---

[46] Department of Labor, Wage and Hour Field Operations Handbook ¶ 32d04 (1989).

[47] 29 U.S.C. §§ 201–219 (1988) (Fair Labor Standards Act).

[48] *See, e.g.,* Pa. Stat. Ann. tit. 43, §§ 333.101–333.115 (Purdon Supp. 1990) (Pennsylvania Minimum Wage Act).

§ 5.19 —Sample Policies

The following examples should be considered in drafting reporting time pay policies:

CLAUSE 5.19(1)
REPORTING TIME PAY—BASIC

If the employee comes to work, punches in, and his or her services are not needed for more than four hours, the employee will be paid for four hours. If the employee is sent home for lack of work after four or more hours' work time, the employee will be paid for eight hours. Maintenance employees called in for emergency repairs will be paid for at least two hours.

CLAUSE 5.19(2)
REPORTING TIME PAY—BASIC (ALTERNATE)

Section 1.   An employee who has been called in to work outside of the employee's regular shift schedule shall be guaranteed a minimum of four (4) hours' work. Call-time pay begins when the employee reports to the assigned work site ready for work. There shall be no duplication of hours.

Section 2.   Call-time shall be paid for at the employee's regular rate of pay or at the employee's overtime rate if the employee qualifies for overtime.

CLAUSE 5.19(3)
REPORTING TIME PAY—INTERMEDIATE

Section 1. Regular Reporting.   Employees reporting for work at their regular time, unless notified prior to leaving for work that day that they are not needed, will be given a minimum of four (4) hours' work on their regular job. If work is not available on their regular jobs, they shall be offered substitute work at their regular hourly rate, including shift differential, to the extent of at least four (4) hours' time. Substitute work means any work within the reasonable capacity of the employee to perform, whether in actual production or assisting in plant cleanup or plant maintenance. If no substitute work is available (at the discretion of the supervisor), the employee shall be paid four (4) hours' call-in pay.

Section 2. No Work Available—Emergencies.   In the event that work is not available due to causes beyond the Company's control, such as strike, fire, riot, flood, storm, utility failure, or lack of material, the reporting pay provisions are not applicable. Employees who report for work will be paid for actual hours worked at their regular job.

CLAUSE 5.19(4)
REPORTING TIME PAY—COMPREHENSIVE

Section 1. Reporting.   If an employee is scheduled or notified to report for work, and reports for work:

a. The employee will be provided with and assigned to a minimum of four hours of work on the job for which the employee is scheduled or notified to report; or

b. In the event that work is not available, the employee will be assigned or reassigned to another job for which the employee is qualified, and which will result in total earnings for the period worked which equals or exceeds the reporting allowance.

Section 2. No Work Available—Payment.   If the employee reports for work and none is available and the employee is released from duty, the employee will be credited with a reporting allowance of four times the standard hourly wage rate of the job (including any applicable additives) for which the employee was scheduled or notified to report.

Section 3. Work Available—Payment.   When the employee starts work and is released from duty before working a minimum of four hours, the employee will be paid for the hours worked and credited with a reporting allowance equal to the standard hourly wage rate of the job for which the employee was scheduled or notified to report multiplied by the unutilized portion of the four-hour minimum. This will not apply in the event that:

a. Failure of utilities beyond the Company's control or Acts of God interfere with work being provided; or

b. The employee is put to work either at his or her own request or if the employee:

(1) Refuses to accept an assignment or reassignment within the first four hours as provided above; or

(2) The Company gives reasonable notice of a change in scheduled reporting time or that the employee need not report.

§ 5.20   Holiday Pay

Although employers may not be required to pay a premium for hours worked on a holiday, many employers do provide additional pay above the employee's regular hourly rate.[49] Employers should clearly specify company-recognized holidays and the applicable rate of pay for holidays worked.

---

[49] *See* Research Institute of America, Employment Coordinator ¶ C-20,701 (1993).

There are a number of issues which must be considered in drafting holiday policies, including:

1. Which holidays will be celebrated
2. When the holidays will be observed
3. Eligibility for the holiday
4. Premium pay if the employee is required to work on a holiday
5. What happens if a holiday occurs during a vacation period
6. Penalties for failure to work on a holiday when the employee is scheduled to work
7. Whether the hours for which an employee is paid but does not work on a holiday will be considered hours of work for overtime purposes.

The number of days designated as holidays varies substantially. The typical number of holidays in the private sector varies from six to ten. The most common holidays are New Year's Day, Memorial Day, Independence Day, Labor Day, Thanksgiving Day, and Christmas Day. Many employers also designate a half-day or full day holiday on Christmas Eve and New Year's Eve, and some designate the day after Thanksgiving. Another frequent practice is to recognize one or more floating holidays. *Floating holidays* are days designated by the employer to provide a four-day weekend and vary from year to year depending on the day of the week on which the fixed holidays are observed.

An eligibility period's completion is frequently a condition precedent to receiving holiday pay. To remove the possibility of employees lengthening the holiday period by calling in sick on the day before or the day after the holiday, employers require the employee to have worked the last scheduled workday before and the first scheduled workday after the holiday in order to receive holiday pay.

Employees who are not required to work on the day the holiday is observed should receive their straight-time rate for the number of hours in their regular workday. For employees who are required to work on a holiday, compensation frequently depends on the reason for working. The policy should anticipate that a holiday may occur during a scheduled vacation period by recognizing:

1. The holiday as a paid day off which will not count against the employee's vacation entitlement, or
2. As a vacation day and a paid holiday for which the employee would receive two days' pay for one day off.

The hours for which an employee is compensated for a holiday may or may not be counted as hours worked for the purpose of entitlement to overtime pay. The handbook should specify how this is treated.

§ 5.21   —Drafting

In drafting holiday pay policies, the following should be considered:

1. Applicable federal[50] or state[51] wage and hour statutes
2. Pay rate for not working
3. Pay rate for working
4. Receipt conditions
5. Nonduplication with other overtime
6. Eligibility
7. Vacation impact
8. Sickness impact
9. Scheduling for weekend holidays
10. Time holiday observation begins and ends
11. Failure of employee to work on a holiday.

§ 5.22   —Sample Policies

The following example should be considered in drafting holiday pay policies:

CLAUSE 5.22(1)
HOLIDAY PAY—BASIC

Hourly nonexempt employees successfully completing their 60 work days of employment are eligible for holiday pay at their regular base pay.

To qualify for holiday pay, an employee must have physically worked the week in which the observed holiday falls. Holiday hours paid for, but not worked, are not included in calculating weekly overtime pay.

The Company observes the following holidays:

New Year's Day	Memorial Day
Independence Day	Labor Day
Thanksgiving Day	Christmas Day

---

[50] 29 U.S.C. §§ 201–219 (1988) (Fair Labor Standards Act).

[51] *See, e.g.*, Pa. Stat. Ann. tit. 43, §§ 333.101–333.115 (Purdon 1991) (Pennsylvania Minimum Wage Act).

CLAUSE 5.22(2)
HOLIDAY PAY—COMPREHENSIVE

Section 1. Holidays.   The following days shall be recognized as holidays:

1.   New Year's Day

2.   Martin Luther King, Jr.'s Birthday

3.   Presidents Day

4.   Primary Election Day

5.   Memorial Day

6.   Flag Day

7.   Independence Day

8.   Labor Day

9.   Columbus Day

10.   Veterans Day

11.   General Election Day

12.   Thanksgiving Day

13.   Christmas Day

Monday shall be recognized as a holiday for all holidays occurring on a Sunday, and Friday for all holidays occurring on a Saturday for those employees on a normal Monday-through-Friday workweek. For other than these employees, the holiday shall be deemed to fall on the day on which the holiday occurs.

Section 2. Payment.   A permanent full-time employee on a Monday-through-Friday workweek shall be paid for any holiday listed in Section 1, if the employee was scheduled to work on that day and if the employee was in an active-pay status on the last half of the employee's scheduled workday immediately prior, and the first half of the employee's scheduled workday immediately subsequent thereto. If a holiday occurs while employees are on leave without pay, they shall be paid for the holiday, if they were scheduled to work on that day and if the employees were in active pay status the last half of their scheduled workday immediately prior and the first half of their scheduled workday immediately subsequent to the leave without pay.

If a holiday is observed while a permanent full-time employee is on sick leave, annual, or other paid leave status, the employee will receive holiday pay and the day will not be charged against sick, annual, or other paid leave credits.

Section 3. Holiday Pay.   If a full-time employee works on any of the holidays set forth in Section 1, the employee shall be compensated at one and one-half times the employee's regular hourly rate of pay for all hours worked on said holiday. The employee shall receive paid time off for all hours worked on a holiday up to a full shift. If the time is worked during the employee's regularly scheduled shift, the paid time off shall be in lieu of holiday pay for that time under this section. Paid time off for time worked outside of the employee's regularly scheduled shift shall not be in lieu of the holiday pay. If a written request is received prior to or within 45 days after the holiday is worked, paid time off shall, subject to management's responsibility to maintain efficient operations, be scheduled and granted as requested by the employee, prior to the holiday or within the 90-calendar-day period succeeding the holiday. If the Company does not schedule paid time off in accordance with the employee's request, or at some other time prior to the end of the 90-calendar-day period, the employee shall be compensated at the employee's regular rate of pay in lieu of paid time off.

Section 4. Holiday Work Equalization.   The Company will attempt to equalize holiday work assignments among permanent full-time employees in the same job classification in the overtime equalization unit during each calendar year. Employees entering established equalization units after the beginning of a calendar year shall be credited for equalization purposes with the amount of holiday work equal to the maximum amount of credited holiday work held by an employee in the same classification in the equalization unit since the beginning of the applicable year. The employer is not required to schedule employees for less than a full shift to equalize holiday work assignments.

Section 5. Part-time Employees.   Part-time employees shall receive holidays on a pro rata basis. Employees, at the Company's option, shall receive either pro-rated paid leave or shall be paid at their regular hourly rate of pay in lieu of such paid leave. Part-time employees shall be compensated at one and one-half times their regular hourly rate of pay for all hours worked on a holiday set forth in Section 1 above.

Section 6. Separation Payment.   A full-time employee separated from the service of the Company for any reason prior to taking paid time off earned by working a holiday listed in Section 1, shall be compensated in lump sum for any unused paid time off the employee has accumulated up to the time of separation.

Section 7. Duplication.   In no event shall an employee be entitled to duplicate holiday payment. There shall be no duplication or pyramiding of any premium pay for the same hours worked. Time worked on holidays during an employee's regular work shift shall not be excluded from hours worked for the purposes of determining eligibility for overtime pay.

§ 5.23   Pay Differentials

Policies may provide pay differentials to employees for performing undesirable tasks, for working undesirable shifts, or in different positions. Pay differentials generally involve additional compensation over the employee's regular rate. Differentials are not regulated by federal or state law.

Generally, employers whose operations require employee scheduling for different shifts provide additional compensation through a pay differential for work on more undesirable shifts to attract employees. A shift differential is paid to compensate an employee for working irregular hours. Because most employees work daytime hours and have the evenings off to enjoy their families, sleep, or other activities, those employees who work other than day shifts should receive additional compensation.

§ 5.24   —Drafting

In drafting pay differential policies, the following should be considered:

1. The need for their use
2. Circumstances under which pay differentials are applicable
3. Eligible employees
4. Pay rates for differentials.

§ 5.25   —Sample Policies

The following examples should be considered in drafting pay differential policies:

CLAUSE 5.25(1)
PAY DIFFERENTIAL—SHIFT PAY DIFFERENTIAL

Section 1. Eligibility.   A shift differential of fifteen cents (15¢) per hour will be paid for any regular shift of 7½ or 8 hours which begins before 6:00 a.m. or at or after 12:00 noon, provided the shift is worked.

Section 2. Overtime.   Any employee who works overtime on a shift on which shift differential is paid shall receive in addition to the appropriate overtime rate the 15:¢per hour shift differential for all overtime hours worked.

Section 3. Call-in.   Employees who are called in on their scheduled day off to work a shift for which shift differential is paid shall receive in addition to the appropriate rate the shift differential for all hours worked.

CLAUSE 5.25(2)
PAY DIFFERENTIAL—SHIFT PAY DIFFERENTIAL (ALTERNATE)

Section 1. Eligibility.   Employees scheduled to work on the afternoon shift shall be paid a premium rate of 30 cents per hour worked. For hours worked on the night shift, a premium rate of 45 cents per hour is paid. For purposes of applying shift differentials, all hours worked during the workday will be considered as worked on the shift the employee is regularly scheduled to start work, except:

a. If the employee is regularly scheduled for the day shift and completes the regular eight (8) hour turn and continues to work into the afternoon shift in excess of four (4) hours, the employee will be paid the afternoon shift differential for all hours worked in excess of four (4) on the afternoon shift.

b. If the employee is regularly scheduled for the day shift, completes the regular eight (8) hour turn, and, after leaving the Company's premises, is called back for the afternoon or night shift within the same workday, the employee will be paid the applicable shift differential for the hours worked on the afternoon or night shift.

Section 2. Shifts.   Shifts are identified as follows:

a. DAY SHIFT—includes all turns regularly scheduled to begin between 6:00 a.m. and 8:00 a.m., inclusive

b. AFTERNOON SHIFT—includes all turns regularly scheduled to begin between 2:00 p.m. and 4:00 p.m., inclusive

c. NIGHT SHIFT—includes all turns regularly scheduled to begin between 10:00 p.m. and 12:00 Midnight, inclusive.

Section 3. Overtime.   Shift differential will be included in the calculation for overtime compensation.

CLAUSE 5.25(3)
PAY DIFFERENTIAL—SUNDAY PREMIUM PAY

A premium of 50 percent of the total earnings for the day is paid for all hours worked on a Sunday. Sunday premium based on the standard hourly wage rate shall be paid for reporting allowance hours.

CLAUSE 5.25(4)
PAY DIFFERENTIAL—RATES OF PAY FOR EMPLOYEE
FILLING FOREMAN POSITION OR SELECTED
FOR SUPERVISORY TRAINING

If an employee is selected to work as an Acting Foreman, the employee will be paid two classes above his or her average rate. If the employee is selected to fill a permanent opening as a Foreman, the employee will be paid his or her average rate if a trial period or pre-job training is required. If, during this period, the employee is required to cover a shift alone without an instructor, the employee will be paid as an Acting Foreman for that time period.

CLAUSE 5.25(5)
PAY DIFFERENTIAL—PAYMENT OF EMPLOYEES
DURING EQUIPMENT RELOCATION

Section 1. Relocation. When equipment is relocated, an employee may be temporarily displaced from his or her job. This displacement may vary from a short period, when the move is relatively easy, to several months when new construction is required at the same position where the old equipment had been located. The following will apply to temporarily displaced employees:

a. If the displacement is for two weeks or less, the employee will fill any available jobs in the department or be referred to another department for that period.

b. If the relocation time is expected to last more than two weeks, the department will utilize a cut back by unit or department seniority, if positions are not readily available for those displaced.

Section 2. Pay Rate. Regardless of the displacement's time length, the employee will be paid his or her actual earnings during this period.

§ 5.26   Training or Education Programs

Policies often review payment for training education programs. Attendance at lectures, meetings, seminars, or training programs need not be counted as working time or compensated[52] if:

1.   Attendance is outside the employee's regular working hours[53]
2.   Attendance is, in fact, voluntary[54]
3.   The course, lecture, or meeting is not directly related to the employee's job duties[55]
4.   The employee does not perform productive work during the attendance.[56]

Training program clauses should require advance written authorization before employees can receive reimbursement for any training or education costs.

---

[52] 29 C.F.R. § 785.27 (1993); *see also* Curtis Mathes Mfg. Co., 73 Lab. Arb. (BNA) 103, 106 (1979) (King, Arb.).

[53] 29 C.F.R. § 785.31 (1993); *see also* Ballou v. General Elec. Co., 433 F.2d 109 (1st Cir.), *cert. denied,* 401 U.S. 1009 (1970) (not compensable).

[54] 29 C.F.R. § 785.28 (1993); *see also* Chepard v. May, 71 F. Supp. 389 (S.D.N.Y. 1947) (compensable when not voluntary).

[55] 29 C.F.R. § 785.29 (1993); *see also* Cassone v. Wm. Edgar John & Assocs., Inc., 185 Misc. 573, 57 N.Y.S.2d 169 (1945) (not compensable).

[56] 29 C.F.R. § 785.27 (1993).

§ 5.27   —Drafting

In drafting training or education program policies, the following should be considered:

1. Applicable federal[57] and state[58] requirements
2. Authorization for program
3. Is program job-related
4. Should employee be compensated or not compensated
5. Is program outside normal work hours
6. Is attendance voluntary or required
7. Employee's eligibility
8. Is program reimbursable or nonreimbursable expense
9. Effect of resignation or termination during course of study.

§ 5.28   —Sample Policies

The following examples should be considered in drafting training or education program policies:

CLAUSE 5.28(1)
TRAINING PROGRAMS

Section 1. Eligibility.   The Company will continue to present training programs and review and upgrade the programs where feasible with the goal of training interested and qualified employees. Among those within a seniority unit who apply from within the classification or classifications determined by the Company as being appropriate for receiving the training, the employee with the greatest length of classification seniority among those with relatively equal qualifications will receive the opportunity for training. If there is no qualified employee within the classification deemed appropriate for training, then the training may be offered to other qualified employees as determined by the Company.

Section 2. Payment.   In-service training that is required by the Company is included in hours of work.

---

[57] 29 U.S.C. §§ 201–219 (1988) (Fair Labor Standards Act).

[58] Pa. Stat. Ann. tit. 43, §§ 333.101–333.115 (Purdon 1991) (Pennsylvania Minimum Wage Act).

CLAUSE 5.28(2)
TRAINING PROGRAMS—TUITION REFUND

Section 1. Eligibility.   Each full-time employee is eligible to apply, through his or her Supervisor, for consideration and prior approval under the Tuition Refund Policy.

Section 2. Courses.   The courses that may be approved for tuition refund consideration are those which:

a. Will directly improve the employee's ability in his or her present position or increase potential in a foreseeable future position with the Company.

b. The course of study must have prior approval and require regular scheduled classroom attendance (not by correspondence) and must be limited to the following levels of instruction:

   (1) Technical or business school or post-high-school level. The amount that may be refunded upon proper prior approval at the technical or business school level will be [amount] per academic year (September through August) based on the attainment schedule below.

   (2) Undergraduate or graduate courses in a recognized college or university.

Section 3. Refund Amount.   The amount that may be refunded upon proper prior approval will be [number] percent of tuition, fees, and required books for [number] credit hours of study per academic year (September through August) at the college or university level.

§ 5.29   Payroll Deductions

Employers must comply with federal[59] and state[60] statutes regarding payroll deductions. Deductions may be either legally mandated or voluntary. Certain deductions may be contrary to law. For example, the following deductions are generally authorized under federal and state statutes for the employee's convenience:

1.   Contributions to and recovery of overpayments under employee welfare and pension plans subject to the Employee Retirement Income Security Act (ERISA)[61]

2.   Contributions authorized in writing by employees or under a collective bargaining agreement to employee welfare and pension plans not subject to the

---

[59] 29 U.S.C. §§ 201–219 (1988) (Fair Labor Standards Act).

[60] Pa. Stat. Ann. tit. 43, §§ 260.1–260.11a (Purdon 1991) (Pennsylvania Wage Payment and Collection Law).

[61] 29 U.S.C. §§ 1001–1368 (1988).

Federal Welfare and Pension Plan Disclosure Act,[62] including group insurance plans, hospitalization insurance, and life insurance

3. Deductions authorized in writing for the recovery of overpayments to employee welfare and pension plans not subject to the Federal Welfare and Pension Plans Disclosure Act[63]

4. Deductions authorized in writing by employees for payments into:

   a. Company-operated thrift plans

   b. Stock option or stock purchase plans to buy securities of the employer or an affiliated corporation at a market price or less, provided such securities are listed on a stock exchange or are marketable over the counter

5. Deductions authorized in writing by employees for payment into employee personal savings accounts, including:

   a. Payments to a credit union

   b. Payments to a savings fund society, savings and loan, or building and loan association

   c. Payments to a bank's savings department for Christmas, vacation, or other savings funds

   d. Payroll deductions for purchase of United States Government bonds

6. Contributions authorized in writing by the employee for charitable purposes, including United Community Fund and similar organizations

7. Contributions authorized in writing by the employee for local area development activities

8. Deductions provided by law, including but not limited to deductions for Social Security taxes,[64] withholding of federal[65] or local income[66] or wage taxes[67] or occupation privilege taxes,[68] and deductions based on court orders.[69]

---

[62] *Id.*

[63] *Id.*

[64] 42 U.S.C. §§ 301–303, 501–504, 901–908, 1101–1108 (1988) (Social Security Act).

[65] 26 U.S.C. §§ 1–9602 (1988) (Internal Revenue Code).

[66] *See, e.g.,* Pa. Stat. Ann. tit. 53, §§ 6901–6924 (Purdon 1972 & Supp. 1993) (local earned income tax).

[67] *See, e.g.,* Pa. Stat. Ann. tit. 53, § 17031 (Purdon 1957) (Philadelphia Wage Tax); *see also* City of Philadelphia v. Kenny, 28 Pa. Commw. 531, 369 A.2d 1343, *cert. denied,* 434 U.S. 923 (1977), *reh'g denied,* 434 U.S. 1025 (1977) (Philadelphia Wage Tax constitutional).

[68] *See, e.g.,* Pa. Stat. Ann. tit. 53, §§ 6901–6924 (Purdon 1972 & Supp. 1993) (occupational privilege tax).

[69] *See, e.g.,* Haines v. General Motors Corp., 603 F. Supp. 471 (S.D. Ohio 1983) (wage garnishment).

9.   Labor organization dues, assessments, and initiation fees, including other labor organization charges authorized by statute[70]

10. Deductions for repayment to the employer of bona fide loans, provided the employee authorizes these deductions in writing either at the time the loan is given or subsequent to the loan

11. Deductions for purchases or replacements by the employee from the employer of goods, wares, merchandise, services, facilities, rent, or similar items, provided these deductions are authorized by the employee in writing or are authorized in a collective bargaining agreement

12. Deductions for purchases by the employee for his convenience of goods, wares, merchandise, services, facilities, rent, or similar items from third parties not owned, affiliated, or controlled directly or indirectly by the employer, if the employee authorizes these deductions in writing

13. Other deductions authorized in writing by employees that are proper and in conformity with the intent or a state's Wage Payment and Collection Law.[71]

§ 5.30   —Drafting

In drafting payroll deduction policies, the following should be considered:

1.   Applicable federal[72] and state[73] wage statutes
2.   Mandatory statutory required deductions
3.   Voluntary or optional deductions
4.   Written authorization for all signed deductions.

§ 5.31   —Sample Policies

The following examples should be considered in drafting payroll deduction policies:

CLAUSE 5.31(1)
PAYROLL DEDUCTIONS—BASIC

Section 1. Permitted Deductions.   Payroll deductions should meet the following guidelines:

---

[70] 29 U.S.C. §§ 151–168 (1988) (National Labor Relations Act).

[71] *See, e.g.,* Pa. Stat. Ann. tit. 43, §§ 260.1–260.11a (Purdon 1991).

[72] 29 U.S.C. §§ 201–219 (1988) (Fair Labor Standards Act).

[73] Pa. Stat. Ann. tit. 43, §§ 260.1–260.11a (Purdon 1991) (Pennsylvania Wage Payment and Collection Law).

a. Required by law or currently available for all regular employees as payment for a fringe benefit, or

b. Currently available for all regular employees as payments toward meeting job-required deposits.

Section 2. Deductions Not Permitted.   Payroll deductions shall not be authorized for the purpose of collecting dues for membership or participation in any organization.

CLAUSE 5.31(2)
PAYROLL DEDUCTIONS—BASIC (ALTERNATE)

The law requires the Company to deduct from the employee's pay federal income tax, Social Security tax, state income tax, local income tax, and occupational privilege tax, which payments shall be turned over by the Company to the appropriate governmental agencies. Wage increases shall not be automatic, but shall be granted as a result of the employer's review. All work-related expenses must have the prior approval of the employee's supervisor. Routine travel costs to and from work are not reimbursable. Reimbursement will be made for mileage, tolls, parking, and so forth, while on Company business, at the then-current Company-approved rate.

CLAUSE 5.31(3)
PAYROLL DEDUCTIONS—COMPREHENSIVE

Section 1. Written Authorization.   The employee's written authorization for payroll deductions shall contain the employee's name, social security number, department employed, and work location.

Section 2. Liability.   The Employee shall indemnify and hold the Company harmless against any and all claims, suits, orders, or judgments brought or issued against the Company as a result of the action taken or not taken by the Company in making any authorized deduction.

§ 5.32   Severance Pay

Employers may be obligated to provide severance pay under certain conditions pursuant to certain federal[74] and state[75] statutes. Severance pay usually involves a special lump sum payment to employees that results from a layoff, resignation, termination, or plant shutdown. The severance pay's amount is usually based on

---

[74] *See, e.g.*, 29 U.S.C. §§ 2101–2109 (1988) (Worker Adjustment and Retraining Notification Act).

[75] *See, e.g.*, Md. Ann. Code art. 41, § 206 (1988) (Maryland Economic Stabilization Act).

the employee's classification and length of service. Enforceable legal obligations may arise from these employment handbook clauses.[76]

§ 5.33 —Drafting

In drafting the severance pay policies, the following should be considered:

1. Applicable federal[77] and state[78] statutes
2. Eligibility
3. Amount
4. Receipt time length.

§ 5.34 —Sample Policies

The following examples should be considered in drafting severance pay policies:

CLAUSE 5.34(1)
SEVERANCE PAY—COMPREHENSIVE

Section 1. Eligibility.   Severance pay will be granted to employees whose termination is initiated by the Company. To be eligible for severance pay, the employee must work to the date agreed upon by the Company in consultation with the Human Resources Department and the employee.

Section 2. Amount.   Two weeks' severance pay is granted for the first year of employment or major portion thereof at the employee's current pay rate. One week's pay is granted for each additional year of service or major portion thereof.

Section 3. Time of Payment.   Every effort should be made to give the employee the severance pay check at the time of separation. If this is not possible, the check will be mailed in accordance with the employee's instructions.

---

[76] *See, e.g.,* Hamilton v. Air Jamaica, Ltd., 750 F. Supp. 1259 (E.D. 1990) (handbook's written severence pay clause created binding employer commitment); Brooks v. Carolina Tel. & Tel. Co., 56 N.C. App. 801, 290 S.E.2d 370 (1982) (handbook's termination pay provision binding); *but see* Morosetti v. Louisiana Land & Exploration, 522 Pa. 491, 564 A.2d 151 (1989) (uncommunicated severance pay policy not binding).

[77] *See, e.g.,* 29 U.S.C. §§ 2101–2109 (1988) (Worker Adjustment and Retraining Notification Act).

[78] *See, e.g.,* Md. Ann. Code art. 41, § 206 (1988) (Maryland Economic Stabilization Act).

CLAUSE 5.34(2)
SEVERANCE PAY—LAYOFF

Employees who are laid off due to lack of work are entitled to severance pay in lieu of notice as follows:

a. Hourly Paid Employees—No termination pay

b. Weekly Paid Employees

    (1) Less than six months of service—no pay

    (2) Six months to one year—three days' pay

    (3) One year to two years—one week's pay

    (4) Over two years—two weeks' pay

c. Flat-Salaried Employees

    (1) Less than three months' service—no pay

    (2) Three months to one year—one week's pay

    (3) One year to five years—two weeks' pay

    (4) Over five years—three weeks' pay.

CLAUSE 5.34(3)
SEVERANCE PAY—TERMINATION

Section 1. Eligibility.   Accrued vacation and sick leave will be paid under the following conditions as a severance payment, provided the employee has a minimum of six months' continuous service as of the termination date, and that he or she:

a. Resigns with a minimum of two weeks' notice, or

b. Is laid off for lack or work, or

c. Resigns to go directly into the armed services.

Section 2. No Payment.   Accrued vacation and sick pay will not be paid as a severance payment if the employee:

a. Has not had six months' continuous service on the active payroll;

b. Was terminated for cause; or

c. Resigns without giving two weeks' notice.

CHAPTER 6

BENEFITS POLICIES

§ 6.1   Introduction

Benefit policies must be drafted with great care. These policies provide employers with an opportunity to promote good employee relations by addressing issues important to employees in addition to their regular compensation. They may, however, also establish binding commitments.[1] Employers should consider the following when drafting benefit policies:

1.   Benefit provisions should clearly state for each benefit eligibility requirements, including who is and who is not eligible

---

[1] *See, e.g.,* Brooks v. Carolina Tel. & Tel. Co., 56 N.C. App. 801, 290 S.E.2d 370 (1982) (handbook's termination pay provision binding).

2. The date on which employees become eligible for each benefit should be clearly defined

3. Conditions for benefit receipt, types and amounts available, and the circumstances under which benefits are forfeited should be set forth

4. Benefit prorating should be specified

5. Benefit policies must comply with applicable federal and state statutes to the extent these benefits are regulated

6. Employers who provide separate materials to employees describing particular benefit programs should only include brief descriptions of these programs in their policies, and these descriptions must be consistent with the specific benefit programs.

This chapter discusses benefit issues involving sick pay,[2] vacation,[3] insurance benefits,[4] profit sharing and retirement,[5] statutory benefits,[6] and so forth.

§ 6.2 Sick Pay

Federal and state statutes do not require employers to provide private sector employees with sick pay. However, certain public sector employers may be required to provide this benefit.[7] Sick leave is generally considered a short-term benefit that enables an employee to be paid for time that the employee was scheduled to work but was unable to because of personal illness or injury.

Employers generally must determine whether to provide sick pay. Policies should set forth the conditions for which sick leave may be used. Sick pay policies may provide that employees will be paid for all or a fraction of their unused sick leave upon an employment separation. When used in policies they may create binding commitments.[8]

---

[2] See §§ **6.2–6.4.**

[3] See §§ **6.5–6.7.**

[4] See §§ **6.8–6.10.**

[5] See §§ **6.11–6.13.**

[6] See §§ **6.14–6.16.**

[7] *See, e.g.,* Pa. Stat. Ann. tit. 24, § 11-1154 (Purdon 1992) (sick leave and pay required for Pennsylvania teachers).

[8] *See, e.g.,* Matson v. Housing Auth., 353 Pa. Super. 588, 510 A.2d 819 (1986) (vacation and sick pay binding).

§ 6.3   —Drafting

In drafting sick pay policies, the following should be considered:

1. Employee's eligibility
2. How earned
3. Accumulation
4. Length of absence
5. Amount of pay
6. Sick pay not counted toward overtime
7. Unused sick pay: is it
   a. Forfeited
   b. Paid
8. Abuse checks.

§ 6.4   —Sample Policies

The following examples should be considered in drafting sick pay policies:

CLAUSE 6.4(1)
SICK PAY—BASIC

Employees who have completed [number of days] and who suffer an injury or illness which prevents them from working and for which the employee is not entitled to workers' compensation, shall be entitled to leave with pay for a maximum of [number of days] lost per calendar year. Employees may carry over unused sick leave from year to year without limit. Employees will not be paid for unused sick leave upon separation from employment. The Company reserves the right to request from employees medical verification for any sick leave used.

CLAUSE 6.4(2)
SICK PAY—COMPREHENSIVE

Section 1. Eligibility.   Employees shall be eligible to use sick leave after [number of days] of service with the Company. Employees shall earn sick leave as of their hiring date in accordance with the following schedule:

Maximum Sick Leave Entitlement Per Year

Sick Leave will be earned at the rate of 6% of all regular hours paid	37.5 Hour Workweek: 117 Hours (15.6 days) 40 Hours Workweek: 124.8 Hours (15.6 days)

Regular hours paid include all hours paid except overtime, standby time, call-time, and full-time out-service training. Work-related disability time shall be included in regular hours paid.

Section 2. Accumulation.   Employees may accumulate sick leave up to a maximum of [number] days.

Section 3. Verification.   A doctor's certificate is required for an absence from work due to sickness for [number] or more consecutive days. For absences of less than three days, a doctor's certificate may be required if the Company has reason to believe that the employee has been abusing the sick leave privilege. The total circumstances of an employee's use of sick leave rather than a numerical formula shall be the basis upon which the Company's determination is made that the employee may be abusing sick leave.

Section 4. Immediate Family Sickness.   When sickness in the immediate family requires the employee's work absence, employees may use not more than [number] days of sick leave entitlement in each calendar year for that purpose. Immediate family is defined as persons residing in the employee's household; that is, the spouse, child, or parent of the employee. The Company may require verification of family sickness.

Section 5. Death.   Employees may use up to [number] days of sick leave for the death of a spouse, parent, stepparent, child, or stepchild and up to three days of leave may be used for the death of a brother, sister, grandparent, grandchild, son- or daughter-in-law, brother- or sister-in-law, parent-in-law, grandparent-in-law, aunt, uncle, or any relative residing in the employee's household.

Section 6. Payment Upon Separation.   Employees who retire shall be paid [amount] of their accumulated unused sick leave to a maximum of [number] days.

Section 7. Sick Leave Anticipation.   Employees who have one or more years of service since their last date of hire may anticipate sick leave to which they become entitled during the then current calendar year unless the Company has reason to believe that the employee has been abusing the leave privilege. Employees with less than one year of service since their last date of hire may not anticipate sick leave.

§ 6.5   Vacation

Although private sector employers need not provide any vacation benefits under federal or state statutes, they may be bound by any vacation policies set forth in their employment policies.[9] Public sector employers, however, may under certain

---

[9] *See, e.g.,* Hamilton v. Air Jamaica, Ltd., 750 F. Supp. 1259 (E.D. Pa. 1990) (vacation policy binding; however, employee was not entitled to recover more than it provided); Matson v. Housing Auth., 353 Pa. Super. 588, 510 A.2d 819 (1986) (vacation and sick pay binding).

conditions be required to provide vacation benefits.[10] Employers are faced with numerous choices in establishing vacation policies and must exercise particular care in their drafting.

There are two basic vacation plan types: the vacation year plan, and the anniversary year plan.[11] The *vacation year plan* is the easiest for an employer to administer. Under this plan, all employees are eligible to take their vacation allotment over a uniform one-year period. The year can be a calendar year, the employer's fiscal year, or any other one-year period.[12] The vacation year plan is easy to administer because it requires the employer to review vacation records only once each year, shortly prior to each vacation year's beginning. During this review, the employer ascertains the vacation amount to which each employee will be entitled during the forthcoming vacation year. Vacation amount, as well as the vacation eligibility, will normally be determined by service length or seniority.

The vacation year plan's disadvantage is the inequity which may arise if the plan is strictly applied to new employees, some of whom may be required to work a full year before being entitled to take vacation and others of whom may receive vacation almost immediately upon employment.[13] For example, if the vacation year coincides with the calendar year, and the vacation plan requires an employee to be employed on the first day of the vacation year to be eligible for vacation, an employee who begins work on January 2 will have to wait 364 days, until the following January 1, before vacation may be taken. However, an employee who begins work on December 31st will be eligible for vacation on the second day of employment. This inequity normally is eliminated by imposing certain eligibility requirements and recognizing pro rata vacation allotments to equalize the plan among all employees.[14]

Under the *anniversary year plan,* employees become entitled to vacation only as of their annual anniversary employment dates. This eliminates the inequity for new employees because all employees will be required to work a full year before being entitled to vacation.[15] It requires greater time expenditures to administer, because the year within which employees may take their vacation allotments varies from employee to employee, necessitating almost daily review of the employees' vacation entitlement.[16]

---

[10] *See, e.g.,* Pa. Stat. Ann. tit. 71, § 741.708 (Purdon 1990) (Pennsylvania Civil Service Act guidelines for holidays, vacations, and sick leave).

[11] For an excellent discussion of vacation pay policies under collective bargaining agreements, *see* N.P. Lareau, Drafting the Union Contract: A Handbook for the Management Negotiator ch. 12 (1989).

[12] *Id.* § 12.02.

[13] *Id.*

[14] *Id.*

[15] *Id.*

[16] *Id.*

§ 6.6 —Drafting

In drafting vacation policies, the following should be considered:

1. Eligibility requirements
2. Conditions
3. Accrual rate
4. Payment
5. Effect of holidays and sickness
6. Payment upon employment separation.[17]

§ 6.7 —Sample Policies

The following examples should be considered in drafting vacation policies:

CLAUSE 6.7(1)
VACATION—COMPREHENSIVE

Section 1. Eligibility.   The amount of vacation employees are entitled to is based on years of service as follows:

Years of Service	Weeks of Vacation
1 but less than 3	1
3 but less than 10	2
10 but less than 17	3
17 but less than 25	4
25 or more	5

Section 2. Eligibility.   To be eligible for a vacation in any calendar year, employees must:

a. Have one year or more of continuous service, and

b. Not have been absent from work for six consecutive months or more in the preceding calendar year; except, in cases of employees who complete one year of continuous service in such calendar year, they shall not have been absent from work for six consecutive months or more during the 12 months following the date of original employment. Employees with more than one year of continuous service, who in any year shall be ineligible for a vacation

---

[17] For additional details regarding vacation policies, *see* Research Institute of America, Employment Coordinator ¶ PM-11,171-11,216 (1993).

by reason of these provisions as a result of an absence on account of layoff or illness, shall receive one week's vacation with pay in such year, if they have not been absent from work for six consecutive months or more in the 12 consecutive calendar months preceding such vacation. Any period of absence while on vacation or while absent due to a compensable disability in the year in which such disability is incurred, or while in military service in the year of reinstatement of employment, shall be excluded in determining the length of absence from work. Continuous service shall be computed from the date of last employment in the event the employee quits or is discharged. There shall be no accumulation of service in excess of the first two years of any continuous period of absence on account of layoff or physical disability (except in the case of compensable disability) in the calculation of service for vacation eligibility.

If an employee quits, retires, dies, or is terminated prior to January 1 of the vacation year, the employee will forfeit the right to receive vacation benefits.

Section 3. Vacation Scheduling.   On or about October 1st of each year, the Company will post a vacation announcement indicating that employees have until the following January 1st to select their vacation preference for the coming year. Most Production employees will be required to take vacation during plant shutdown. Employees with a minimum of plant seniority may also be required to work during the plant shutdown. The balance of regular vacation, if any, will be allocated on the basis of department seniority provided the allocation does not interfere with the department's proper operation.

Most Maintenance Department employees are required to work during the plant shutdown and may not initially request more than 3 weeks of vacation entitlement during the period from Memorial Day until Labor Day. After all Maintenance Department employees have been granted their first choice of vacation by seniority, employees can request weeks in excess of 3.

If an employee transfers from one department to another, vacation will be based on the original schedule, provided the schedule is not precluded by department operations or is not in conflict with the schedules of more senior employees in the new department.

Employees may work in lieu of vacation time off for any week's entitlement in excess of the length of time of the plant shutdown. If scheduled to work during the shutdown, the employee may be required to take vacation at some other time during the year, provided the vacation does not conflict with vacation schedules of employees with more department seniority or with efficient department operation. Vacations are not cumulative and must be taken in the calendar year, with the following exceptions:

   a. If Christmas week is a shutdown week, employees may schedule vacation by drawing on next year's vacation allowance; or

b. The payroll week containing New Year's Day can be taken as vacation charged to either the preceding or the next following vacation year.

Section 4. Vacation Rate Per Hour.   Employees will be paid for their weeks of vacation at their average rate of earnings per hour for the prior calendar year. Average rate of earnings per hour will be computed by:

a. Totaling

 1. Pay received for all hours worked (total earnings including premium for overtime, holiday. Sunday and shift differential),

 2. Vacation pay, including pay in lieu of vacation but excluding vacation bonus, and

 3. Pay for unworked holidays, and

b. Dividing such earnings by the total of

 1. Hours worked,

 2. Vacation hours paid, including hours for which pay in lieu of vacation was paid, and

 3. Unworked, paid holiday hours.

Average rate of earnings will be adjusted to reflect intervening general wage changes and retroactive pay adjustment, if any, for the job or jobs performed or paid for.

Section 5. Vacation Hours.   Hours of vacation pay for each vacation week will be the average hours per week worked by the employee in the prior calendar year. Any weeks not having 32 hours of actual work will be excluded from the calculation. Average hours per week worked will be computed by:

a. Totaling the following hours in payroll weeks with 32 or more hours of actual work:

 1. Hours worked,

 2. Hours paid for unworked holidays; and

b. Dividing these hours by the number of weeks in which 32 or more hours were worked.

The minimum number of hours paid for each week of vacation will be 40, and the maximum number of hours paid for each week of vacation will be 48. Employees who did not work in the prior year will have their vacation pay computed on the basis of their last calculated vacation rate and hours, adjusted to reflect intervening general wage changes.

Section 6. Vacation for Part-Time Employees.   Part-time employees will be paid their average hours per week worked in the prior calendar year, without regard to the 40-hour minimum guarantee.

CLAUSE 6.7(2)
VACATION—COMPREHENSIVE (ALTERNATE)

Section 1. Eligibility.   An employee shall be eligible for vacation after 30 days of employment with the Company. Employees shall earn vacation leave as of their date of hire. Leave shall be earned according to the following schedule:

Service	Per Year	Annual Leave Entitlement Per Month
Less than 12 months	10 days	$5/6$ days
12 months to 180 months	15 days	$1\,1/4$ days
180 months or more	20 days	$1\,2/3$ days

Employees shall earn annual leave credits for each month in which they are in compensable status for ten or more working days.

Section 2. Payment Rate.   Vacation pay shall be paid at the employee's regular straight-time rate in effect for the employee's regular job on the payday immediately preceding the employee's vacation period.

Section 3. Scheduling.   Vacations shall be scheduled and granted for time periods requested by the employee subject to the Company's responsibility to maintain efficient operations. If the nature of the work makes it necessary to limit the number of employees on vacation at the same time, the employee with the greatest seniority as it relates to total years of continuous service with the Company shall be given priority.

Section 4. Holidays.   If a holiday occurs during the work week in which vacation is taken by an employee, the holiday shall not be charged to vacation leave.

Section 5. Sickness.   Employees who become ill during their vacation will not be charged vacation leave for the period of illness provided they furnish satisfactory proof of the illness upon return to work.

Section 6. Work.   For employees required to work during their scheduled vacation period who are unable to reschedule their vacation during the calendar year due to work demands, the calendar year shall be extended for 90 days for rescheduling purposes.

Section 7. Separation Payment.   Employees separated from the Company for any reason prior to taking their vacation shall be compensated in a lump sum for the unused vacation they have accumulated up to the separation time.

Section 8. Accrual.   Employee may carry over 30 days of unused vacation leave from one year to next.

CLAUSE 6.7(3)
VACATION—COMPREHENSIVE (ALTERNATE)

Section 1. Period.   The vacation period is the calendar year beginning January 1 and continuing through December 31. As used in this policy, month and year mean full calendar periods. Also, the term service refers to regular employment, and excludes part-time and temporary workers.

Section 2. Eligibility.

Eligibility	Vacation in Current Calendar Year
Began work between 6/2 and 12/31 of current calendar year	None
Began work between 1/1 and 6/1 of current calendar year	One week, after six months of service
Completed one year of service in current year	Two weeks, after six months of service
Completed ten years of service in current year	Three weeks
Completed 20 years of service in current year	Four weeks

Section 3. Carryover.   Vacation must be taken during the calendar year in which it is accrued. Employees may not accumulate vacation from year to year.

Section 4. Pay Instead of Vacation.   Employees may not choose to forego their vacation and elect to receive additional pay instead of the time off.

Section 5. Scheduling.   Vacations may be scheduled throughout the year, at the discretion of the department supervisor, who will consider adequate staffing levels at times of peak demand. If two or more employees request the same vacation time and this presents a conflict with work demands, the supervisor will consider length of service in apportioning vacation time among those who have applied for the same period.

Section 6. Holidays and Illnesses During Vacation.   If a paid holiday occurs during an employee's vacation, the employee may extend that vacation by another day or agree to take the day at another time mutually agreeable to the supervisor and the employee. Illness during a vacation will not extend the scheduled period or convert the absence to sick leave, except if the employee is hospitalized or becomes disabled for an extended period of time.

Section 7. Vacation Pay.   Sales personnel on basic salary plus commission will receive their current weekly base salary plus the weekly average of their year-to-date commissions for each week of vacation. Straight commission or draw sales personnel will receive their weekly average year-to-date commissions for each week of vacation, but not less than their current weekly draw. Draw will not be paid during vacation. All other non-sales employees will receive their current base salary and shift differential, if applicable, for each week of vacation.

Section 8. Advance Vacation Pay. Employees may receive advance vacation checks if they are taking a full week of vacation or have been requested to take vacation because of a plant shutdown. Employees must request advance checks one week before taking vacation.

Section 9. Vacation Pay on Employment Separation. When employment is terminated, entitlement to vacation pay is determined by the reason for the termination. If an employee is discharged or resigns, accrued vacation will be prorated for the year at the rate of 1/12 annual vacation pay for each month worked since the preceding January 1st, less any vacation already taken. If the termination is because of layoff, retirement, or death, the employee or his estate will be eligible for payment for all unused vacation accrued in the current year.[18]

§ 6.8 Insurance Benefits

The precise insurance benefits to be provided may be set forth in employment policies in their entirety, in summary fashion, by mere reference, or not at all. It is generally the insurance carrier's contract that defines the employees or former employees who are eligible to receive the benefits.

Insurance benefits generally cover medical, dental, prescription, life, or disability. To avoid inconsistent statements, employers should distribute to employees the insurance carrier's booklets regarding these benefits and should not include complete information in their policies. Policies should merely provide general insurance descriptions and refer employees to the plan booklets for further information. Federal or state statutes do not require an employer to provide any insurance benefits other than those that are statutorily mandated.[19]

§ 6.9 —Drafting

In drafting insurance benefit policies, the following should be considered:

1. Details of benefits should not be set forth in the policy
2. Employees should be referred to the insurance carrier's plan booklet to avoid coverage inconsistencies

---

[18] *Id.* ¶ PM-11,181.

[19] See §§ **6.14–6.16** regarding social security, workers' compensation, and unemployment compensation statutorily mandated benefits.

3. Eligibility requirements should conform with the insurance provider's

4. Benefit type offered:
   a. Hospitalization
   b. Medical
   c. Dental
   d. Prescription
   e. Disability
   f. Life insurance
   g. Other

5. Payment made by
   a. Employer
   b. Employee
   c. Copayment.

§ 6.10   —Sample Policies

The following examples should be considered in drafting insurance benefit policies:

CLAUSE 6.10(1)
INSURANCE BENEFITS—BENEFIT HIGHLIGHTS

The Company's benefit program is made up of various benefit plans that have been designed to work together to provide employees and their dependents with security under a variety of circumstances. Highlights of these benefit plans are contained in this section of the Company's Employment Handbook. They provide only an overview of the Company's benefit program for full-time employees and do not describe all of the various plan limitations. For these details, the individual plan documents should be consulted. Individual plan documents may be obtained from the Human Resources Department.

PLAN	BENEFIT PROVIDED	PARTICIPATION BEGINS	PAID BY
COMPREHENSIVE MEDICAL PLAN:	A comprehensive plan providing a broad range of medical benefits for you and your dependents, payable after a deductible and co-insurance amount of covered expenses per indi-	Following completion of the [number] days of employment	Company

PLAN	BENEFIT PROVIDED	PARTICIPATION BEGINS	PAID BY
	vidual have been met. The current maximum out-of-pocket cost per individual is $300 ($600 per family).		
DENTAL PLAN:	Dental benefits of 100%, 85%, or 50% of "covered charges" for you and your dependents, up to a calendar year maximum of $1000 per individual.	Following the completion of [number] days of employment.	Company
SICKNESS AND ACCIDENT PLAN:	Continuation of a portion of pay during total disability due to sickness or off-the-job accidents, for a period based on length of service.	Following completion of [number] days of employment	Company
OCCUPATIONAL DISABILITY PLAN:	For employees disabled by an occupational injury or illness, an amount equal to the greater of Statutory Workers' Compensation payments or the Company's sickness and accident plan.	Immediate	Company
LIFE INSURANCE PLAN:	Life insurance coverage related to your earnings.	Following completion of [number] days of employment.	Company
TOTAL AND PERMANENT DISABILITY PLAN:	A portion of your basic life insurance, payable in monthly installments, if you be-	Following completion of [number] days of employment.	Company

PLAN	BENEFIT PROVIDED	PARTICIPATION BEGINS	PAID BY
	come totally and permanently disabled, which reduces the amount of your life insurance coverage.		
ACCIDENTAL DEATH AND DISMEMBERMENT PLAN:	Additional life insurance coverage for death or dismemberment resulting from an accident.	Following completion of [number] days of employment.	Company
TRAVEL ACCIDENT PLAN:	Additional life insurance coverage for death or dismemberment while traveling on a common carrier.	Following completion of [number] days of employment.	Company
GENERAL RETIREMENT PLAN:	Monthly pension income based on length of service and average earnings, provided you are hired before age 60 and work 10 years or to age 65.	Age 25 and 1 year of service (upon satisfaction of these requirements, prior service will be credited in accordance with plan provisions).	Company

CLAUSE 6.10(2)
INSURANCE BENEFITS—COMPREHENSIVE

Section 1. Life Insurance.   The Company will assume the entire cost of the insurance coverage for eligible employees as set forth in the currently existing life insurance plan.

Section 2. Medical.   The Company shall provide each full time employee with 100% paid coverage under the present Blue Cross/Blue Shield and Major Medical Plan. In addition it shall provide dependency coverage where the dependents of the employee qualify under this Plan.

CLAUSE 6.10(3)
INSURANCE BENEFITS—COMPREHENSIVE (ALTERNATE)

Section 1. Medical.   All full-time employees are eligible for hospitalization. Employees may elect coverage under HMO or Blue Cross/Blue Shield, Major Medical coverage. This cost will be paid by the Company. The Company will pay [number] percent for family coverage and the remaining [number] percent will be paid by the employee. Part-time employees may participate at their own expense. A booklet will be given to all employees describing the benefits in detail. Enrollment will be effective after [number] days of employment.

Section 2. Dental.   All full-time employees are eligible for dental coverage. Employees may elect coverage under Blue Shield. This cost will be paid by the Company. The Company will pay [number] percent for family coverage and the remaining [number] percent will be paid by employee. Part-time employees may participate at their own expense. A booklet will be given to all employees describing the benefits. Enrollment will be effective after [number] days of employment.

Section 3. Life Insurance.   All full-time employees will be eligible for life insurance coverage, including accidental death and dismemberment benefits. The coverage amount will be the equivalent of one year's earnings and premiums will be paid by the Company. Enrollment will be effective after [number] days of employment.

CLAUSE 6.10(4)
INSURANCE BENEFITS—COMPREHENSIVE (ALTERNATE)

The Company recognizes the need for insured protection for employees and their families in case of illness or accident. It provides a comprehensive hospital and surgical group plan, a major medical program, and drug prescription coverage. The plan provides coverage for expenses incurred in hospitalization, surgical procedures, maternity costs, excess major medical needs, and prescription drugs for all employees. Further details are set forth in the plan documents for each plan. Copies of these plan documents may be obtained from the Human Resources Department. Full-time employees become eligible for this insurance protection program on the first day of the month after completion of their orientation period. The Company pays the entire cost for the individual employee only and coverage for dependents is available at a reduced rate.

§ 6.11 Profit Sharing and Retirement

With the exception of plans for governmental employees, the Employee Retirement Income Security Act (ERISA)[20] regulates employee benefit plans, including profit sharing and retirement plans for almost all employees. In addition, the Multi-employer Pension Plan Amendment Act (MPPAA)[21] imposes further requirements.

Employment policies covering profit sharing and retirement plans should contain general statements setting forth the existence of these plans, the benefits available, and which employees are eligible. For additional information regarding these plans, employees should be referred to separate summary plan descriptions.

---

[20] 29 U.S.C. §§ 1001–1368 (1988).

[21] *Id.* §§ 1381–1461.

Absent these precautions, unwanted employer binding commitments may be created.[22]

§ 6.12 —Drafting

In drafting profit sharing and retirement policies, the following should be considered:

1. Details of benefits should not be set forth
2. Eligibility requirements should conform with the plan's documents
3. Employees should be referred to each respective plan's documents to avoid coverage inconsistencies
4. Clauses should be reviewed by an experienced benefits counselor.

§ 6.13 —Sample Policies

The following examples should be considered in drafting profit sharing and retirement policies:

CLAUSE 6.13(1)
PROFIT SHARING/RETIREMENT PLAN

A Profit Sharing/Retirement Plan has been established for the benefit of the employees in a trust fund separate from the Company. This trust is funded by a percentage of the Company's profits, calculated at the end of each fiscal year on July 31, along with the earnings of previous deposits and investments. Eligibility and other details are explained in a separate booklet available from the Human Resources Department.

CLAUSE 6.13(2)
PROFIT SHARING PLAN

The Company has a plan by which it contributes a proportion of its profit to a trust for the benefit of its employees. This plan, called the Profit Sharing Plan, provides employees with an opportunity to benefit or share, by means of deferred compensation, in the Company's financial success. Assuming the Company operates profitably, the benefits will normally be paid out during an employee's retirement and will supplement any social security benefits received. All employees are eligible to participate in the plan after one year of employment. Please refer to the Profit Sharing Plan booklet for the program's specific details.

---

[22] *See* McKelvey v. Spitzer Motor Center, Inc., 46 Ohio App. 3d 75, 545 N.E.2d 1311 (1988) (employee bonus plan based on employer's annual profit created binding commitment).

CLAUSE 6.13(3)
RETIREMENT PLAN

The Company has a retirement plan. This is a voluntary plan to which the Company and eligible employees contribute a fixed percentage of earnings. Employees 21 years of age or older and who have completed two years of continuous employment may participate. The Retirement Plan is described in detail in a special booklet available from the Human Resources Department.

CLAUSE 6.13(4)
RETIREMENT PLAN (ALTERNATE)

A booklet which describes the Company's Retirement Plan will be made available to employees when they become eligible to participate. Eligibility is open to any employee:

1. Completing at least one full year of continuous service; and

2. 21 years or older.

CLAUSE 6.13(5)
RETIREMENT PLAN (ALTERNATE)

Full-time employees working 20 or more hours per week are eligible to participate in the Company's Retirement Plan. Employees will be admitted to the Plan when they have (a) completed one year of service and (b) have reached their 21st birthday. The plan is paid fully by the Company, and detailed information is available from the Human Resources Department.

CLAUSE 6.13(6)
RETIREMENT PLAN—TAX SHELTERED ANNUITY

To provide financial security, the Company provides the opportunity to participate in a Tax Sheltered Annuity Program. Employees may have a portion of their wages or salary set aside tax free from federal income tax only and taxable at time of withdrawal as a long-term investment for their retirement years. For further information regarding this program, consult the Human Resources Department.

§ 6.14   Statutory Benefits

Certain benefits are mandated by federal[23] and state[24] statutes that may not be waived by employees. These benefits include employer contributions to unem-

---

[23] *See, e.g.,* 26 U.S.C. §§ 3301–3311 (1988) (federal Unemployment Compensation Act).

[24] *See, e.g.,* Cal. Lab. Code § 132a (West 1971) (Workers' Compensation Act).

ployment compensation insurance,[25] workers' compensation insurance,[26] and so-cial security.[27] Employers should inform employees of the employer expense incurred in funding these benefits for them to obtain some understanding regarding the employer's responsibility for these contributions. Employment policies may also provide general descriptions of these benefits, including eligibility requirements and the means for obtaining benefits.

§ 6.15 —Drafting

In drafting statutory benefit policies, the following should be considered:

1. Applicable federal and state statutes
2. Type of benefits
3. Brief benefit description
4. Eligibility
5. Employer cost.

§ 6.16 —Sample Policies

The following examples should be considered in drafting statutory benefit policies:

CLAUSE 6.16(1)
STATE UNEMPLOYMENT COMPENSATION

Furloughed employees should be registered for state unemployment compensation benefits. Generally, employees who are terminated or quit a job are not eligible to receive these benefits. Company-paid payroll taxes provide the funds to pay unemployment compensation benefits.

CLAUSE 6.16(2)
WORKERS' COMPENSATION

Workers' compensation is a state-mandated program of medical and disability income payments made to or on behalf of workers or their survivors for any work-related illness, injury, or fatality that arises out of the course of their employment. Consult the Human Resources Department for details.

---

[25] 26 U.S.C. §§ 3301–3311 (1988) (federal Unemployment Tax Act).

[26] *See, e.g.,* Cal. Lab. Code § 132a (West 1971).

[27] 42 U.S.C. §§ 301–303, 501–504, 901–908, 1101–1108 (1988) (federal Social Security Act).

CLAUSE 6.16(3)
WORKERS' COMPENSATION (ALTERNATE)

All employees are covered by the state Worker's Compensation Act. One of the objectives of the Worker's Compensation Act is to "provide sure, prompt and reasonable income and medical benefits to work accident victims." The cost of this insurance is paid by the Company. Employees should report any injury received while working the day it occurs and complete an incident report of the accident immediately.

CLAUSE 6.16(4)
WORKERS' COMPENSATION (ALTERNATE)

As required by law, the Company provides workers' compensation coverage for accidents or injuries arising from the course of employment. In connection with this coverage, all accidents or injuries occurring at any time in which the Company may be involved, no matter how minor, must be reported immediately to the Company.

CLAUSE 6.16(5)
SOCIAL SECURITY

The federal government requires a deduction to be made from an employee's pay for Social Security benefits, and requires the Company to match this deduction. Employees should keep their Social Security cards and receipts of deductions for their own records. Questions about Social Security should be directed to the Social Security Administration, at (Address) . The Human Resources Department will also assist if requested.

CHAPTER 7

LEAVES OF
ABSENCE POLICIES

§ 7.1 Introduction

Employment policies may provide for many different leaves of absences. Leaves of absence are temporary absences from employment without loss of employment status. The following are generally common to leaves of absence:

1. Eligibility requirements
2. Conditions for utilizing the leave
3. Payment status
4. Effect of the leave on benefit accrual
5. Leave duration.

Policies frequently cover leave of absence issues involving medical,[1] pregnancy,[2] bereavement,[3] personal,[4] military service,[5] jury duty,[6] voting,[7] family and medical,[8] or other matters.

§ 7.2 Medical Leave

Medical leaves are generally provided for medical disabilities or conditions that prevent employees from performing their job duties. The Family and Medical Leave Act of 1993 may affect their granting.[9] They may be used in addition to paid sick leave or in conjunction with a disability insurance plan. Employers may require employees to submit medical statements establishing the existence and duration of any disability and may limit leaves to periods of actual disability. They may be paid or unpaid. Leaves for periods other than actual disability should be treated as personal leaves.

§ 7.3 —Drafting

In drafting medical leave policies, the following should be considered:

---

[1] See §§ **7.2–7.4.**

[2] See §§ **7.5–7.7.**

[3] See §§ **7.8–7.10.**

[4] See §§ **7.11–7.13.**

[5] See §§ **7.14–7.16.**

[6] See §§ **7.17–7.19.**

[7] See §§ **7.20–7.22.**

[8] See §§ **7.23–7.26.**

[9] P.L. 103.3 (Feb. 5, 1993) (Family and Medical Leave Act of 1993). See also §§ **7.23–7.26.**

1. Federal[10] or state[11] requirements
2. Eligibility requirements
3. Time length
4. Compensation status
5. Reporting requirements
6. Extension criteria
7. Verification requirements.

§ 7.4   —Sample Policies

The following examples should be considered in drafting medical leave policies:

CLAUSE 7.4(1)
MEDICAL LEAVE—BASIC

Leaves of absence due to injury or illness may be granted for extended time periods if the employee is under the care of a qualified medical doctor and with the concurrence of the Company medical department. The limit for medical leaves of absence is 18 months. A written note from the employee's doctor stating the general nature of the illness and the expected period of absence must be sent to the Company as soon as possible after the onset of the illness or injury. Following concurrence by the Company doctor, the employee will be notified that he or she has been placed on a medical leave of absence.

CLAUSE 7.4(2)
MEDICAL LEAVE—COMPREHENSIVE

Section 1. Eligibility.   Extended leave without pay for illness may be granted, upon an employee's written request, for a period of at least two consecutive weeks but not more than six consecutive months. The request, which shall be submitted in advance of the leave if circumstances permit, shall include proof of illness or disability in the form of a doctor's certificate which shall state a prognosis and expected return date. The Company is not required to grant subsequent leave without pay for this purpose.

Section 2. Extension.   Upon the employee's request, an extension of up to an additional six months of leave without pay for illness may be granted provided the employee provides proof of continuing illness or disability in the form of a doctor's certificate which shall state a prognosis and expected date of return.

---

[10] See P.L. 103.3 (Feb. 5, 1993) (Family and Medical Leave Act of 1993). See also §§ **7.23–7.26.**
[11] *See, e.g.,* New Jersey Family and Medical Leave Act.

Section 3. Return to Work.   Upon certification from the employee's doctor that the employee is able to return to work, the employee shall be offered his or her same or a similar position. If a position is not available, the employee shall be offered another position. If the employee refuses an offer of a same or similar position, the employee shall be separated from employment. If the employee accepts an alternate position, his pay rate shall be for that position and not for the one previously held.

Section 4. Other Benefits.   Employees shall be required to use accumulated sick and/or vacation leave prior to the commencement of a leave without pay.

§ 7.5   Pregnancy Leave

Federal statute requires that pregnancy disability policies be identical to the employer's other nonoccupational disability policies.[12] This means that any sick leave or other disability benefit offered to a male suffering from an illness or injury must be extended to a pregnant female for the period she is disabled by her pregnancy. A more restricted disability definition may not be applied to pregnancy than to other disabilities.[13]

Employers are under no obligation to extend benefits to a female employee for periods she is not disabled by pregnancy, nor may they require that the employee quit working for specified periods before or after delivery.

Extending benefits to a female employee for periods after delivery that she is not disabled for child care purposes imposes an obligation to extend similar benefits to males for child care purposes.[14] Not to do so constitutes sex discrimination. Employers must exercise caution to avoid discriminatory pregnancy policies. States also may impose additional requirements on employers.[15]

§ 7.6   —Drafting

In drafting pregnancy leave policies, the following should be considered:

1.   Applicable federal[16] and state[17] statutory requirements
2.   Eligibility requirements

---

[12] 42 U.S.C. §§ 2000e-1 to 2002-2017 (1988) (Civil Rights Act of 1964).

[13] *Id.*

[14] *See,* Byrd v. Unified School Dist., 453 F. Supp. 621 (E.D. Wis. 1978) (similar leave for males); *see also* Newport News Shipbuilding & Dry Dock Co. v. EEOC, 462 U.S. 669 (1983) (Pregnancy Discrimination Act provides protection for female company employees on payroll as well as for male employee spouses). *See also* P.L. 103.3 (Feb 5, 1993) (Family and Medical Leave Act of 1993); §§ 7.23–7.26.

[15] *See, e.g.,* Pa. Stat. Ann. tit. 43, §§ 951–963 (Purdon 1991) (Pennsylvania Human Relations Act).

[16] 42 U.S.C. §§ 2000e-1 to 2002-2017 (1988) (Civil Rights Act of 1964).

[17] Pa. Stat. Ann. tit. 43, §§ 951–963 (Purdon 1991) (Pennsylvania Human Relations Act).

3. Verification prior to and upon return to work
4. Coordination with other disability benefits
    a. Sick leave
    b. Vacation leave
    c. Disability policy
5. Time length
6. Additional leave after disability
    a. Eligibility
        (1) Males
        (2) Females
    b. Time length
    c. Compensation status
        (1) Paid
        (2) Unpaid.

§ 7.7   —Sample Policies

The following examples should be considered in drafting pregnancy leave policies:

CLAUSE 7.7(1)
PREGNANCY LEAVE—BASIC

Employees who become pregnant may continue to work until they are certified as unable to work by their physicians. At that point they are entitled to receive weekly income from the Company's Disability Insurance Plan. When the employee comes back to work, she is entitled to return to the same or equivalent job with no loss of service or other rights or privileges. Should the employee fail to return to work when released by her doctor, she will be considered to have voluntarily terminated her employment.

CLAUSE 7.7(2)
PREGNANCY LEAVE—COMPREHENSIVE

Section 1. General.   All employees who become pregnant shall be granted pregnancy leave upon request.

Section 2. Granting Leave.

a. An employee shall submit written notification to her immediate supervisor stating the anticipated duration of the leave at least two weeks in advance, if circumstances permit. Leaves shall be granted for a time period not to exceed six months. Upon the request of the employee and at the Company's discretion, leaves may be extended or renewed for a period not to exceed six months. In no case shall the total amount of leave exceed 12 months.

b. The employee shall not be required to leave prior to childbirth unless she can no longer satisfactorily perform her position's duties.

c. While an employee is on pregnancy leave, the duties of her position shall either be performed by remaining staff and the position kept vacant or they shall be performed by a substitute employee.

Section 3. Re-employment.   Every employee has the right to return to the same position in the same classification she held before going on pregnancy leave or to an equivalent position with regard to pay and skill.

Section 4. Seniority Rights.   Upon return from pregnancy leave, an employee shall retain all seniority and pension rights that had accrued up to the time of her leave, including those rights accrued during the approved pregnancy leave without pay.

Section 5. Annual and Sick Leave.   An employee who is on pregnancy leave without pay is entitled to use accrued sick leave for the period that she is unable to work, as certified by a physician, and all accrued vacation and personal leave. All other periods of leave related to pregnancy leave shall be leave without pay. Unused leave shall be carried over until her return. An employee shall not earn annual and sick leave while she is on pregnancy leave without pay.

§ 7.8   Bereavement Leave

Employment policies may provide leave for a specified period due to a close family member's death, with or without pay or with partial pay. Clauses should specify eligibility requirements and leave conditions, including the employee's relationship to the deceased. It also should indicate any documentation that employees must submit upon return from the leave.

§ 7.9   —Drafting

In drafting bereavement leave policies, the following should be considered:

1. Eligibility requirements
2. Time length
3. Relationship to the deceased
4. Compensation
5. Verification.

§ 7.10   —Sample Policies

The following examples should be considered in drafting bereavement leave policies:

CLAUSE 7.10(1)
BEREAVEMENT LEAVE

Section 1. Eligibility.   When death occurs to an employee's current spouse, mother, father, current mother-in-law, current father-in-law, son, daughter, grandparents, grandchildren, brother, or sister (including stepfather, stepmother, stepchildren, stepbrother, or stepsister when they have lived with the employee in an immediate family relationship), the employee will, upon request, be excused and paid for up to a maximum of three paid days. These days must be scheduled on days during the period beginning with the day of death and extending up to and including the day of the funeral; provided, however, one day shall be the day of the funeral.

Section 2. Payment.   Payment for each day will be eight times the employee's average straight-time hourly earnings. Employees will not receive bereavement pay when it duplicates pay received for time not worked for any other reason. Time paid for bereavement will not be counted as hours worked for determining overtime or premium pay. Procedure for payment requires completion and submission to the Human Resources Department of an "Authorization for Bereavement Pay" form. This form is to be completed by the employee's supervisor.

CLAUSE 7.10(2)
BEREAVEMENT LEAVE (ALTERNATE)

Section 1. Full-Time Employees.   Full-time employees are entitled to three consecutive leave days with pay for a death in the immediate family (current spouse, child, mother, father, sister, brother, stepchildren, legal guardian). Employees are entitled to one leave day with pay to attend the funeral for the death of grandparents or current mother/father-in-law. Other unpaid excused time, if needed, may be granted.

Section 2. Part-Time Employees.   Part-time employees shall receive one day off with pay for funeral services if that date is a regularly scheduled working day for a death and two additional days excused without pay for death in the immediate family (current spouse, child, mother, father, sister, brother, stepchildren, legal guardian, grandparents, and current father/mother- in-law).

CLAUSE 7.10(3)
BEREAVEMENT LEAVE WITH SICK LEAVE

Section 1. Eligibility.   Employees shall be allowed $1\frac{1}{4}$ days of sick leave for each month of service. Sick leave shall be earned by an employee for any month in which the employee is in compensable status for ten or more working days. Employees shall be eligible to take sick leave after 30 days' service with the Company.

Section 2. Accumulation.   Employees shall earn sick leave from their date of hire and may accumulate sick leave up to a maximum of 200 days.

Section 3. Verification.   A doctor's certificate is required for an absence from work due to sickness for three or more consecutive days. For absence of less than three days, a doctor's certificate may be required when, in the Company's opinion, the employee has been abusing sick leave privileges.

Section 4. Immediate Family Sickness.   Employees may use not more than three (3) days of sick leave, in any calendar year, when sickness in the immediate family requires the employee's absence from work. Immediate family is defined as current spouse or child of the employee residing in the employee's household. The Company may require proof of family sickness.

Section 5. Death.   Employees may use up to five days of sick leave for the death of a current spouse, parent, or child, and up to three days of leave may be used for the death of a brother, sister, grandparent, grandchild, current son- or daughter-in-law, current brother- or sister-in-law, current parent-in-law, current grandparent-in-law, or any relative residing in the employee's household.

§ 7.11   Personal Leave

Personal leave provisions are as varied as the employment policies that contain them. Personal leave should be available only to conduct the employee's necessary personal business that cannot be conducted during normal business hours or to attend to an unforeseen emergency. Personal leave may end up to be additional vacation days.

Employers may provide nonmedical personal leaves of absence in accordance with their needs. Policies should include the general parameters and requirements for these leaves. Employers should retain discretion to consider all relevant factors before determining whether to grant personal leaves. Documentation should also cover the basis for leave decisions in order to counter any possible discrimination claims.

§ 7.12   —Drafting

In drafting personal leave policies, the following should be considered:

1. Eligibility requirements
2. Leave length
3. Compensation
4. Verification.

§ 7.13   —Sample Policies

The following examples should be considered in drafting personal leave policies:

CLAUSE 7.13(1)
PERSONAL LEAVE—BASIC

A leave of absence without pay for a full-time employee may be granted at the discretion of the President and/or Personnel Manager. The request must be in writing to your department head, stating the reasons and dates for the leave of absence. The leave may not exceed three months.

Sick leave and vacation do not accrue during a leave of absence. Vacation time that has accrued at the time of request will be granted when the leave begins. Hospitalization and life insurance will be canceled during a leave of absence. An employee, however, desiring continued coverage during leave, may obtain it by paying the premiums in advance. Insurance benefits will be effective on the first of the month following the employee's return. Other benefits will start immediately. The employee will be given preference for the first available position for which he/she is qualified. If the employee does not return to work as scheduled, he will be considered terminated.

CLAUSE 7.13(2)
PERSONAL LEAVE—COMPREHENSIVE

Section 1. Eligibility.   All permanent full-time employees shall be eligible for two (2) personal leave days per calendar year.

Section 2. How Earned.   One personal leave day shall be earned the first half of each calendar year (January 1 to June 30) and one personal leave day shall be earned during the second half of each calendar year (July 1 to December 31). The employee must have 30 days' service in pay status in each half calendar year in order to earn the personal leave entitlement.

Section 3. Scheduling.   Personal leave shall be scheduled and granted for time periods requested by the employee subject to the Company's responsibility to maintain efficient operations. If the nature of the work makes it necessary to limit the number of employees on personal leave at the same time, the employee with the greatest seniority as it relates to total years of continuous Company service shall be give his or her choice of personal leave in the event of any conflict in selection.

Section 4. Participation Prior to Earning.   Personal leave to which an employee may become entitled during the calendar year may be granted at the Company's discretion before it is earned. An employee who is permitted to anticipate leave and who subsequently terminates employment shall reimburse the Company for those personal leave days used but not earned.

Section 5. Nonaccrual.   Personal leave days shall be noncumulative from calendar year to calendar year. If an employee is required to work on his or her scheduled personal leave day and is unable to reschedule the personal day during the calendar year due to the work demands, the calendar year shall be extended for 90 days for rescheduling purposes.

Section 6. Illness.   An employee who becomes ill while on personal leave will not be charged personal leave for the period of illness provided he or she furnishes satisfactory proof of the illness upon return to work.

Section 7. Part-Time Employees.   All part-time employees who are in pay status for 30 days in each one-half calendar year shall be eligible for $\frac{1}{2}$ paid personal leave per day per $\frac{1}{2}$ calendar year.

§ 7.14   Military Leave

Employers are required by federal[18] and state[19] statutes to reinstate veterans to their former or similar positions if the veterans left their positions for military service and these rights are exercised within the requisite period. Military leave must also be granted for periodic active duty under certain circumstances. Employment policies should include a general provision that military leave will be provided if legal requirements are met.

§ 7.15   —Drafting

In drafting military leave policies, the following should be considered:

1.   Applicable federal[20] and state[21] statutes
2.   Discretionary matters
    a.   Compensation
    b.   Time Length

---

[18] 38 U.S.C. §§ 2021(a)(A)(i), 2021(a)(B), 2021(b)(1), 2024 (1988) (Vietnam Era Veterans Readjustment Assistance Act, guaranteeing the right to re-employment upon satisfactory completion of military service and prohibiting termination "without cause" within one year after re-employment).

[19] *See, e.g.,* Pa. Stat. Ann. tit. 51, §§ 7301–7311 (Purdon 1976) (Pennsylvania military leave requirements).

[20] 38 U.S.C. §§ 2021(a)(A)(i), 2021(a)(B), 2021(b)(1), 2024 (1988) (Vietnam Era Veterans Readjustment Assistance Act).

[21] *See, e.g.,* Pa. Stat. Ann. tit. 51, §§ 7301–7311 (Purdon 1976) (Pennsylvania military leave requirements).

§ 7.16   —Sample Policies

The following examples should be considered in drafting military leave policies:

CLAUSE 7.16(1)
MILITARY LEAVE—COMPREHENSIVE

Section 1. Eligibility.   Full-time employees who, as members of the organized reserves of the Armed Forces of the United States or of the state national guard, must perform active duty at an annual encampment or are called up to perform emergency duty, will be paid for each of these duties, up to a maximum of two weeks per year, provided the employee has completed one or more years of Company service before the end of the calendar year in which the annual encampment or call-up began. Emergency duty is defined as flood, storm, riot, and other civil commotion control.

Section 2. Payment.   Employees will receive for this period of active duty the difference between the total amount paid by the Government for the entire period of active duty (not including travel, subsistence, and quarters allowance for the employee only) and the amount calculated by multiplying the number of days the employee would have worked had the employee not been on active duty (plus any holiday in this period which would not have been worked) by eight times the employee's average straight-time hourly rate of earnings (including applicable incentive earnings but excluding shift differential, cost-of-living, and Sunday and overtime premiums) during the last payroll period worked (excluding annual plant shutdown) prior to active duty. If the period of encampment exceeds two weeks in any calendar year, pay shall be based upon the first two weeks the employee would have worked during the period.

Where the employee does not serve a full two-week period at the time of the emergency call-up and subsequently is recalled within the calendar year for additional emergency duty, the employee will be paid for no more than 10 working days per calendar year for emergency duty.

Section 3. Verification.   Employees shall submit a military pay voucher or if that is not available, shall request a military pay form from the Payroll Department to be completed by a military commander, executive, or payroll officer. One of these two forms must be submitted to the Payroll Department before any adjustment will be made.

CLAUSE 7.16(2)
MILITARY LEAVE—COMPREHENSIVE (ALTERNATE)

Section 1. Eligibility.   Employees who are members of reserve components of the Armed Forces are entitled to a leave with pay on all working days not exceeding 15 days in any calendar year during which they are engaged in field training authorized by the Federal Forces. Employees who are members of the state's National Guard are entitled to leave with pay on all working days during which they shall, as members of the National Guard, be engaged in the active service of the state or in authorized field training.

   Section 2. Military Service—Employment Status. Whenever an employee is drafted at any time into the active military service of the United States or enlists in time of war or armed conflict, he shall be granted a military leave without pay. The term drafted shall mean to be drafted, to be ordered into active military service as a member of a reserve component of the Armed Forces, or in any way to enter or remain involuntarily in active military service for such period as is necessary to satisfy one's draft obligation. While an employee is on military leave, duties shall either be performed by remaining employees and his or her position kept vacant or they shall be performed by a temporary substitute.

§ 7.17   Jury or Witness Duty Leave

A strong public policy implicit in federal and state constitutions,[22] statutes,[23] and decisional law[24] encourages jury service. Statutory protections generally entitle an employee to take time off for jury duty or for a court appearance as a witness when reasonable notice is given to the employer.[25] The employer is prohibited from terminating or discriminating against an employee for taking time off for this purpose.

§ 7.18   —Drafting

In drafting jury or witness duty policies, the following should be considered:

   1.   Applicable federal[26] and state[27] statutes
   2.   Compensation
      a.   Paid
      b.   Unpaid
   3.   Verification.

---

[22] *See* K. Decker, Employee Privacy Law and Practice ch. 3 (John Wiley & Sons, Inc. 1987) [hereinafter Decker, Privacy Law].

[23] *See, e.g.*, 28 U.S.C. § 1875 (1988) (Judiciary and Judicial Procedure Act; prohibits employee termination for service on federal grand or petit juries).

[24] *See, e.g.*, Nees v. Hocks, 272 Or. 210, 536 P.2d 512 (1975) (employee wrongfully terminated for expressing desire to serve on a jury).

[25] *See, e.g.*, Cal. Lab. Code § 203(c) (West 1971) (California's statute prohibiting termination for jury service).

[26] *See, e.g.*, 28 U.S.C. § 1875 (1988) (Judiciary and Judicial Procedure Act).

[27] *See, e.g.*, Cal. Lab. Code § 203(c) (West 1971) (California's jury service statute).

§ 7.19   —Sample Policies

The following examples should be considered in drafting the handbook's jury or witness duty policies:

CLAUSE 7.19(1)
JURY OR WITNESS DUTY LEAVE—DIFFERENCE IN PAY

Upon receiving a summons to report for jury or witness duty, an employee shall on his or her next working day present the summons to his or her immediate superior. The employee shall be excused from employment for the day or days required in serving as a juror or witness in any court created by the United States or the State of [state's name]. This shall be considered an excused absence. Full-time employees shall be entitled to their usual compensation less any fee or compensation received from serving as jurors or witnesses upon written presentation to the Company.

CLAUSE 7.19(2)
JURY OR WITNESS DUTY LEAVE—DIFFERENCE IN PAY

Employees will be granted leave if they are called for jury duty or subpoenaed as a witness. The Company will pay the difference between the employee's regular pay and the amount received from jury duty. This applies to all employees during regularly scheduled work days.

CLAUSE 7.19(3)
JURY OR WITNESS DUTY LEAVE—UNPAID

Employees called for jury duty or subpoenaed to attend court shall be granted unpaid leaves while attending court. Evidence of this duty in the form of a subpoena or other written notification shall be presented to the employee's immediate supervisor as far in advance as practicable.

§ 7.20   Voting Time Leave

Voting is a general society obligation.[28] A strong public policy implicit in federal and state constitutions,[29] statutes,[30] and decisional law[31] encourages voting. Some

---

[28] *See* Decker, Privacy Law §§ 2.40, 7.24.

[29] *Id.* ch. 3.

[30] *See, e.g.,* Cal. Elec. Code § 14350 (West 1977) (California's statute requiring employee time off for voting).

[31] *See, e.g.,* Bell v. Faulkner, 75 S.W.2d 612 (Mo. App. 1984) (refusing to vote as employer wished).

states require that an employee be given time off to vote.[32] Employment hand-books may address this subject matter.

§ 7.21 —Drafting

In drafting voting time leave policies, the following should be considered:

1. Applicable state[33] statutes
2. Requests for voting time should be made in advance of the election date to not unnecessarily interfere with employer requirements
3. Proof that voting time was used by the employee
4. Voter registration verification by having the employee sign an authorization to vote form indicating:
    a. That the employee is an eligible registered voter for the subject election
    b. That falsification may result in employee discipline up to and including termination.

§ 7.22 —Sample Policies

The following examples should be considered in drafting voting policies:

CLAUSE 7.22(1)
VOTING TIME LEAVE—COMPREHENSIVE

Section 1. Time Off.   Company employees are entitled to vote at general, primary, or presidential primary elections. When registered voter-employees do not have sufficient time outside of regular working hours to vote, they may take off so much working time as will, when added to their voting time outside their working hours, enable them to vote. Employees shall be allowed time off for voting only at the beginning or end of their regular working shifts, whichever allows them the most free time for voting and the least time off from their regular working shift, unless otherwise mutually agreed. Employees who are election officers may absent themselves from employment on election day without being subject to demotion, suspension, or termination.

Section 2. Compensation.   Employees may take off so much time as will enable them to vote, but not more than two hours of which shall be compensated.

---

[32] *See, e.g.*, Cal. Elec. Code § 14350 (West 1977) (California's statute requiring time off for voting).

[33] *Id.*

Section 3. Time-Off Notice.   If an employee knows or has reason to believe that time off is needed to vote, he or she must give the Company at least five working days' notice that time off is desired for voting.

§ 7.23   Family and Medical Leave

The Family and Medical Leave Act (FMLA) requires employers of 50 or more employees to provide up to 12 weeks of leave during any 12-month period.[34] The leave may be taken for one or more of the following reasons:

1. Birth of a child
2. Adoption of a child or placement of a foster child
3. To care for a sick spouse, child, or parent
4. Employee's own serious health condition.

Any eligible employee who takes family or medical leave must be returned to the same position held prior to the leave or an equivalent position. The employer must also maintain group health coverage for the employee during the leave period.

The Act covers any business entity or individual that employs 50 or more employees for each working day during each of 20 or more calendar work weeks in the current or the preceding calendar year. The calendar work weeks need not be contiguous.

Employer includes a partnership, sole proprietorship, corporation, business trust, or virtually any organized group that is engaged in commerce. It also includes public agencies, such as state and local governments, the U.S. Postal Service, and certain other agencies of the federal government. There are exceptions, however, for employees who are not subject to civil service and for elected and appointed officials. To determine whether an employer meets the 50-or-more-employee test, all employees—full- and part-time, temporary and permanent—are to be counted. For example, an employer who has one full-time employee and 50 part-time, seasonal employees each day for 20 work weeks during the year will be subject to the law.

To be eligible for family or medical leave, an employee must have been employed by the employer:

1. For at least 12 months
2. For at least 1,250 hours during the prior 12-month period.

Employees with one year of service who worked, on average, 24 hours or more a week during the entire prior year are eligible for family or health leave. Eligible

---

[34] P.L. 103.3 (Feb. 5, 1993) (Family and Medical Leave Act of 1993).

employees are entitled to 12 work weeks of leave during any 12-month period. Both women and men are entitled to take family or medical leave, if otherwise eligible.

Leave must be granted for one or more of the following reasons:

1. Birth of the employee's child to care for the child
2. Placement of a child with the employee for adoption or foster care
3. To care for the employee's spouse, child, or parent who has a serious health condition
4. Due to a serious health condition that renders the employee incapable of performing the conditions of his or her job.

A *serious health condition* is defined as an illness, injury, impairment, or physical or mental condition that involves inpatient care in a hospital, hospice, or residential medical care facility, or continuing treatment by a health care provider.

The Act limits the amount of family leave that must be granted when a husband and wife are employed by the same employer. Under the Act, the aggregate amount of leave that the shared employer must give the spouses during any 12 months is limited to 12 work weeks if the leave is for the birth or placement of a child or to care for a sick parent. The law is unclear as to the amount of leave when each spouse has a sick parent who needs care.

The Act does not require paid family or health leave. Leave may consist of paid leave, but whether leave is paid or not is the employer's discretion. However, an employee may choose or the employer may require that any of the employee's available accrued paid vacation, personal, family, or sick leave be substituted for any part of the 12-week leave period. Once any paid leave is used up, the remainder of the 12 weeks of leave may be unpaid.

Where the necessity for leave is foreseeable due to the expected birth or placement of a child, the employee must provide at least 30 days' notice of the employee's intention to take leave. If the birth or placement requires leave to begin in less than 30 days, the employee must provide this notice as soon as practicable.

Where the necessity for leave is due to a family member's or the employee's own serious health condition and is foreseeable, based on planned medical treatment, the employee must:

1. Give at least 30 days' notice (or notice as soon as practicable, if treatment starts in less than 30 days)
2. Make a reasonable effort to schedule the treatment so as not to unduly disrupt the operations of the employer, subject to the approval of the health care provider.

Where the need for leave is unforeseeable, only notice as soon as practicable is required.

An employer may require that any leave request based on a family member's or the employee's own serious health condition be supported by certification of a health care provider. The employee must provide a copy of the certification to the employer in a "timely manner." The certification must contain:

1. Date the serious health condition began

2. Probable duration of condition

3. Appropriate medical facts regarding condition

4. If the leave is based on care of a spouse, child, or parent, a statement that the employee is needed to provide the care and an estimate of the length of time that need will continue

5. If the leave is based on the employee's own serious health condition, a statement that the employee is unable to perform the functions of his or her job

6. In the case of intermittent leave or leave on a reduced schedule for planned medical treatment, the dates the treatment is expected to be given and the duration of the treatment.

The Act allows an employer to require the employee to provide later recertifications "on a reasonable basis." Moreover, an employer can require an employee to report periodically on his or her status and intentions of returning to work. Finally, the Act allows the employer to require each employee taking leave due to the employee's serious health condition to obtain certification that the employee is able to resume work.

With limited exceptions, any eligible employee who takes leave is entitled to be restored to his or her old job or to an equivalent position with equivalent pay, benefits, and other terms and conditions of employment. No employment benefits that accrued before the date leave began can be lost. However, an employee is not entitled to an accrual of any seniority or employment benefits that occur during the period of leave. An employer may deny job restoration to certain highly compensated employees. This exception applies to any salaried eligible employee who is among the highest paid 10 percent of employees of the employer who work within 75 miles of the facility where the employee taking leave works. The exception only applies, however, if:

1. The denial of job restoration is necessary to prevent "substantial and grievous economic injury" to the employer's operations

2. The employer notifies the employee of its intent to deny restoration when the employer first determines such economic injury would occur

3. When leave has begun, the employee elects not to return to work after receiving such notice.

The employer must maintain coverage under any group health plan for any employee who takes family or medical leave. The coverage must be continued for the duration of the leave at the same level and under the same conditions coverage would have been provided if no leave had been taken.

However, if an employee fails to return to work after the period of leave expires, the employer may recover the premium the employer paid for coverage during the leave period. Exceptions exist when the employee does not return to work due to the continuation, recurrence, or onset of a serious health condition of a family member or the employee that would otherwise entitle the employee to take leave or due to other circumstances beyond the employee's control.

The employer may require that an employee claiming an inability to return to work due to a continuation, recurrence, or onset of a serious health condition provide certification from a health care provider to that effect.

It is unlawful for an employer to interfere, restrain, or deny the exercise of rights given under the Act. An employer cannot terminate or in any other manner discriminate against employees for taking advantage of their rights to family and medical leave or opposing the employer's denial of those rights.

An employee claiming a violation of the Act may bring suit in any state or federal court against an employer on the employee's own behalf and that of all similarly situated employees. Any employer found to have violated the FMLA will be liable to any eligible employee affected by the violation for:

1. Damages equal to any wages, salary, employment benefits, or other compensation denied or lost by reason of the violation

2. When no compensation or benefits have been lost (for example, when leave was denied and the employee continued to work), damages equal to any actual monetary losses suffered by the employee due to the violation (such as the cost of providing care to a family member) plus interest on the above damages.

The court may also impose liquidated damages equal to the actual damages and interest described above. Such liquidated damages may be waived by the court when the employer acted in good faith and had reasonable grounds for believing it was not in violation. If judgment is awarded to the employee, the employer will also be required to pay a reasonable attorney's fee, reasonable expert witness fees, and other court costs incurred by the employee. Finally, if appropriate, the court may order equitable relief such as employment, reinstatement, and promotion of the employee.

The employee may also complain to the Department of Labor (DOL), which shall investigate and attempt to resolve the complaint. If the complaint cannot be resolved, the DOL may bring court action to recover the damages or other relief available to the employee in a civil action. The employee's right to bring an action will terminate on the filing of an action by the DOL. The DOL may also seek an injunction retraining violations of the law by the employer.

Any lawsuits by the employee or the government must be commenced within two years of the last event constituting a violation for which relief is sought. If the violation is willful, the statute of limitations is extended to three years.

An employer must make, keep, and preserve records regarding compliance with the Act. In addition, each employer must conspicuously post a notice containing information about the Family and Medical Leave Act and information on how to file a charge for violation of the law. Failure to post can result in a penalty of up to $100 for each offense.

§ 7.24   —Drafting

In drafting family and medical leave policies, the following should be considered:

1. Applicable federal[35] and state statutory requirements
2. Eligibility requirements
3. Verification prior to and upon return to work
4. Coordination with other benefits
   a. Sick leave
   b. Vacation leave
   c. Disability policy
5. Time length
6. Additional leave
   a. Eligibility
      (1) Males
      (2) Females
      (3) Spouses
   b. Time length
   c. Compensation status
      (1) Paid
      (2) Unpaid.

§ 7.25   —Sample Policies

The following examples should be considered in drafting family and medical leave policies:

---

[35] P.L. 103.3 (Feb. 5, 1993) (Family and Medical Leave Act of 1993).

CLAUSE 7.25(1)
FAMILY AND MEDICAL LEAVE

Section 1. Family and/or Medical Leave. A family and/or medical leave of absence is an approved absence available to eligible employees for up to 12 weeks of unpaid leave per year under particular circumstances that are critical to the family's life. Leave may be taken:

a. Upon the birth of the employee's child

b. Upon the placement of a child with the employee for adoption or foster care

c. When the employee is needed to care for a child, spouse, or parent who has a serious health condition

d. When the employee is unable to perform the functions of his or her position because of a serious health condition.

Section 2. Scope. This policy shall apply to all family and medical leaves of absence except to the extent that this type of leave is covered under other paid Company employment benefit plans or policies for any part of the 12 weeks of leave to which the employee may be entitled under this policy. If an employee is entitled to paid leave under another Company benefit plan or policy, the employee must take that paid leave first.

Section 3. Eligibility. An employee must have been employed for at least 12 months and must have worked at least 1,250 hours during the 12-month period preceding the commencement of the leave. If the employee on leave is a salaried employee and is among the highest paid 10 percent of Company employees within 75 miles, and if keeping the job open for the employee would result in substantial economic injury to the Company, reinstatement to the employee on leave to an equivalent position with equivalent employment benefits as well as other terms and conditions of employment can be denied. In this situation the employee may be given an opportunity to return to other work, if available.

Section 4. Basic Regulations and Conditions of Leave.

a. The Company will require medical certification to support a claim for leave for an employee's own serious health condition or to care for a seriously ill child, spouse, or parent. For the employee's own medical leave, the certification must include a statement that the employee is unable to perform the functions of his or her position. For leave to care for a seriously ill child, spouse, or parent, the certification must include an estimate of the amount of time the employee will be needed to provide care. In its discretion, the Company may require a second medical opinion and periodic recertifications at its own expense. If the first and second opinions differ, the Company, at its own expense, may require the binding opinion of a third health care provider, approved jointly by the Company and the employee.

b. If medically necessary for a serious health condition of the employee or his or her spouse, child, or parent, leave may be taken on an intermittent or reduced leave schedule. If leave is requested on this basis, however, the Company may require the employee to transfer temporarily to an alternative position that better accommodates recurring periods of absence or a part-time schedule, provided that the position has equivalent pay and benefits.

c. Spouses who are both employed by the Company are entitled to a total of 12 weeks of leave instead of 12 weeks each for the birth or adoption of a child or for the care of a sick parent.

Section 5. Notification and Reporting Requirements.   When the need for leave is foreseeable, including the birth or adoption of a child, or planned medical treatment, the employee must provide reasonable prior notice and make efforts to schedule leave so as not to disrupt Company operations. In cases of illness, the employee will be required to report periodically on his or her leave status and intention to return to work.

Section 6. Status of Employee Benefits During Leave of Absence.

a. Any employee who is granted an approved leave of absence is advised to provide for the retention of his or her group insurance coverages by arranging to pay the premium contributions during the period of unpaid absence.

b. In the event that an employee elects not to return to work upon completion of an approved unpaid leave of absence, the Company may recover from the employee the cost of any payments made to maintain the employee's benefit coverage unless the failure to return to work was for reasons beyond the employee's control. Benefit entitlements based upon length of service will be calculated as of the last paid work day prior to the start of the unpaid leave of absence.

Section 7. Procedures.

a. A Request for Family and Medical Leave of Absence Form must be originated in duplicate by the employee. This form should be completed in detail, signed by the employee, submitted to the immediate supervisor for proper approval, and forwarded to the Human Resources Department. If possible, the form should be submitted 30 calendar days in advance of the leave's effective date.

b. All requests for family and medical leaves of absence due to illness will include the following sufficient medical certification attached to a completed Request for Family and Medical Leave of Absence stating:

(1) The date on which the serious health condition commenced

(2) The probable duration of the condition

(3) The appropriate medical facts within the knowledge of the health care provider regarding the condition.

In addition, for purposes of leave to care for a child, spouse, or parent, the certificate should give an estimate of the amount of time that the employee will be needed to provide this care. For purposes of leave for an employee's illness, the certificate must state that the employee is unable to perform the functions of his or her position. In the case of certification for intermittent leave or leave on a reduced leave schedule for planned medical treatment, the dates on which this treatment is expected to be given and the duration of this treatment must be stated.

CLAUSE 7.25(2)
FAMILY AND MEDICAL LEAVE

Section 1. Eligibility.   All employees who have been with the Company for at least 12 months and have worked at least 1,250 hours within the previous 12-month period are eligible for family and/or medical leave of absence. Employees are eligible to take up to 12 weeks of unpaid leave in any 12-month period under four circumstances that are critical to the life of a family. Leave may be taken:

a. Upon the birth of the employee's child

b. Upon the placement of a child with the employee for adoption or foster care

c. When the employee is needed to care for a child, spouse, or parent who has a serious health condition

d. When the employee is unable to perform the functions of his or her position because of a serious health condition.

Section 2. Definitions.

a. "Serious health condition" means an illness, injury, impairment, or physical or mental condition involving either in-patient care or continuing treatment by a health care provider.

b. "Health care providers" include doctors of medicine, osteopathy, or any other person determined by the Secretary of Labor to be capable of providing health care services.

Section 3. Return to Work.   When an employee is able to return to active employment, he or she shall be returned to the same or an equivalent position with equivalent employee benefits and compensation and other conditions of employment. *Equivalent* means substantially the same but not exactly equal. However, if the employee on leave is a salaried employee and is among the highest paid 10 percent of Company employees within 75 miles, and if keeping the job open for the employee would result in substantial economic injury to the Company, reinstatement to the employee on leave can be denied. In this situation, however, the employee will be given an opportunity to return to work.

Section 4. Other Leaves.   This policy shall apply to all family and medical leaves of absence except to the extent that these leaves are covered under other paid employment benefit plans or policies for any part of the 12 weeks of leave to which the employee may be entitled under this policy. In other words, if an employee is entitled to paid leave under another benefit plan or policy, the employee must take the paid leave first.

Section 5. Medical Certification.   The Company will require medical certification to support a claim for leave for an employee's own serious health condition or to care for a seriously ill child, spouse, or parent. For the employee's own medical leave, the certification must include a statement that the employee is unable to perform the functions of his or her position. For leave to care for a seriously ill child, spouse, or parent, the certification must include an estimate of the amount of time the employee will be needed to provide care. In its discretion, the Company may require a second medical opinion and periodic recertifications at its own expense. If the first and second opinions differ, the Company, at its own expense, may require the binding opinion of a third health care provider, approved jointly by the Company and the employee.

Section 6. Scheduling Leave.   Leave may be taken on an intermittent or reduced leave schedule if medically necessary for a serious health condition of the employee or his or her spouse, child, or parent. If leave is requested on this basis, however, the Company may require the employee to transfer temporarily to an alternative position that better accommodates recurring periods of absence or a part-time schedule, provided that the position has equivalent pay and benefits.

Spouses who are both employed by the Company are entitled to a total of 12 weeks of leave (rather than 12 weeks each) for the birth or adoption of a child or for the care of sick parent.

When the need for leave is foreseeable, such as the birth or adoption of a child, or planned medical treatment, the employee must provide reasonable prior notice and make efforts to schedule leave so as not to disrupt Company operations. In cases of illness, the employee will be required to report periodically on his or her leave status and intention to return to work.

Section 7. Insurance Coverages.   Any employee who is granted an approved leave of absence under this policy is advised to provide for the retention of his or her group insurance coverages by arranging to pay his or her portion of the premium contributions during the period of unpaid absence. In the event that an employee elects not to return to work upon completion of an approved unpaid leave of absence, the Company may recover from the employee the cost of any Company payments made to maintain the employee's coverage unless the failure to return to work was for reasons beyond the employee's control. Benefit entitlements based upon length of service will be calculated as of the last paid work day prior to the start of the leave of absence.

Section 8. Requesting Leave Procedure.   Any employee requesting a leave must complete a Request for Family and Medical Leave of Absence Form and submit it to the immediate supervisor for proper approval and forward it to the Human Resources Department. If possible, the form should be submitted 30 calendar days in advance of the effective date of the leave. All requests for family and medical leave of absence due to illness will include the following sufficient medical certification attached to a completed Request for Family and Medical Leave of Absence Form stating:

a. The date on which the serious health condition commenced

b. The probable duration of the condition

c. The appropriate medical facts within the knowledge of the health care provider regarding the condition.

In addition, for purposes of leave to care for a child, spouse, or parent, the certificate should give an estimate of the amount of time that the employee will need to provide such care. For purposes of leave for an employee's illness, the certificate must state that the employee is unable to perform the functions of his or her position. In the case of certification for intermittent leave or leave on a reduced leave schedule for planned medical treatment, the dates on which this treatment is expected to be given and the duration of this treatment must be stated.

§ 7.26   —Sample Forms

The following examples should be considered for use with family and medical leave requests.

FORM 7.26(1)
FAMILY AND MEDICAL LEAVE REQUEST FORM

Employee Name: _____   SS#: _____

I. INSTRUCTIONS

At least thirty (30) calendar days prior to beginning a leave, eligible employees must complete this Family and Medical Leave Request Form and submit it to their immediate supervisor unless the event is unforeseeable and/or when leave is solely due to a serious medical condition of the employee. The immediate supervisor should verify information on this form (i.e. normal work schedule, paid time off available, etc.), date and sign the form, and submit it to the Human Resources Department. If leave is for a serious medical condition of the employee or a family member, or if "YES" is checked for a Short-Term Disability, please have the attached Certification of Physician or Practitioner completed and returned to the Human Resources Department.

II. NOTICE

You have requested a leave of absence under the Company's Family and Medical Leave Policy. This notice is provided to you in accordance with federal regulations and is intended to explain your rights and obligations under our Family and Medical Leave Policy. If you have any questions after reviewing this notice, you should review your copy of the Company's Family and Medical Leave Policy or contact the Human Resources Department.

1. The leave you have requested will _____ will not _____ be counted against your annual family and medical leave entitlement.

2. All employees on family and medical leave shall be restored to the same or an equivalent job upon returning from leave.

3. You will be required to substitute accrued paid leave for family and medical leave.

4. If you fail to return to work upon completion of your family and medical leave, you will be liable for any health insurance premiums paid by the Company on your behalf during your leave.

5. If your leave is due to a serious personal health condition or is necessary to care for a family member with such a condition, you are required to submit a Medical Certification to the Human Resources Department prior to beginning your leave. Thirty (30) calendar day updates from your physician are also required. Failure to submit a Medical Certification form will result in a denial of leave.

6. Prior to returning to work, you will be required to submit a Fitness For Duty Certificate signed by your physician to the Human Resources Department. The Company reserves the right to obtain additional medical opinions regarding your fitness for duty at the completion of any medical leave.

III. EMPLOYEE INFORMATION

NAME: _____   DATE: _____

DEPARTMENT: _____   ( ) Regularly Scheduled
                                             Full-time

DATE OF HIRE: _____   ( ) Regularly Scheduled
                                             Part-time

NORMAL WORK SCHEDULE: _____ days per week

                       _____ hours per day

REASON FOR LEAVE:

( ) Birth or Adoption of Child

        Child's Date of Birth: _____

              or

        Date Adopted/Foster Child was placed in your care: _____

( ) Serious Medical Condition of Employee or Family Member

    Name of Family Member: _____

    Relationship of Employee: _____

( ) Other: (explain) _____

Leave will be taken as:

    ( )   Block of time

    ( )   Intermittent Leave

    ( )   Reduced Work Schedule

Available paid time off:

    Vacation Hours: _____

    Personal Leave Hours: _____

    Compensatory Time Hours: _____

    Sick Leave Hours: _____

    Sick Leave Res. Hrs.: _____

    Short-Term Disability: ( ) Yes   ( ) No

    Long-Term Disability: ( ) Yes   ( ) No

(Estimated Dates)

    Date leave to begin: _____

    Return to work date: _____

    Total length of leave: _____

IV. DISPOSITION

Your request for family and medical leave has been:

                                 Granted: ____ Denied: ____

    Inclusive Dates: _____ to _____

Reason:

_____

I have read and fully understand my rights and obligations under the Family and Medical Leave Act of 1993 as set forth on the required posting notice.

_____   _____

(Employee's Signature)   (Date)

_____   _____

(Human Resources Department   (Date)

_____   _____

(Immediate Supervisor's Signature)   (Date)

FORM 7.26(2)
U.S. DEPARTMENT OF LABOR
FORM WH-320
CERTIFICATION OF PHYSICIAN OR PRACTITIONER

Family and Medical Leave Act of 1993

1. Employee's Name: _____

2. Patient's name (if other than employee): _____

3. Diagnosis: _____

    _____

    _____

    _____

    _____

4. Date condition commenced: _____

    Probable duration of condition: _____

5. Regimen of treatment to be prescribed (Indicate number of visits, general nature and duration of treatment, including referral to other provider of health services. Include schedule of visits or treatment if it is medically necessary for the employee to be off work on an intermittent basis or to work less than the employee's schedule of hours per day or days per week.):

    (a) By physician or practitioner:

        _____

        _____

        _____

    (b) By another provider of health services, if referred by physician or practitioner:

        _____

        _____

        _____

If this certificate relates to care for the employee's seriously ill family member, skip items 7, 8 and 9 and proceed to items 10 through 14. Otherwise, continue below:

Check "Yes" or "No" in the boxes below, as appropriate:

    Yes   No

7. [ ] [ ]   Is inpatient hospitalization of the employee required?

8. [ ] [ ]   Is employee able to perform work of any kind? (If "No," skip Item 9).

9. [ ] [ ]   Is employee able to perform the functions of employee's position? (Answer after reviewing statement from employer of essential functions of employee's position; or, if none provided, after discussing with employee.)

For certification relating to care for the employee's seriously ill family member, complete items 10 through 14 below as they apply to the family member and proceed to item 15 on reverse side:

    Yes   No

10. [ ] [ ]   Is inpatient hospitalization of the family member (patient) required?

11. [ ] [ ]   Does (or will) the patient require assistance for basic medical, hygiene, nutritional needs, safety or transportation?

12. [ ] [ ]   After review of the employee's signed statement (*See* Item 14 below), is the employee's presence necessary or would it be beneficial for the care of the patient? (This may include psychological comfort.)

13.   Estimate the period of time care is needed or the employee's presence would be beneficial:

_____

_____

       Item 14 is to be completed by the employee needing family leave.

14.   When family leave is needed to care for a seriously ill family member, the employee shall state the care he or she will provide and an estimate of the time period during which this care will be provided, including a schedule if leave is to be taken intermittently or on a reduced work schedule:

_____

_____

_____

15.   Signature of physician or practitioner:

_____

16.   Date: _____

17.   Type of Practice (field or specialization, if any): _____

Employee signature:

_____

Date: _____

(See definitions)

DEFINITIONS

"Serious health condition" means an illness, injury, impairment or physical or mental condition that involves:

—any period of incapacity or treatment connected with inpatient care (i.e., an overnight stay) in a hospital, hospice, or residential medical-care facility;

—any period of incapacity requiring absence of more than three (3) calendar days from work, school, or other regular daily activities that also involves continuing treatment by (or under the supervision of) a health care provider; or,

—continuing treatment by (or under the supervision of) a health care provider for a chronic or long-term health condition that is incurable or so serious that, if not treated, would likely result in a period of incapacity of more than three (3) calendar days, and for prenatal care.

"Health care provider" means:

—doctors of medicine or osteopathy authorized to practice medicine or surgery by the state in which the doctor practices; or

—podiatrists, dentists, clinical psychologists, optometrists, and chiropractors (limited to manual manipulation of the spine to correct a subluxation as demonstrated by x-ray to exist) authorized to practice, and performing within the scope of their practice, under state law; or

—nurse practitioners and nurse-midwives authorized to practice, and perform within the scope of their practice, as defined under state law; or,

—Christian Science practitioners listed with the First Church of Christ, Scientist in Boston, Massachusetts. [Where an employee or family member is receiving treatment from a Christian Science practitioner, an employee may not object to any requirement from an employer that the employee or family member submit to examination (not treatment) to obtain a second or third certification from a health care provider other than a Christian Science practitioner.]

CHAPTER 8

EMPLOYEE DATA VERIFICATION POLICIES

235

§ 8.1   Introduction

Employment policies may address other matters that do not involve introductory,[1] compensation,[2] benefit,[3] leave of absence,[4] or discipline, performance, layoff and dispute resolution[5] matters. These policies may fit into a variety of categories, including employee data verification,[6] records,[7] medical concerns,[8] information, collection and distribution,[9] workplace concerns,[10] and concerns outside the workplace.[11] The use of these policies should be reviewed by each employer based upon their need for addressing this subject matter. Among these other policies are credit checks,[12] arrest records,[13] criminal convictions,[14] fingerprints,[15]

---

[1] See ch. 4.

[2] See ch. 5.

[3] See ch. 6.

[4] See ch. 7.

[5] See **§ 8.13.**

[6] See ch. 9.

[7] See ch. 9.

[8] See ch. 10.

[9] See ch. 11.

[10] See ch. 12.

[11] See ch. 13.

[12] See **§§ 8.3–8.6.**

[13] See **§§ 8.7–8.9.**

[14] See **§§ 8.10–8.12.**

[15] See **§§ 8.13–8.15.**

photographs,[16] immigration,[17] reference checks,[18] skill testing,[19] employment records,[20] medical records,[21] physical examinations,[22] smoking,[23] employee assistance programs,[24] alcohol and drugs,[25] acquired immune deficiency syndrome,[26] safety,[27] searches,[28] monitoring,[29] surveillance,[30] polygraphs,[31] literature solicitation and distribution,[32] whistleblowing,[33] dress and grooming,[34] spouses,[35] nepotism,[36] third party representation,[37] religious accommodation,[38] privacy misconduct,[39] sexual harassment,[40] video display monitoring,[41] outside employment,[42] loyalty,[43] conflicts of interest,[44] off-duty non-criminal misconduct,[45] off-duty criminal misconduct,[46] and residency.[47]

---

[16] See §§ **8.16–8.19.**

[17] See §§ **8.20–8.25.**

[18] See §§ **8.26–8.33.**

[19] See §§ **8.34–8.38.**

[20] See ch. 9.

[21] See ch. 9.

[22] See ch. 10.

[23] See ch. 10.

[24] See ch. 10.

[25] See ch. 10.

[26] See ch. 10.

[27] See ch. 11.

[28] See ch. 11.

[29] See ch. 11.

[30] See ch. 11.

[31] See ch. 11.

[32] See ch. 11.

[33] See ch. 12.

[34] See ch. 12.

[35] See ch. 12.

[36] See ch. 12.

[37] See ch. 12.

[38] See ch. 12.

[39] See ch. 12.

[40] See ch. 12.

[41] See ch. 12.

[42] See ch. 13.

[43] See ch. 13.

[44] See ch. 13.

[45] See ch. 13.

[46] See ch. 13.

[47] See ch. 13.

§ 8.2   Introduction to Employee Data Verification

After an application is submitted, employers use various procedures to verify employee information. Data verification may occur with or without the individual's consent or knowledge.

Verification is the selection method that checks applicant information accuracy.[48] Almost every qualification an applicant offers for employment consideration can be verified. Verification sources include previous employers, schools, colleges, military records, certifying or licensing bodies, public records, and so forth. Public records include those from courts, law enforcement agencies, licensing bureaus, tax assessors, and financial departments.

Some verification sources are more accurate than others. Verifying a college degree can be accomplished by contacting the college registrar, while a driver's license can be checked with the state driver's license department. However, it is sometimes more difficult to obtain accurate information from previous employers. Employers may be more cooperative when the information request is accompanied by an applicant-signed release.[49]

Information accuracy can be substantially increased by informing applicants that the information they furnish will have a direct bearing upon their hiring.[50] Also, applicants should be instructed that the information they furnish will be carefully verified. These procedures greatly decrease the inconsistency between information furnished by applicants and that obtained through verification.

Some companies provide employers with services that include verifying job experience, work performance, attendance, training, education, criminal convictions, motor vehicle driving records, military records, and so forth.[51] These companies also conduct applicant background searches and provide comprehensive reports by reviewing workers' compensation claims, credit bureau records, bankruptcy filings, and interviews with coworkers and neighbors to determine an applicant's reputation regarding honesty, alcohol, drug abuse, and so forth.

Verification information may be irrelevant and not job-related. To safeguard employee interests and minimize employer litigation exposure, procedures and policies must be developed to counteract these problems. This section reviews policies relevant to employment data verification that are inherent in credit

---

[48] *See generally* D. Myers, Human Resources Management: Principles and Practice (2d ed. 1992) [hereinafter Myers, Human Resources].

[49] See ch. 4.

[50] Myers at 267.

[51] *Id.* at 268.

checks,[52] arrest records,[53] criminal convictions,[54] fingerprints,[55] photographs,[56] immigration requirements,[57] reference checks,[58] and skill testing.[59]

§ 8.3 Credit Checks

Credit information collection, maintenance, use, and disclosure present significant employee concerns by potentially revealing non-job-related data. This information may be used by employers in evaluating applicants and/or employees for hiring, promotion, reassignment, or retention. Sometimes credit information is obtained for non-job-related purposes. Personal finances are generally not relevant to the job applied for or held.

Federal[60] and state[61] statutes place certain restrictions on credit information used for employment purposes. Non-job-related credit reports may violate federal[62] and state[63] FEP statutes. A requirement that applicants and employees have a good credit record may have to be justified by a legitimate job-related business necessity.[64]

§ 8.4 —Drafting

In drafting credit check policies, the following should be considered:

---

[52] See §§ **8.3–8.6.**

[53] See §§ **8.7–8.9.**

[54] See §§ **8.10–8.12.**

[55] See §§ **8.13–8.15.**

[56] See §§ **8.16–8.19.**

[57] See §§ **8.20–8.25.**

[58] See §§ **8.26–8.33.**

[59] See §§ **8.34–8.38.**

[60] *See, e.g.,* 15 U.S.C. §§ 1681–1681(t) (1988) (Fair Credit Reporting Act); *see also* K. Decker, Employee Privacy Law and Practice §§ 2.5, 6.7 (John Wiley and Sons, Inc. 1987) [hereinafter Decker, Privacy Law].

[61] *See, e.g.,* Cal. Civ. Code §§ 1785.1–1786.56 (West 1985) (California Fair Credit Reporting Act); *see also* Decker, Privacy Law §§ 2.23, 6.7.

[62] *See, e.g.,* 42 U.S.C. §§ 2000e-1 to 2002-17 (1988) (Civil Rights Act of 1964); *see also* Decker § 2.8.

[63] *See, e.g.,* Pa. Stat. Ann. tit. 43, §§ 951–963 (Purdon 1991) (Pennsylvania Human Relations Act); *see also* Decker, Privacy Law § 2.25.

[64] *See* United States v. Chicago, 549 F.2d 415 (7th Cir. 1977) (credit check for police officer not job-related); *see also* Decker, Privacy Law § 6.7.

1. Review applicable federal[65] and state[66] statutes
2. Select a reputable credit agency and periodically review the choice
3. Notify the applicant and/or employee that a credit check will be performed and indicate:
   a. The types of information expected to be collected that are not collected on the application, and, as to information regarding character, general reputation, and mode of living, each area of inquiry
   b. The techniques that may be used to collect the information
   c. The sources that are expected to provide the information
   d. The parties to whom and circumstances under which information about the individual may be disclosed without authorization and the information that may be disclosed
   e. The statutory procedure by which the individual may gain access to any resulting record
   f. The procedures the individual may use to correct, amend, or dispute any collected record
   g. That information in any report prepared by a consumer reporting agency may be retained by that organization and subsequently disclosed by it to others
4. Obtain the applicant's and/or employee's written consent for undertaking a credit check
5. Not share the information received regarding an applicant and/or employee with potential creditors
6. Limit credit checks to job-related information and purposes
7. Consider credit information highly confidential and sensitive
8. Certify that credit information will only be used for job-related purposes[67]

§ 8.5 —Sample Policies

The following should be considered in drafting credit check policies:

POLICY 8.5(1)
CREDIT CHECK POLICY

Section 1. Definitions.   For the purposes of this policy, the following terms shall mean:

---

[65] *See, e.g.,* 15 U.S.C. §§ 1681–1681(t) (1988) (Fair Credit Reporting Act).

[66] *See, e.g.,* Cal. Civ. Code §§ 1785.1–1786.56 (West 1985) (California Fair Credit Reporting Act).

[67] *See* Privacy Protection Study Commission, Personal Privacy In An Informational Society 250–51 (1977) [hereinafter Privacy Protection Study Commission, Report].

a. *Consumer report.*   Any report containing information relating to an individual's credit record or manner of obtaining credit directly from a creditor of the individual or from a consumer reporting agency; and also shall include information pertaining to an individual's character, general reputation, personal characteristics, or mode of living obtained through personal interviews with neighbors, friends, or associates of the individual reported on, or others with whom he or she is acquainted or may have knowledge concerning any of these information items.

b. *Consumer reporting agency.*   Any person who, for monetary fees or dues, regularly engages in assembling or evaluating employment information to be used regarding individuals.

c. *Employment purposes.*   A report used by the Company for evaluating an individual for employment, promotion, reassignment, retention, and so forth.

d. *Individual.*   A person who has applied for employment or who is currently employed by the Company.

Section 2. Procurement.   The Company shall request a consumer report only for legitimate employment purposes, which must be job-related.

Section 3. Written Permission.   The Company shall procure a consumer report only after written permission from the individual has been received.

Section 4. Information Inspection.   The Company shall, upon request and proper identification of any individual, allow the inspection of any and all consumer reports maintained regarding that individual.

Section 5. Confidentiality.   The Company shall maintain all consumer report information in strict confidence and shall not disclose it absent the individual's written permission.

§ 8.6   —Credit Check Consent Form

The following should be used to safeguard the employer's interest in requesting credit-related information from an applicant or employee:

FORM 8.6(1)
CREDIT CHECK CONSENT FORM

Based on the requirements of the job for which I am applying, I authorize __(Company's Name)__ to conduct a job-related credit check.

_____   _____
Date   Applicant/Employee's Name

§ 8.7   Arrest Records

Many employers believe that arrest history is critical, or at least relevant, to employment.[68] Arrest information raises employee privacy concerns because it indicates only that a law enforcement agency believed that probable cause to arrest existed for some offense. It does not reflect guilt, nor that the person actually committed the offense.

Refusing employment or terminating employees because of arrest records is not permitted absent evidence that it is job-related to the employer's business.[69] Even when a legitimate pre-employment inquiry is made regarding arrest records, an applicant's rejection based solely on an arrest record may violate federal[70] and state[71] FEP statutes.

§ 8.8   —Drafting

In drafting arrest record policies, the following should be considered:

1. Applicable federal[72] and state[73] statutes
2. That a differentiation be made between arrest and conviction
3. That a careful evaluation be made of the frequency and severity of arrests
4. Age at time of the arrest
5. The elapsed time since an arrest
6. The whole individual: i.e., his or her aptitudes, abilities, interests, and educational level, rather than one aspect of personal history
7. The job's nature and its relation to the employability of those with arrest records
8. Geographic location of the incidents involved

---

[68] *See* Decker, Privacy Law § 6.8.

[69] *See* Gregory v. Litton Sys., Inc., 316 F. Supp. 401 (C.D. Cal. 1970), *aff'd with modifications not here relevant,* 472 F.2d 631 (9th Cir. 1972) (arrest record inquiries prohibited); *see also* Decker, Privacy Law §§ 2.32, 6.8.

[70] *See, e.g.,* 42 U.S.C. §§ 2000e-1 to 2002-17 (1988) (Civil Rights Act of 1964); *see also* Decker, Privacy Law §§ 2.8, 2.32, 6.8.

[71] *See, e.g.,* Pa. Stat. Ann. tit. 43, §§ 951–963 (Purdon 1991) (Pennsylvania Human Relations Act); *see also* Decker, Privacy Law §§ 2.25, 2.32, 6.8.

[72] *See, e.g.,* 42 U.S.C. §§ 2000e-1 to 2002-2017 (1988) (Civil Rights Act of 1964).

[73] *See, e.g.,* Pa. Stat. Ann. tit. 43, §§ 951–963 (Purdon 1991) (Pennsylvania Human Relations Act).

§ 8.9   —Sample Policies

The following example should be considered in drafting arrest record policies:

POLICY 8.9(1)
ARREST RECORD POLICY

Section 1. Conviction.   A "conviction" shall include a plea, verdict, or finding of guilt, regardless of whether sentence is imposed by a court.

Section 2. Collection.   The Company shall not ask an applicant or employee to disclose, through any written form or verbally, information concerning an arrest or detention that did not result in conviction or information concerning a referral to and participation in any pretrial or posttrial diversion program.

Section 3. Use.   The Company shall not seek from any source or utilize as a factor in determining any employment condition including hiring, promotion, termination, apprenticeship, or any other training program leading to employment, any record of arrest or detention that did not result in conviction or any record regarding a referral to and participation in any pretrial or posttrial diversion program.

Section 4. Exception.   The Company may ask an applicant or employee about an arrest for which the applicant or employee is out on bail or on his or her own recognizance pending trial.

§ 8.10   Criminal Convictions

Criminal convictions present different employee concerns than do arrests.[74] A conviction is a societal judgment regarding an individual's actions. Unlike arrests, a conviction record is complete. Guilt and accountability have been finalized.

Employees tend to be uneasy about conviction information collection, maintenance, use, and disclosure. Even though an employer may take legitimate employment actions based on criminal convictions when it correlates the offense's nature, gravity, and time elapsed since the conviction to job-relatedness, concerns remain over subsequent use and disclosure.[75] Conviction record use may violate federal[76] and state[77] FEP statutes.

---

[74] See §§ **8.3–8.6.** *See also* Decker, Privacy Law § 6.9.

[75] *See, e.g.*, Richardson v. Hotel Corp. of Am., 332 F. Supp. 519 (E.D. La. 1971), *aff'd mem.*, 468 F.2d 951 (5th Cir. 1972) (legitimate employee termination for conviction); *see also* Decker, Privacy Law § 6.9.

[76] *See, e.g.*, 42 U.S.C. §§ 2000e-1 to 2002-17 (1988) (Civil Rights Act of 1964); *see also* Decker, Privacy Law §§ 2.8, 2.32, 6.8.

[77] *See, e.g.*, Pa. Stat. Ann. tit. 43, §§ 951–963 (Purdon 1991) (Pennsylvania Human Relations Act); *see also* Decker, Privacy §§ 2.25, 2.32, 6.9.

§ 8.11 —Drafting

In drafting criminal conviction policies, the following should be considered:

1. Applicable federal[78] and state[79] statutes
2. The job and its responsibilities
3. The time, nature, and number of convictions
4. Each conviction's facts
5. Each conviction's job-relatedness
6. The length of time between a conviction and the employment decision
7. Employment history before and after the conviction
8. Rehabilitation efforts
9. Whether the particular conviction would prevent job performance in an acceptable businesslike manner
10. Age at the time of the conviction
11. The conviction's geographic location

§ 8.12 —Sample Policies

The following example should be considered in drafting criminal conviction policies:

POLICY 8.12(1)
CRIMINAL CONVICTION POLICY

Section 1. Conviction.   A "conviction" shall include a plea, verdict, or finding of guilt, regardless of whether sentence is imposed by a court.

Section 2. Conviction's Use.   The Company may consider any conviction as a possible justification for the refusal, suspension, revocation, or termination of employment when it directly relates:

a. To the applicant's possible performance in the job applied for; or

b. To the employee's possible performance in the job which the employee holds.

Section 3. Conviction's Job-Relatedness.   In determining whether a conviction is job-related, the Company will consider, among other things:

---

[78] *See, e.g.,* 42 U.S.C. §§ 2000e-1 to 2002-2017 (1988) (Civil Rights Act of 1964).

[79] *See, e.g.,* Pa. Stat. Ann. tit. 43, §§ 951–963 (Purdon 1991) (Pennsylvania Human Relations Act).

a. The job and its responsibilities;

b. The time, nature, and number of convictions;

c. Each conviction's facts;

d. Each conviction's job-relatedness;

e. The length of time between a conviction and the employment decision;

f. Employment history before and after the conviction;

g. Rehabilitation efforts;

h. Whether the particular conviction would prevent job performance in an acceptable businesslike manner;

i. Age at the time of the conviction; and

j. The conviction's geographic location.

Section 4. Excluded Convictions.   The Company will not consider:

a. Convictions which have been annulled or expunged;

b. Convictions of a penal offense for which no jail sentence may be imposed; or

c. Conviction of a misdemeanor in which the period of twenty years has elapsed since the conviction's date and during which there has been no subsequent arrest or conviction.

§ 8.13   Fingerprints

Fingerprinting has generally been considered a valid employer collection method related more to verifying information than to compulsory incriminating fact extraction.[80] Despite its primary use in verifying information, some states regulate fingerprinting to limit employer abuses.[81] Statutes may prohibit an employer from requiring that an applicant or employee be fingerprinted for the purpose of furnishing information to a third party, as a condition precedent to securing or retaining employment, where this information could be used to the applicant's or employee's detriment.[82]

---

[80] *See* Decker, Privacy Law § 6.10.

[81] *See, e.g.,* Cal. Labor Code § 1051 (West 1971) (California's statute regulating fingerprinting); *see also* Decker, Privacy Law §§ 2.33, 6.10.

[82] *See, e.g.,* Cal. Labor Code § 1051 (West 1971) (California's statute regulating fingerprinting); *see also* Decker, Privacy Law §§ 2.33, 6.10.

§ 8.14 —Drafting

In drafting fingerprint policies, the following should be considered:

1. Review applicable statutes[83]
2. To verify employee identity, where this is in doubt, or for receipt of an employee benefit
3. Verify identity for meeting immigration requirements

§ 8.15 —Sample Policies

The following example should be considered in drafting fingerprint policies:

POLICY 8.15(1)
FINGERPRINT POLICY

The Company shall not require, as a condition to securing or retaining employment, that an applicant or employee be fingerprinted where fingerprints could be used to the applicant's or employee's detriment in a non-job-related situation.

§ 8.16 Photographs

Photographing employees during the initial hiring process raises objections, in that race, color, national origin, sex, age, and disability may be unnecessarily revealed for non-job-related use.[84] These employee interests have been protected primarily under federal[85] and state[86] FEP statutes. However, employers have been permitted to photograph employees at the workplace when a legitimate job-related business purpose existed.[87] Legitimate employee photographing may be used to improve safety, for example, or to identify employees who are violating employer rules.

---

[83] *Id.*

[84] *See* Decker § 6.11.

[85] *See, e.g.,* 42 U.S.C. §§ 2000e-1 to 2002-17 (1988) (Civil Rights Act of 1964); *see also* Decker, Privacy Law §§ 2.7–2.12, 6.11.

[86] *See, e.g.,* Pa. Stat. Ann. tit. 43, §§ 951–963 (Purdon 1991) (Pennsylvania Human Relations Act); *see also* Decker, Privacy Law §§ 2.25, 6.11.

[87] *See, e.g.,* Thomas v. General Elec. Co., 207 F. Supp. 792 (W.D. Ky. 1962) (permissible to take motion pictures to study plant layout and evaluate employee jobs); *see also* Decker, Privacy Law §§ 6.11, 7.14, 7.19.

§ 8.17   —Drafting

In drafting photograph policies, the following should be considered:

1.   Review applicable federal[88] and state[89] statutes
2.   Not require photographs on applications or at interviews
3.   Use photographs only for legitimate business purposes; i.e., for job performance monitoring
4.   Obtain employee consent when photographs are used in employer literature or advertisements

§ 8.18   —Sample Policies

The following example should be considered in drafting photograph policies:

POLICY 8.18(1)
PHOTOGRAPH POLICY

The Company shall not require, as a condition to securing or retaining employment, that an applicant or employee be photographed where photographs could be used to the applicant's or employee's detriment in a non-job-related manner.

§ 8.19   —Photograph Consent Form

A consent to use employee photographs should be executed at hiring, and may take the following form:

FORM 8.19(1)
PHOTOGRAPH CONSENT

The Company may use my name, picture, or likeness for any advertising, publicity, or other legitimate business purpose, regardless of whether I am employed by the Company when the name, picture, or likeness is used. This consent is given in consideration of my employment. The legitimate use of my name, picture, or likeness will not result in an invasion of privacy, defamation, intentional infliction of emotional distress, or a violation of any other property right that I may have. I understand that I will receive no additional consideration, compensation, or benefit if my name, picture, or likeness is used. Any negatives, prints, or other material for printing or

---

[88] *See, e.g.,* 42 U.S.C. §§ 2000e-1 to 2002-2017 (1988) (Civil Rights Act of 1964).

[89] *See, e.g.,* Pa. Stat. Ann. tit. 43, §§ 951–963 (Purdon 1991) (Pennsylvania Human Relations Act).

reproduction in connection with the use of my name, picture, or likeness will be the Company's property.

_____   _____
Date   Employee

_____
Witness

§ 8.20 Immigration

The Immigration Reform and Control Act of 1986 (IRCA)[90] creates an additional recordkeeping requirement for employers in an attempt to curtail illegal immigration into the United States. It requires every employer to ask applicants for specific written verification establishing that they can be employed. Civil and criminal penalties may be imposed on employers who knowingly hire or recruit an alien.

IRCA prohibits employers from discriminating against applicants based on their national origin. It is an unfair immigration-related employment practice to discriminate against any individual in hiring, recruitment, or termination because of that individual's national origin or citizenship status.

The potential for employer problems exists in the collection of age, national origin, or other potentially discriminatory data required by IRCA. To minimize employer intrusions by not obtaining sensitive applicant data, the required IRCA information should not be collected until the applicant pool has been sufficiently narrowed prior to hiring. Once collected, it should be maintained separate from the employee's personnel file, to prevent disclosures that could have a discriminatory impact. This will minimize employee challenges arising out of federal[91] or state[92] FEP statutes.

---

[90] Immigration Reform and Control Act of 1986, Pub. L. No. 99-603, 100 Stat. 3359 (codified in scattered sections of 7 U.S.C. § 2025; 8 U.S.C. §§ 1101, 1152–53, 1160–61, 1184, 1186–87, 1252, 1254–55a, 1258–59, 1321, 1324–24b, 1357, 1364–65; 18 U.S.C. § 1546; 20 U.S.C. §§ 1091, 1096; 29 U.S.C. §§ 1802, 1813, 1816, 1851; 42 U.S.C. §§ 303, 502, 602–03, 672–73, 1203, 1320b–7, 1353, 1396b, 1436a, 1437r); _see also_ Decker, Privacy Law §§ 2.20, 6.12.

[91] _See, e.g.,_ 42 U.S.C. §§ 2000e-1 to 2002-17 (1988) (Civil Rights Act of 1964); _see also_ Decker, Privacy Law §§ 2.7–2.12.

[92] _See, e.g.,_ Pa. Stat. Ann. tit. 43, §§ 951–963 (Purdon 1991) (Pennsylvania Human Relations Act); _see also_ Decker, Privacy Law § 2.25.

§ 8.21   —Guidelines for Completing the Employment Eligibility Verification Form (Form I-9)

The following are guidelines for completing Form I-9[93] (Employment Eligibility Verification Form).

Verifying Employment Eligibility.   The Immigration Reform and Control Act of 1986 (IRCA) requires employers to hire only citizens and aliens who are authorized to work in the United States. The Employment Eligibility Verification Form (Form I-9) has been developed for verifying that persons are eligible to work.[94] IRCA requires an employer to:

1. Have all employees complete Form I-9 when they begin working
2. Check documents establishing employee identity and eligibility to work
3. Properly complete Form I-9
4. Retain Form I-9 for at least three years
5. Retain Form I-9 until one year after the person leaves employment, if the person is employed for more than three years
6. Present Form I-9 for inspection to an Immigration and Naturalization Service (INS) or Department of Labor (DOL) officer upon request

Unlawful Discrimination.   If the employer has four or more employees, the employer may not discriminate against any individual other than an unauthorized alien in hiring, terminating, recruiting, or referring for a fee because of that individual's national origin or, in the case of a citizen or intending citizen, because of his or her citizenship status.

The Civil Rights Act of 1964 (Title VII) and the remedies against discrimination it provides are applicable. Title VII prohibits discrimination against any individual on the basis of national origin in hiring, termination, assignment, compensation, and other employment terms and conditions. National origin discrimination claims against employers with 15 or more employees should be filed with the Equal Employment Opportunity Commission (EEOC).

Under IRCA, national origin discrimination charges against employers with four through fourteen employees, and citizenship discrimination charges against employers with four or more employees, should be filed with the Office of Special Counsel in the Department of Justice. Discrimination charges may be filed either by the person who believes that he or she was discriminated against in employment on the basis of national origin or citizenship status, by a person on their

---

[93] Adapted from the Handbook for Employers, Immigration and Naturalization Service (June 1987).

[94] See § **8.25.**

behalf, or by INS officers who have reason to believe that discrimination has occurred. Discrimination charges must be filed within 180 days of the discriminatory act. The Office of Special Counsel will notify the employer by certified mail within 10 days upon receipt of a discrimination charge. After investigating the charge, the Special Counsel may file a complaint with an administrative law judge. If the Special Counsel does not file a complaint within 120 days of receiving the charge, the person making the charge (other than an INS officer) may initiate the filing of a complaint with an administrative law judge. The administrative law judge will conduct a hearing and issue a decision.

Employers found to have engaged in discriminatory practices will be ordered to cease the prohibited practices. They may also be ordered to:

1. Hire, with or without back pay, individuals directly injured by the discrimination

2. Pay a fine of up to $1,000 for each individual discriminated against, or up to $2,000 for each individual in cases of employers previously fined

3. Keep certain records regarding applicant and employee hiring

Should a court decide that the losing party's claim has no reasonable basis in fact or law, the court may award attorneys' fees to prevailing parties other than the United States.

Penalties for Prohibited Practices. If an investigation reveals that an employer has violated IRCA regarding employees hired after November 6, 1986, INS may take action. Violations of IRCA include civil penalties for:

1. *Hiring or continuing to employ unauthorized employees.* Employers determined to have knowingly hired unauthorized employees or to be continuing to employ persons knowing that they are or have become unauthorized may be fined as follows:

    a. First violation of not less than $250 and not more than $2,000 for each unauthorized employee

    b. Second violation of not less than $2,000 and not more than $5,000 for each unauthorized employee

    c. Subsequent violations of not less than $3,000 and not more than $10,000 for each unauthorized employee

2. *Failing to comply with recordkeeping requirements.* Employers who fail properly to complete, retain, and present for inspection the Form I-9 as required by law may be fined as follows:

    a. Civil fines of not less than $100 and no more than $1,000 for each employee for whom the form was not completed, retained, or presented

   b. In determining penalties, consideration shall be given to the business's size, good faith efforts to comply, the seriousness of the violation, and whether the violation involved unauthorized employees

3. *Requiring indemnification.* Employers found to have required a bond or indemnity from an individual against liability may be fined $1,000 and ordered to make restitution, either to the person who was required to pay the indemnity, or, if that person cannot be located, to the United States Treasury

4. *Recruiting unauthorized seasonal agricultural workers outside the United States.* Employers who knowingly recruit unauthorized workers outside the United States to perform seasonal agricultural labor may face the same penalties as for hiring unauthorized workers, unless the workers recruited have been granted Special Agricultural Worker (SAW) status

Criminal penalties for violation of IRCA include:

1. *Engaging in a pattern or practice of knowingly hiring or continuing to employ unauthorized employees.* Employers convicted for having engaged in a pattern or practice of knowingly hiring unauthorized aliens after November 6, 1986, may be fined as follows:

   a. Fines of up to $3,000 per employee and/or six months imprisonment

   b. The same penalties apply to engaging in a pattern or practice of recruiting unauthorized seasonal agricultural workers outside the United States

   c. Criminal sanctions will be reserved for serious or repeated violations

2. *Engaging in fraud, false statements, or otherwise misusing visas, immigration permits, and identity documents.* Persons who use fraudulent identification or employment eligibility documents or documents that were lawfully issued to another, or who make a false statement or attestation for purposes of satisfying the employment eligibility requirements may be imprisoned for up to five years, or fined, or both

Persons for Whom Form I-9 Must Be Completed.

1. For persons hired after May 31, 1987, a Form I-9 must be completed:

   a. Within three business days of the date of the hire

   b. If the person is employed for less than three days, the employer must complete Form I-9 before the end of the employee's first working day

2. Employers need not complete Form I-9 for:

   a. Persons hired before November 7, 1986

   b. Persons hired after November 6, 1986, who left employment before June 1, 1987

    c.   Persons employed for domestic work in a private home on an intermittent or sporadic basis

    d.   Persons who provide labor and are employed by a contractor providing contract services such as employee leasing

    e.   Persons who are independent contractors

How to Complete Form I-9.   Form I-9 contains two sections. The employee completes the first section containing Steps 1, 2, and 3. If a preparer or translator assists the employee, the preparer or translator completes Step 4. The second section, containing Steps 5 and 6, should be completed by the employer.

When completing Form I-9, the employee will need to provide a document or documents that establish identity and employment eligibility. Some documents establish both identity and employment eligibility. These documents appear in List A on the bottom half of the Form I-9. Other documents establish identity alone (List B) or employment eligibility alone (List C). If the person does not provide a document from List A, he or she must produce one from List B and one from List C.

The employer should review the document or documents provided by the person. Documents should appear to be genuine and relate to the individual.

If employees cannot complete Section 1 by themselves or need the form translated, someone may assist them. The preparer or translator should read the form to the employee, help with Step 1 and Step 2 as needed, have the employee sign or mark the form, and follow Step 4.

If a minor under age 16 cannot produce a List A document or one of the identity documents on List B, he or she is exempt from producing one if:

    1.   A parent or legal guardian completes Section 1 and writes in the space for the minor's signature the words, "minor under age 16"

    2.   The parent or legal guardian completes the "Preparer/Translator Certification"

    3.   The employer writes in Section 2 the words, "minor under age 16" under List B in the space after the words, "Document Identification #"

If this procedure is followed, the minor must still procure a List C document showing employment eligibility.

Instructions for Recruiters and Referrers for a Fee.   IRCA's provisions also apply to those who recruit persons and refer them to potential employers in return for a fee, and to those who refer or provide documents or information about persons to employers in return for a fee. The provisions do not apply to persons who recruit for their own company or business. Union hiring halls that refer union members or nonunion individuals who pay membership dues are not considered to be recruiters or referrers for a fee.

Starting June 1, 1987, they should complete Form I-9 when a person they refer to an employer is hired by that employer. The form should be completed within three business days of the hire.

Recruiters and referrers may designate agents to complete the verification procedures on their behalf, including national associations or employers. If the employer who hires the referred individual is designated as the agent, the employer need only provide the recruiter or referrer with a Form I-9 photocopy. Recruiters or referrers who designate someone to complete the verification procedures on their behalf are still responsible for compliance with IRCA, and may be found liable for violations.

Recruiters and referrers must retain the Form I-9 for three years after the date the referred individual was hired by the employer. They must also present forms for inspection to an INS or DOL officer after three days' advance notice. The penalties also apply to recruiting and referring unauthorized employees for a fee which occurs on or after June 1, 1987.

Applicable Documents for Verifying Employment Eligibility.   Certain documents have been designated for determining IRCA employment eligibility. (The employee must provide a document or documents that establish identity and employment eligibility.)

Some documents establish both identity and employment eligibility. These are listed on the Form I-9 under List A, "Documents That Establish Identity and Employment Eligibility." If a person does not provide a document from List A, he or she must provide one document that establishes identity and one document that establishes employment eligibility.

To establish identity, the person must provide a document in List B. To establish employment eligibility, one of the immigration documents in List C must be furnished.

If an employee is unable to provide the required document or documents within three days, he or she must at least produce, within three days, a receipt showing that he or she has applied for the document. The employee must produce the document itself within 21 days of hiring.

LIST A

Documents That Establish Identity and Employment Eligibility

1.   United States Passport
2.   Certificate of United States Citizenship (INS Form N-560 or N-561)
3.   Certificate of Naturalization (INS Form N-550 or N-570)
4.   Unexpired foreign passport which:

  a. Contains an unexpired stamp reading "Processed for I-551. Temporary Evidence of Lawful Admission for permanent residence. Valid until _____. Employment authorized"; or

  b. Has attached thereto a Form I-94 bearing the same name as the passport and containing an employment authorization stamp, so long as the period of endorsement has not yet expired and the proposed employment is not in conflict with any restrictions or limitations identified on the Form I-94

5. Alien Registration Receipt Card (INS Form I-151) or Resident Alien Card (INS Form I-551), provided that it contains a photograph of the bearer

6. Temporary Resident Card (INS Form I-688)

7. Employment Authorization Card (INS Form I-688A)

LIST B

Documents That Establish Identity

For individuals 16 years of age or older:

1. State-issued driver's license or state-issued identification card containing a photograph or, if the driver's license or identification card does not contain a photograph, identifying information should be included listing name, date of birth, sex, height, color of eyes, and address

2. School identification card with a photograph

3. Voter's registration card

4. United States military card or draft record

5. Identification card issued by federal, state, or local government agencies

6. Military dependent's identification card

7. Native American tribal documents

8. United States Coast Guard Merchant Mariner Card

9. Driver's license issued by a Canadian government authority

For individuals under age 16 who are unable to produce one of the documents listed above:

1. School record or report card

2. Clinic doctor or hospital record

3. Daycare or nursery school record

LIST C

Documents That Establish Employment Eligibility

1. Social Security number card, other than one which has printed on its face "not valid for employment purposes," that must be a card issued by the Social Security Administration; a facsimile such as a metal or plastic reproduction that people can purchase is not acceptable

2. An original or certified copy of a birth certificate issued by a state, county, or municipal authority bearing an official seal

3. Unexpired INS employment authorization

4. Unexpired reentry permit (INS Form I-327)

5. Unexpired Refugee Travel Document (INS Form I-571)

6. Certification of Birth issued by the Department of State (Form FS-545)

7. Certification of Birth Abroad issued by the Department of State (Form DS-1350)

8. United States Citizen Identification Card (INS Form I-197)

9. Native American tribal document

10. Identification Card for use of Resident Citizen in the United States (INS Form I-179)

§ 8.22   —Temporary United States Visas Suitable for Employment

In administering requirements under the Immigration Reform and Control Act of 1986, the following should be considered regarding visas:[95]

1. B-1 (Business Visitor)
   a. Uses

   Permits entry by an alien:

   (i) To participate in commercial transactions, to negotiate contracts, to consult with business associates, to litigate, to participate in scientific, educational, professional or business conventions or conferences, or to undertake independent research

---

[95] Based upon and used with permission from Pivec, *The Immigration Reform and Control Act of 1986: Compliance Requirements for Public Employers,* 14 Current Mun. Probs. 160, Appendix A (1987), copyright 1987 by Mary E. Pivec.

(ii) Who is otherwise classifiable as an H-1, coming to perform services for which no salary will be paid by a United States source

(iii) Already employed abroad coming to undertake training in the United States who would otherwise be classifiable as an H-3 and who will continue to receive salary from the foreign employer alone

(iv) To furnish technical information and assistance under the Foreign Assistance Act

(v) Who is a personal or domestic servant of an employer in the United States who holds temporary status as a B, E, F, H, I, J, or L under certain specified circumstances

b. Duration of Stay

(i) Issued for one year or more depending upon governmental reciprocity, subject to unlimited revalidation

(ii) Permits United States entry for six months, stay subject to renewal in six-month increments through INS district office

c. Method of Procurement

Alien applies at a United States consular post abroad

d. Documentation

(i) Nonimmigrant visa application

(ii) Proof of foreign employer's sponsorship and/or reasonably permanent employment or business connections and/or family, social, cultural, or other associations abroad are sometimes required

e. Comments

(i) United States employer may pay living expenses for B-1 business visitor

(ii) Honorarium or other fees may also constitute allowable expenses

2. E-1/E-2 (Treaty Traders & Investors)

a. Uses

Entry by managers, executives, and specialized-knowledge employees pursuant to a treaty of trade or commerce between the United States and the same country of which the employer and the visa applicant are nationals

b. Duration of Stay

(i) Issued for four-year periods by United States consulate posts abroad, subject to unlimited revalidation so long as the visa holder remains in treaty employment in the United States

(ii) Issued by INS stateside for two-year periods in connection with a status change request

c.   Methods of Procurement

Alien either applies at a United States consular post abroad or, if already in the United States, at the INS district office with jurisdiction in the United States

d.   Documentation

Proof of the following is required:

(i)   That the alien will be employed as a manager, executive, or specialized-knowledge employee

(ii)   That his or her nationality is the same as that of the treaty employer

(iii)   That 51 percent of the trade of the United States treaty entity is with the treaty country

(iv)   That the treaty employer is owned or incorporated in the treaty country

(v)   That the United States entity is well established and is a growing concern

(vi)   In the case of treaty investment visas, that the United States investment is substantial and appropriate to the scope of the enterprise

e.   Comments

Spouses of treaty traders and investors are permitted to work but are not permitted to adjust to permanent resident status in the United States if such work was performed

3.   F-1 (Academic Students)

a.   Uses

F-1 visa holders or academic students may receive work permission from the INS for off-campus employment:

(i)   After completion of one full year of study in the United States, provided the student can demonstrate economic necessity due to unforeseen circumstances arising subsequent to entry or change to student status

(ii)   For practical training purposes in connection with completion of an academic program

b.   Duration of Stay

(i)   F-1 students may remain in the United States for the duration of their academic program and any approved period(s) of practical training, plus 60 days

(ii)   No more than 12 months of practical training may be approved, regardless of the number of academic programs engaged in

    c. Method of Procurement

        (i)   F-1 students must receive approval from the INS prior to engaging in off-campus employment which is other than practical training

        (ii)   F-1 students must apply for practical training approval, whether to be obtained during vacation periods, or following completion of studies, from the INS

    d. Documentation

    Proof that comparable training is unavailable in the student's home country, but that employment opportunities in the field are now or will be available at home upon training completion in the United States

    e. Comments

    Students should be cautioned against applying for practical training rather than an H-1 visa if qualified, since proposed INS regulations would prohibit a status change to H-1 if practical training has been used

4. H-1 (Temporary Workers of Distinguished Merit and Ability)

    a. Uses

    Employment in the United States by professionals or other persons of distinguished merit and ability

    b. Duration of Stay

        (i)   May be issued initially for three years

        (ii)   Renewable for additional two years, provided no change in circumstances occurs

        (iii) Approval of sixth year subject to extraordinary documentation requirements

        (iv) New petition will not be entertained until the alien has spent one year abroad

    c. Method of Procurement

        (i)   Employer files I-129B petition in duplicate with the INS regional adjudication center with jurisdiction over the place of employment

        (ii)   Alien obtains visa at designated United States consular post abroad or applies for a status change with the INS in the United States if maintaining status

    d. Documentation

        (i)   Employer must show that:

            a. The alien's position is professional in nature

            b. The alien possesses the requisite education and/or experience requirement

        c. The Alien's Intended stay is temporary in nature

        d. The H-1 classification is not being sought principally to enable the employee to enter the United States permanently in advance of the availability of a visa number

    (ii) The alien must show that:

        a. He or she has not abandoned his or her foreign residence

        b. He or she will return abroad before his or her authorized stay terminates

e. Comments

    (i) Recently proposed regulations, if adopted, may severely restrict the class of persons eligible for H-1 visas, particularly in the business and management areas

    (ii) Spouses of H-1 visa holders are classified as H-4's and are not permitted to work under that classification

5. J-1 (Exchange Visitors)

  a. Uses

  Persons in training for employment in United States companies or affiliates abroad

  b. Duration of Stay

    (i) Business and industrial trainees—18 months

    (ii) Teachers and instructors—two years

    (iii) Research scholars—three years

  c. Method of Procurement

    (i) The authorized employer or agency issues an eligibility certificate for exchange visitor status

    (ii) The alien is interviewed for eligibility at a United States consular post abroad

  d. Documentation

  The alien must show:

    (i) That the intended activities in the Untied States conform to the program description

    (ii) That the skills to be acquired in the United States will be useful in the home country

    (iii) That the alien will maintain a residence abroad, while residing in the United States, which he or she has no intention of abandoning

  e. Comments

    (i) In many cases, J visa holders cannot change status to the H or L category or adjust to permanent resident status

    (ii) In most cases, J visa holders must return to the home country for a period of two years at the expiration of their approved program; the INS does not view waivers of this requirement favorably

    (iii) Participation in more than one exchange visitor program requires special State Department approval

    (iv) Spouses of J-1 visa holders (J-2s) are permitted to work only upon a showing that it is necessary for the support of the spouse and children of the J-1

    (v) Exchange visitor program skills are limited by country according to United States Information Agency bulletin

6. L-1 (Intracompany Transferees)

  a. Uses

Employment in the United States by managers, executives, and specialized-knowledge personnel (professional and nonprofessional) employed abroad by the sponsor employer or an affiliate, for at least one year prior to application for intracompany transfer

  b. Duration of Stay

    (i) Issued initially for a period up to three years pursuant to an approved employer petition

    (ii) A two-year extension is available to accomplish the original purpose for admission

    (iii) Maximum approved stay—six years; sixth year subject to extraordinary documentation requirements

    (iv) If the United States employer is newly opened, the initial term is limited to one year; the petition will be reexamined thereafter to determine bona fides

  c. Method of Procurement

    (i) Employer files I-129B petition in duplicate with the INS regional adjudication center with jurisdiction over the place of employment

    (ii) Alien obtains visa at a designated United States consular post abroad, or applies for a status change through the INS

  d. Documentation

Employer must show:

    (i) That the alien's position is managerial or executive, or that it involves specialized knowledge

    (ii) That the alien was employed in the qualifying capacity for one year abroad prior to the petition (United States employment does not count)

(iii) That it is a parent, branch, affiliate, subsidiary, or joint venture partner of the transferring firm abroad

(iv) That it will continue to do business in at least one country abroad after the transfer; regular, systematic, and continuous provision of goods and/or services, not the mere presence of an agent or an office abroad

(v) If the alien is being transferred to a new United States office, lease or purchase agreement and proof of financial liability to pay the alien

(vi) If the alien is an owner or major shareholder, that there is an assignment abroad available posttransfer

(vii) That the L-1 is not being sought principally to enable the alien to enter the United States permanently in advance of the availability of a visa number

(viii) The alien may have to show prospects of work abroad post-temporary United States assignment; prior employment history in the United States and abroad will be relevant

e. Comments

(i) Blanket L-1 petitions are currently available where the employing entity has transferred five managers or executives into United States positions within the prior year

(ii) Highly advantageous status if the alien later seeks adjustment to permanent residence since the labor certification recruitment procedure can be waived for L-1 executives and managers

(iii) The spouse and children of an L-1 alien (classified as L-2) are not authorized to accept employment

§ 8.23 —Counterfeit Document Detection

In determining the legitimacy of documents presented for Immigration Reform and Control Act verification, employers should:

1. Be aware of the document's information

2. Determine whether the information pertains to the individual presenting the document: i.e., if the person appears to be 18 and the identification says 45, there is a problem; if a man presents an identification with a woman's picture, there is also a problem

3. Look for alterations of an official document through erasures, photograph substitutions, and so forth; official documents are never altered but are replaced

4. Check to be sure the document is squarely cut

5. Ascertain that printing and engraving is parallel with the document's edges, along with being sharp, clear, and unbroken

6. View documents as suspect where printing and engraving is dull, unclear, broken, or blurred

7. Not deny employment to someone based on a suspect document, but should contact the local INS office for verification of the document's number

8. Check with the state employment agency to determine if it has a certification process to verify an applicant's documents through the INS and issue a letter of certification to potential employers, with the certification letter serving as eligibility proof

§ 8.24   —Sample Policies

The following example should be considered in drafting Immigration Reform and Control Act of 1986 policies:

POLICY 8.24(1)
UNLAWFUL IMMIGRATION DISCRIMINATION

The Company will not discriminate against any individual other than an unauthorized alien in hiring, disciplining, terminating, recruiting, and so forth because of that individual's national origin or, in the case of a citizen or intending citizen, because of his or her citizenship status.

§ 8.25   —Employment Eligibility Verification Form
(Form I-9)

The following form is required to be completed for employee eligibility verification under the Immigration Reform and Control Act of 1986:

FORM 8.25(1)
EMPLOYMENT ELIGIBILITY VERIFICATION (FORM I-9)

1 | EMPLOYEE INFORMATION AND VERIFICATION: (To be completed and signed by employee.)

Name: (Print or Type) Last	First	Middle	Birth Name
Address: Street Name and Number	City	State	ZIP Code
Date of Birth (Month/Day/Year)		Social Security Number	

I attest, under penalty of perjury, that I am (check a box):

☐ 1. A citizen or national of the United States.

☐ 2. An alien lawfully admitted for permanent residence (Alien Number A _____) .

☐ 3. An alien authorized by the Immigration and Naturalization Service to work in the United States (Alien Number A _____ ,
or Admission Number _____ , expiration of employment authorization, if any _____).

I attest, under penalty of perjury, the documents that I have presented as evidence of identity and employment eligibility are genuine and relate to me. I am aware that federal law provides for imprisonment and/or fine for any false statements or use of false documents in connection with this certificate.

Signature	Date (Month/Day/Year)

PREPARER/TRANSLATOR CERTIFICATION (To be completed if prepared by person other than the employee). I attest, under penalty of perjury, that the above was prepared by me at the request of the named individual and is based on all information of which I have any knowledge.

Signature	Name (Print or Type)		
Address (Street Name and Number)	City	State	Zip Code

2 | EMPLOYER REVIEW AND VERIFICATION: (To be completed and signed by employer.)

Instructions:

Examine one document from List A and check the appropriate box, **OR** examine one document from List B **and** one from List C and check the appropriate boxes.
Provide the *Document Identification Number* and *Expiration Date* for the document checked.

List A Documents that Establish Identity and Employment Eligibility	List B Documents that Establish Identity	and	List C Documents that Establish Employment Eligibility
☐ 1. United States Passport ☐ 2. Certificate of United States Citizenship ☐ 3. Certificate of Naturalization ☐ 4. Unexpired foreign passport with attached Employment Authorization ☐ 5. Alien Registration Card with photograph	☐ 1. A State-issued driver's license or a State-issued I.D. card with a photograph, or information, including name, sex, date of birth, height, weight, and color of eyes. (Specify State)_____) ☐ 2. U.S. Military Card ☐ 3. Other (Specify document and issuing authority) _____		☐ 1. Original Social Security Number Card (other than a card stating it is not valid for employment) ☐ 2. A birth certificate issued by State, county, or municipal authority bearing a seal or other certification ☐ 3. Unexpired INS Employment Authorization Specify form # _____
Document Identification # _____	*Document Identification* # _____		*Document Identification* # _____
Expiration Date (if any) _____	*Expiration Date (if any)* _____		*Expiration Date (if any)* _____

CERTIFICATION: I attest, under penalty of perjury, that I have examined the documents presented by the above individual, that they appear to be genuine and to relate to the individual named, and that the individual, to the best of my knowledge, is eligible to work in the United States.

Signature	Name (Print or Type)	Title
Employer Name	Address	Date

Form I-9 (05/07/87)
OMB No. 1115-0136

U.S. Department of Justice
Immigration and Naturalization Service

EMPLOYEE DATA VERIFICATION

> **NOTICE:** Authority for collecting the information on this form is in Title 8, United States Code, Section 1324A, which requires employers to verify employment eligibility of individuals on a form approved by the Attorney General. This form will be used to verify the individual's eligibility for employment in the United States. Failure to present this form for inspection to officers of the Immigration and Naturalization Service or Department of Labor within the time period specified by regulation, or improper completion or retention of this form, may be a violation of the above law and may result in a civil money penalty.

Section 1. Instructions to Employee/Preparer for completing this form

Instructions for the employee.

All employees, upon being hired, must complete Section 1 of this form. Any person hired after November 6, 1986 must complete this form. (For the purpose of completion of this form the term "hired" applies to those employed, recruited or referred for a fee.)

All employees must print or type their complete name, address, date of birth, and Social Security Number. The block which correctly indicates the employee's immigration status must be checked. If the second block is checked, the employee's Alien Registration Number must be provided. If the third block is checked, the employee's Alien Registration Number *or* Admission Number must be provided, as well as the date of expiration of that status, if it expires.

All employees whose present names differ from birth names, because of marriage or other reasons, must print or type their birth names in the appropriate space of Section 1. Also, employees whose names change after employment verification should report these changes to their employer.

All employees must sign and date the form.

Instructions for the preparer of the form, if not the employee.

If a person assists the employee with completing this form, the preparer must certify the form by signing it and printing or typing his or her complete name and address.

Section 2. Instructions to Employer for completing this form

(For the purpose of completion of this form, the term "employer" applies to employers and those who recruit or refer for a fee.)

Employers must complete this section by examining evidence of identity and employment eligibility, and:
- checking the appropriate box in List A *or* boxes in both Lists B and C;
- recording the document identification number and expiration date (if any);
- recording the type of form if not specifically identified in the list;
- signing the certification section.

NOTE: Employers are responsible for reverifying employment eligibility of employees whose employment eligibility documents carry an expiration date.

Copies of documentation presented by an individual for the purpose of establishing identity and employment eligibility may be copied and retained for the purpose of complying with the requirements of this form and no other purpose. Any copies of documentation made for this purpose should be maintained with this form.

Name changes of employees which occur after preparation of this form should be recorded on the form by lining through the old name, printing the new name and the reason (such as marriage), and dating and initialing the changes. Employers should not attempt to delete or erase the old name in any fashion.

RETENTION OF RECORDS.

The completed form must be retained by the employer for:
- three years after the date of hiring; or
- one year after the date the employment is terminated, whichever is later.

> Employers may photocopy or reprint this form as necessary.

U.S. Department of Justice
Immigration and Naturalization Service

OMB #1115-0136
Form I-9 (05/07/87)
☆ U.S.G.P.O.: 1987- 183-918/69085

For sale by the Superintendent of Documents, U.S. Government Printing Office
Washington, D.C. 20402

§ 8.26   Reference Checks

Reference information is frequently collected or disclosed absent the employee's knowledge.[96] It often involves former employers who may be solicited without the employee's knowledge or consent.

Reference checks represent another employer effort to compile and verify the most complete and accurate information regarding applicants. From the former employer's perspective, detailed reference requests present a litigation risk against the former employer by the former employee. Many employers limit their reference request response to verifying the former employee's employment dates, job title, and salary. However, requesting detailed references from former employers is one precaution an employer can take during the hiring process to limit its vulnerability to employment litigation.

Some states statutorily regulate employee references.[97] Federal[98] or state[99] FEP statutes, along with claims for invasion of privacy[100] and defamation,[101] may also offer employee protection.

A defense to a defamation claim is that a former employer has a qualified privilege to communicate in good faith when responding to an inquiry by one with a legitimate information interest. The former employer has the burden of establishing good faith and that the recipient had a legitimate information interest.

By failing to request references, the employer may risk negligent hiring liability.[102] Negligent hiring arises out of employee acts committed while in the employer's service but outside the employee's employment scope. While an employer generally is not liable for employee acts outside of the employment's scope, employer liability for negligent hiring has been found where an employee was responsible for others' safety or security.[103]

---

[96] *See* Decker, Privacy Law § 6.13.

[97] *See, e.g.,* Cal. Labor Code §§ 1050, 1052 (West 1971) (California's statute regulating employee references); *see also* Decker, Privacy Law § 2.34.

[98] *See, e.g.,* 42 U.S.C. §§ 2000e-1 to 2002-17 (1988) (Civil Rights Act of 1964); *see also* Decker, Privacy Law §§ 2.7–2.12.

[99] *See, e.g.,* Pa. Stat. Ann. tit. 43, §§ 951–963 (Purdon 1991) (Pennsylvania Human Relations Act); *see also* Decker, Privacy Law § 2.25.

[100] *See, e.g.,* Cummings v. Walsh Constr. Co., 561 F. Supp. 872 (S.D. Ga. 1983) (invasion of privacy without broad public disclosure); *see also* Decker, Privacy Law §§ 4.3, 6.13.

[101] *See, e.g.,* Lewis v. Equitable Life Assurance Soc'y, 361 N.W.2d 875 (Minn. Ct. App. 1985), *aff'd in pertinent part,* 389 N.W.2d 876 (Minn. 1986) (defamation where false termination reason given to employees); *see also* Decker, Privacy Law §§ 4.4, 6.13.

[102] *See, e.g.,* Welch Mfg., Div. of Textron, Inc. v. Pinkerton's, Inc., 474 A.2d 436 (R.I. 1984) (prior company theft by a security guard); Burch v. A & G Assocs., Inc., 122 Mich. App. 798, 333 N.W.2d 140 (1983) (assault committed by a driver); *see also* Decker, Privacy Law § 6.22.

[103] *See, e.g.,* Welch Mfg., Div. of Textron, Inc. v. Pinkerton's, Inc., 474 A.2d 436 (R.I. 1984) (prior company theft by a security guard); Burch v. A & G Assocs., Inc., 122 Mich. App. 798, 333 N.W.2d 140 (1983) (assault committed by a driver); *see also* Decker, Privacy Law § 6.22.

§ 8.27   —General Considerations

In the narrowest sense, references are those individuals listed by an applicant who can furnish pertinent information about the applicant's qualifications.[104] Normally, references are requested as part of the application. References are sometimes considered valueless, because applicants may only use persons whom they feel will provide favorable information, and because the information furnished is usually subjective and/or not job-related. Reference problems can be minimized by placing the following constraints on applicants:

1. Applicants should be instructed to list only those references who have known the applicant for a given time period and have direct knowledge of the applicant's qualifications as they relate to the job's specifications

2. Request the applicant briefly to justify why the reference is qualified to provide this information

3. Applicants should be requested to sign releases waiving their rights to review information furnished by a reference

4. References should be sent a copy of the waiver, indicating that the applicant has waived review rights

5. References should be sent a copy of the job specifications and requested to use their knowledge to compare the applicant's qualifications with the job's specifications

6. References should be contacted in person or by telephone to discuss an applicant's qualifications or to verify information

§ 8.28   —Reference Check Methods

Proper reference checking is time-consuming. It demands personal involvement and extends beyond having someone make telephone calls to references listed on an application. Possible approaches to reference-checking include:

1. Meeting with the applicant's references because:
    a. People are much more willing to be open in person
    b. It provides the opportunity to interpret facial expressions and body language which may, in addition to words, indicate how the reference actually feels about the applicant's prior work performance
2. Using the telephone
3. Checking references by mail

---

[104] Myers, Human Resources at 258.

§ 8.29   —Providing References

In providing references, the following should be considered:

1. Review the legal aspects concerning what information can be disclosed absent an employee's consent
2. Check that the human resources staff has distributed procedures and policies regarding information disclosure:
    a. Content
    b. Circumstances
    c. Eligible persons
3. Ensure that the information's accuracy is substantiated by factual records
4. Communicate the procedure and policy regarding references
5. Instruct all personnel that they are not to discuss another employee's performance with those outside the company
6. Maintain a policy of truthfulness and accuracy in making employee evaluations, especially in cases involving termination decisions
7. Ensure that communications, whether oral or written, internal or external, concern job-related matters only
8. Use a written release, where possible, to obtain the employee's consent to provide information to prospective employers and to release the employer from all claims that might arise from providing references
9. Centralize the process of providing references
10. Provide information on a need-to-know basis only.[105]

§ 8.30   —Reference Checking

In checking references, the following should be considered:

1. Obtain the employee's written permission to check references
2. Check references before making the final job offer
3. If a discrepancy exists between facts or recommendations, a more extensive investigation should be undertaken
4. Be skeptical of all subjective evaluations, especially those that do not include verifiable acts or behavior
5. View silence as an indication for further investigation; an employer may attempt to avoid wrongful termination litigation by negotiating a settlement with an employee that includes no unfavorable references

---

[105] *See* Lotito & Bryant, *Reference Checking: Are the HR Professional's Hands Tied?,* Hum. Resource Mgmt. Legal Rep. 5 (Spring 1988).

6. Obtain as many references as possible, and investigate all of them before the applicant is hired

7. Interview the applicant thoroughly and make complete notes of the interview

8. Ask the applicant to explain any gaps in employment history

9. Ask the applicant to state what his or her previous supervisor or manager would say if asked about the applicant's job qualifications

10. Encourage the applicant to sign a form releasing information from former employers

11. Although expensive, the use of a commercial service to investigate the applicant may be desirable, especially for higher-level positions or positions of a sensitive nature.[106]

§ 8.31   —Sample Policies

The following example should be considered in drafting reference policies:

POLICY 8.31(1)
REFERENCE CHECKING POLICY

Absent an employee or a former employee's written consent, the Company will not provide information, except name, job title, and employment dates, regarding its current or former employees unless required by federal or state law or court order. All employee information requests must be referred to the Human Resources Department. Supervisors or other employees are not permitted to respond to a reference request. Telephone inquiries will not be answered. Only written inquiries from the person seeking the information on that person's letterhead with name and title will be considered.

§ 8.32   —Information Release Form

The following forms should be used by employers when requesting references on behalf of applicants or employees:

FORM 8.32(1)
INFORMATION RELEASE FORM

I, __(Name)__ , hereby authorize the Company to release the following information regarding my employment with the Company to __(Company's Name, Person, etc.)__ :

---

[106] *Id.* at 6–7.

Information List

_____

_____

_____

_____

_____

Date: _____   _____
                                                Signed

FORM 8.32(2)
INFORMATION RELEASE FORM (ALTERNATE)

Employment reference for:

_____

S.S.N.: _____

Job Title: _____

I have stated to the _____ (Company's Name) _____
that I was employed by you as a _____ (Position Title) _____.
I request that the following information be furnished by you for reference purposes
to this employer and I consent to you providing this information regarding my past
employment, work performance, attendance record, abilities, and reason for my
employment separation.

                            _____
                                        (Name)

_____
          (Date)

Employed as: _____

From: _____ To: _____

Reason for leaving: _____

_____

_____

Would you re-employ this individual: _____

Please check below the rating that most accurately describes this individual:

	Satisfactory	Unsatisfactory
Work Quality	_____	_____
Work Quantity	_____	_____
Cooperation	_____	_____
Supervision	_____	_____
Attendance	_____	_____

Other remarks regarding job-related performance that may be relevant to the position requested: _____

_____

_____

_____

_____

(Name)

_____

(Position)

_____

(Company)

_____

(Address)

_____

(Telephone)

_____

(Date)

§ 8.33 —Telephone Reference Check

The following form should be used by employers when requesting references on behalf of applicants or employees through a telephone reference check.

FORM 8.33(1)
TELEPHONE REFERENCE CHECK

Applicant's name: _____

Person contacted: _____ Title: _____

Company: _____

Business type: _____

Address: _____

Telephone: _____

Dates of employment: _____

_____

_____

Position: _____

Job functions: _____

_____

Work quality: _____

_____

_____

Work quantity: _____

_____

_____

Initiative: _____

_____

_____

Work habits: _____

_____

_____

Cooperation with others: _____

_____

_____

Attendance: _____

_____

_____

Limitations: _____

_____

_____

Reason for separation: _____

_____

_____

Would you re-employ? _____ Why/Why not? _____

_____

_____

Would you recommend the applicant for this position (describe position)? _____

_____

Why/Why not? _____

_____

Completed by: _____

Position title: _____

Date: _____

§ 8.34   Skill Testing

For employers, a desire exists to fill jobs with employees qualified for the work assigned. This desire, combined with only a vague knowledge of what the law exacts as prerequisites for skill testing, presents important employee privacy considerations.[107]

It has generally been held that skill testing offers an objective standard by which to predict job performance. Some tests, however, eliminate ethnic minorities from certain positions by favoring education levels typical of a white, middle-class background.[108] Performance by the economically disadvantaged on such tests has been poor.

---

[107] *See* Decker, Privacy Law § 6.18.

[108] *See* United States v. South Carolina, 434 U.S. 1026 (1978); Dothard v. Rawlinson, 433 U.S. 321 (1977); Washington v. Davis, 426 U.S. 229 (1976); Albemarle Paper Co. v. Moody, 422 U.S. 405 (1975); Griggs v. Duke Power Co., 401 U.S. 424 (1971); United States v. Georgia Power Co., 474 F.2d 906 (5th Cir. 1972); Hicks v. Crown Zellerbach Corp., 319 F. Supp. 314 (E.D. La. 1970); Hobson v. Hansen, 269 F. Supp. 401 (D.D.C. 1967).

Educational and industrial psychologists have played a major role in developing tests that attempt to predict job performance.[109] These tests remove some of the subjectivity used in employee selection. Employment testing has developed into a highly sophisticated and technical field with its own language, its own standards, and its own complex methodology.[110]

Test is a generic word encompassing a systematic method of measuring applicant qualifications through pencil and paper instruments, oral questions, the performance of exercises, or the manipulation of objects.[111] Tests may be commercially prepared or custom-constructed by an employer or consultant. Tests can be grouped into the following categories:[112]

1. *Achievement test,* which measures the extent of a person's knowledge or competence within a field

2. *Aptitude test,* which measures innate or acquired capacities to learn an occupation

3. *Interest inventory,* which, while nominally a test, is more a self-assessment of interests that either correlate to those of individuals who are successfully employed in a particular occupation or can otherwise be used to determine an individual's suitability for a particular job

4. *Manual dexterity or motor test,* which measures a number of motor functions, including reaction time, quickness of arm movements, multilimb coordination, and finger dexterity

5. *Mental ability test,* which measures the ability to reason, perceive relationships, understand numerical properties, and solve quantitative problems

6. *Performance test,* which measures demonstrated performance, usually on a piece of equipment

7. *Sensory test,* which measures hearing and vision, including color vision

---

[109] *See, e.g.,* American Psychological Association, Principles for the Validation and Use of Personnel Selection Procedures (rev. ed. 1980).

[110] *See* Guardians Ass'n of N.Y. City Police Dep't v. Civil Serv. Comm'n, 630 F.2d 79, 89 (2d Cir. 1980), where the court noted that testing is:

> not primarily a legal subject; it is part of the general field of educational and industrial psychology, and possesses its own methodology, its own body of research, its own experts, and its own terminology. The transition of a technical study such as this into a set of legal principles requires a clear awareness of the limits of both testing and law. It would be entirely inappropriate for the law to ignore what has been learned about employment testing in assessing the validity of these tests. At the same time, the science of testing is not as precise as physics or chemistry, nor its conclusions as provable. While courts should draw upon the findings of experts in the field of testing, they should not hesitate to subject these findings to both the scrutiny of reason and the guidance of Congressional intent.

[111] Myers, Human Resources at 250.

[112] Myers at 251–257.

  8. *Situational test,* which is a generic term for a variety of exercises that measure an applicant's responses to workplace situations

  9. *Competitive group exercise,* which assigns roles to applicants, who receive various instructions concerning how the role should be played

10. *In-basket test,* which evaluates applicants' abilities to handle a work basket of events representative of those encountered on the job they are seeking

11. *Computer game,* which measures the ability of applicants to evaluate information, usually quantitative data, plan responses, and make decisions

12. *Work sample,* which measures an applicant's performance on an important job task representative of what could actually occur on the job

13. *Role playing (RP),* which is typically two persons playing assigned roles; however, RP differs from group exercises with assigned roles because only two people are involved. It is used to test for applicant knowledge, training, skills, and abilities in handling employee performance appraisal interviews, evaluating employee ideas, assisting employees in receiving help for personal problems, and resolving disciplinary problems

14. *Assessment center (AC),* a selection method in which participants engage in multiple exercises, some of which are simulations, and their performance is appraised by pooled assessments of trained assessors

Testing can have a significant impact on information collection, maintenance, use, and disclosure. Depending upon the test, it may reveal information affecting employee speech, beliefs, information, association, and lifestyle. These concerns are essentially protected by federal[113] and state[114] FEP statutes.

FEP statutes generally require that a protected classification not be a factor in employment selection.[115] If a selection procedure has a disproportionate impact that excludes protected persons, its use is unlawful unless the procedure is demonstrably a reasonable job performance measure; i.e., unless it is job-related or justified by business necessity.[116]

Under the Civil Rights Act of 1964 (Title VII),[117] the Uniform Guidelines on Employee Selection Procedures have been developed.[118] The Guidelines define a *selection procedure* broadly as any measure, combination of measures, or

---

[113] *See, e.g.,* 42 U.S.C. §§ 2000e-1 to 2002-17 (1988) (Civil Rights Act of 1964); *see also* Decker, Privacy Law §§ 2.7–2.12.

[114] *See, e.g.,* Pa. Stat. Ann. tit. 43, §§ 951–963 (Purdon 1991) (Pennsylvania Human Relations Act); *see also* Decker, Privacy Law § 2.25.

[115] *See* Melanson v. Rantoul, 536 F. Supp. 271 (D.R.I. 1982).

[116] *See* Griggs v. Duke Power Co., 401 U.S. 424 (1971).

[117] 42 U.S.C. §§ 2000e-1 to 2002-17 (1988) (Civil Rights Act of 1964); *see* Decker, Privacy Law § 2.8.

[118] 43 Fed. Reg. 38290, 29 C.F.R. § 1607.1 *et seq.* (1993). The Uniform Guidelines, as published by the Office of Federal Contract Compliance and Procedures (OFCCP), are found at 41 C.F.R. pt. 60-3.

procedure used as a basis for an employment decision,[119] including hiring, promotion, membership, referral, retention, selection, training, or transfer.[120] Selection procedures include traditional paper and pencil tests, performance tests, training programs, probationary periods, informal or casual interviews, unscored application forms, and physical, educational, and work experience requirements.[121]

Title VII does not prohibit employers from giving or acting on the results of a professionally developed ability test where the test, its administration, and action on it are not designed, intended, or used to discriminate.[122] However, a professionally developed test must be job-related.[123]

§ 8.35 —Skill Testing Effectiveness and Propriety

The following should be considered regarding skill testing effectiveness and propriety:

1. Objectivity, by identifying characteristics of mind and skill necessary for a particular job while disregarding race, religion, politics, sex, residence, age, and so forth

2. Validity, in that the test actually measures what it purports to measure by evaluating applicants in exactly the same relationship to one another as they would stand after on-the-job performance

3. Reliability as a consistent measuring instrument, in that a person taking the same test on different occasions should receive substantially the same score each time

§ 8.36 —Skill Testing Use Determinations

In determining whether testing should be used, the following should be considered:

1. A determination of the selection objective: a given position, occupation, program, career, and so forth

2. A determination of basic selection standards: what skills and knowledge are necessary

---

[119] 29 C.F.R. § 1607.16Q (1993).

[120] *Id.* § 1607.2B.

[121] *Id.* § 1607.16Q.

[122] 42 U.S.C. § 2000e-2(h) (1988).

[123] *See* Griggs v. Duke Power Co., 401 U.S. 424 (1971).

3.   Labor market, for determining whether qualified applicants are available for testing

4.   Cost utility: whether the testing can be done economically without becoming extremely costly

§ 8.37 —Drafting

In drafting skill testing policies, the following should be considered:

1.   Review applicable federal[124] and state[125] statutes
2.   Do not over-rely on tests
3.   Use other screening methods, including interviews, background verifications, and reference checks, along with tests
4.   Use test results as added information, not to terminate an employee
5.   Contact the test's developer to recheck the test if someone receives an extremely poor score but has good recommendations, job performance, and so forth
6.   Use tests at the end of the hiring process when applicants have been narrowed to the best choices
7.   Maintain test score confidentiality
8.   Ensure that the test is job-related and does not measure extraneous non-job-related factors

§ 8.38 —Sample Policies

The following example should be considered in drafting skill testing policies:

POLICY 8.38(1)
TESTING POLICY

Section 1. Testing Procedures.   In addition to written, oral, and performance tests, the Company may authorize an evaluation of education and experience, medical tests, physical strength and physical agility tests, and other types of tests, singly or in combination as job-related circumstances warrant. For promotional tests, the Company may authorize other performance criteria involving seniority and performance evaluations developed under a uniform system.

---

[124] 42 U.S.C. §§ 2000e-1 to 2002-17 (1988) (Civil Rights Act of 1964).

[125] *See, e.g.*, Pa. Stat. Ann. tit. 43, §§ 951–63 (Purdon 1991) (Pennsylvania Human Relations Act).

Section 2. Test Scheduling.   The Company shall give due consideration to the convenience of the applicants, consistent with its needs, in determining dates, times, and locations of tests.

Section 3. Security.

a. The Company will establish appropriate procedures to ensure that all applicants for a test are given equal opportunity to demonstrate their qualifications in that:

   (i)   The Company will establish proper precautions to prevent an unauthorized person from securing in advance questions or other materials to be used in a test, unless the questions or materials are available to all applicants; and

   (ii) When the conditions under which a test is held have materially impaired its competitive nature or worth in assessing qualifications, the Company will order that the tests or appropriate sections thereof, if severable, be cancelled. New tests or parts of tests may be substituted, if possible.

b. The Company will establish appropriate procedures to ensure that the identity of the applicants in all tests does not adversely affect the objective rating or scoring of test papers.

c. The Company will disqualify an applicant who impersonates another or has another person impersonate himself or herself in connection with a test, or who uses or attempts to use unauthorized aids or assistance, including copying or attempting to copy from or helping or attempting to help another applicant in any part of a test, or who otherwise seeks to attain undue advantage in connection with the test.

d. No applicant in a test shall copy, record, or transcribe any test question or answer, or remove from the testing room any question sheet, answer sheet, booklet, scrap papers, notes, or other papers or materials related to the test's content. Applicants shall be notified of this action and no examiner, proctor, monitor, or other person charged with the supervision of an applicant or group of applicants shall have authority to waive it. The Company may disqualify a candidate or refuse to certify an eligible person who violates this section.

Section 4. Preservation of Test Records.   The Company shall ensure that the following documents are maintained as official records:

a. The test's original copy;

b. The test's description;

c. The test's instructions;

d. The scoring keys or other scoring standards used;

e. The examiners' reports; and

f. The resulting eligible list.

Section 5. Test Paper Inspection.

a. The Company will, upon request of an applicant, authorize the applicant to inspect his or her test documents in the presence of an authorized Company official. The inspection shall not include authorization to copy test instructions, questions, or answers, and will be conducted to maintain security of the testing program.

b. The Company may authorize review of the application and test papers of an applicant, upon request and for official purposes, by law enforcement or other public officials where there are legitimate inspection reasons. Copies of test materials will not be made available except as provided by applicable statutes or regulations.

c. The Company will authorize the disclosure of applications and test papers to a private individual only where the individual seeking access can demonstrate a clear necessity to pursue a legitimate legal right. The Company will take necessary precautions to avoid disclosure of the identities of the persons whose applications and test papers are being examined. Where it is evident that the information release would operate to prejudice or impair a person's reputation or personal security, access to the information shall be denied.

Section 6. Information Regarding Unsuccessful Applicants. Except as provided in Section 5 (Test Paper Inspection), the test papers of applicants who failed all or part of a test or who voluntarily withdrew from the test shall not be exhibited or disclosed nor shall information be released concerning their test participation.

CHAPTER 9

WORKPLACE
RECORD POLICIES

§ 9.1   Introduction to Workplace Records

Considerable employment information is collected, maintained, used, and disclosed by employers.[1] This information is used to hire, discipline, terminate, place, transfer, promote, demote, train, compensate, and provide full or partial fringe benefits. Information may be collected, maintained, used, or disclosed without employee notice, knowledge, or consent.

Employment record confidentiality and integrity is important for both employees and employers, in that non-job-related information may be collected, maintained, or used. These records, usually referred to as *personnel files,* generally contain the employee's personal, employment, and medical history. *Personal history* concerns prior background and work history. *Employment history* details current work history regarding wages, promotions, disciplinary actions, commendations, sick days, vacation days, positions held, and performance evaluations.

---

[1] *See* Decker, Privacy Law §§ 7.2–7.4.

Medical history contains information about the employee's physical and psychological health. This section reviews policies and procedures relevant to employment records involving personal[2] and medical[3] information.

§ 9.2   Employment Records

Employer methods for collecting, maintaining, accessing, using, and disclosing employment information vary.[4] Certain employment record aspects are regulated by federal[5] and state[6] statutes. These statutes generally set forth what employment information may be collected, along with providing for employee access and the right to review and copy record contents. Some statutes permit employees to place a counterstatement in the record when information is incorrect or challenged.

Various states require employers to permit employees to inspect their personnel records.[7] This includes records that have been used to determine employment qualifications, promotion, compensation, or disciplinary action up to and including termination. The employer is required to maintain the personnel files at the place the employee reports to work or to make them available there upon reasonable notice.

Some statutes mandate that certain employment information be maintained by employers.[8] Employee record privacy is thus affected, because employers, despite legal restrictions, may use detailed application blanks,[9] interviews,[10] and

---

[2] See §§ **9.2–9.8.**

[3] See §§ **9.9–9.12.**

[4] *See* Decker, Privacy Law § 7.3.

[5] *See, e.g.,* 5 U.S.C. § 552a (1988) (Privacy Act of 1974); *see also* Decker, Privacy Law §§ 2.3–2.4.

[6] *See, e.g.,* Pa. Stat. Ann. tit. 43, §§ 1321–1324 (Purdon 1991) (Pennsylvania's statute regulating personnel file inspection); *see also* Decker, Privacy Law §§ 2.30–2.31.

[7] *See, e.g.,* Pa. Stat. Ann. tit. 43, §§ 1321–1324 (Purdon 1991) (Pennsylvania's statute regulating personnel file inspection); *see also* Decker, Privacy Law §§ 2.30–2.31.

[8] See § **9.5.** *See, e.g.,* 42 U.S.C. §§ 2000e-1 to 2002-17 (1988) (Civil Rights Act of 1964).

[9] See ch. 4. *See, e.g.,* Gregory v. Litton Sys., Inc., 316 F. Supp. 401 (C.D. Cal. 1970), *aff'd with modifications not here relevant,* 472 F.2d 631 (9th Cir. 1972) (arrest record inquiries prohibited); *see also* Decker, Privacy Law §§ 2.32, 6.4, 6.8.

[10] See §§ ch. 4. *See, e.g.,* Richardson v. Hotel Corp. of Am., 332 F. Supp. 519 (E.D. La. 1971), *aff'd mem.,* 468 F.2d 951 (5th Cir. 1972) (legitimate employee termination for convictions); *see also* Decker, Privacy Law § 6.5.

similar questionable information collection devices involving polygraph examinations,[11] honesty tests,[12] credit checks,[13] and so forth.

In providing employment information, the employee relinquishes control of sensitive personal information, along with the opportunity to verify the accuracy of information that may be developed from these disclosures. Collecting inaccurate employment information is possible because each employer has its own recordkeeping system.

Employers frequently receive requests for employment information from other employers, social workers, insurance companies, credit bureaus, government officials, and union business agents. The employee initially revealed this information to obtain employment or to maintain it. Disclosure may occur for a purpose unrelated to employment that is against the employee's best interest. Through these disclosures, the employee again loses control of sensitive personal information as well as the opportunity to verify the information's accuracy. Dependence upon the employer's good will or personal values creates problems over what *confidentiality* means for employment records.

Employment records may result in privacy claims arising out of invasion of privacy,[14] defamation,[15] intentional infliction of emotional distress,[16] negligent maintenance or disclosure of employment records,[17] fraudulent misrepresentation,[18] and public policies.[19] A state constitutional privacy right may protect personnel files from disclosure to third parties.[20] Employee requests to review

---

[11] *See, e.g.,* People v. Hamilton, 125 A.D.2d 1000, 511 N.Y.S.2d 190 (1986) (employer could be held liable for invasion of privacy where polygraph examiner sexually abused females by touching and asking intimate questions); *see also* Decker, Privacy Law § 6.19.

[12] *See, e.g.,* Minnesota v. Century Camera, Inc., 309 N.W.2d 735 (Minn. 1981) (employer honesty test use); *see also* Decker, Privacy Law §§ 2.35, 6.20.

[13] See ch. 8. *See, e.g.,* United States v. Chicago, 459 F.2d 415 (7th Cir. 1977) (credit check for police officer not job-related); *see also* Decker, Privacy Law § 6.7.

[14] *See, e.g.,* Quinones v. United States, 492 F.2d 1269 (3d Cir. 1974) (release of inaccurate personnel file); *see also* Decker, Privacy Law § 4.3.

[15] *See, e.g.,* Wendler v. DePaul, 346 Pa. Super. 479, 499 A.2d 1101 (1985) (negative employee performance evaluation); *see also* Decker, Privacy Law § 4.4.

[16] *See, e.g.,* Hall v. Macy Dep't Stores, 242 Or. 131, 637 P.2d 126 (1981) (security investigator made false statement, during interview of young female clerk regarding cash register shortage, that he had proof of her theft and threatened prosecution); *see also* Decker, Privacy Law § 4.6.

[17] *See, e.g.,* Bulkin v. Western Kraft E., Inc., 422 F. Supp. 437 (E.D. Pa. 1976) (negligent maintenance of employment records); *see also* Decker, Privacy Law § 4.7.

[18] *See, e.g.,* Hall v. Integon Life Ins. Co., 454 So. 2d 1338 (Ala. 1984) (plaintiff entitled to trial on fraudulent misrepresentation claim based on statements that termination would only be for gross misconduct); *see also* Decker, Privacy Law § 4.8.

[19] *See, e.g.,* Frampton v. Central Ind. Gas. Co., 260 Ind. 249, 297 N.E.2d 425 (1973) (filing workers' compensation claim); *see also* Decker, Privacy Law § 4.10.

[20] *See, e.g.,* Board of Trustees of Stanford Univ. v. Superior Court, 119 Cal. App. 3d 516, 174 Cal. Rptr. 160 (1981) (California Constitution protection of personnel file disclosure to third parties); *see also* Decker, Privacy Law §§ 3.9–3.11.

personnel files of co-employees may violate the co-employee's right guaranteed by a state constitution.[21] The employer, as the private information's custodian, cannot waive employee privacy rights that are constitutionally guaranteed this protection.[22]

Contractual litigation theories are also applicable to employment record privacy interests.[23] Employee interests may receive protection in employment contracts,[24] restrictive covenants,[25] employment handbooks and policies,[26] and collective bargaining agreements.[27]

9.3 —Drafting

In drafting employment record policies, the following should be considered:

1. Applicable federal[28] and state[29] statutes.
2. A uniform system of collecting, maintaining, accessing, using, and disclosing employment information.
3. Collecting employment information by reviewing:[30]
   a. The number and types of records maintained
   b. Information items

---

[21] *See, e.g.,* Board of Trustees of Stanford Univ. v. Superior Court, 119 Cal. App. 3d 516, 174 Cal. Rptr. 160 (1981) (California Constitution protection of personnel file disclosure to third parties); *see also* Decker, Privacy Law §§ 3.9–3.11

[22] *See, e.g.,* Board of Trustees of Stanford Univ. v. Superior Court, 119 Cal. App. 3d 516, 174 Cal. Rptr. 160 (1981) (California Constitution protection of personnel file disclosure to third parties); *see also* Decker, Privacy Law §§ 3.9–3.11.

[23] *See* Decker, Privacy Law §§ 4.11–4.15.

[24] *See, e.g.,* Landrum v. J.F. Pritchard & Co., 139 Ga. App. 393, 228 S.E.2d 290 (1976) (employer's promise to pay a salary was adequate consideration for the employee's promise to work, to assign the employer inventions, or not to compete with the employer); *see also* Decker, Privacy Law § 4.12.

[25] *See, e.g.,* Tabs Assocs., Inc. v. Brohawn, 59 Md. App. 330, 475 A.2d 1203 (1984) (restrictive covenant to prevent future trade secret misuses); *see also* Decker, Privacy Law § 4.13.

[26] *See, e.g.,* Toussaint v. Blue Cross & Blue Shield of Mich., 408 Mich. 579, 292 N.W.2d 880 (1980) (employment handbook may create binding employer commitments); *see also* Decker, Privacy Law § 4.14.

[27] Singer Co., 85 Lab. Arb. (BNA) 152 (1985) (Yarowsky, Arb.) (employer must inform employees of personnel file entries); *see also* Decker, Privacy Law § 4.15.

[28] *See, e.g.,* 42 U.S.C. §§ 2000e-1 to 2002-2017 (1988) (Civil Rights Act of 1964); 42 U.S.C. §§ 12101–12213 (Supp. 1992) (Americans with Disabilities Act);

[29] *See, e.g.,* Pa. Stat. Ann. tit. 43, §§ 1321–1324 (Purdon) (Pennsylvania's statute regulating personnel file inspection).

[30] *See* Privacy Protection Study Commission, Report at 235.

   c. Information uses made within the employer's decisionmaking and non-decisionmaking structure

   d. Information disclosure made to those other than the employer

   e. The extent to which employees are aware and regularly informed of the uses and disclosures that are made of this information

4. Fair information collection procedures and policies concerning applicants, employees, and former employees that:[31]

   a. Limit information collection to that which is job-related

   b. Inform what records will be maintained

   c. Inform of the uses to be made of this information

   d. Adopt procedures to assure information accuracy, timeliness, and completeness

   e. Permit review, copying, correction, or information amendment

   f. Limit internal use

   g. Limit external disclosures, including disclosures made without authorization, to specific inquiries or requests to verify information

   h. Provide for a regular policy compliance review

   i. Contain an employment application with a waiver authorizing the employer to disclose employee file contents to those to whom the employee grants access; e.g., reference checks by subsequent employers, and to make a credit check where applicable

   j. Indicate on the file when and where these employee reviews took place

   k. Restrict information access to those with a need to know and those who are authorized outside of the employer, i.e., law enforcement officials, government agencies, and so forth

   l. That information retention conforms to applicable law[32]

   m. A privacy clause

§ 9.4   —Employment Record Inspection Procedures

An employee's right to inspect his or her personnel file, however, is not absolute. Statutes may not grant an employee a right to inspect any records relating to an investigation of a possible criminal offense or to reference letters maintained by the employer.[33] The employer is entitled to impose reasonable restrictions upon

---

[31] *Id.* at 237–38.

[32] See § **9.5.**

[33] *See, e.g.,* Pa. Stat. Ann. tit. 43, §§ 1321–1324 (Purdon 1991) (Pennsylvania's statute regulating personnel file inspection); *see also* Decker, Privacy Law §§ 2.30, 7.3.

an employee's access to his or her personnel file.[34] These may take various forms, including:[35]

1. Requiring the employee to submit a written request to inspect his or her personnel file
2. Allowing inspection only by appointment
3. Allowing inspection only during regular business hours
4. Allowing inspection only on the employee's own time
5. Allowing inspection only in the presence of an employer representative
6. Limiting inspection frequency
7. Allowing employees to copy or obtain copies of their own personnel files
8. Permitting employee amendment of this information
9. Documenting inspection dates by employee

§ 9.5   —Employment Record Retention and Posting

Certain federal statutes require that employers collect, maintain, post, and disclose various forms of employment information.[36] Among these are the following.

Civil Rights Act of 1964 (Title VII)[37]

Records to Be Retained	Time Period
A. Any personnel or employment record made or kept by an employer, including applications and records having to do with hiring, promotion, demotion, transfer, layoff, termination, pay rates, compensation terms, and selection for training or apprenticeship	A. Six months from the date of making the record or taking the personnel action involved, whichever occurs later
B. Personnel records relevant to a discrimination charge or action brought by the Attorney General	B. Until final disposition of the charge or action

[34] *See, e.g.,* Pa. Stat. Ann. tit. 43, §§ 1321–1324 (Purdon 1991) (Pennsylvania's statute regulating personnel file inspection); *see also* Decker, Privacy Law §§ 2.30, 7.3.

[35] Privacy Protection Study Commission, Report app. 3 at 35–43.

[36] For an exhaustive list of other federal statutes and their requirements, *see* Policy and Practice Series (BNA) (1993).

[37] 42 U.S.C. §§ 2000e-1 to 2002-17 (1988); *see* Decker, Privacy Law § 2.8.

Records to Be Retained	Time Period
against the employer, including records relating to the charging party and to all other employees holding similar positions, applications or test papers completed by an unsuccessful applicant and by all other candidates for the same position	
C. For apprenticeship programs: 1. A chronological list of names and addresses of all applicants, dates of application, sex, and minority group, or file of written applications containing the same information; and other records pertaining to apprenticeship applicants, including test papers, interview records, and so forth	C. Retained for: 1. Two years or the period of the successful applicant's apprenticeship, whichever is later
2. Any other record made solely for completing report EEO-2 or similar reports	2. One year from due date of the report
D. Employers with 100 or more employees must file a copy of EEO-1—Employer Information Report	D. Current report must be retained indefinitely; six months

POSTING REQUIREMENT CONSOLIDATED EEO POSTER

Age Discrimination in Employment Act (ADEA)[38]

Records to Be Retained	Time Period
A. Payroll records containing each employee's name, address, date of birth, occupation, rate of pay, and compensation earned per week	A. Three years

---

[38] 29 U.S.C. §§ 621–634 (1988); see Decker, Privacy Law § 2.9.

Records to Be Retained	Time Period
B. Personnel records relating to: 　1. Job applications, resumes, or other replies to job advertisements, including applications for temporary positions and records pertaining to failure or refusal to hire 　2. Promotion, demotion, transfer, selection for training, layoff, recall, or termination 　3. Job orders submitted to an employment agency or union 　4. Test papers in connection with employer-administered aptitude or other employment tests 　5. Physical examination results considered in connection with a personnel action 　6. Job advertisements or notices to the public or employees regarding openings, programs, or opportunities for overtime work	B. One year from the date of the personnel action to which the record relates, except 90 days for applications and other applicant pre-employment records for temporary jobs
C. Employee benefit plans, written seniority or merit rating systems	C. Period plan or system is in effect plus one year
D. Personnel records, including the above, relevant to an action commenced against the employer	D. Until final disposition of the enforcement action

Americans with Disabilities Act[39]

Records to Be Retained	Time Period
Similar to those required by the Civil Rights Act of 1964 (42 U.S.C. §§ 2000e-1 to 2002-17 (1988)).	Record and reporting requirements of the Civil Rights Act of 1964, Title VII (42 U.S.C. §§ 2000e-1 to 2002-17 (1988)) should be applied to meet minimum considerations for this statute.

[39] 42. U.S.C. §§ 12111–12117 (Supp. 1992); *see* Decker, Privacy Law § 2.12A.

Vocational Rehabilitation Act of 1973[40]

Records to Be Retained	Time Period
(Federal contractors/subcontractors) A. For handicapped applicants and employees, complete and accurate employment records required by the Act. The Department of Labor suggests that this requirement may be met by annotating the application or personnel form of the handicapped applicant or employee to indicate each vacancy, promotion, and training program for which he or she was considered, including a statement of reasons for any rejection that compares the handicapped individual's qualification to those of the person selected, as well as any accommodations considered. Descriptions of accommodations actually undertaken also should be attached	A. One year
B. Records regarding complaints and actions taken under the Act	B. One year

Executive Order No. 11246 (Affirmative Action) (September 24, 1965, as amended)[41]

Records to Be Retained	Time Period
(Federal contractors, subcontractors) Written affirmative action programs and supporting documentation, including required utilization analysis and evaluation; other records and documents relating to compliance	Not specified

[40] 29 U.S.C. §§ 701–796i (1988); *see* Decker, Privacy Law § 2.10.

[41] Executive Order No. 11246 (federal contractors), 3 C.F.R. § 339 (1964–1965 compilation), reprinted in 42 U.S.C. § 2000e note, issued on Sept. 24, 1965, as amended; *see* Decker, Privacy Law § 2.12.

Records to Be Retained	*Time Period*
with applicable EEO nondiscrimination and affirmative action requirements, including records and documents on nature and use of tests, test validations, and test results as required; and compliance with construction industry EEO plans and requirements	

Occupational Safety and Health Act of 1970[42]

Records to Be Retained	*Time Period*
A. Log & Summary of Occupational Injuries and Illnesses, briefly describing recordable causes of injury and illness, extent and outcome of each incident, and summary totals for calendar year (Effective January 1, 1983, the following industries are exempt: retail trade, finance, insurance and real estate, and services)	A. Five years following the end of the year to which they relate
B. Supplementary Record, containing more detailed information for each occurrence of injury or illness	B. Five years following the end of the year to which they relate
C. Complete and accurate records of all medical examinations required by the law	C. Duration of employment plus 30 years, unless a specific OSHA standard provides a different time period
D. Records of any personal or environmental monitoring of exposure to hazardous materials	D. 30 years

---

[42] 29 U.S.C. §§ 651–678 (1988); *see* Decker, Privacy Law § 2.13.

POSTING REQUIREMENT OSHA POSTER

Immigration Reform and Control Act of 1986[43]

Records to Be Retained	Time Period
Form I-9, Employment Eligibility Verification, must be completed by all employers for all new employees hired after November 7, 1986. This form must be completed within three days after hiring	Must be retained for three years after the employee's hiring or for one year after employment termination, whichever is later

§ 9.6   —Employment Record Confidentiality

Regarding confidentiality, it should initially be ascertained whether the employee has a reasonable privacy expectation in the employment information. When this reasonable privacy expectation exists, information should not be released absent employee consent or authorization. In evaluating disclosure interests, the following should be considered:

1. The request's originator
2. The request's purpose
3. The relationship between the employee and employer regarding any third party requesting this information
4. Restricting disclosure to job-related information
5. Information accuracy
6. A privacy interest in not releasing the information
7. A statutory or other duty requiring or not requiring information disclosure

§ 9.7   —Sample Policies

The following examples should be considered in drafting employment record policies:

---

[43] Pub. L. No. 99-603 (Nov. 6, 1986), 100 Stat. 3359 (codified in scattered sections of 7 U.S.C. § 2025; 8 U.S.C. §§ 1101, 1152–53, 1160–61, 1184, 1186–87, 1252, 1254–55a, 1258–59, 1321, 1324–24b, 1357, 1364–65; 18 U.S.C. § 1546; 20 U.S.C. §§ 1091, 1096; 29 U.S.C. §§ 1802, 1813, 1816, 1851; 42 U.S.C. §§ 303, 502, 602–03, 672–73, 1203, 1320b-7, 1353, 1396b, 1436a, 1437r); *see also* Decker, Privacy Law §§ 2.20, 6.12.

POLICY 9.7(1)
EMPLOYMENT RECORDS

Section 1. Employee.   Any person currently employed or subject to recall after layoff or leave of absence with a right to return to a position with the Company or a former employee who has terminated services within the preceding year.

Section 2. Open Records.   The Company shall, upon an employee's request, which the Company may require to be in writing, permit the employee to inspect any personnel documents which are, have been, or are intended to be used in determining that employee's qualifications for employment, promotion, transfer, additional compensation, termination, or other disciplinary action, except as provided in Section 9 (Exceptions). The inspection right encompasses personnel documents in the possession of a person, corporation, partnership, or other association having a contractual agreement with the Company to keep or supply a personnel record. An employee may request all or any part of his or her records, except as provided in Section 9 (Exceptions). The Company shall grant at least two inspection requests by an employee in a calendar year when requests are made at reasonable intervals, unless otherwise provided in a collective bargaining agreement. The Company shall provide the employee with the inspection opportunity within seven working days after the employee makes the request or, if the Company can reasonably show that the deadline cannot be met, the Company shall have an additional seven working days to comply. The inspection shall take place at a location reasonably near the employee's place of employment and during normal working hours. The Company may allow the inspection to take place at a time other than working hours or at a place other than where the records are maintained if that time or place would be more convenient for the employee. Nothing in this policy shall be construed as a requirement that an employee be permitted to remove any personnel records or any part of these records from the place on the Company's premises where the records are made available for inspection. The Company retains the right to protect its records from loss, damage, or alteration to ensure the integrity of its records. If an employee demonstrates that he or she is unable to review his or her personnel record at the employing unit, the Company may, upon the employee's written request, mail a copy of the requested record to the employee.

Section 3. Copies.   The employee may obtain a copy of the information or part of the information contained in the employee's personnel record. The Company may charge a fee for providing a copy of the information. The fee shall be limited to the actual cost of duplicating the information.

Section 4. Personnel Record Inspection by Designated Representatives.   An employee who is involved in a current grievance against the Company may designate in writing a representative of the employee's union, collective bargaining unit, or other representative to inspect the employee's personnel record which may have a bearing on the grievance's resolution, except as provided in Section 9 (Exceptions). The Company shall allow the designated representative to inspect that employee's personnel record in the same manner as provided under Section 2 (Open Records).

Section 5. Personnel Record Correction. If the employee disagrees with any information contained in the personnel record, a removal or correction of that information may be mutually agreed upon by the Company and the employee. If an agreement cannot be reached, the employee may submit a written statement explaining the employee's position. The Company shall attach the employee's statement to the disputed portion of the personnel record. The employee's statement shall be included whenever that disputed portion of the personnel record is released to a third party as long as the disputed record is a part of the file. The inclusion of any written statement attached in the record, without further comment or action by the Company, shall not imply or create any presumption of Company agreement with its contents.

Section 6. Disclosure of Disciplinary Action: Written Notice.

a. The Company shall not disclose a disciplinary report, letter of reprimand, or other disciplinary action to a third party, to a party who is not a part of the Company's organization, or to a party who is not a part of a labor organization representing the employee, without written notice as provided in this section.

b. The written notice to the employee shall be by first-class mail to the employee's last known address and shall be mailed on or before the day the information is disclosed.

c. This section shall not apply if:

   (i) The employee has specifically waived written notice as part of a written, signed employment application with another employer;

   (ii) The disclosure is ordered to a party in legal action or arbitration; or

   (iii) Information is requested by a government agency as a result of a claim or complaint by an employee, or as a result of a criminal investigation by the agency.

Section 7. Review of Record Prior to Release of Information. The Company shall review a personnel record before releasing information to a third party and, except when the release is ordered to a party in a legal action or arbitration, delete disciplinary reports, letters of reprimand, or other records of disciplinary action which are more than four years old.

Section 8. Record of Nonemployment Activities. The Company shall not gather or keep a record of an employee's association, political activities, publications, communications, or nonemployment activities, unless the employee submits the information in writing or authorizes the Company in writing to keep or gather the information. This prohibition shall not apply to the activities that occur on the Company's premises or during the employee's working hours which interfere with the performance of the employee's legitimate job duties or the duties of other employees or activities, regardless of when and where occurring, which constitute criminal conduct or may reasonably be expected to harm the Company's property, operations, business, or could by the employee's action cause the Company financial liability. A record which is kept by the Company as permitted under this section shall be part of the personnel record.

Section 9. Exceptions.   The right of the employee or the employee's designated representative to inspect his or her personnel records does not apply to:

a. Reference letters for that employee;

b. Any portion of a test document, except that the employee may see a cumulative total test score for either a section of or the entire test document;

c. Materials used by the Company for management planning, including but not limited to judgments, external peer review documents or recommendations concerning future salary increases and other wage treatments, management bonus plans, promotions, and job assignments, or other comments or ratings used for the Company's planning purposes;

d. Information of a personal nature about a person other than the employee if disclosure of the information would constitute a clearly unwarranted invasion of the other person's privacy;

e. Records relevant to any other pending claim between the Company and employee which may be discovered in a judicial proceeding; and

f. Investigatory or security records maintained by the Company to investigate criminal conduct by an employee or other activity by the employee which could reasonably be expected to harm the Company's property, operations, or business or could by the employee's activity cause the Company financial liability, unless and until the Company takes adverse personnel action based on information in the records.

Section 10. Administration.   The Director of Human Resources or an authorized representative shall administer and enforce the provisions of this policy.

Section 11. Complaints.   If an employee alleges that he or she has been denied his or her rights under this policy, he or she may file a complaint with the Human Resources Department. The Human Resources Department shall investigate the complaint. The Human Resources Department shall attempt to resolve the complaint by conference, conciliation, or persuasion.

POLICY 9.7(2)
EMPLOYMENT RECORDS—PRIVATE EMPLOYER

Section 1. Purpose.   To establish policies and procedures for the collection, maintenance, access, use, and disclosure of employee information.

Section 2. Objectives.   To provide a uniform system of collecting, maintaining, accessing, using, and disclosing employee information, along with preserving and protecting the personal privacy of all wage and salaried employees.

Section 3. Personnel Records.

a. An employment record is to be established for each employee upon hiring.

b. Official employment records for current employees are to be maintained by the Human Resources Department.

c. Documents maintained in official employment records are classified permanent or temporary, as defined in Sections 4 (Record Access) and 6 (Type of Information Kept). Permanent information will always remain in the official employment record when an employee transfers or terminates. Temporary information is to be retained for four years, unless otherwise indicated, and then is to be removed in accordance with Section 7 (Request for Information).

d. The following information is specifically prohibited from being placed in official employment records:

   (i)   Arrest records, upon acquittal or when formal charges have been dropped;

   (ii)   Investigative material regarding a civil, criminal, or administrative investigation of alleged wrongdoing by an employee which resulted in the employee's acquittal;

   (iii)   National identification;

   (iv)   Racial identification, except data used in support of the Company's affirmative action program;

   (v)   Ethnic information;

   (vi)   Political affiliation;

   (vii)   Religious affiliation;

   (viii) Written criticisms of which an employee is not aware; and

   (ix)   Financial disclosure information.

Section 4. Record Access.

a. Official employment records are to be secured in locked file cabinets during nonwork hours. Operating instructions for computer terminals are to be accessible only to persons designated by the Human Resources Department to operate the terminals and are to be secured during nonwork hours.

b. Only the Human Resources Department and its designees are to have access to official employment records, to data maintained on the computer system file, and to computer-produced reports.

c. The following are to have access to all information in official employment records and to information on the computer system when needed in the performance of their duties, provided that requests for access are made to the Human Resources Department:

(i)   President;

(ii)   Division head and designees;

(iii)   Affirmative action officer;

(iv)   An employee's department director;

(v)   An employee's immediate supervisor and those in direct chain of command above the immediate supervisor; and

(vi)   The Human Resources Department.

d. Employees and persons with written permission of employees have the right to review official employment records and reference files. Reviews must be conducted in the presence of the Human Resources Department at times amenable to both, and an employee may have a representative present. Employees may request copies of documents in their employment records; however, they are not permitted to alter, remove, add, or replace any documents. The Human Resources Department may charge reasonable fees when requested to provide copies of all materials contained in the official employment record or when frequent requests for copies of materials are received from the same employee.

e. Employees have a right to submit rebuttals to any material in their official employment records. Rebuttals are to be acknowledged by the Human Resources Department. Rebuttals and acknowledgments shall become part of the official employment record in the same permanent or temporary category as the material being rebutted. If rebuttals are submitted by inactive employees, the acknowledgment and rebuttal shall both be included in the former employee's official employment record.

f. "Permanent information" is formal documentation of a person's current employment status and employment history.

g. "Temporary information" is information which does not make a significant contribution to a person's employment record or which becomes outdated or inaccurate because of the passage of time.

Section 5. Responsibilities.

a. The Director of Human Resources is required to maintain a record of all employees and to develop standards for the establishment and maintenance of employment records.

b. Heads of departments are to ensure that necessary procedures and safeguards are implemented in accordance with this policy.

c. Human Resources Department officers are to be the custodians of personnel records. Custodians are to disclose and withhold employee information in accordance with this policy and are to ensure that information under their control is not accessible to unauthorized persons.

d. The Human Resources Department is to store and control official employment records of inactive employees until the year of the individual's 75th year of birth. At that time, the folders are to be burned or shredded. In addition, the Human Resources Department is to provide information to departments, former employees, and other authorized persons, as prescribed in this policy.

e. The Human Resources Department shall audit this policy's implementation and review complaints and appeals concerning information delays or denials. The Human Resources Department shall also review all subpoenas and other written judicial orders seeking information.

f. All personnel having access to official employment records or to data maintained on the computer files or to the computer-produced reports, directly or through someone else, are to disclose and withhold information in accordance with this policy and are to ensure that information under their control is not accessible to unauthorized persons.

Section 6. Type of Information Kept.

a. This is not an all-inclusive list of information appropriate for maintenance in official employment records. Questions regarding the appropriateness of maintaining other data should be referred to the Human Resources Department. The following types of information are permanent and must be included in official employment records:

(i) Latest employment application;

(ii) Employee notifications regarding appointment, promotion, demotion, involuntary retirement, resignation by reason of abandonment of position, layoff, reassignment, transfer, salary changes (except general pay increases), termination, suspension, disciplinary notices, and temporary assignment in a higher job classification;

(iii) Absence and leave records;

(iv) Last five annual performance evaluations;

(v) Employee-initiated acknowledgments of temporary employment or unusual employment conditions, such as the certificate required of minors;

(vi) Employee requests and responses concerning voluntary retirement, voluntary separation, transfer, demotion, and leaves of absence other than vacation, sick, or personal;

(vii) Employee benefit records;

(viii) Current payroll deduction authorizations including, but not limited to, group life insurance, retirement, medical/hospital insurance, workers' compensation, federal and state withholding tax, earned income tax, union dues, credit union, and tax-sheltered annuities;

(ix) Letters of commendation, cost reduction awards, management improvement awards, exceptional increments, awards for excellence, professional organization or society awards, and any other form of official recognition given an employee that relates to his or her duties and responsibilities; and

(x)   Significant training records.

b. The following types of information are temporary and are to be purged from official employment records:

(i)   Reference letters;

(ii)   Caution, reprimand, admonishment, or warning letters;

(iii) Oral reprimand confirmations;

(iv)   Nonpermanent performance evaluations;

(v)   Professional affiliations;

(vi)   Out-service and in-service training of limited significance to an employee's development; and

(vii) Periodic health examination records required by federal or state regulations.

c. Reference information is subject to access by employees. Only the following employee information may be maintained for reference purposes by departments not maintaining official employment records:

(i)   Name and home address;

(ii)   Social security number;

(iii) Job classification title;

(iv)   Job description, performance objectives, and performance standards;

(v)   Data necessary to verify payrolls;

(vi)   Attendance records;

(vii) Emergency telephone numbers; and

(viii) Copies of last five performance evaluations.

d. Supervisors' or managers' notes and records on matters involving discipline or performance on specific work assignments may be maintained separately from the official employment record and are not subject to employee access.

e. If a personnel action is amended, only information concerning the amended action is to be maintained. The original personnel action and any rescinded personnel actions are to be removed from an official employment record.

Section 7. Request for Information.

a. Requests for employment information disclosure are to be handled as follows:

(i)   An employee's home address may be furnished to police or court officials upon written request showing that an indictment has been returned against an employee or a complaint, information, accusation, or other writ has been filed against an employee and the home address is needed to serve a summons, warrant, or subpoena.

(ii)   An employee's social security number and home address may be furnished to taxing authorities upon written request.

(iii)   Medical information may be furnished:

    (A)   When it is needed to aid medical treatment and an employee is not able to provide the information;

    (B)   To a federal or state investigative agency when requested information is required to verify adherence to regulations.

(iv)   Any information available to an employee from his or her own official employment record may be released upon written employee authorization.

(v)   The Director of Human Resources is to be notified immediately of the receipt of any subpoena or other written judicial order seeking information not listed in Section 7.1(i) above. The Human Resources Department, in conjunction with the Company's general counsel, will make a determination as to the response to a subpoena or judicial order. Should a subpoena appear on its face to be relevant to the legal proceeding and not to be overly broad in scope, and without a compelling policy or legal reason to be contrary, the Company will make the requested records available. However, before complying with a subpoena, the employee will be given an opportunity to consult with a private attorney to seek to have the subpoena quashed. Should the Human Resources Department be unable to contact the employee, it will, by certified mail, return receipt requested, mail notification of the subpoena to the employee's last known address.

(vi)   Federal and state law enforcement and investigative agencies are to be provided, upon request, information deemed a public record. Requests from these agencies for nonpublic information are to be honored only if requested information is determined to be relevant to the investigation or audit and is within statutory authority of the requesting agency. Employment records are not to be released. Questions concerning the release of this information should be referred to the Director of Human Resources.

(vii)   Following the release of nonpublic information to a federal or state investigative agency, due to a subpoena or otherwise, the Human Resources Department shall notify the employee in writing of what information was released.

(viii)   Replies to inquiries from a prospective employer concerning specific reasons for an employee's employment separation are to indicate only whether the separation was voluntary or involuntary. Particular circumstances or issues involved in an involuntary separation are not to be disclosed without the employee's written authorization, or when authorized by the Human Resources Department.

b. Official employment records are to be reviewed at least once every two years or when an employee transfers or is terminated. Information within the files is to be maintained in chronological order. Temporary information fours years old or older is to be removed. Oral and written reprimands are to be maintained for two years if no similar incidents occur. Employees are to be notified when documents are removed from their folders and are to be given 10 calendar days to request these documents. Documents not needed for current or pending disciplinary or grievance actions or not requested by employees are to be destroyed.

c. Requests to review official employment records by employees are to be responded to as follows:

   (i)   Employees are to be advised that they may choose to travel to the location where the official employment record is maintained. Travel expenses or unpaid leave will not be authorized for this purpose;

   (ii)   Upon request, the contents of an employee's official employment record may be duplicated and forwarded for review;

   (iii) The Human Resources Department will attach a signed statement to the file certifying that the entire contents of the record were copied and contained in the record sent to the employee; and

   (iv)   Employees may be charged reasonable fees for the cost of reproducing material in their official employment records.

Section 8. Access to Inactive Records.   The Human Resources Department will provide access to inactive official employment records to clearly identified former employees or persons with letters of authorization from former employees.

Section 9. Administration.   The Human Resources Department will review compliance with this policy. Departments will be advised of areas of noncompliance and corrective actions required. If any procedure in this policy conflicts with any provision in a collective bargaining agreement, which provision is otherwise lawful, the provision of the collective bargaining agreement shall control.

POLICY 9.7(3)
EMPLOYMENT RECORDS—PUBLIC EMPLOYER

Section 1. Purpose.   To establish policies and procedures for the collection, maintenance, access, use, and disclosure of personnel information.

Section 2. Objectives.   To provide a uniform system of collecting, maintaining, accessing, using, and disclosing personnel information, along with preserving and protecting the personal privacy of all wage and salaried employees, and to provide for the public's right to know.

Section 3. Personnel Records.

a. All personnel records of employees, active and inactive, are employment records. An employment record is to be established for each employee upon hiring.

b. Official employment records for active employees are to be maintained by the Personnel Bureau.

c. The Personnel Bureau is the official repository of all personnel records on inactive employees.

d. Documents maintained in official employment records are classified permanent or temporary, as defined in Sections 4 (Record Access) and 6 (Type of Information Kept). Permanent information will, in all cases, remain in the official employment record when an employee transfers or terminates. Temporary information is to be retained for four years, unless otherwise indicated, and then is to be removed in accordance with Section 7 (Request for Information).

e. The following information is specifically prohibited from being placed in official employment records:

   (i) Arrest records, upon acquittal or when formal charges have been dropped;

   (ii) Investigative material regarding a civil, criminal, or administrative investigation of alleged wrongdoing by an employee which resulted in the employee's acquittal;

   (iii) National identification;

   (iv) Racial identification, except data used in support of an affirmative action program;

   (v) Ethnic information;

   (vi) Political affiliation;

   (vii) Religious affiliation;

   (viii) Written criticisms of which an employee is not aware; and

   (ix) Code of Conduct financial disclosure forms and supplementary employment information.

Section 4. Record Access.

a. Official employment records are to be secured in locked file cabinets during nonwork hours. Operating instructions for computer terminals are to be accessible only to persons designated by the Personnel Bureau to operate the terminals, and are to be secured during nonwork hours.

b. Only the Personnel Bureau and its designees shall have access to official employment records, to data maintained in the employment records, to data maintained on the computer file, and to computer-produced reports.

c. The following are to have access to all information in official employment records and to information on the computer file, when needed in the performance of their duties, provided that requests for access are made to the Personnel Bureau:

(i)   Governor and Lieutenant Governor;

(ii)   Agency head and designees;

(iii)   Agency affirmative action officer;

(iv)   An employee's bureau director;

(v)   An employee's immediate supervisor and those in direct chain of command above the immediate supervisor.

(vi)   Members of the Bureaus of Personnel, Labor Relations, and Affirmative Action, Office of Administration (OA); and

(vii)   Designated staff of the State Civil Service Commission.

d. Employees, and persons with written permission of employees, have the right to review official employment records and reference files. Reviews must be conducted in the presence of the Personnel Bureau or designee at times amenable to both, and an employee may have a representative present. Employees may request copies of documents in their records; however, they are not allowed to alter, remove, add, or replace any documents. The Personnel Bureau may charge reasonable fees when requested to provide copies of all materials contained in the official employment records, or when frequent requests for copies of materials are received from the same employee.

e. Employees have a right to submit rebuttals to any material in their official employment records. Rebuttals are to be acknowledged by custodians. Rebuttals and acknowledgments shall become part of the official employment record in the same permanent or temporary category as the material being rebutted. If rebuttals are submitted by inactive employees, the Personnel Bureau will acknowledge the rebuttal and both the rebuttal and the acknowledgment will be included in the former employee's official employment record.

f. "Public information" consists of name; employment department, board, commission, system, or council; position title; date of birth; biweekly salary; appointment date; voting county; headquarters county; type of service (civil service or non-civil service); pay status; and employee benefits. The above is not an all-inclusive list of public information. Any other requests for information that may be considered public are to be forwarded to the Personnel Bureau.

g. "Permanent information" is formal documentation of a person's current employment status and employment history.

h. "Temporary information" is information which does not make a significant contribution to a person's employment record or which becomes outdated or inaccurate because of the passage of time.

Section 5. Responsibilities.

a. The Director of Personnel is required to maintain a record of all employees and to develop standards for the establishment and maintenance of employment records.

b. Heads of agencies are to ensure that necessary procedures and safeguards are implemented in accordance with this policy.

c. Personnel officers are to be custodians of personnel records. They are to disclose and withhold employee information in accordance with this policy, and are to ensure that information under their control is not accessible to unauthorized persons.

d. The Personnel Bureau is to store and control official employment records of inactive employees until the year of the individual's 75th year of age. At that time, the folders are to be burned or shredded. In addition, the Personnel Bureau is to provide information to agencies, former employees, and other authorized persons, as prescribed in this policy.

e. The Personnel Bureau shall audit this policy's implementation and review complaints and appeals concerning information delays or denials. The Personnel Bureau shall also review all subpoenas and other written judicial orders seeking information.

f. All personnel having access to official employment records, to data maintained on the computer file, or to computer-produced reports, directly or through someone else, are to disclose and withhold information in accordance with this policy, and are to ensure that information under their control is not accessible to unauthorized persons.

Section 6. Type of Information Kept.

a. This is not an all-inclusive list of information appropriate for maintenance in official employment records. Questions regarding the appropriateness of maintaining other data should be referred to the Personnel Bureau. The following types of information are permanent and must be included in official employment records:

   (i)   Latest employment application;

   (ii)   Employee notifications regarding appointment, promotion, demotion, involuntary retirement, resignation by reason of abandonment of position, furlough, reassignment, transfer, salary changes (except general pay increases), dismissal, suspension, change in Civil Service status, and temporary assignment in a higher classification;

   (iii) Out-of-ordinary leave records;

   (iv)   Last five annual performance evaluation reports;

   (v)   Employee-initiated acknowledgements of temporary employment or unusual employment conditions, such as the certificate required of minors;

    (vi)   Employee requests and agency responses concerning voluntary retirement, voluntary separation, transfer, demotion, and leaves of absence other than annual, sick, or personal;

    (vii)   Current payroll deduction authorizations including, but not limited to, group life insurance, retirement, medical/hospital insurance, workers' compensation, federal and state withholding tax, earned income tax, union dues, credit union, and tax-sheltered annuities;

    (ix)   Letters of commendation, cost reduction awards, management improvement awards, exceptional increments, Governor's Award for Excellence, professional organization or society awards, and any other form of official recognition given an employee that relates to his or her employment duties and responsibilities;

    (x)   Department of Defense Form DD-214 when used for employment purposes; and

    (xi)   Significant training records.

  b. The following types of information are temporary and are to be purged from official employment records:

    (i)   Reference letters;

    (ii)   Caution, reprimand, admonishment, or warning letters;

    (iii)   Oral reprimand confirmations;

    (iv)   Nonpermanent performance evaluations;

    (v)   Professional affiliations;

    (vi)   Out-service and in-service training of limited significance to an employee's development; and

    (vii)   Periodic health examination records required by federal or state regulations.

  c. Reference information is subject to access by employees. Only the following employee information may be maintained for reference purposes by offices not maintaining official employment records:

    (i)   Name and home address;

    (ii)   Social security number;

    (iii)   Job classification title;

    (iv)   Job description, performance objectives, and performance standards;

    (v)   Data necessary to verify payrolls;

    (vi)   Attendance records;

    (vii)   Emergency telephone numbers; and

    (viii) Copies of last five performance evaluations.

d. Supervisors' or managers' notes and records on matters involving discipline or performance on specific work assignments may be maintained separately from the official employment records, and are not subject to employee access.

e. If a personnel action is amended, only information concerning the amended action is to be maintained. The original personnel action and any rescinded personnel actions are to be removed from the employment record.

Section 7. Request for Information.

a. Requests for nonpublic information are to be handled as follows:

(i)   An employee's home address may be furnished to police or court officials upon written request showing that an indictment has been returned against an employee or a complaint, information, accusation, or other writ has been filed against an employee and the home address is needed to serve a summons, warrant, or subpoena.

(ii)   An employee's social security number and home address may be furnished to taxing authorities upon written request.

(iii)   Medical information may be furnished:

(A)   When it is needed to aid medical treatment and an employee is not able to provide the information.

(B)   To a federal or state investigative agency when requested information is required to verify adherence to regulations.

(iv)   Any information available to an employee from his or her own official employment record may be released upon written authorization of the employee.

(v)   The Director of Personnel is to be notified immediately of the receipt of any subpoena or other written judicial order seeking information not listed in Section 7.a(i). The Director of Personnel, in conjunction with the Office of General Counsel, will make a determination as to the response to a subpoena or judicial order. Should a subpoena appear on its face to be relevant to the legal proceeding and not to be overly broad in scope, and without a compelling policy or legal reason to the contrary, the Personnel Bureau will make the requested records available. However, before complying with a subpoena, the employee may consult with a private attorney to seek to have the subpoena quashed. Should the Personnel Bureau be otherwise unable to contact the employee, it will, by certified mail, return receipt requested, mail notification of the subpoena to the employee's last known address.

(vi)   Nonpublic information may be released to governmental investigative personnel when needed in the performance of their official duties. Proper identification must be provided and requesters must state specifically what information is needed. The Personnel Bureau shall determine whether the requested information is relevant to the investigation's nature or audit and is within statutory authority of the investigating agency. Only information deemed relevant and within statutory authority is to be provided. The following agencies are to be provided nonpublic information upon request:

(A)   Human Relations Commission;

(B)   Auditor General;

(C)   Office of General Counsel;

(D)   State Police; and

(E)   Attorney General.

If it is determined that the requested information is irrelevant to the stated request's reason, the requester is to be advised that the request can be referred to the Director of Personnel, or the requester can seek a subpoena.

(vii)   Federal and state law enforcement and investigative agencies are to be provided, upon request, information deemed a public record. Requests from these agencies for nonpublic information are to be honored only if requested information is determined to be relevant to the investigation or audit and is within statutory authority of the requesting agency. Entire employment records are not to be released unless all information contained is relevant to the investigation or audit. Questions concerning the release of this information should be referred to the Personnel Bureau. If it is determined that requested information is irrelevant or not within statutory authority, the requester is to be advised that the request can be referred to the Director of Personnel, or the requester can seek a subpoena.

(viii)   Following the release of nonpublic information to a federal or state investigative agency, due to a subpoena or otherwise, the Personnel Bureau shall notify the employee in writing of what information was released.

(ix)   Replies to inquiries from a prospective employer concerning specific reasons for an employee's employment separation are to indicate only whether the separation was voluntary or involuntary. Particular circumstances or issues involved in an involuntary separation are not to be disclosed without written authorization of the employee, or when authorized by the Personnel Bureau.

(x)   The Personnel Bureau shall release pertinent employment information when an employee is requesting a transfer from one agency to another, or when an employee is to be reemployed within 60 calendar days of termination. The following information, in addition to public information, is to be provided to another agency upon written request indicating that the employee is being considered for employment:

(A)   Performance evaluations;

(B)   Caution, reprimand, admonishment, or warning letters;

    (C)   Oral reprimand confirmations;

    (D)   Suspension and termination letters;

    (E)   Commendation letters;

    (F)   Leave records;

    (G)   Training records; and

    (H)   Employment history data (consisting of the above data on file from each agency in which the employee was employed).

The Personnel Bureau is to notify an employee of what information has been referred to the requesting agency. If an individual is not subsequently accepted for transfer or reemployment, all information is to be returned to the forwarding agency. Use of this information for any other purpose is strictly prohibited.

b.   Official employment records are to be reviewed at least once every two years or when an employee transfers or is terminated. Information within the files is to be maintained in chronological order. Temporary information four years old or older is to be removed. Oral and written reprimands are to be maintained for two years if no similar incidents occur. Employees are to be notified when documents are removed from their folders and are to be given 10 calendar days to request these documents. Documents not needed for current or pending disciplinary or grievance actions or not requested by employees are to be destroyed.

c.   Requests to review official employment records by employees located at facilities other than where the records are maintained are to be responded to as follows:

    (i)   Employees are to be advised that they may choose to travel to the location where the official employment record is maintained. Travel expenses and administrative leave will not be authorized for this purpose.

    (ii)   Upon request, the contents of an employee's official employment record are to be duplicated and forwarded for review.

    (iii)   The Personnel Bureau will attach a signed statement to the file certifying that the entire contents of the record were copied and are contained in the record sent to the employee.

    (iv)   Employees may be charged reasonable fees for the cost of reproducing material in their official employment records.

d.   Before records of transferring employees are sent to gaining agencies, the Personnel Bureau shall ensure that they contain all appropriate permanent documents, and that the terminated employee's name, social security number, and year of birth are correctly entered. Records are to be safeguarded during transit and receipted for by gaining agencies. Losing agencies may retain the names, addresses, social security numbers, and copies of personnel history cards of transferred and terminated employees. Those agencies using United States mail to transfer folders should use third- or fourth-class rates.

e. Records of transferring employees are to be provided to gaining agencies. The Personnel Bureau should notify the employee of information provided to the requesting agency.

f. Official employment records of terminated employees are to be sent to the Personnel Bureau within 60 calendar days of termination, except those of employees with pending grievances, appeals, or other formal actions requiring retention. When the formal action is resolved, the folder should be sent to the Personnel Bureau immediately. Each agency is to provide a list of its personnel who are authorized to have access to inactive folders.

Section 8. Access to Inactive Records.   The Personnel Bureau will provide access to inactive official employment records as follows:

a. Public information will be provided within a reasonable time period to anyone upon request:

b. Nonpublic information will be furnished to clearly identified former employees or persons with authorization letters from former employees;

c. Any previous employing agency will be provided access to official employment records. Records will be made available only to persons authorized by an agency to have access;

d. Records will be made available to agencies in which an inactive employee has not had previous employment upon:

    (i)   Written request by the agency indicating the employee has been employed and the record is needed for active employment use; or upon

    (ii)   Written authorization from the most recent employment agency; or upon

    (iii)   Employee authorization.

Section 9. Administration.   The Personnel Bureau will review compliance with this policy. Agencies will be advised of areas of noncompliance and corrective actions required. If any procedure in this policy conflicts with any provision in a collective bargaining agreement, which provision is otherwise lawful, the provision of the collective bargaining agreement shall control.

POLICY 9.7(4)
EMPLOYMENT RECORD CONFIDENTIALITY

Section 1. Confidentiality.   The Company shall make reasonable efforts to keep in confidence and not to disclose to any third party, or use for the benefit of any party other than the Company, the employee's confidential and proprietary documentation which is or has been disclosed to the Company. This information shall be protected by the same security procedures as are used by the Company in protecting its own trade secrets and other confidential data, and shall be examined by and disclosed to only those persons who may require the information in the course of their legitimate job-related duties.

Section 2. Exceptions.   The requirement of confidential treatment shall not apply:

a. To information that was in the public domain prior to the Company's receipt of it or has subsequently become part of the public domain by publication or otherwise, except by the Company's wrongful act;

b. Information that was in the Company's possession prior to its receipt and was not acquired directly or indirectly from the employee;

c. Information independently developed by the Company; and

d. Information received by the Company from a third party as to which the Company reasonably believes it has no confidentiality obligation.

§ 9.8   —Employment Record Inspection Forms

The following policy should be considered regarding employment record inspection:

FORM 9.8(1)
EMPLOYMENT RECORD INSPECTION

Upon submission of a written request to the Human Resources Department, an employee may examine his or her personnel file's contents. Within a reasonable time after the request's receipt, the employee will be notified of a time, during regular business hours, when the employee on his or her free time may inspect the file's contents. The file, or any of its contents, may not be removed from the inspection place; however, the employee may take notes or by written request receive copies of file material for a reasonable copying charge. An employee who disagrees with file material should bring this to the Human Resources Director's attention. If no satisfactory resolution occurs, the employee may insert into the personnel file his or her position statement. This statement will become a permanent part of the employee's personnel folder and will accompany the contested document at all times. The employee's personnel file will not be disclosed to anyone outside the Company except in compliance with a lawfully served subpoena or statutory requirement.

FORM 9.8(2)
EMPLOYMENT RECORD INSPECTION

Section 1. Review.   Employees and other persons with written permission of affected employees have the right to review their official employment records. All reviews must be conducted in the presence of the Human Resources staff, at times amenable to both, and an employee may have a representative of his or her choosing present. Employees and/or their representatives may request document copies; however, they are not allowed to alter, remove, add, or replace any documents. Reasonable fees may be charged by the Human Resources Department when document copies are requested.

Section 2. Rebuttals.   Employees may submit rebuttals to any material contained in their official employment records. Rebuttals are to be acknowledged by the Human Resources Department. Rebuttals and acknowledgments shall become part of the official employment record.

§ 9.9   Medical Records

Medical records may contain employee personal details regarding age, life history, family background, medical history, present and past health or illness, mental and emotional health or illness, treatment, accident reports, laboratory reports, and other scientific data from various sources. They may also contain medical providers' notes, prognoses, and reports of the patients' response to treatment. Should this medical information be disclosed, it could cause embarrassment, humiliation, damage to family relationships, or even employment termination.[44]

Medical record technology changes, through third-party payment,[45] government medical care participation,[46] and recordkeeping system computerization, have expanded medical information's amount, type, and accessibility.[47] These records may be sought for various reasons. They may be important to legal actions,[48] public health evaluation and occupational health research,[49] third-party payment,[50] employment,[51] credit rating,[52] and other health care provider use.[53]

---

[44] *See* Decker, Privacy Law § 7.4.

[45] Third-party payment includes payment of medical expenses by government insurance carriers and the employer. H. Schuchman, Confidentiality of Medical Records 6 (1982) [hereinafter Schuchman, Medical Records].

[46] Government payment for health care involves Medicaid, which provides aid for medical payments to low-income individuals. The program is state-administered and federally reimbursed. Schuchman, Medical Records at 78, 81, 88–89.

[47] *See generally* Boyer, *Computerized Medical Records and the Right to Privacy: The Emerging Federal Response,* 25 Buffalo L. Rev. 37 (1975) (discussing computerization of clinical medicine, statistical research and policy planning, and medical treatment payment).

[48] *See* United States v. Westinghouse Elec. Corp., 638 F.2d 570 (3d Cir. 1980) (this may arise through court-ordered disclosure or subpoenas).

[49] Occupational health research involves investigations of employment conditions and employee health to determine if materials used in that environment negatively affect employee health. This is provided for by OSHA. 29 U.S.C. § 669 (1982); *see* Decker, Privacy Law § 2.13.

[50] *See* Winslade, *Confidentiality of Medical Records: An Overview of Concepts and Legal Policies,* 3 J. Legal Medicine 497, 509 (1982).

[51] E. Hayt, Medico-Legal Aspects of Hospital Records 187 (1977).

[52] Schuchman, Medical Records at 4.

[53] On the federal level, the Privacy Act of 1974 includes medical records in its access provision, in that "Each [federal] agency that maintains a system of records shall—upon request by any individual to gain access to his record to any information pertaining to him which is contained

Employee medical information disclosure to employers may also create privacy problems. This may arise when an employee is disciplined for apparent alcohol or drug abuse before any test is requested.[54] The employer should inform the employee that he or she may vindicate his or her condition by taking an examination. If the employee consents to a medical examination but refuses to provide a written authorization for disclosure of the results, the employer may circumvent the authorization requirement by asking the doctor for an opinion limited to whether the employee is qualified to work.

To minimize potential challenges to discipline imposed following an employee's refusal to release medical information, clear instructions should be given to the employee. The employee should be specifically advised that he or she may be disciplined based on the employer's information then available, even if the employee refuses to submit to an examination or the employee continues to refuse to authorize test result disclosure.

A privacy interest in medical records has been partially acknowledged,[55] and the employee privacy interest in preserving medical record confidentiality has been recognized by federal[56] and state[57] statutes. Society's legitimate need for this information may supersede an employee privacy interest even though an employee's medical records, which may contain intimate personal facts, are entitled to privacy protection.[58] Employee privacy rights must be evaluated against the public interest represented by certain government investigations.[59]

Employers should take precautions to protect medical information confidentiality by restricting access to managerial employees who have a legitimate job-related business interest in obtaining the information. Except in emergency situations, employers should avoid seeking medical information directly from an

---

in the system; permit him . . . to review the record and have a copy made . . . ." 5 U.S.C. § 552a(d)(1) (1988); *see also* Decker, Privacy Law § 2.4.

[54] *See, e.g.,* Conveyor Co., 38 Lab. Arb. (BNA) 1141, 1143 (1962) (Roberts, Arb.) (employer's inherent right to require physical examinations); *see also* Decker, Privacy Law § 7.4.

[55] *See, e.g.,* 5 U.S.C. § 552a (1988) (Privacy Act of 1974, forbidding medical record disclosure without written consent, unless covered by specific statutory exception); *see also* United States v. Westinghouse Elec. Corp., 638 F.2d 570, 577 (3d Cir. 1980) (explicitly recognizing constitutional employee medical record privacy right); General Motors Corp. v. Director of NIOSH, 363 F.2d 163, 166 (6th Cir. 1980) (implicitly recognizing constitutional privacy right), *cert. denied,* 454 U.S. 877 (1981); *see also* Decker, Privacy Law §§ 2.4, 2.31, 7.4.

[56] *See, e.g.,* 29 U.S.C. §§ 651–678 (1988) (Occupational Safety and Health Act); *see also* Decker, Privacy Law § 2.13.

[57] *See, e.g.,* Md. Ann. Code art. 100 § 95A(a)–(e) (1979) (Maryland's statute protecting medical record privacy); *see also* Decker, Privacy Law § 2.31.

[58] United States v. Westinghouse Elec. Corp., 638 F.2d 570, 577 (3d Cir. 1980) (recognizing constitutional employee medical privacy right).

[59] *See, e.g.,* 29 U.S.C. §§ 651–678 (1988) (Occupational Safety and Health Act); *see also* Decker, Privacy Law §§ 2.13, 7.4.

employee's physician without prior employee consent. Employee hospital records should be accorded similar deference.[60]

Various states restrict dissemination of medical information in the custody of health care providers, and also strictly limit an employer's use and disclosure of employee medical information.[61] Employers should refrain from collecting, maintaining, using, disclosing, or knowingly permitting employees to use or disclose medical information which the employer possesses, without the employee having first signed an authorization permitting this use or disclosure.

Employers must establish appropriate procedures to ensure medical information confidentiality and protection from unauthorized collection, maintenance, use, and disclosure. Procedures may include instructions regarding confidentiality to employees handling files, and security systems restricting file access.

§ 9.10 —Drafting

In drafting medical record policies, the following should be considered:

1. Applicable federal[62] and state[63] statutes;
2. Medical information disclosure
3. The relationship between the employee and employer regarding any third party requesting the information
4. The employee's privacy interest in not releasing the information
5. The employer's statutory or other duty to disclose the information
6. Identity of the person making the request
7. The request's purpose
8. When an employee who is the subject of medical information maintained by an employer requests correction or amendment, the employer should:
   a. Disclose to the employee, or to a person designated by him or her, the identity of the medical information's source;
   b. Make the correction or amendment within a reasonable time period if the person who was the information's source concurs that the information is inaccurate or incomplete;
   c. Establish a procedure for an employee who is the subject of employer medical information to present supplemental information for inclusion

---

[60] *See* Dalprin Co., 83-2 Lab. Arb. Awards (CCH) ¶ 8,555 (1983) (Dybeck, Arb.).

[61] *See, e.g.,* Md. Ann. Code art. 100, § 95A(a)–(e) (1979) (Maryland's statute protecting medical record privacy); *see also* Decker, Privacy Law §§ 2.31, 7.4.

[62] *See, e.g.,* 29 U.S.C. §§ 651–678 (1988) (Occupational Safety and Health Act); 42 U.S.C. §§ 12101–12213 (Supp. 1992) (Americans with Disabilities Act).

[63] *See, e.g.,* Md. Ann. Code art. 100, § 95A(a)–(e) (1979) (Maryland's statute protecting medical record privacy); *see also* Decker, Privacy law §§ 2.31, 7.4.

in the employer's medical information, provided that the supplemental information's source is also included.[64]

10. Employer authorization for disclosure of medical records should:

  a. Be handwritten by the employee

  b. Be separate from any other language present on the same page

  c. Be signed and dated by the employee

  d. State the names, employer functions, or persons authorized to disclose the information

  e. State the names, employer functions, persons, or entities authorized to receive the information

  f. State the limitations on the medical information's use by those authorized to receive it

  g. Provide a date after which the employer is no longer authorized to disclose the information

  h. Provide the employee with a copy of the authorization

§ 9.11   —Medical Record Confidentiality

In maintaining medical record confidentiality, the employer must consider:

1. Record types involved
2. The information
3. The potential for harm should disclosure occur
4. The disclosure's effect on the physician-patient relationship
5. Safeguards against inadvertent or accidental disclosure
6. Statutory or public interest reasons requiring disclosure

§ 9.12   —Sample Policies

The following examples should be considered in drafting medical record policies:

POLICY 9.12(1)
MEDICAL RECORD COLLECTION

Section 1. Medical Record Collection Authorization.   For the Company to obtain medical information from an employee, the employee will be required to sign an authorization. The Company shall provide a copy of the authorization to

---

[64] Privacy Protection Study Commission, Report at 263.

the employee upon demand. The Company shall disclose any limitations on the use of the information to the person to whom it is communicated. The Company shall not be liable for any unauthorized use of the medical information if it has attempted in good faith to communicate the limitations of use. The Company will honor any cancellation or modification of the authorization by the employee upon receipt of written notice.

Section 2. Lack of Medical Record Authorization.   If an employee refuses to execute an authorization, the Company will not discriminate against the employee in terms or conditions of employment on the basis of that refusal. However, the Company may take necessary action against an employee, including discipline up to and including termination, in the absence of medical information due to the employee's refusal to sign an authorization. Should the Company be unable to ascertain an employee's ability to perform a job function due to a physical condition, discipline or termination may be appropriate despite the employee's refusal to release medical information. Regardless of whether an employee consents to submit to a test which would evaluate alcohol or drug abuse, the Company has the right to discipline an employee based on other information available to it.

Section 3. No Authorization Required.   The Company is not required to obtain employee authorization for release of medical records in the following circumstances:

a.   The information is compelled by judicial or administrative process;

b.   The information is relevant in a lawsuit, arbitration, grievance, or other claim or challenge to which the Company and employee are parties and in which the employee has placed in issue his or her medical history, medical or physical condition or treatment;

c.   For administering and maintaining employee benefit plans, workers' compensation, and for determining eligibility for paid and unpaid leave from work for medical reasons; and

d.   Disclosure to a provider of health care.

POLICY 9.12(2)
MEDICAL RECORD RELEASE

Section 1. Release.   The Company shall provide medical information that it has collected or maintained regarding its employees. This information shall be provided upon written request of an employee, a former employee, or the employee's designated representative to furnish any medical report pertaining to the employee. This information extends to any medical report arising out of any physical examination by a physician or other health care professional and any hospital or laboratory tests which examinations or tests are required by the Company as a condition of employment or arising out of any injury or disease related to the employee's employment. However, if a physician concludes that presentation of all or any part of an employee's medical record directly to the employee will result in serious medical harm to the employee, he or she shall so indicate on the medical record, in which case a copy shall be given to a physician designated in writing by the employee.

Section 2. Cost Reimbursement.   The Company may require the employee, former employee, or the employee's designated representative to pay the reasonable cost of furnishing report copies.

POLICY 9.12(3)
MEDICAL RECORD CONFIDENTIALITY

The Company shall maintain medical information confidentiality regarding applicants, employees, and former employees. It shall furnish only medical information to a physician designated in writing by the applicant, employee, or former employee. However, the Company may use or supply medical examination information in response to subpoenas, requests to the Company by any governmental agency, and in arbitration or litigation of any claim or action involving the Company.

CHAPTER 10

WORKPLACE
MEDICAL POLICIES

§ 10.1   Introduction to Medical Concerns

Workplace medical concerns are gaining importance through the growing awareness of alcohol and drug abuse and through the uncertainty over acquired immune deficiency syndrome (AIDS). Employees and employers are increasingly confronted with serious questions regarding how medical privacy concerns should be balanced. This section reviews medical concerns arising out of physical examinations,[1] smoking,[2] employee assistance programs,[3] alcohol and drug abuse,[4] AIDS,[5] and safety.[6]

---

[1] See §§ **10.2–10.4.**

[2] See §§ **10.5–10.7.**

[3] See §§ **10.8–10.11.**

[4] See §§ **10.12–10.34.**

[5] See §§ **10.35–10.45.**

[6] See §§ **9.96–9.98.**

§ 10.2 Physical Examinations

The employer's right to require applicants to undergo a physical examination is considered basic to the hiring process.[7] Physical examinations may be administered at the final hiring process step after an employment offer has been made that is contingent upon satisfactory completion of the physical examination.[8] Situations also arise that necessitate requiring physical examinations during the employment relationship.[9]

Employers may, unless restricted by a collective bargaining agreement, require employees to have physical examinations under legitimate job-related circumstances.[10] This need may arise where an employee desires to return to work following an accident, sick leave, or extended layoff, has exercised a bid on a job requiring greater physical effort, or so forth.[11] It has also been acknowledged that "this right is not an absolute one exercisable at the whim" of the employer that "cannot be arbitrarily insisted upon without reasonable grounds."[12] Unreasonable requests for physical examinations could expose employers to liability under federal[13] and state[14] FEP statutes.

§ 10.3 —Drafting

In drafting physical examination policies, the following should be considered:

1. Conditions for administering
   a. Before hiring
   b. After hiring
      (1) Accidents
      (2) Sick leave
      (3) Layoff
      (4) Job bids

---

[7] *See* Conveyor Co., 38 Lab. Arb. (BNA) 1141 (1962) (Roberts, Arb.) (employer's good faith right to require physical examination). *See also* Decker, Privacy Law § 6.15A.

[8] *See* 42 U.S.C. §§ 12101–12213 (Supp. 1992) (Americans with Disabilities Act).

[9] *See, e.g.,* Pittsburgh Plate Glass Co., 52 Lab. Arb. (BNA) 985 (1969) (Duff, Arb.) (employer's right to require physical examination after sick leave).

[10] *Id.*

[11] *See, e.g.,* Chris-Craft Corp., 27 Lab. Arb. (BNA) 404 (1956) (Bothwell, Arb.) (employer could require physical examination in recall).

[12] Conchemco, Inc., 55 Lab. Arb. (BNA) 54, 97 (1970) (Ray, Arb.).

[13] *See, e.g.,* 42 U.S.C. §§ 2000e-1 to 2002-17 (1988) (Civil Rights Act of 1964); *see also* Decker, Privacy Law §§ 2.7–2.12.

[14] *See, e.g.,* Pa. Stat. Ann. tit. 43, §§ 952–963 (Purdon 1991) (Pennsylvania Human Relations Act); *see also* Decker, Privacy Law § 2.25.

2. Partial or full payment by

   a. Applicant

   b. Employee or

   c. Employer

3. Result of disputes

4. Establishing relationships with one or more physicians because the physician:

   a. Understands the job's physical requirements

   b. Is able to provide a faster conclusion regarding employment eligibility

   c. Is familiar with required paperwork

   d. Provides a more convenient means for dialogue with the human resources staff

5. Employing a full- or part-time physician on a retainer and/or one of a group of physicians.

§ 10.4   —Sample Policies

The following examples should be considered in drafting physical examination policies:

POLICY 10.4(1)
PHYSICAL EXAMINATION—HEALTH CARE EMPLOYER

As an employment condition, employees will be required at the Company's cost to have a pre-employment physical examination completed by a physician currently licensed to practice in [state's name]. A written statement from the examining physician shall verify that the individual is free from communicable diseases that may disqualify him or her for the position for which he or she is seeking employment. A written report of a chest x-ray completed within the past 60 days or a tuberculin skin test (Mantoux) done within 72 hours after the employee reports to work will also be required. All employees with a positive reaction from the skin test will be required to have a chest x-ray at their expense. During employment, the Company at its cost reserves the right to require employees as a condition to continuing or maintaining employment to undergo periodic physical examinations.

POLICY 10.4(2)
PHYSICAL EXAMINATION REQUIRED

To determine medical fitness for employment, the Company may require employee physical examinations, when it is deemed advisable for health and safety, by a Company-employed physician. The Company may also require applicants to be physically examined at the Company's expense. Should an employee be found medically unfit to work at his or her assigned job, the Company will furnish the employee a copy of the physician's report or a physician's statement. Any applicant or employee may also be examined at his or her own expense by a physician selected by him or her and the physician's report may be submitted to the Company for consideration.

POLICY 10.4(3)
PHYSICAL EXAMINATION REQUIRED FOR CONTAGIOUS
DISEASES OR FOR SANITARY MEASURES

Section 1. Contagious Diseases.   The Company may require physical examinations for contagious diseases. To protect the lives and well-being of all, employees with untreated or incurable contagious diseases may be given an unpaid medical leave, laid off, or terminated, depending upon the medical evaluation.

Section 2. Sanitary Measures.   The Company may require a physical examination of any employee should it appear necessary as a sanitary or safety measure. The physical examination shall be made by the Company's physician at the Company's expense.

POLICY 10.4(4)
PHYSICAL EXAMINATION AFTER ACCIDENT OR SICKNESS

Section 1. Physical Examination Required.   If an employee has been absent because of accident or sickness, the Company may require a physical examination by a physician of the Company's choice. Following the examination, if it is determined that the sickness or accident may subject the employee to other or continued sickness or accidents, he or she will not be allowed to return to work.

Section 2. Result Disputes.   Should the employee disagree with the Company physician's decision, he or she may be examined by a physician of his or her own choosing, provided that notification of this intent is given to the Company within three (3) calendar days after the Company has denied the right to return to work. Any costs incurred by this physician will be paid by the employee.

If the employee's physician indicates that the employee can return to work, the Company will be notified in writing by the physician making the determination. The notification must be given to the Company not later than thirty (30) calendar days from the date the employee has been notified that he or she has been denied the right to return to work.

If the matter cannot be resolved, the Company's and the employee's physician will select a third physician to whom to submit their respective findings. The third physician may examine the employee and make a determination concerning the employee's status. Any expense incurred by the third physician will be shared equally by the Company and the employee. The third physician's finding will be considered by the Company in determining whether the employee should be returned to work.

POLICY 10.4(5)
PHYSICAL EXAMINATIONS FOR EMPLOYEES IN HAZARDOUS JOBS

To protect employees while working on jobs that may constitute health hazards, employees may, upon the Company's request or the employee's, be given a Company-paid physical examination. If the examination is made by a Company physician, the physical examination report, upon the employee's written request, will be sent to the employee's physician.

POLICY 10.4(6)
PHYSICAL EXAMINATION EMPLOYEE COMPENSATION

The Company may require employee physical examinations or tests made by its physician at its expense. Where possible, the physical examination will be scheduled during the employee's normal working hours. The Company will compensate the employee for the time involved at the employee's applicable pay rate for a Company-required physical examination that occurs during the employee's normal working hours or outside the employee's normal working hours.

POLICY 10.4(7)
PHYSICAL EXAMINATION INFORMATION AVAILABLE
TO EMPLOYEE'S PHYSICIAN

Employee physical examinations may be arranged by the Company only when necessary and only after notifying the employee with an explanation of the specific reasons for the examination. Report copies of these physical examinations and medical treatments will be maintained by the Company in its Medical Department and will be available to the employee's physician, if authorized in writing by the employee.

POLICY 10.4(8)
PHYSICAL EXAMINATION CONFIDENTIALITY

The Company will maintain physical examination result confidentiality. These results shall be furnished only to the employee's designated physician upon the employee's written authorization; provided that the Company may use or supply physical examination results in response to subpoenas, requests to the Company by any governmental agency authorized by law to obtain these reports, and in arbitration or litigation of any claim or action involving the Company.

POLICY 10.4(9)
PHYSICAL EXAMINATION RESULTS DISPUTE: MEDICAL ARBITRATOR

Section 1. Physical Examinations Required.   An applicant, before being hired, must meet certain job-related health and physical fitness standards as determined by a physical examination given by a Company-designated physician. After employ-ment, periodic physical examinations may be offered or required to aid an employee in improving health or to enable the Company to ensure its employees' health.

Section 2. Results.   An applicant/employee, upon request, shall have the oppor-tunity to discuss his or her physical examination's results with the Company's physi-cian. Upon the applicant's/employee's request, the information will be made available to his or her personal physician.

Section 3. Result Disputes.   Should the Company's physician determine that an applicant/employee cannot perform the job applied for or currently held because of an existing medical condition, and should a dispute arise between the Company's physician and the employee's personal physician regarding this determination, a complaint may be filed with the Human Resources Department.

If the complaint is not resolved by the Human Resources Department, the appli-cant/employee, the Company's physician, and the applicant's/employee's personal physician shall exchange x-rays, laboratory test reports, and physical examination reports within ten (10) calendar days of the date the complaint was filed with the Human Resources Department.

If, after exchanging of x-rays and reports, final agreement cannot be reached re-garding the medical findings and conclusions, the applicant/employee may, within fourteen (14) calendar days after the exchange, refer the dispute to the Company's President, who shall attempt to resolve the problem by examining all available med-ical evidence.

If a dispute still exists regarding the applicant's/employee's medical condition af-ter the Company President's review, the dispute may be presented to an impartial medical arbitrator selected by mutual agreement of the parties in accordance with the following:

a. Within fourteen (14) calendar days following the dispute's referral to the Company's President, all x-rays and reports shall be forwarded to the medical arbitrator.

b. Within fourteen (14) calendar days thereafter, the medical arbitrator shall con-duct whatever employee examination is deemed necessary and appropriate, and shall meet with the two physicians, along with any medical experts, to discuss the findings.

c. Within fourteen (14) calendar days thereafter, the medical arbitrator shall sub-mit to the Company and the applicant/employee a written determination.

d. Any of the time limits provided herein may be extended by the parties' mutual written agreement.

e. The charges and expenses of the medical arbitrator shall be paid equally by the parties.

f.   The determination of the medical arbitrator shall be final and binding on the parties and the applicant/employee involved.

§ 10.5   Smoking

Workplace smoking is changing rapidly.[15] Employers are increasingly taking steps to curtail workplace smoking. Permitting or not regulating workplace smoking makes employers vulnerable to challenges by nonsmoking employees. Mounting concern over smoking's effects on the health, productivity, and morale of smokers and nonsmokers has combined with changing social attitudes about smoking to begin reversing the notion that smoking is an acceptable public practice. Awards for unemployment,[16] disability,[17] and medical treatment[18] have been made to nonsmokers, and union grievances under collective bargaining agreements are increasingly dealing with this issue.[19] Employment handbooks have also served as the basis for disciplining or terminating smoking employees.[20]

Smoking is becoming an activity that an employee does within the confines of his or her home, but not at the workplace or in public. Privacy questions concern the employer's liability if smoking is or is not restricted, and whether only nonsmokers can be hired.

While discrimination against smokers does not rise to that prohibited by federal[21] and state[22] FEP statutes, it certainly affects an employment interest. It may be a non-job-related criterion that controls employment distribution, especially when employers do not hire smokers or restrict smoking outside the workplace. By not confining job-relatedness criteria to the workplace, employers could deny opportunities based on what occurs outside the workplace.

---

[15] *See* Decker § 7.7.

[16] *See, e.g.,* Lapham v. Commissioner, Unemployment Compensation Bd., 103 Pa. Commw. 144, 519 A.2d 1101 (1987) (failure to curtail workplace smoking constitutes compelling and necessitous reason for leaving employment and entitling one to unemployment compensation); *see also* Decker, Privacy Law § 7.7.

[17] *See, e.g.,* Schober v. Mountain Bell Tel., 96 N.M. 376, 630 P.2d 1231 (1980) (disability); *see also* Decker, Privacy Law § 7.7.

[18] *See, e.g.,* Fuentes v. Workmen's Compensation Appeals Bd., 16 Cal. 3d 1, 547 P.2d 449, 128 Cal. Rptr. 673 (1976) (worker's compensation); *see also* Decker, Privacy Law § 7.7.

[19] *See, e.g.,* H-N Advertising & Display Co., 88 Lab. Arb. (BNA) 329 (1986) (Heekin, Arb.) (employer's failure to convene joint safety committee to review plant conditions and to make recommendations regarding employer's smoking policy violated collective bargaining agreement); *see also* Decker, Privacy Law § 7.7.

[20] *See* Hatfield v. Johnson Controls, 7 I.E.R. Cas. (BNA) 758 (E.D. Mich. 1992) (supervisor properly terminated under handbook's just cause provision for smoking in restricted area).

[21] *See, e.g.,* 42 U.S.C. §§ 2000e-1 to 2002-17 (Civil Rights Act of 1964); *see also* Decker, Privacy Law §§ 2.7–2.12.

[22] *See, e.g.,* Pa. Stat. Ann. tit. 43, §§ 952–963 (Purdon 1991) (Pennsylvania Human Relations Act); *see also* Decker, Privacy Law § 2.25.

When using employment as an incentive to control how employees act at home, employers decide or circumscribe what is done in private. This could be a guise under which to discriminate if statistics establish that certain minority, national origin, or age groups smoke more than others.

§ 10.6 —Drafting

In drafting smoking policies, the following should be considered:

1. Applicable statutes[23]
2. Establish a smoking policy, which may be either voluntary or a total prohibition
3. For unionized employers, meet with the union to discuss the smoking policy
4. Consult employees for their input
5. Communicate the policy
6. Require all employees to follow the policy
7. Establish smoking and nonsmoking areas
8. Make smoke cessation classes available for persons who want to stop smoking
9. Improve ventilation to minimize smoking's health hazard
10. Where employees have a medically proven reaction to smoke, separate those persons from smokers, but do not terminate them
11. Where smoking presents a work safety hazard, due to paints, chemicals, or explosives, adopt and implement a smoking ban that is reasonable
12. Investigate smoking complaints

§ 10.7 —Sample Policies

The following examples should be considered in drafting smoking policies:

POLICY 10.7(1)
SMOKING POLICY

Smoking is prohibited in areas designated as "No Smoking." Smokers should remember to be considerate of nonsmoking employees and customers.

A reminder from the Surgeon General: "Quitting Smoking Now Greatly Reduces Serious Risks to Your Health."

---

[23] *See, e.g.,* Pa. Stat. Ann. tit. 35, §§ 1221, 1223.1–.5, 1230.1, 1235.1 (Purdon Supp. 1993) (Pennsylvania's Clean Indoor Act).

POLICY 10.7(2)
SMOKING POLICY

Section 1. Purpose and Background.   This policy is designed to promote employee health and safety and the conduct of Company business. It is not intended to totally prohibit smoking on the Company's premises, but does restrict it to certain areas.

Smoking poses a significant risk to the smoker's and nonsmoker's health. It can damage sensitive technical equipment and can be a safety hazard. In sufficient concentrations, sidestream smoke can be annoying to nonsmokers. It may be harmful to individuals with heart and respiratory diseases or allergies related to tobacco smoke.

Smoking is a complex problem that concerns elements of a psychological and physiological addiction. Many individuals require assistance to eliminate smoking from their lives. It is not a problem that can be solved completely by prohibition or restriction. This policy is intended to assist employees in finding a reasonable accommodation between those who do not smoke and those who do, and demonstrates the Company's desire to improve the health of all employees.

Section 2. Policy.   It is the Company's policy to respect the nonsmoker's and the smoker's rights in Company buildings and facilities. When these rights conflict, the Company and its employees should endeavor to find a reasonable accommodation. When an accommodation is not possible, the nonsmoker's rights should prevail.

Section 3. Prohibited Areas.   Smoking is not permitted:

a. In areas with sensitive equipment, computer systems, or where records and supplies would be exposed to hazard from fires, ashes, or smoke;

b. Where combustible fumes can collect, as in garage and storage areas, areas where chemicals are used, and all other designated areas where an occupational safety or health hazard might exist;

c. In confined areas of general access, as in libraries, medical facilities, cashier waiting lines, elevators, restrooms, stairwells, copy rooms, lobbies, waiting rooms, fitness centers, and so forth;

d. Where Company premises are frequently visited by customers, such as public offices and customer service areas; and

e. The Company may designate other locations where smoking specifically is not permitted.

Section 4. Work Areas.   In work areas where space is shared by two or more persons, an effort shall be made to accommodate individual smoking preferences to the degree reasonably possible. When requested, managers and supervisors shall make a reasonable attempt to separate persons who smoke from those who do not.

Employees may designate their private offices as smoking or nonsmoking areas. Visitors to private work areas should honor the employee's wishes.

In Company vehicles, including Company-sponsored van pools, smoking shall be permitted only when there is no objection from one or more of the occupants.

Section 5. Areas of Common Use.   In meetings and enclosed locations, including conference rooms and classrooms, smoking will not be permitted. Breaks and appropriate access to public areas may be scheduled to accommodate smoker needs.

In enclosed common-use locations, including cafeterias, dining areas, employee lounges, and auditoriums, smoking shall be permitted only in identified smoking sections, providing there is adequate ventilation and they are not normal customer areas. Smoking is permitted in corridors. Employees and visitors are expected to honor the smoking and nonsmoking designations and to be considerate of nonsmokers in their vicinity.

POLICY 10.7(3)
SMOKING POLICY

Section 1. Purpose and Background.   This smoking ban policy is designed to provide the Company's employees with a more healthy workplace environment. Implementation of this policy is a direct result of several compelling health and safety issues indicating that:

   a.   An increasing number of health conscious people are legitimately concerned about the impact on their health of smoke in the workplace;

   b.   Smoking poses a significant risk to the smoker's and non-smoker's health;

   c.   The U.S. Surgeon General has defined nicotine as an addicting substance and has released compelling statistics on the impact of smoke inhalation, whether active or passive, on our health;

   d.   Smokers and nonsmokers will benefit from a firm, definitive, yet thoughtfully implemented policy; and

   e.   Smoke can damage sensitive equipment and be a safety hazard.

Section 2. Objective.   An essential part of this policy's implementation is the recognition that the elimination of smoking in all Company facilities and Company owned vehicles is done for the benefit of all employees, guests, and friends of the Company. The hazards of smoking have an impact on all employees and require the cooperation of all employees.

Section 3. Implementation.   Maintaining the Company's commitment to its employees as its single greatest asset, the Company is implementing its policy as follows:

a. **Phase 1:** A period of employee education consisting of this policy's communication, assistance for smokers in dealing with smoking restrictions, and education of nonsmokers about their role in this effort.

b. **Phase 2:** A six month transition period beginning ___(date)___ and ending ___(date)___, during which indoor smoking at all locations will be permitted only in *specifically designated areas.* These areas are: ___(List permitted smoking areas)___

_____

_____

_____

_____

_____

_____

c. **Phase 3:** Beginning on ___(date)___, a *complete ban* on all smoking in any Company facilities will be imposed. Additionally, all smoking in Company owned or leased vehicles will be prohibited.

§ 10.8   Employee Assistance Programs (EAP)

Employee assistance programs (EAPs) help employees and their families to recognize and overcome personal problems that interfere with employee work performance.[24] They are an extension of the performance evaluation process. Problem areas covered may involve job dissatisfaction, supervisor or coworker conflicts, job performance anxiety, alcohol and drug abuse, emotional problems, marital problems, gambling problems, financial problems, and so forth. Because employer confidentiality is required to make EAPs function properly, confidentiality breaches may result in employee privacy litigation.[25]

EAPs require considerable planning and operational expertise to function properly. In addition to administering the EAP, various actions must be taken to ensure that the program operates efficiently. Efficient operation means that the program prevents employee problems and identifies, treats, and rehabilitates those employees who are troubled.

---

[24] *See* Decker, Privacy Law § 7.8.

[25] *See, e.g.,* Brotherhood of Maintenance v. Burlington N., 802 F.2d 1016 (8th Cir. 1986) (stressing the importance of EAP confidentiality); *see also* Decker, Privacy Law § 7.8.

§ 10.9 —Drafting

In drafting EAP policies, the following should be considered:

1. Confidentiality and privacy in:
   a. Recordkeeping
   b. Coding records to prevent inadvertent identification of those who are enrolled
   c. Limiting supervisor access
   d. Keeping EAP records separate from employee personnel or medical records
2. EAP services offered
   a. Alcohol and drug abuse
   b. Family matters
   c. Personal problems
3. Communicating EAP services to employees and their families by:
   a. Employee education
   b. Orienting managers, supervisors, and union representatives
4. Procedures for individuals referred by managers, supervisors, and/or union representatives
5. Procedures for use by employees and their families
6. The EAP's location
7. The EAP's coordination with medical and disability benefit plans
8. Outside agency versus Company provision of the EAP regarding:
   a. The EAP provider's malpractice liability insurance
   b. The EAP staff's qualifications

§ 10.10 —EAP Brochure

In acquainting employees with an EAP's existence, the employer should consider the following brochure:

BROCHURE 10.10(1)
EAP BROCHURE

The Company has established an Employee Assistance Program (EAP). The EAP is a confidential, personal counseling service for employees and members of their immediate households. It is designed to assist in resolving personal and job-related problems that could possibly affect employee work performance.

The (Name of group providing the EAP) will offer employees confidential access to trained counselors. They will be available 24 hours a day, seven days a week, by telephone and outside the workplace to help overcome problems that might affect the employee's personal life or job.

The questions and answers in this brochure describe the Company's EAP counseling services and how to use them.

Q.   What is the Employee Assistance Program?
A.   The program offers professional assistance to Company employees. You or members of your immediate family may receive confidential, professional assistance to help resolve personal and job-related problems. The Company pays for the EAP's services. It is designed to allow the employee or members of his or her immediate family to seek help on their own on any subject.
Q.   How does the EAP work?
A.   The Company has retained the services of the   (Name of group providing the EAP), which specializes in personal problem assessment and refers individuals to a variety of professional resources to receive help. There is no charge for the EAP service. Where the EAP counselor advises referral services, potential cost will be discussed if the cost is not covered by the EAP or the Company's benefit plans. A 24-hour telephone service is available to make appointments. Any employee or member of his or her immediate household may initiate a request.
Q.   Is the EAP confidential?
A.   Yes. Once a person has become an EAP client, information about the basic personal problem or the treatment will not be revealed to the Company without the client's knowledge and consent, except as permitted or required by law. Records are kept confidential in accord with professional codes of ethics and applicable federal and state regulations. However, critical situations requiring third-party warnings, medical emergencies, and appropriate legal action may require information release without client consent. Where, in the EAP counselor's professional judgment, the employee's situation poses a significant potential health or safety risk to the Company, or other employees, the EAP counselor will require the employee to inform the Company of this fact, but not the nature of the problem, and will confirm with the Company that this contact was made.
Q.   What kinds of problems will the EAP deal with?
A.   A wide range of problems from job or family to feeling depressed and not knowing why. Examples of EAP services include alcohol or drug abuse, financial or legal problems, marital difficulties, family problems of any type, job-related problems, and so forth.
Q.   But are not these private problems? What right does the Company have to interfere with the employee's personal life?
A.   Certainly these are personal problems and the Company is not attempting to interfere in employees' personal lives. The EAP service is voluntary. It is there as a fringe benefit, but also recognizes the Company's interest in retaining productive employees by providing help so problems can be corrected before affecting work.

Q.   What does a Company referral to the EAP mean?

A.   The Company may refer an employee to the EAP based on job performance, attendance, observable aberrant behavior, and so forth. A Company referral to the EAP will be kept confidential.

Q.   Who will pay the cost of EAP counseling or other professional services that might be necessary?

A.   The EAP sessions are free for the employee and/or immediate family members to assist in evaluating and addressing personal concerns. If a referral to an outside professional resource is required, it will be at the individual's expense. The EAP counselor will try to minimize employee cost by making referrals to the most appropriate agency. The Company's health insurance and other benefits may cover some of the outside services and time away from work when subsequent treatment is required.

BROCHURE 10.10(2)
EAP BROCHURE

Introduction

Employee Assistance Programs (EAP's) began in the United States in the 1930's and now are in use throughout the country. This growth is the result of the recognition by increasing numbers of employers and employee organizations that nonwork-related problems can seriously interfere with job performance and with an employee's sense of well being. Help sought early can prevent the development of serious personal and work problems.

Over the years many employees have turned to their colleagues, the Company, and to others for assistance for themselves or family members with marital problems, family difficulties, alcoholism concerns, mental health problems, and so forth. Employees have not always known where to turn for the appropriate help. The Company's EAP is a response to this need.

The Company's EAP is a response to this need in providing a no-cost, confidential, professional counseling service designed to assist employees in securing appropriate help.

The Company is pleased that it has been able to arrange its EAP with   (EAP provider's name) . This EAP provider has had many years of experience in helping individuals and families evaluate and deal with a variety of problems.

Marital/Family Problems

The anxiety of a domestic problem can create havoc in the family and directly affect the performance of the most stable individual. Among these problems are: marital discord; separation; the stresses and increased responsibilities following divorce; the reaction of children to the loss of a parent; sibling, peer, and school difficulties; parent-child tensions; experimentation with alcohol and drugs; and so forth.

What are expected behaviors in these situations? Which need patience? In which would a program of counseling be helpful? The Company's EAP can provide assistance in sorting out these problems.

Mental Health

The stress of modern life at work and in our private lives sometimes creates tension that can be eased by talking with a professional listener. Mental health difficulties can occur in the best adjusted individuals. Irritability, anxiety, increased distractedness, and so forth can be the result of stress. Work becomes more difficult and relating to others becomes less enjoyable.

Sometimes it takes only a sympathetic ear to help. Some symptoms are a result of an immediate crisis while others are indicative of more severe or of longer-standing problems. A trained EAP counselor can help sort out what, if any, treatment is needed.

Addiction

Early EAPs gained employer and employee acceptance in dealing with alcoholism counseling programs that were designed to help employees whose work was marred by absenteeism and unsatisfactory job performance. While experience has indicated that there are many other factors that can adversely affect performance, alcoholism, drugs, and other addictions, including prescription and nonprescription drugs, remain increasingly serious workplace problems. Early intervention can be very effective in treating these addiction-related problems. There are outpatient and inpatient programs available. Treatment success can reach the 80 percent level, particularly if problems are dealt with early.

Aging

With the increasing age of the general population, families are more often confronted with problems of older family members. Resources are available to aid families in understanding the aging process regarding its physical and emotional components. Families can learn which problems are reversible and which are not, along with what alternatives and treatments are available. The EAP counselor can provide information and referrals concerning nursing home placement, payment resources, medical assistance, and so forth.

Other Problems

The EAP counselor is in a position to suggest resources or to offer advice on other problems that might be affecting the lives of employees or their families; i.e., the location of financial counselors, the existence of special service organizations, and so forth. In many cases, people just do not know where to turn to find the help they need. The Company's EAP program can arrange for a referral to the proper facility or resource.

Procedure

If you or a member of your family needs help in any of the areas described above, or if you should simply want to explore an area of concern, call the Company's EAP counseling service and schedule an appointment. At that time, you will be given an appointment scheduled within five (5) working days of your call. If you feel your problem is an emergency, let the EAP counselor know and an earlier appointment will be arranged.

You may be able to work out a solution to your difficulty in one or two sessions with an EAP counselor. If another type of counseling or treatment is appropriate, the EAP counselor will facilitate the referral.

The EAP counselor will discuss costs, coverage, and so forth regarding the Company's program. The Company's medical benefits program will usually pay part or all of the cost associated with counseling or treatment. Should the Company's benefits not cover the counseling or treatment, you will be informed of the cost and what you must pay before the service is provided.

The Company assures you that all EAP counseling and treatment will be kept in complete confidence. No identifying data will be available to the Company nor will the participants in the EAP be identified as the counseling center's clients.

It is not the Company's objective or intention to interfere with the private lives of employees or their families. An EAP can aid employees in dealing more effectively with situations that can interfere with their sense of well being and that do not undermine their functioning and performance as employees. The Company sincerely hopes that employees and their families will avail themselves of the EAP services that are being offered.

§ 10.11   —Sample Policies

The following examples should be considered in drafting EAP policies:

POLICY 10.11(1)
EMPLOYEE ASSISTANCE PROGRAM

Section 1. Purpose.   The Company has always been concerned with its employees' health and well-being. Because of these concerns, an Employee Assistance Program (EAP) has been developed to aid employees who develop medical or behavioral problems. Some of these problems include alcohol and drug abuse, marital, family, gambling, legal, financial, psychological, medical, or behavioral difficulties.

Section 2. General Coverage.   Employee effectiveness can deteriorate for many reasons. Often it is personal or family problems that affect job performance. The Company's EAP is designed to help employees with these problems, including directing them to appropriate professional services. Employees or their family members who are suffering from any type of personal problem are encouraged to voluntarily seek diagnostic counseling and treatment services available under the EAP.

Section 3. Alcohol and Drug Abuse Coverage.   The following are aspects of the Company's EAP regarding alcohol and drug abuse:

a.   Alcoholism along with drug abuse is a significant problem;

b.   The Company recognizes alcohol and drug abuse as treatable diseases;

c.   An employee with an alcohol or drug abuse problem will receive the same careful consideration that is extended to employees suffering from any other disease; and

d.   For the purposes of the EAP, *alcohol and drug abuse* is defined as the continuing use of alcoholic beverages or drugs that definitely and repeatedly interferes with health or job performance.

Section 4. Job Performance Coverage.   The following are aspects of the Company's EAP regarding job performance:

a.   Job performance is the key to recognition of a need for EAP services; and

b.   Employees whose deteriorating job performance does not respond to normal corrective action should be referred to the EAP, if the supervisor believes that the poor job performance is caused by a medical or behavioral problem.

Section 5. Supervisor Participation.   Supervisors should understand that they are not expected to be qualified to diagnose alcoholism, drug abuse, other personal problems, or to make judgments about the behavioral problem causes. It is the employee who is responsible for accepting and complying with a supervisor's referral to the EAP. This employee responsibility includes:

a.   Following the treatment prescribed; and

b.   An employee's refusal to accept diagnosis and treatment will be handled in the same way that similar refusals or treatment failures are handled for other illnesses, when the result of the refusals or failures continues to affect job performance.

Section 6. Confidentiality.   All records and activities within the EAP will be preserved in accordance with Company policies on privacy and confidentiality of sensitive records.

POLICY 10.11(2)
EMPLOYEE ASSISTANCE PROGRAM

Section 1. Eligibility.   All employees and their immediate family members covered by employee insurance benefits who desire assistance in dealing with a personal problem are covered by the Company's Employee Assistance Program (EAP).

Section 2. Primary Services Provided by the EAP to the Company and Its Employees. A qualified professional EAP counselor:

a. Evaluates the employee problem and identifies the problem to the employee if he or she did not recognize it initially;

b. Gives motivational counseling, including helping the employee recognize how the problem has been affecting his or her life;

c. Makes a referral to an appropriate resource within the community; i.e., private practitioners, county-funded agencies, hospitals, and so forth;

d. Assures that there is assistance available to the employee which the employee can afford through Company insurance or otherwise;

e. Monitors the employee's progress through periodic progress checks at intervals the EAP counselor feels necessary for the problem involved;

f. Returns the employee to productive employment;

g. When an individual voluntarily participates in the EAP, information regarding the name of the individual, the nature of the problem under treatment, and counselling records are maintained in strictest confidence; and

h. When the Company has made a referral to the EAP in conjunction with the Company's Alcohol and Drug Policy, the Company will:

   (i)   Be informed regarding whether or not the employee is participating in the program;

   (ii) Whether the employee is active or inactive in whatever therapy has been recommended;

   (iii) Be given a prognosis as to how well the employee is expected to progress; and

   (iv) Be notified where a referred employee refuses help or fails to continue with the prescribed therapy.

Section 3. EAP Primary Services Provided to the Company. The following EAP services are provided:

a. Technical assistance is provided on the implementation of the personnel policy, review of benefit package, and its impact on the EAP program;

b. Training for managers and supervisors as deemed appropriate by the Company concerning the EAP's operation and their role in implementing it regarding:

   (i)   How to recognize troubled employees through documented job performance; and

   (ii) A discussion of disciplinary procedures and the use of objective confrontation techniques.

c. Program promotion and publicity regarding the availability of EAP services including posters, payroll stuffers, and so forth; and

d. Employee education, talks, and media presentations to all Company employees to introduce them to the EAP services being offered and to answer
their questions.

§ 10.12 Alcohol and Drugs

Employers are developing alcohol and drug abuse programs to increase workplace
productivity and safety.[26] Medical testing procedures are a significant part of
these programs.

Regardless of the benefits that testing may provide concerning workplace productivity and safety, it presents important employment policy considerations. By
its very nature, testing intrudes upon the employee's solitude and physical integrity. When testing is administered to detect employee alcohol or drug use, in-
trusiveness increases in complexity and degree.

Private and public sector employers implementing these programs are subject
to privacy limitations under the United States Constitution[27] and certain state
constitutions.[28] Statutory obligations may exist regarding an employer's requirement to rehabilitate employees who abuse alcohol or drugs.[29]

Various federal[30] and state[31] FEP statutes may affect drug testing when it has
a disproportionate adverse effect on minorities, certain national origin groups,
and so forth. Searching or testing employees may subject employers to liability
under various litigation theories, including invasion of privacy, defamation, and
false imprisonment.[32] Invasion of privacy may provide protection in safeguarding
an employee's solitude, seclusion, and private affairs.[33] Before conducting a drug
search, an employer should limit the employee's privacy expectations by giving
prior notice that searches can occur.[34] When the employer creates a privacy expectation through a handbook or employment policy, it may be required to follow

---

[26] *See* Decker, Privacy Law § 7.9.

[27] U.S. Const. amend. IV; *see also* Decker, Privacy Law § 3.5.

[28] *See, e.g.,* Cal. Const. art. 1; *see also* Decker, Privacy Law §§ 3.9–3.11.

[29] *See, e.g.,* Cal. Lab. Code §§ 1025–1028 (West Supp. 1993) (California's statute requiring alcohol and drug rehabilitation programs).

[30] *See, e.g.,* 42 U.S.C. §§ 2000e-1 to 2002-17 (1988) (Civil Rights Act of 1964); *see also* Decker,
Privacy Law §§ 2.7–2.12.

[31] *See, e.g.,* Pa. Stat. Ann. tit. 43, §§ 951–963 (Purdon 1991) (Pennsylvania Human Relations
Act); *see also* Decker, Privacy Law § 2.25.

[32] *See generally* Decker, Privacy Law ch. 4.

[33] Restatement (2d) of Torts § 652b (1977); *see also* Decker § 4.3.

[34] See ch. 10. *See, e.g.,* K-Mart Corp. v. Trotti, 677 S.W.2d 632 (Tex. Ct. App. 1984), *writ refused
per curiam,* 686 S.W.2d 593 (Tex. 1985); *see also* Decker, Privacy Law § 7.9.

that policy.[35] The search's scope may also impose employer liability.[36] Finally, publicly disclosing private facts about a drug test's results may impose liability.[37]

§ 10.13   —Drafting

In drafting alcohol and drug policies, the following should be considered:

1. Applicable federal[38] and state[39] statutes
2. Drug testing necessity
3. Employee group or category to be tested
4. Giving notice to all affected employees
5. Receiving employee consent to test and to disclose test results
6. Selecting a reputable laboratory to analyze employee samples
7. The employer's response to employees who have a positive test result or who refuse to take a test
8. Arranging for a confirming test on positive samples
9. Guarding against disclosure of information about employees obtained through the tests
10. Limiting alcohol or drug testing to situations where on-the-job impairment is evident
11. Having supervisors document behavior that suggests alcohol or drug impairment
12. Interviewing employees about illnesses or prescription drugs that may adversely affect their job performance
13. Implementing or strengthening restrictions on the use or possession of alcohol or drugs on employer property during work hours

---

[35] See ch. 10. *See, e.g., See* Baggs v. Eagle-Picher Indus., Inc., 7 I.E.R. Cas. (BNA) 318 (6th Cir. 1992) (employees terminated upon refusing to submit to drug test or upon testing positive failed to state claim based on progressive language in handbook because handbook expressly stated that disciplinary steps may not always be followed). Rulon-Miller v. International Business Machs., 162 Cal. App. 3d 241, 208 Cal. Rptr. 524 (1984) (employer policy ensuring privacy expectation); *see also* Decker, Privacy Law §§ 4.14, 7.9.

[36] *See, e.g.,* O'Brien v. Papa Gino's, 780 F.2d 1067 (1st Cir. 1986) (use of polygraph examination to probe employee's drug use outside the workplace); *see also* Decker, Privacy Law § 7.9.

[37] *See, e.g.,* Bratt v. International Business Machs. Corp., 785 F.2d 352 (1st Cir. 1986) (invasion of privacy liability for disclosing private medical information); *see also* Decker, Privacy Law §§ 4.3, 7.9.

[38] *See, e.g.,* 41 U.S.C. §§ 701–707 (1989) (Drug-Free Workplace Act); 42 U.S.C. §§ 12101–12213 (Supp. 1992) (Americans with Disabilities Act).

[39] *See, e.g.,* Minn. Stat. §§ 181.950–.957 (West Supp. 1993) (Minnesota's statute regulating testing).

14. Ensuring that the facts and circumstances that created the reasonable suspicion are documented, where testing is performed based on a reasonable suspicion
15. Providing an opportunity for the union to participate in establishing an alcohol and drug testing program, by bargaining with the union over the changes in work rules or practices resulting from adopting a testing program under a collective bargaining agreement.[40]

§ 10.14 —Privacy Considerations

To balance employee privacy rights present in alcohol or drug testing, employers should consider:

1. Limiting initial testing to employee jobs involving a significant risk to other employees or to the public
2. Testing only when there is significant evidence of suspected abuse that arises from alcohol- or drug-impaired job performance
3. Being certain that the employee is aware that he or she is being tested specifically and only for drugs
4. Keeping findings confidential
5. Confirming all positive results through alternate tests
6. Stressing alcohol and drug rehabilitation as part of any testing program.

§ 10.15 —Alcohol and Drug Testing Program Implementation Considerations

The following should be considered in implementing an alcohol and drug testing program:[41]

1. Familiarize managers, supervisors, and employees with the problem of workplace alcohol and drug abuse
2. Develop an alcohol and drug abuse policy
3. Communicate the policy to everyone

---

[40] *See* Littler, Mendelson, Fastiff & Tichy, *Responding to Drug and Alcohol Abuse in the Workplace,* in The 1987 Employer B, B-31 (1987) [hereinafter Littler, 1987 Employer]. Littler, Mendelson, Fastiff & Tichy prepare this publication on an annual basis for Business Laws, Inc. of 8228 Mayfield Road in Chesterland, Ohio 44026; telephone (216) 729-7996. This publication is an excellent reference source for human resource professionals and attorneys as an annual update of employment laws.

[41] *See* McLanahan, *Annotated Checklist: Employer Programs to Control Drug and Alcohol Abuse,* in Employment Problems in the Workplace 39-88 (J. Kauff ed. 1986).

4. Enforce the policy consistently
5. Test for alcohol and drug abuse by considering:
   a. *Announced testing,* in that:
      (i) It offers employees no surprises;
      (ii) It may be less objectionable; and
      (iii) The employer's responsibility to explain the testing's rationale may be lessened because it becomes part of the employee's routine
   b. *Random testing,* in that:
      (i) Testing is done unannounced;
      (ii) Employees are selected randomly;
      (iii) Employees are selected without arbitrary, capricious, or discriminatory reasons
   c. *Reasonable cause testing,* in that:
      (i) It may be used where suspicion exists;
      (ii) It may be done after physical or behavioral signs indicate testing appropriateness or after a suspicious workplace occurrence
6. Obtain proper test results by:
   a. Ensuring that the container is clean and not contaminated
   b. Observing chain of custody procedures to ensure that the sample is not lost or altered
   c. Selecting a qualified laboratory
   d. Recognizing the error inherent in the test method used
7. Understand the meaning of a positive test result regarding:
   a. Testing as a report of facts about body chemistry and not about behavior
   b. Accidental or legitimate exposure
   c. Employment relation
8. Legal considerations regarding:
   a. Search and seizure
   b. Procedural due process
   c. Fair employment practices
   d. Privacy considerations
9. Make the testing program routine by:
   a. Including it as part of the employer's everyday operation
   b. Automatic compliance
10. Do testing right by:
    a. Spending money for quality laboratory services
    b. Treating test results as confidential
    c. Not abusing employee privacy rights

11.   Utilize an employee assistance program (EAP)
12.   Conduct thorough and proper investigations of suspected violations
13.   Know the applicable statutes and regulations
14.   Be firm but fair in practicing good employee relations

§ 10.16   —Minimizing Liability

To minimize employer liability for employee privacy claims arising out of alcohol and drug testing, the following should be considered:[42]

1.   *Obtain a release/authorization.* Before an applicant/employee is tested for alcohol or drugs, the employer should obtain test consent. The consent form should solicit information regarding prescription drug use or nonprescription medication to eliminate false positives. For example, therapeutic cold medicines, such as Contac and Sudafed, can create a false positive for amphetamine use. The consent form may help protect the employer against claims for invasion of privacy, defamation, false imprisonment, assault and battery, and so forth

2.   *Do a follow-up test.* An initial screening test indicating a positive result should be verified by a confirmation test for all employees. Employers may wish to perform confirmation tests for applicants where:
   a.   There are few applicants, to minimize an additional test's costs
   b.   The initial test is positive regarding an otherwise highly qualified applicant
   c.   The applicant desires confirmation in contesting an adverse employment decision

3.   *Safeguard the specimen.* The specimen should be marked in the applicant's/employee's presence and a documented chain of custody maintained to ensure that the specimen is correct. Selecting a reliable laboratory is essential.

4.   *Restrict test disclosure.* Test results should not be publicized. Even when the drug tests are considered accurate and there is no risk of publication of a false fact, they should not be disclosed.

5.   *Use split samples.* The specimen should initially be split into two samples. Every sample should be preserved for a reasonable time period; i.e., 60 to 90 days. During this period, the employee who provided the sample should be permitted to have the sample evaluated independently by a confirmation test at his or her own expense. An employee who has the opportunity to

---

[42] *See* Redeker & Segal, *Drug and Alcohol Testing: Legal and Practical Considerations,* 7 Bureau of Nat'l Affairs Communicator 2, 20 (Fall 1987).

confirm the test results independently may be less likely to challenge those results. Where applicants are not permitted independently to confirm their test results because they may not be informed of the test's results, a separate sample should be retained in case the applicant challenges an adverse employment decision.

§ 10.17   —Recognizing Impairment

Managers and supervisors should be instructed to observe employees closely where alcohol- and drug-impaired job performance is suspected. The following should be considered by managers and supervisors in recognizing and determining whether an employee is under the influence of alcohol or drugs while at the workplace:

1. Employee physical characteristics:
   a. Smell of alcohol on breath
   b. Slurred speech
   c. Disorientation, in that the employee does not know where he or she is, what day it is, and so forth
   d. Lack of motor coordination
   e. Mood and attitude, in that the employee is belligerent, moody, ecstatic, more open, and more nervous than usual
   f. Skin color pale or flushed
   g. Excessive restroom trips
   h. Bloodshot eyes or dilated pupils
2. Other impairment indicia:
   a. Witnesses who observe the drinking of alcohol or ingestion of drugs
   b. Bottles, cans, or cups with traces of alcohol or drugs
   c. Confessions of the employee regarding the use of alcohol or drugs
   d. Other employee confessions
   e. Traces of drugs or drug paraphernalia
   f. Marijuana smell
   g. Congregation of employees in remote areas or in areas that employees usually do not frequent, such as closets, storerooms, stairwells, and so forth[43]
3. Symptoms of specific types of alcohol or drug impairment:
   a. Alcohol
      (i) Alcohol odor on breath or clothes
      (ii) Missing items in liquor cabinet, liquor that tastes watered down

---

[43] *See* Littler, 1987 Employer at B-32.

    (iii)   Slurred speech, uncoordination

    (iv)   Sleeping more than usual or at odd times

    (v)   Physical complaints that fit the "hangover" description; that is, morning nausea, headache, woolly mouth, fatigue, and thirst

    (vi)   Excessive use of mouthwash, breath fresheners, and so forth

    (vii)   Use of other drugs, including tobacco

    (viii)   Excusing the behavior of friends who drink or defending the right to drink before the legal drinking age

b. Cocaine

    (i)   Sleeping problems

    (ii)   Runny nose, nasal sores

    (iii)   Headaches

    (iv)   Lowered appetite

    (v)   Decreased sexual drive

    (vi)   Problems at home, school, work, with relationships, or financial difficulties

    (vii)   Depressed, irritable, fatigued

    (viii)   Redness of skin from scratching; that is, "coke bugs"

    (ix)   Dilated pupils, tremors, nausea

    (x)   Talkativeness, fever, rapid heartbeat

    (xi)   Drug-related paraphernalia; that is, small spoons, small mirrors, small vials, razor blades, straws, and so forth

c. Marijuana

    (i)   A sweet odor similar to burnt rope in a room, on clothes, and so forth

    (ii)   Roach remnants; that is, a small butt end of a marijuana cigarette

    (iii)   Joint; that is, a hand rolled cigarette, usually with the ends twisted or crimped

    (iv)   Roach clips; that is, holders of the roach, including common items such as paper clips, bobby pins, or hemostats

    (v)   Seeds or leaves in pockets or possessions

    (vi)   Rolling papers or pipes, usually hidden somewhere

    (vii)   Eyedrops for covering up red eyes

    (viii)   Excessive use of incense, room deodorizers, or breath fresheners

    (ix)   Devices for keeping the substance, including boxes, cans, or even concealed containers such as a soft drink can with a screw-off lid

    (x)   Eating binges

    (xi)   Appearance of intoxication, yet no smell of alcohol

(xii) Excessive laughter

(xiii) Yellowish stains on finger tips from holding the cigarette.[44]

§ 10.18   —Disciplining for Alcohol or Drug Abuse

In disciplining for alcohol or drug abuse, the following should be considered:

1. Was the employee intoxicated or under the influence of drugs at the workplace?
2. Is drinking or drug use part of other types of employee misconduct?
3. Does the employee's artificially induced mental state result in his or her inability to perform job duties?
4. Does the employee's drinking or drug use have a deleterious effect on the morale of other employees?
5. Has the employee made efforts to rehabilitate himself or herself after being warned of losing his or her job?
6. Does the employer have clear policies and rules prohibiting possession or use of alcohol or drugs at the workplace?
7. Has the employer publicized the policies and rules sufficiently so that all employees are aware of their existence?
8. Depending upon the seriousness of the policy or rule violation, has progressive discipline been considered?

§ 10.19   —Pre-employment Testing

The following procedures are important to the success of any pre-employment alcohol or drug testing program:

1. Give each applicant, before final hiring, a pre-employment drug test
2. Have each applicant read and sign the employer's pre-employment drug testing consent form, which should include the following:
    a. Statement of alcohol and drug policy
    b. Disqualification for employment consideration of those with positive test results
    c. A hold harmless agreement for test result use
    d. Authorization to release test results to the employer
    e. Optional second testing on the same sample at the applicant's expense

---

[44] *See* U.S. Department of Justice Drug Enforcement Administration, *Let's All Work to Fight Drug Abuse* 6, 10, 15 (1989).

f. A written disclosure of what medication the applicant has taken prior to the test

g. A copy of the signed form, which should be retained with the applicant's file while the applicant brings the original to the laboratory or clinic

§ 10.20   —Probable Cause Testing Guidelines

In undertaking probable cause testing, the employer should consider the following:

1. The employer must personally observe abnormal employee behavior, along with the appearance, behavior, speech, or breath odor of the employee before the employee is required to provide a specimen

2. At the time of the test, the employee must be given a form to list the use of prescription and nonprescription medications, along with being given a proper explanation of the importance of accurately furnishing this information

3. If an employee is required to sign a consent form to authorize a laboratory or clinic to test a sample and release results to the employer, the employer cannot require the employee to waive any claim or cause of action under the law

4. The employee is to be given a copy of the specimen collection procedures at the time of the test

5. The employee must either void directly into a tamper-resistant urine bottle, or use a wide-mouth clinic specimen container that must be transferred in the employee's full view into a urine bottle

6. The specimen must be immediately sealed and labeled in the employee's presence and initialed by the employee

7. The chain-of-possession form must be completed properly

8. Testing must be done by a properly licensed and certified laboratory.

§ 10.21   —Urine Drug Analysis Report Contents

A urine drug analysis report should include the following:

1. The drugs and metabolites included in the test

2. The cutoff limits for each assay, including screening and confirmation

3. The methodology employed in each assay; i.e., enzyme multiplied immunoassay technique (EMIT), radioimmunoassay (RIA), gas chromatography/mass spectrometry (GC/MS), and so forth

4. The drugs and/or metabolites confirmed as positive

§ 10.22   —Letter Introducing Company Alcohol and Drug Policy

In introducing the employer's alcohol and drug policy, the following letter to employees should be considered:

FORM 10.22(1)
LETTER INTRODUCING COMPANY ALCOHOL AND DRUG POLICY

Dear ___(Employee's Name)___ :

We are all aware that alcohol and drug abuse is a major problem throughout our society. As you know, the Company has made a commitment for a work environment free from alcohol and drug substances. The Company's primary objectives are employee health and safety, along with fulfilling obligations to the public and customers, protecting private and public property, and preserving the confidence placed in the Company.

The Company has been carefully considering how best to fulfill these responsibilities. As a result, the Company has prepared an Alcohol and Drug Abuse Policy. The Company's purpose is to discourage alcohol and drug abuse so all can benefit from a healthy and safe workplace. Here are some highlights of the Alcohol and Drug Abuse Policy that will become effective on ___(Date)___ :

1.   *Voluntary Assistance.* An employee who voluntarily seeks assistance on a timely basis through the Employee Assistance Program (EAP) or the Company's Medical Department for any problem, including an alcohol- or drug-related problem, may do so without jeopardizing employment status, providing that prescribed treatment is followed and work performance is acceptable. In some cases temporary reassignment may be necessary.

2.   *Alcoholic Beverages.* Employees shall not consume alcoholic beverages during regular or overtime working hours, during paid or unpaid meal periods when the employee will be returning to work following the meal period, or during working hours when representing the Company away from Company facilities. Also, employees shall not report to work under the influence of alcoholic beverages or possess alcoholic beverages on Company property.

3.   *Other Substances Which Alter Mental or Physical Capacity.* Use, possession, sale, or purchase of other substances that may alter mental or physical capacity while on the job or on Company property is prohibited. Employees shall not report to work under the influence of these substances.

4.   *Searches.* To help ensure a work environment free of alcohol and drugs, the Company may search an employee's personal effects located on Company property and the employee's work area.

5.   *Physical/Clinical Tests.* Employees may be physically examined and/or clinically tested:

a.   When there are reasonable grounds for believing an employee is either under the influence of or is improperly using alcohol or drugs in violation of the policy;

b.   As part of Company-required physical examinations; or

c.   As a follow-up to a rehabilitation program.

6.   *Prescribed Treatment.* An employee undergoing prescribed medical treatment with a substance that may alter physical or mental capacity must report this to the Medical Department.

7.   *Reporting Violations.* An employee who observes or has knowledge of a violation of the Alcohol and Drug Abuse Policy by another employee or others has an obligation promptly to report the violation to his or her immediate supervisor and/or the Human Resources Department. Any supervisor who receives this report or who observes this violation must report the information to the responsible supervisor and/or the Human Resources Department.

8.   *Imminent Threat to Safety.* In any instance where there exists an imminent threat to safety of persons or property as a result of apparent unfitness for duty, an employee shall immediately contact his or her supervisor and the Human Resources Department.

9.   *Disciplinary Action.* Unlawful involvement with alcohol and drugs on or off the job is a serious conduct breach. Violations of the Alcohol and Drug Abuse Policy will result in disciplinary action up to and including termination.

10. *Law Enforcement Notification.* Where criminal violations are involved or suspected, appropriate law enforcement agencies will be notified.

11. *Applicability.* The Alcohol and Drug Abuse Policy applies to all Company employees, regardless of work location or employment status.

All of us have a responsibility for diligent, professional performance, and conduct that demonstrates trust of the public and our fellow employees. Because of this, please cooperate with the Company in implementing this policy so we can provide a healthy and safe workplace.

This is an important topic, and I am sure each of us can understand the need to adhere strictly to the requirements outlined herein. If you have any questions concerning this matter, please contact your supervisor promptly.

Thank you for your continued cooperation.

Very truly yours,

_____

President

§ 10.23   —Follow-up Letter Clarifying Company's Alcohol and Drug Policy

The following letter should be considered in explaining the employer's alcohol and drug policy:

FORM 10.23(1)
LETTER CLARIFYING COMPANY ALCOHOL AND DRUG POLICY

Dear ___(Employee's Name)___ :

I wrote to you recently about the Company's Alcohol and Drug Abuse Policy and the procedures that have been established to maintain a work environment free from alcohol and drugs. In that letter, plans and procedures were outlined. Over the past several weeks the Company has discussed the program with supervisors, who were asked to meet with you.

The Company now has the benefit of the feedback from these reviews and meetings. The purpose of this letter is to clarify some matters and to advise you of steps being taken to address certain concerns as follows:

1. *Test Samples.* At the time a sample is collected, it will be divided into two containers. One container will be sent to the laboratory for analysis; the second will be retained by the Medical Department. If the first sample is found to be positive, the second container will be analyzed. If the contents of the second container are found to be positive, the results will be considered positive; if the contents of the second container are found to be negative, the results of both analyses will be considered negative. The second container will be discarded upon receipt of a negative test result.

2. *Review Committee.* A committee has been established to review all cases where a positive result is reported after processing both sample containers. The Committee is chaired by _(Name)_, Director of Human Resources. If the Committee determines that there is a reason to question the reported result, the individual will be offered the opportunity to provide a second sample, or to accept the results of the first sample.

3. *Personnel Action on a Confirmed Positive Test Result.* Concern and questions were expressed about the availability of rehabilitation. It is important for people who have a problem with alcohol or drugs to take the initiative to obtain help. Seeking help will not affect continued employment where job performance is acceptable.

   In the event of any confirmed positive test, the Company will consider all the circumstances. This consideration will include the individual's ability to have avoided a violation and any current or prior rehabilitation effort. If there are cases where an attempt at rehabilitation rather than termination is acceptable to the Company, the appropriate action to be taken before a return to work would include:

a.   A disciplinary suspension, without pay of any type from the Company.

b.   Successful participation in and completion of a recognized professional rehabilitation program. Rehabilitation programs requiring absence from work will be reviewed by the Company on a regular basis to determine if continued participation in the program is appropriate.

c.   Following rehabilitation and prior to a potential work return, the employee must provide written proof of completing the rehabilitation program and must also outline any follow-up action required by the program. The proof supplied by the individual will be reviewed by the Company's Human Resource Department and Medical Department to determine if the proof is satisfactory to the Company.

d.   The employee must participate fully in any follow-up programs recommended by the rehabilitation agency, the Employee Assistance Program (EAP), and the Company's Medical Department. Failure to provide proof of satisfactory participation in the follow-up programs will subject the employee to disciplinary action up to and including termination.

e.   The employee will be subject to extra, unscheduled testing for 24 months following rehabilitation.

f.   If the employee returns to work, he or she may be temporarily or permanently removed from his or her current position and made eligible for less critical assignments, where a position is available for which he or she is qualified.

g.   A confirmed positive analysis during or following rehabilitation will result in termination.

4.   *Call Out.* There has been some concern about an employee being called to report for unscheduled work when he or she may not be fully fit. Should that occur, advise your supervisor or the person contacting you of the facts so that your fitness for duty can be discussed. The purpose is to assure that people reporting to work are fit for duty. The Company recognizes that on occasion people may not be fit for unscheduled work calls. However, if that is a frequent ocurrence, the Company will have to evaluate the situation. Also, employees who are on call are expected to be fit for duty when and if called.

The Company's intention is to provide a healthy and safe workplace for you that is free of alcohol and drugs. Employees have a right to expect this.

Thank you for sharing your concerns about the program and accepting the need for an effective program. I ask for your support in making the program a success.

Very truly yours,

_____

President

§ 10.24   —Letter Outlining Company's Procedures for a Positive Test Result

The following letter should be considered in informing employees of the procedures that will be taken where a positive test occurs:

FORM 10.24(1)
LETTER OUTLINING PROCEDURES FOR POSITIVE TEST RESULT

Dear ___(Employee's Name)___ :

I am requesting and recommending that the following steps be taken when the Medical Department reports a positive drug screen result to the Human Resources Department:

1. The Human Resources Department will instruct the employee who has tested positive on initial drug screening to contact the Medical Department as soon as possible to make an appointment.

2. All Employee Assistance Program (EAP) correspondence and verbal communications regarding treatment, counselling, and employee follow-up will be through the Medical Department only. The information will be confidential. The Human Resources Department will instruct the EAP counselors to have employees sign information release forms for this purpose.

3. The Medical Department will keep the Human Resources Department apprised of the employee's progress in the rehabilitation program.

4. The Medical Department reserves the right to randomly test the employee during and after rehabilitation has been completed. The Human Resources Department will be kept informed of testing results.

5. Any and all work restrictions will be determined by the Medical Department. The Human Resources Department and the employee's supervisor will be informed in writing of any work restrictions, if restrictions are deemed medically necessary.

Very truly yours,

_____

Medical Director

§ 10.25   —Sample Policies

The following examples should be considered in drafting alcohol and drug policies:

POLICY 10.25(1)
ALCOHOL AND DRUGS—BASIC

Alcoholic beverages are not permitted on the Company's premises, at Company-sponsored functions, or in Company-owned vehicles. Illegal controlled substances are not permitted on the Company's premises, at Company-sponsored functions, or in Company-owned vehicles. This policy applies to any prescription drugs that may have an adverse impact on an employee's ability to work safely while using these drugs. It is the employee's responsibility to have his or her physician's permission to work while using the prescription medicine and to inform the Company of this so it can make an evaluation.

POLICY 10.25(2)
ALCOHOL AND DRUGS—SMALL COMPANY
(UNDER 100 EMPLOYEES)

Section 1. Introduction. The use, possession, distribution, or sale of alcohol or drugs anywhere at work is prohibited and considered a willful violation of Company policy which can result in employee discipline up to and including termination. All employees have the responsibility to report to work in a fit condition and to perform their jobs without unnecessary risk to themselves or other individuals regarding health and safety.

Section 2. Applicability. All employees, whether salaried or hourly, will be subject to alcohol and drug screening as a result of:

1. Involvement is a serious workplace accident or serious safety-related incident as determined by the Company:

   a. A *serious workplace accident* is any accident resulting in lost-time injury to the employee and/or involvement in an accident resulting in the lost-time injury of another individual and/or property damage.

   b. A *serious workplace incident* is any incident presenting a substantial risk of lost-time injury or property damage.

2. Being identified as unfit for work as determined by the Company. Unfit for work involves the identification of employees by designated Company personnel as not safely or competently performing their jobs and presenting unnecessary risk to themselves or others.

3. As part of all Company-required physical examinations or evaluations as required by law, regulation, or other cause as determined by the Company, including pre-employment examinations.

Section 3. Test Failure. Any employee unable to pass alcohol and drug screening will be removed from work and referred to the Company's Employee Assistance Program (EAP), and may be subject to disciplinary action up to and including termination. The employee, upon returning to work, may be required to undergo unannounced drug testing over a twelve (12) month period. Subsequent violations may result in discipline up to and including termination. Refusal to have alcohol and drug screening or referral to the EAP, as required in this policy, will subject the employee to immediate discipline up to and including termination.

Section 4. Applicants.   All applicants, regardless of intended payroll status, must undergo physical examinations which may include alcohol and drug screening as a part of pre-employment processing.

Section 5. Statement of Understanding.

(Please Print) I, (Name) , have read this policy and had it explained to me, and I understand its contents, and consent to screening for alcohol or drugs.

Employee Signature _____

Date _____

POLICY 10.25(3)
ALCOHOL AND DRUGS—MEDIUM-SIZED COMPANY
(100 TO 1,000 EMPLOYEES)

Section 1. Introduction.   Alcohol and drug abuse in the workplace reflect a national problem. The development of a Company policy for dealing with these problems, along with appropriate management, supervisor, and employee education when implementing this policy, are important in addressing this.

Section 2. Statement on Alcohol and Drugs.   The Company has a strong commitment to its employees to provide an alcohol- and drug-free work environment. Likewise, the Company is committed to its customers, local businesses, and the general public to operate its business safely and prudently. Consistent with this commitment, the Company has formulated this policy regarding alcohol and drugs.

Section 3. Purposes.   The purposes of this policy are:

a. To establish and maintain a healthy and safe working environment for all employees;

b. To ensure the reputation of the Company and its employees as good, responsible citizens;

c. To reduce accidental injury to person or property;

d. To reduce absenteeism, tardiness, and indifferent job performance and

e. To provide assistance toward rehabilitation for any employee who seeks the Company's help in overcoming any addiction to, dependence upon, or problem with alcohol or drugs.

Section 4. Definitions.

a. *Alcohol or alcoholic beverage* means any beverage that may be legally sold and consumed and that has an alcoholic content in excess of .5% by volume.

b. *Drug* means any substance other than alcohol capable of altering the mood, perception, pain level, or judgment of the individual consuming it.

c. *Prescribed drug* means any substance prescribed for the individual consuming it by a licensed medical practitioner.

d. *Illegal drug* means any drug or controlled substance the sale or consumption of which is illegal under federal or state law.

e. *Employee* means any person employed by the Company, including but not limited to those persons in a temporary, part-time, or full-time status; all levels of management and supervision responsibility; and all areas of production, sales, and distribution.

f. *Unfit condition* means any employee identified by designated Company personnel as not safely or competently performing their job and presenting unnecessary risk to themselves or others.

g. *Workplace accident* means any accident resulting in lost time, injury to self, and/or involvement in an accident which results in the lost-time injury of another individual and/or property damage.

h. *Serious safety-related incident* means any incident presenting a substantial risk of lost-time injury or property damage.

i. *Motor vehicle accident* means any employee involved in a motor vehicle accident while operating a Company-owned or leased vehicle.

Section 5. Alcoholic Beverages.   The following are prohibited regarding alcoholic beverages:

a. No alcoholic beverage will be brought into, possessed, or consumed on the Company's premises, Company property, Company vehicles, or during any on-duty status with the Company.

b. Drinking or being under the influence of alcoholic beverages while on duty is cause for discipline up to and including termination.

c. Any employee whose off-duty alcohol abuse results in excessive absenteeism or tardiness, or is the cause of accidents or poor work, will be referred to the Employee Assistance Program (EAP) for rehabilitation. If the employee refuses or fails rehabilitation, he or she shall be subject to discipline up to and including termination.

Section 6. Prescription Drugs.   The following are prohibited regarding prescription drugs:

a. No prescription drug shall be brought upon the Company's premises by any person other than the person for whom the drug is prescribed by a licensed medical practitioner, and the drug shall be used only in the manner, combination, and quantity prescribed.

b. Any employee whose prescription drug abuse results in excessive absenteeism or tardiness, or is the cause of accidents or poor work, will be referred to the Employee Assistance Program (EAP) for rehabilitation. If the employee refuses or fails rehabilitation, he or she shall be subject to discipline up to and including termination.

c. Any employee undergoing prescribed medical treatment with a controlled substance that may affect job performance should report this treatment to his or her supervisor. A controlled substance's use as part of a prescribed medical treatment is not grounds for disciplinary action, although it is important for the Company to know the use is occurring. It may, however, be necessary to change an employee's job assignment while the employee is undergoing treatment.

Section 7. Illegal Drugs.   The following are prohibited regarding illegal drugs:

a. The use of an illegal drug, controlled substance, or the possession of one at or outside the workplace is subject to discipline up to and including termination.

b. The sale, trade, or delivery of illegal drugs or controlled substances by an employee to another person is cause for discipline up to and including termination.

c. The occasional, recreational, or off-duty use of illegal drugs will not be excused and will subject the employee to discipline up to and including termination. The Company's understanding indicates that employee involvement with illegal drugs, even recreationally, may be expected to result in:

   (i) Financial and domestic difficulties causing:

      (A) Unstable performance

      (B) Theft

   (ii) Embarrassment to the Company due to:

      (A) Employee arrests

      (B) Poor customer relations, unsatisfactory work, short tempers, and so forth.

Section 8. General Prohibited Conduct.   Any employee found to be using, selling, possessing, trafficking in, or under the influence of any alcoholic beverage or drug on Company property, or while performing assigned duties off Company property, will be considered in willful violation of Company policy and will be subject to appropriate disciplinary action up to and including termination. Employees may be suspended with or without pay pending completion of an investigation. The Company reserves the right to search employee personal effects and the work area of an employee suspected to be involved in alcohol or drug abuse activities.

Section 9. Employee Assistance Program.   Any employee who desires assistance in dealing with a personal, alcohol, or drug dependency problem may seek help, voluntarily, in confidence, by contacting the Employee Assistance Program (EAP). These individuals must be capable of performing their assigned duties and must cease all involvement with alcohol and drugs that will impact their job with the Company. They must enroll in and complete a prescribed treatment program. Employees undergoing counseling or treatment will not be exempt from the Company's rules, policies, procedures, or disciplinary application.

Section 10. Safety of Work Force, Work Rules, Blood and Urine Tests.   To ensure the safety of the workplace and the work force, the following work rules will apply to all employees effective upon receipt of notice of this policy:

    a. Each employee, as a condition of continued employment, will be required, upon request of Company supervisory personnel, to:

        (i)   Submit to search of any vehicle brought upon or parked upon Company premises;

        (ii) Submit to search of any pocket, package, purse, briefcase, tool box, lunch box, or other container brought upon Company premises, including personal belongings;

        (iii) Submit to search of desk, file cabinet, and so forth.

    b. The Company reserves the right to require, at its discretion, where it suspects alcohol or drug abuse, that an employee, as a condition of continued employment, be physically examined and/or clinically tested for the presence of alcohol or drugs by qualified medical personnel as a result of:

        (i)   Being identified by supervision as appearing to be in an unfit condition, as determined by the Company;

        (ii) Involvement in a serious workplace accident or serious safety-related incident as determined by the Company;

        (iii) Involvement in a motor vehicle accident while operating a Company-owned or leased vehicle;

        (iv) Being absent from work for three or more consecutive days; or

        (v)   Any other circumstance, incident, or occurrence that leads the Company to suspect alcohol or drug abuse.

Section 11. Job Applicants.   All job applicants, regardless of intended payroll status, must successfully undergo alcohol and drug screening as part of pre-employment processing.

Section 12. Rejection of Treatment or Failure of Rehabilitation.   Any employee who refuses to submit to testing or has a positive result from an alcohol or drug test will be referred to the Employee Assistance Program (EAP) to complete successfully a prescribed treatment program. Any employee who subsequently violates this policy, has a future positive test result, refuses to have alcohol or drug testing, or refuses to use the EAP as required by this policy, will be subject to discipline up to and including termination. An employee with a positive result from an alcohol or drug test may request an immediate confirmation test on the original specimen at his or her own expense. If the result of the confirmation test is negative, the Company will reimburse the employee.

Section 13. Confidentiality. All information obtained in the course of testing, rehabilitation, and treatment of employees with alcohol and drug abuse problems shall be protected as confidential medical information and shall be kept separate from the employee's official personnel file. Only those who have a need to know shall be given access to this information. The importance of this confidentiality to the Company and its employees cannot be overemphasized.

Section 14. Effective Date and Notice to Employees. The policies set forth herein are effective immediately upon notice to employees. Each present employee will be furnished a copy of this policy and will sign a receipt for it. Future employees will each be furnished a copy before hiring.

ALCOHOL AND DRUG ABUSE POLICY RECEIPT AND ACKNOWLEDGMENT

I, ___(Name)___ , hereby acknowledge that I have received a copy of the ___(Employer's Name)___ Alcohol and Drug Abuse Policy and understand that it is my obligation and responsibility to read this policy and comply with its terms.

_____
(Signature)

_____
(Date)

POLICY 10.25(4)[45]
ALCOHOL AND DRUGS—LARGE COMPANY
(OVER 1,000 EMPLOYEES)

Section 1. Purpose. To support the Company's commitment to protect the health and safety of the public and its employees, this policy is designed for maintaining an alcohol- and drug-free workplace.

Section 2. Applicability. This policy has Company-wide applicability.

Section 3. Definitions.

a. *Alcohol.* Any beverage that may be legally sold and consumed and that has an alcoholic content in excess of .5% by volume.

---

[45] *See generally* Edison Electric Institute Human Resource Management Division, EEI Guide to Effective Drug and Alcohol Fitness for Duty Policy Development (rev'd Aug. 1985) [hereinafter Edison Electric Institute, Policy Development].

b. *Disciplinary action.* Action taken against an employee found to be in violation of Company policies.

c. *Drug.* Any physical- or mind-altering substance or any "controlled substance" or "controlled dangerous substance" as defined by federal and state statutes. These include, but are not limited to, any nonprescribed drug, narcotic, heroin, cocaine, or marijuana, or a prescribed drug which is abused or not used in accordance with a physician's evaluation.

d. *Employee.* All employees regardless of work location or employment status.

e. *Responsible supervisor.* The supervisor to whom the employee reports.

Section 4. Requirements. Employees shall not consume alcoholic beverages during regular or overtime working hours, during paid or unpaid meal periods when the employee will be returning to work following the meal period, or during working hours when representing the Company away from Company facilities. Additionally, employees shall not report to work under the influence of alcoholic beverages or possess alcoholic beverages on Company property.

The use, possession, sale, or purchase of other substances which may alter mental or physical capacity, which substances include, but are not limited to, nonprescribed drugs, narcotics, marijuana, or other "controlled substances" or "controlled dangerous substances" as defined by federal or state statutes while on the job or on Company property is prohibited. Employees shall not report to work under the influence of these substances.

The unlawful involvement with alcohol or drugs on or off the job is a serious conduct breach. Each employee has an obligation to advise the Company of any known violations of these requirements. Violations of these requirements will result in disciplinary action up to and including termination.

The Company also applies the intent of these requirements to maintain a safe work environment free of alcohol and drugs to all contractors, business invitees, visitors, and guests to Company property.

Section 5. Drug and Alcohol Testing. To help ensure an alcohol- and drug-free workplace, the Company may search an employee's personal effects located on Company property, the work area of an employee, and physically examine and/or clinically test employees for the presence of alcohol or drugs during working hours.

Employees may be physically examined and/or clinically tested for the presence of alcohol or drugs:

a. Where there are reasonable grounds for believing an employee is either under the influence of or is suspected of using alcohol or drugs;

b. As part of any Company-required physical examination;

c. As a follow-up to a rehabilitative program;

d. On a random basis where health and safety requirements necessitate this.

If the alcohol or drug test reveals positive results, the employee will be suspended pending joint evaluation by the affected manager, Human Resources Department, and Medical Department. Employees whose physical examinations and/or test results are positive are subject to disciplinary action up to and including termination. If the test results are negative, the matter will be closed.

All applicants and all Company employees whose assignment will make them an "employee" shall be physically examined and/or chemically tested for the presence of alcohol and drugs. The employment process will be terminated for all individuals whose examinations and/or tests are positive.

Section 6. Voluntary Assistance.   An employee who voluntarily seeks assistance on a timely basis through the Employee Assistance Program or the Company's Health Services Department for an alcohol- or drug-related problem, prior to the Company identifying the problem, may do so without jeopardizing their employment status, providing that prescribed treatment is followed and work performance is acceptable. In some cases temporary reassignment may be necessary.

Section 7. Prescribed Treatment.   If an employee is undergoing a prescribed medical treatment with a substance that may alter physical or mental capacity, he or she must report this to the Medical Department.

Section 8. Reporting Violations.   Any supervisor who observes or receives a violation report must, as soon as practicable, report the information to the responsible supervisor, and/or the Human Resources Department.

Any employee who observes or has knowledge of a violation, whether by an employee or others, has an obligation promptly to report this to his or her immediate supervisor and/or the Human Resources Department.

Section 9. Imminent Threat to Safety.   In any instance where there exists an imminent threat to safety of persons or property, an employee shall immediately contact the manager, supervisor, or the Human Resources Department.

Section 10. Responsible Supervisor Action.   Supervisors must assure that all employees are familiar with and comply with this policy. They must notify the Human Resources Department of any known or suspected violation. When a responsible supervisor observes or receives a report of a possible violation, he or she shall:

a. Confirm that the Human Resources Department has been advised.

b. Follow further directions of the Human Resources Department, which may include conducting an initial evaluation.

c. If the responsible supervisor is asked to conduct an initial evaluation, he or she shall report the results to the Human Resources Department. If no apparent violation has occurred, the matter will be closed.

d. Determine in conjunction with the Human Resources Department whether it is advisable or necessary to suspend an employee, with or without pay, or re-assign him or her pending completion of the investigation.

e. Recommend any proposed disciplinary action and ensure that the recommendation is reviewed, approved, and implemented by the Human Resources Department.

When a supervisor observes or receives a report of a possible violation by others, including contractors, business invitees, visitors or guests, he or she shall:

a. Advise the individual's responsible supervisor if that individual is a contractor or sponsor for access to the facility of a business invitee, visitor, or guest.

b. Advise the Human Resources Department.

c. Provide further assistance or cooperation as may be requested.

Section 11. Human Resources. It is the Human Resource Department's responsibility to:

a. Review recommended disciplinary actions and ensure that the actions are in accordance and consistent with Company procedure.

b. Assemble a complete, comprehensive, and coherent file on the incident, where personnel action is taken.

c. Ensure that appropriate procedures and policies are communicated to all employees.

d. Ensure that appropriate division/departments are notified and participate in the recommendations resulting from investigations.

Section 12. Other Responsibilities. The following are other responsibilities in administering this policy and are not intended to supersede other requirements:

a. All employees must:

(i)   Become informed and comply with the policy;

(ii) Cooperate with investigations;

(iii) Report any known policy violation; and

(iv) Immediately respond to imminent threat to the safety of person or property.

b. Department managers must:

(i)   Ensure that all subordinates are conversant with and comply with the policy; and

(ii) Review investigative reports and disciplinary action recommendations.

c. Human Resources must:

   (i)   Communicate this procedure and policy to all employees, including new hires;

   (ii) Arrange for alcohol and drug testing; and

   (iii) Review investigative reports and recommend disciplinary action.

d. Medical Department must:

   (i)   Supervise physical examinations and testing for presence of alcohol or drugs; and

   (ii) Apprise the Human Resources Department and the responsible supervisor of the results of any the examinations or tests.

§ 10.26   Drug-Free Workplace Act

The Drug-Free Workplace Act of 1988 applies to all employers with a federal government contract of $25,000 or more for the procurement of property or services.[46] Violation of the act can lead to suspension of payments and/or termination of the contract and even debarment for a period of up to five years.

The act sets forth specific requirements expected of federal contractors in providing a drug-free workplace by requiring them to:

1. Develop a statement to employees:

   a. Notifying employees that the unlawful manufacture, distribution, dispensation, possession, or use of a controlled substance is prohibited in the workplace;

   b. Identifying the specific disciplinary actions that the employer will take against employees for violating the prohibitions; and

   c. Providing that as an employment condition, the employee will:

      (1) Abide by the terms of the employer's policy; and

      (2) Notify the employer of any criminal drug statute conviction for a workplace violation no later than five days after the conviction

2. Give each covered employee a copy of the policy

3. Develop a drug-free awareness program that informs employees about:

   a. The employer's policy of maintaining a drug-free workplace;

   b. The dangers of workplace drug abuse;

   c. Available drug counseling, rehabilitation, and employee assistance programs; and

---

[46] 41 U.S.C. §§ 701–707 (1988) (Drug-Free Workplace Act).

   d.   The penalties the employer may impose on the employee for drug vio-
         lations and convictions

4.   Notify the federal contracting agency within ten days after receiving actual
       notice of an employee's conviction for a workplace violation

5.   Impose a sanction on or require the satisfactory participation in a drug
       abuse assistance or rehabilitation program by any employee who is con-
       victed of a workplace violation within 30 days after receiving notice from
       the employee of a conviction; and

6.   Make a good faith effort to continue to maintain a drug-free workplace
       through implementation of the Act's requirements.

   Set forth below is a suggested policy for federal contractors to use in meeting
the act's requirements.

POLICY 10.26(1)
ALCOHOL, DRUG, AND CONTROLLED SUBSTANCE ABUSE

Section 1. Introduction.   Alcohol, drug, and controlled substance abuse in the
workplace reflects a national problem. The development of a Company policy for
dealing with these problems along with appropriate management, supervision, and
employee education are important in addressing this problem.

Section 2. Statement on Alcohol, Drugs, and Controlled Substances.   The
Company has a strong commitment to its employees to provide an alcohol, drug,
and controlled substance-free work environment. Likewise, the Company is committed to the community in providing this type of workplace. Consistent with this commitment, the Company has formulated its policy regarding alcohol, drug, and
controlled substance abuse.

Section 3. Purposes.   The purposes of the Company's policy are:

a.   To establish and maintain a healthy and safe working environment for all
      employees;

b.   To ensure the reputation of the Company and its employees as good, responsi-
      ble citizens;

c.   To reduce accidental injury to person or property;

d.   To reduce absenteeism, tardiness, and indifferent job performance; and

e.   To provide assistance toward rehabilitation for any employee who seeks the
      Company's help in overcoming any addiction to, dependence upon, or prob-
      lem with alcohol, drugs, or controlled substances.

Section 4. Applicability.   This policy is applicable to all employees.

Section 5. Definitions.

a. **Alcohol.** Any beverage that may be legally sold and consumed and that has an alcoholic content in excess of .5% by volume.

b. **Company.** The ___(Company's name)___ .

c. **Disciplinary action.** Action taken by the Company against an employee, up to and including termination, who is found to be in violation of the Company's alcohol, drug, and controlled substance abuse policy.

d. **Drug.** Any physical or mind-altering substance or any "controlled substance" or "controlled dangerous substance" as defined by federal and state statutes. These include, but are not limited to, any nonprescribed drug, narcotic, heroin, cocaine, or marijuana, or a prescribed drug which is abused or not used in accordance with a physician's evaluation.

e. **Employee.** All Company employees regardless of work location or employment status.

Section 6. Training.   The Company will develop an awareness program regarding alcohol, drug, and controlled substance abuse that informs employees of:

a. The Company's policy on alcohol, drugs, and controlled substance abuse;

b. The dangers of alcohol, drug, and controlled substance abuse;

c. The availability of Company assisted services and programs for counseling and rehabilitation for alcohol, drug, and controlled substance abuse problems; and

d. The Company's penalties for employees involved with alcohol, drug, or controlled substance abuse violations or convictions.

Section 7. General Prohibited Conduct.   Any employee found to be unlawfully using, manufacturing, selling, distributing, dispensing, possessing, trafficking in, or under the influence of any alcoholic beverage or drug on Company property or while performing assigned duties off of Company property will be considered in violation of this policy.

Section 8. Policy Violation.   Employees violating this policy will be subject to appropriate disciplinary action up to and including termination. Employees may be suspended with or without pay pending completion of an investigation. The Company reserves the right to search employee personal effects brought on the Company's property along with the employee's work area when an employee is suspected of being involved in alcohol, drug, or controlled substance abuse activities. Employees must notify the Company of any criminal drug statute conviction for a workplace violation within five (5) calendar days after the conviction.

Section 9. Employee Assistance.   Any employee who desires assistance in dealing with a personal, alcohol, drug, or controlled substance abuse problem may seek help, voluntarily, in confidence, by contacting the Human Resources Department.

These individuals must be capable of performing their assigned duties and must cease all involvement with alcohol, drugs, or controlled substances that will impact their job duties with the Company. Employees may be required as a condition of retaining employment to enroll in and complete a prescribed treatment program. Employees undergoing counseling or treatment will not be exempt from the Company's rules, policies, procedures, or disciplinary application.

Section 10. Confidentiality.   All information obtained in the course of assistance, counseling, rehabilitation, or treatment of employees with alcohol, drug, or controlled substance abuse problems shall be protected as confidential medical information and shall be kept separate from the employee's official personnel file. Only those persons who have a need to know shall be given access to this information. The importance of this confidentiality to the Company and its employees cannot be overemphasized.

Section 11. Effective Date and Notice to Employees.   The policies set forth herein are effective immediately upon notice to employees. Each present employee will be furnished a copy of this policy and will sign a receipt for it. Future employees will each be furnished a copy of the policy prior to hiring and will also be required to sign a receipt for it.

ALCOHOL, DRUG, AND CONTROLLED
SUBSTANCE ABUSE POLICY
RECEIPT AND ACKNOWLEDGMENT

I,   __(name)__ , hereby acknowledge that I have received a copy of the __(company's name)__   Alcohol, Drug, and Controlled Substance Abuse Policy, and I understand that it is my obligation and responsibility as a condition of my employment to read this policy and comply with its terms.

_____   _____
(Date)   (Signature)

POLICY 10.26(2)
ALCOHOL, DRUG, AND CONTROLLED SUBSTANCE ABUSE

Under the terms of the Drug-Free Workplace Act, the Company is required to give you a copy of its official policy statement concerning the establishment of an alcohol and drug-free workplace.

Please sign below to indicate that:

1. You have received this statement

2. You have read it or been informed or its content

3. You agree to abide by this policy in all respects

NOTE: THIS ACT REQUIRES YOU TO ACKNOWLEDGE AND AGREE TO THE ABOVE AS A CONDITION OF CONTINUED EMPLOYMENT

Acknowledged and agreed:

_____

Signature

_____

Print Name

_____

Department

_____

Date

Please return this form to the Human Resources Office within ten (10) calendar days of receipt.

ALCOHOL AND DRUG-FREE AWARENESS PROGRAM

The Company recognizes that the misuse of alcohol and drugs is a serious problem with legal, physical, and social implications for the Company, employees, and the community. Because of this, the Company is very much concerned, especially since alcohol and drug abuse can affect employee health, safety, efficiency, and productivity.

Alcohol and drugs shall be defined as those outlined under the Drug-Free Workplace Act.

The unlawful manufacture, distribution, dispensing, possession, or use of a controlled substance or possession or use of alcohol is prohibited on any site or vehicle owned, leased, or utilized by the Company. Any employee in violation of this policy will be subject to immediate disciplinary action up to and including termination.

Employees are required to notify the Company of any criminal drug statute conviction for a violation occurring on any site or vehicle owned, leased, or utilized by the Company. Upon notification, the Company will take one of the following actions:

1. Disciplinary action up to and including termination and/or

2. Required participation in an alcohol or drug rehabilitation program.

Further information concerning the Company's policy is available from the Human Resources Department. Set forth below is an overview of the Drug-Free Workplace Act of 1988:

1. **Application/Coverage.** The Act applies to all federal agencies and covers recipients of procurement contracts, including purchase orders, totaling $25,000 or more; any individuals awarded contracts, regardless of grant size. *Exceptions:* Contractors or grantees who perform work outside the U.S. are not subject to the Act. Hospitals and banks and other financial institutions are not covered unless they receive procurement contracts or grants that meet the Act's requirements.

2. **Compliance Date.** The Act's requirements apply to contracts and grants awarded on or after March 18, 1989.

3. **Certification Requirement.** As a precondition to receiving a contract or grant, employers must certify that they will maintain a drug-free workplace by:

    a. Publishing an anti-drug policy statement

    b. Providing employees with a copy of the statement

    c. Establishing a drug awareness and education program for employees

    d. Stipulating that, as a condition of employment, employees must abide by the anti-drug policy and report any criminal convictions for drug-related activity in the workplace

    e. Notifying the appropriate federal agency of employee drug-related activity in the workplace convictions

    f. Taking appropriate disciplinary actions against workplace substance abusers and

    g. Making a "good faith" effort to comply with the Act's requirements.

4. **Drug Testing.** Drug testing is not addressed in the Act.

5. **Employer Noncompliance Sanctions.** Contractors and grantees that provide a false certification or otherwise fail to abide by the Act's terms are subject to suspension of contract or grant payments, termination of the contract or grant, and debarment for up to five years.

6. **Employee Sanctions.** Employers informed about criminal convictions of employees for illegal activity in the workplace are required to take appropriate disciplinary action up to and including termination.

§ 10.27 —Department of Transportation Alcohol and Drug Regulations

Congress authorized creation of required procedures for transportation employers to follow when conducting workplace alcohol and drug testing.[47] Department

---

[47] 49 C.F.R. pt. 40 (1993).

of Transportation (DOT) agency regulations designate which employees are subject to testing. Transportation employers, including self-employed individuals, must follow these procedures for testing officers, employees, agents, and contractors. In *Teamsters v. Department of Transportation,*[48] it was determined that the Federal Highway Administration regulations requiring all interstate motor carriers to conduct drug testing of drivers operating vehicles weighing more than 26,000 pounds, carrying 15 or more passengers, or transporting hazardous materials were constitutional on their face. The regulations require annual random testing for:

1. At least 50 percent of drivers during the first biennial medical examination following implementation of the program
2. Pre-employment testing
3. Testing after "reportable" accidents that involve a fatality, an injury demanding immediate medical treatment away from the scene of the accident, or at least $4,400 in property damage.

In permitting "random" screening, the court found that the government had a compelling interest in promoting safety and deterring drug use in the trucking industry, and drivers had reduced privacy expectations because of the highly regulated nature of their industry. The mandated procedures for specimen collection minimize intrusions on privacy and the element of surprise is necessary to accomplish the government's purpose. The following policies implement the procedures suggested by these regulations.

POLICY 10.27(1)
DOT ALCOHOL AND DRUG POLICY

Section 1. Applicability.   This policy applies to drivers who are subject to the driver qualification requirements of the Federal Motor Carrier Safety regulations. The testing requirements apply to driver-applicants, driver-employees, and contract or leased drivers. A driver is covered if, at any point during the year, the driver operates a vehicle:

a. With gross vehicle weight rating or gross combination vehicle weight rating of 26,001 pounds or more

or

With any weight used to transport hazardous materials in a quantity that requires placarding.

and

---

[48] 6 I.E.R. Cas. (BNA) 647 (9th Cir. 1991).

b. When the vehicle is used on public highways to transport property in interstate commerce.

Section 2. Use Prohibited.   No driver will use a Schedule I drug of the Schedule of Controlled Substances of the Drug Enforcement Agency or an amphetamine, narcotic, or any other habit-forming drug, including alcohol. The schedule of drugs includes, but is not limited to, opiates, opium derivatives, hallucinogenic substances, depressants, and stimulants. The driver shall not consume any of these controlled substances while off duty or on duty. Any violation of this policy may result in discipline up to and including termination.

Section 3. Impairment Prohibited.   No driver will report for work or will drive impaired because of any drug or controlled substance. A driver may use a substance administered by or under the instructions of a physician who has advised the driver that the substance will not affect the driver's ability to safely operate a motor vehicle. "Impaired" means under the influence of a substance so that the driver's motor senses—i.e., sight, hearing, balance, reaction, reflex, or judgment—either are or may be presumed affected. Any violation of the policy may result in discipline up to and including termination.

Section 4. Possession Prohibited.   No driver at any work site shall possess any controlled substance, lawful or unlawful, which could result in impaired performance, with the exception of substances administered by or under the instructions of a physician. "Work site" means any motor vehicle, office, building, yard, or other property operated by the Company, or any other location at which the driver is to perform Company work. "Possess" means to have either in or on the driver's person, personal effects, motor vehicle, or areas substantially entrusted to the driver's control. Any violation of this policy may result in discipline up to and including termination.

Section 5. Substance Screening Procedures.   For purposes of assuring compliance with the Federal Motor Carrier Safety regulations and this policy, employee-drivers and new applicants for positions as drivers will be subject to alcohol and drug screening. "Screening" means testing of urine to determine use or impairment.

a. **Pre-Employment Testing.** Prior to assuming a driving position, all applicants will be subject to substance screening. Refusal to submit to screening will make it impossible to medically qualify the applicant, and the applicant therefore cannot be employed as a driver.

b. **Biennial Testing.** Drivers are required to submit to controlled substance testing at least once every two years during the medical examination required by the Federal Motor Carrier Safety regulations. Refusal to submit to testing will make it impossible to medically qualify the driver, and the driver therefore cannot continue to be employed as a driver and he or she will be subject to discipline up to and including termination.

c. **Probable Suspicion Testing.** When there is reasonable evidence to suspect that a driver has reported to work or is working impaired, the driver may be subject to substance screening. Refusal to submit to screening will be considered as a positive test result and the driver will be subject to discipline up to and including termination.

Section 6. Test Results.   Test results are reviewed to determine whether there is an indication of controlled substance use. The results are confidential. The Company's Medical Review Officer will be the sole custodian of the individual test results. They will not be released to any additional parties without the tested employee's written authorization. The Medical Review Officer will advise the Company only as to whether the test results are negative or positive.

Section 7. Employee Assistance Program (EAP).   All employees subject to the driver qualification requirements of the Federal Motor Carrier Safety regulations will receive sixty (60) minutes of formal training on the effects of alcohol and drugs. In addition, if the driver has a personal problem involving physical illness, emotional distress, chemical dependency, financial or legal trouble, marital or family problems that affects job performance and needs assistance to resolve it, the driver should contact the Company's EAP provider to arrance a confidential consultation. The initial evaluation is free. Additional professional services may be covered by the Company's health benefits.

Section 8. Behavioral Categories.   Employees with alcohol and drug abuse problems fall into one of two behavioral categories. The first, or "Type I," is the clearly impaired condition, when the employee is visibly impaired and evidences obvious and severe signs of impairment, involving lack of balance, slurred speech, dilated pupils, drowsiness, and so forth. The second, or "Type II," is the employee who, although not evidencing immediate obvious and severe signs of impairment, does evidence less severe behavioral patterns, possibly over a time period.

   a. **"Type I" Impairment.**   When an employee with this behavior is encountered, the supervisor should:

   1. **First,** find a witness (a trained supervisor, if possible) to accompany him or her in confronting the employee. Consideration should also be given to asking the union steward to be present.

   2. **Second,** advise the employee that his or her conduct appears to be impaired and that because of concern over the employee's and others' safety, he or she cannot commence or continue to work until the impairment is diagnosed and remedied. The supervisor must be sure not to attempt to diagnose the impairment's cause. This Behavior that appears to be impaired by substance abuse can be caused by a number of legitimate medical reasons.

   3. **Third,** advise the employee that he or she is requested to go with a Company employee to an approved medical facility to determine the impairment's cause. This will include a urine sample for laboratory testing.

       (a) If the employee refuses to go to the medical facility, he or she should be advised that refusal will result in disciplinary action up to and including termination.

(b)   If the employee still refuses to go to the medical facility, the supervisor should offer to have the employee driven to his or her home, other local residence, or a nearby hotel.

(c)   If the employee refuses and insists on leaving on his or her own, the supervisor should advise the employee that for the safety of the motoring public, he or she will have to advise the police of the employee's impaired condition. The employee should not be allowed to leave in a Company vehicle. If the employee does leave, the supervisor should call the police and advise them of the incident.

4.   **Fourth,** if the employee agrees to go to the medical facility, he or she should be taken to the medical facility by another Company employee who should advise the medical facility of the employee's conduct and ask the facility to evaluate the impaired employee.

5.   **Fifth,** the employee should be advised that he or she is suspended pending the medical diagnosis.

(a)   If the medical diagnosis indicates a non-alcohol or non-drug-induced impairment, the employee should be requested to return to work after treatment and obtaining a written release from the attending physician.

(b)   If the medical diagnosis indicates an alcohol-induced impairment or the presence of any controlled substance or illegal drug in the employee's body system, the employee will be subject to discipline up to and including termination. No employee will be allowed to return to work without evidence of having entered some type of rehabilitation program, to be approved by the Company, within ten (10) business days of receiving notice of the medical diagnosis. The Company will assist in locating a program if the employee desires assistance. Continued employment with the Company will be conditioned upon no recurrences of alcohol-induced impairment or the presence of any controlled substance or illegal drug in the employee's body system while working and written evidence from the rehabilitation facility of participation in and successful completion of a rehabilitation program.

6.   **Sixth,** fill out the "Supervisor's Guide to Impaired Work Behaviors" form the same day and note on that form all dates, times, conduct, length of observation period, statements, witnesses, and any other events relevant to the incident. Submit the form to the office as soon as possible.

b.   **"Type II" Impairment.** If an employee has more subtle signs of physical impairment of some nature, including attendance problems, lack of energy, frequent nausea, and so forth, the supervisor should complete a "Supervisor's Guide to Impaired Work Behavior" form. The supervisor should then approach the employee, with a witness if possible, to discuss the problem. The employee should be advised as to the nature of the behavior observed by the supervisor or co-employees and the basis for the supervisor's concern. The employee should be offered assistance from the Company to obtain outside help to deal with his or her problem. If the employee rejects this offer of assistance, he or she should be advised that he or she may be requested to be evaluated at a medical facility if the conduct discussed is observed at a later date. If the supervisor later decides to have an evaluation performed, the same steps as set forth in Section 8(a) should be followed.

Section 9. Drug and Alcohol Disciplinary Guidelines.   If an employee is subject to disciplinary procedures due to a medical diagnosis indicating an alcohol-induced impairment or the presence of any controlled substance or illegal drug in the employee's body system, or the employee refuses to submit to a substance screening test required by DOT regulations, the following guidelines should be followed:

a.   The employee shall be granted a leave of absence on a one-time basis, for a maximum of sixty (60) calendar days.

b.   The employee, within ten (10) calendar days after receiving notice of the medical diagnosis, must initiate the rehabilitation process and notify the Company.

c.   The employee must begin the rehabilitation process fifteen (15) calendar days after electing to do so.

d.   The employee shall be granted reinstatement on a one-time basis if the employee successfully completes a program of evaluation and, if necessary, treatment as approved by a physician.

e.   All costs for rehabilitation over and above that paid for by the employee's health benefits must be paid by the employee.

f.   Upon being reinstated, the employee will be subject to additional tests for alcohol or drugs without prior notice within twelve (12) months after the employee's return to employment. A positive test result or a refusal to submit to testing shall result in termination without the receipt of a prior warning letter.

Supervisors' Guide to Impaired Work Behavior

Employee's Name: _____

Date of Observation: _____

Time of Observation: From: _____ A.M.   _____ P.M.

To: _____ A.M.   _____ P.M.

Location: _____

The behaviors listed below are examples of changes you might observe in an individual employee.

Use this form:

_____   When you believe than an employee's performance is impaired and you want to identify and record the basis for your conclusion.

_____ When you notice a change in an employee and you want to evaluate whether there are other changes as well.

_____ When you wish to discuss an apparent, but not immediate or severe, impairment with an employee and you want to be specific about the changes you have seen.

Observed Personal Behavior: Check All Appropriate Items

1. **Physical signs or conditions**

_____ Weariness, exhaustion	_____ Unsteady walk
_____ Untidiness	_____ Falling
_____ Yawning excessively	_____ Changes in appearance after lunch or break
_____ Blank stare	
_____ Slurred speech	

2. **Mood**

_____ Appears to be depressed all the time

_____ Irritable

_____ Suspicious

_____ Complains about others

_____ Emotional outbursts

_____ Mood changes after lunch or break

3. **Actions**

_____ Withdrawn or improperly talkative

_____ Spends excessive amount of time on telephone or in the bathroom

_____ Argumentative

_____ Displays violent behavior

4. **Absenteeism**

_____ Acceleration of absenteeism and tardiness, especially Mondays and Fridays

_____ Frequent unreported absences

_____ Usually high incidence of colds, flu, upset stomach, headaches

_____ Frequent use of unscheduled vacation time

_____ Leaving work area more than necessary (e.g., frequent trips to car, water fountain, or bathroom)

5. Other observed actions or behavior: _____

_____

_____

_____

Above behavior witnessed by:

Signed: _____ Date: _____

Signed: _____ Date: _____

This form must be prepared within twenty-four (24) hours of the behavior's observation.

POLICY 10.27(2)
DOT ALCOHOL AND DRUGS POLICY

Section 1. Introduction.   Alcohol and drug abuse in the workplace reflect a national problem. The development of a Company policy for dealing with these problems, along with appropriate management, supervisor, and employee education when implementing this policy, are important in addressing this.

Section 2. Statement on Alcohol and Drugs.   The Company has a strong commitment to its employees to provide an alcohol- and drug-free work environment. Likewise, the Company is committed to its customers, local businesses, and the general public to operate its business safely and prudently. Consistent with this commitment, the Company has formulated this policy regarding alcohol and drugs.

Section 3. Purposes.   The purposes of this policy are:

a. To establish and maintain a healthy and safe working environment for all employees;

b. To ensure the reputation of the Company and its employees as good, responsible citizens;

c. To reduce accidental injury to person or property;

d. To reduce absenteeism, tardiness, and indifferent job performance; and

e. To provide assistance toward rehabilitation for any employee in accordance with the Company's Employee Assistance Program (EAP).

Section 4. Definitions

a. "Alcohol or alcoholic beverage" means any beverage that may be legally sold and consumed and that has an alcoholic content in excess of .5% by volume.

b. "DOT" means the Department of Transportation.

c. "Drug" means any substance other than alcohol capable of altering the mood, perception, pain level, or judgment of the individual consuming it.

d. "Employee" means any person employed by the Company, including but not limited to those persons in a temporary, part-time, or full-time status; all levels of management, administration, and supervision responsibility; and all areas of production, sales, and distribution.

e. "Illegal drug" means any drug or controlled substance the sale or consumption of which is illegal under federal or state law.

f. "Motor vehicle accident" means any motor vehicle accident in which an employee is involved while operating a Company-owned or leased vehicle.

g. "MRO" means Medical Review Officer.

h. "Prescribed drug" means any substance prescribed for the individual consuming it by a licensed medical practitioner.

i. "Serious safety-related incident" means any incident presenting a substantial risk of lost-time injury or property damage.

j. "Unfit condition" means the condition of any employee identified by designated Company personnel as not safely or competently performing his or her job and presenting unnecessary risk to self or others.

k. "Workplace accident" means any accident resulting in lost time, injury to self, and/or involvement in an accident which results in the lost-time injury of another individual and/or property damage.

Section 5. Alcoholic Beverages. The following are prohibited regarding alcoholic beverages:

a. No alcoholic beverage will be brought into, possessed, or consumed on the Company's premises, Company property, or Company vehicles.

b. Any employee whose alcohol abuse results in excessive absenteeism or tardiness, or is the cause of accidents or poor work, may be referred to the Employee Assistance Program (EAP) for rehabilitation. If the employee refuses or fails rehabilitation, he or she shall be subject to discipline up to and including termination.

Section 6. Prescription Drugs. The following are prohibited regarding prescription drugs:

a. No prescription drug shall be brought upon the Company's premises by any person other than the person for whom the drug is prescribed by a licensed medical practitioner, and the drug shall be used only in the manner, combination, and quantity prescribed.

b. Any employee whose prescription drug abuse results in excessive absenteeism or tardiness, or is the cause of accidents or poor work, may be referred to the Employee Assistance Program (EAP) for rehabilitation. If the employee refuses or fails rehabilitation, he or she shall be subject to discipline up to and including termination.

c. Any employee undergoing prescribed medical treatment with a controlled substance that may affect job performance shall report this treatment to his or her supervisor, including providing the supervisor with a list of medications. Use of a controlled substance as part of a prescribed medical treatment is not grounds for disciplinary action, although it is important for the Company to know the use is occurring. It may, however, be necessary to change an employee's job assignment while the employee is undergoing treatment.

Section 7. Illegal Drugs.   The following are prohibited regarding illegal drugs:

a. The use of an illegal drug or controlled substance, or the possession of one, at or outside the workplace is subject to discipline up to and including termination.

b. The sale, trade, or delivery of illegal drugs or controlled substances or conspiring in the sale, trade, or delivery of illegal drugs or controlled substances by an employee to another person is cause for discipline up to and including termination.

c. The occasional, recreational, or off-duty use of illegal drugs will not be excused and will subject the employee to discipline up to and including termination. The Company's understanding indicates that employee involvement with illegal drugs, even recreationally, may be expected to result in:

   (1)   Financial and domestic difficulties causing:

      (a)   Unstable performance

      (b)   Theft

   (2)   Embarrassment to the Company due to:

      (a)   Employee arrests

      (b)   Poor customer relations, unsatisfactory work, short tempers, and so forth.

Section 8. Prohibited Conduct.

a. **General.** Any employee found to be using, selling, possessing, trafficking in, or under the influence of any alcoholic beverage or drug while engaged in a work-related activity will be considered in violation of Company policy and will be subject to appropriate disciplinary action up to and including termination. Employees may be suspended with or without pay pending completion of an investigation. The Company reserves the right to search employee personal effects, work area(s), and vehicle(s) of an employee suspected to be involved in alcohol or drug abuse activities.

b. **Conviction for Driving While Intoxicated.** Any employee whose Company duties involve driving who is convicted of driving while intoxicated at or outside the workplace is subject to immediate disciplinary action up to and including termination, along with loss of Company vehicle privileges.

Section 9. Safety of Work Force, Work Rules, and Testing. To ensure the safety of the workplace and the work force, the following work rules apply to all employees effective upon receipt of notice of this policy:

a. Each employee, as a condition of continued employment, will be required, upon request of Company supervisory personnel, to:

    (1) Submit to search of any vehicle brought upon or parked upon Company premises;

    (2) Submit to search of any pocket, package, purse, briefcase, tool box, lunch box, or other container brought upon Company premises, including personal belongings; or

    (3) Submit to search of desk, file cabinet, and so forth.

b. The Company reserves the right to require, at its discretion, when it suspects alcohol or drug abuse, that an employee, as a condition of continued employment, be physically examined and/or clinically tested for the presence of alcohol or drugs by qualified medical personnel as a result of:

    (1) Being identified by supervision as appearing to be in an unfit condition, as determined by the Company;

    (2) Involvement in a serious workplace accident or serious safety-related incident as determined by the Company;

    (3) Involvement in a motor vehicle accident while operating a Company-owned or leased vehicle; or

    (4) Any other circumstance, incident, or occurrence that leads the Company to suspect alcohol or drug abuse.

Section 10. Job Applicants. All job applications, regardless of intended payroll status, must successfully undergo alcohol and drug screening as part of the pre-employment processing.

Section 11. Testing.

a. **General Procedures.** In cases in which an employee is acting in an abnormal manner and at least one supervisor (two, if available) has probable suspicion to believe that the employee is under the influence of alcohol or drugs, the Company may require the employee to go to a medical clinic to provide specimens for laboratory testing. If requested, the employee will sign a consent form authorizing the clinic to obtain specimens and release the results of the laboratory testing to the Company's Medical Review Officer, in the case of Department of Transportation (DOT) covered employees, and the testing results to the Company.

b. **Refusal.** A refusal to provide a specimen will constitute a presumption of guilt and the employee will be subject to termination. For a non-DOT-covered employee who is unable to provide a specimen after a reasonable waiting period (not to exceed one (1) hour), the Company may take whatever action may be necessary up to and including termination. In DOT-covered cases, if the employee is unable to produce sixty (60) milliliters (ml.) of urine, he/she shall be given fluids to drink and shall remain at the collection site under observation until able to produce a 60-ml. specimen, or until eight (8) hours have passed. If still unable to produce a 60-ml. specimen, the employee shall be referred for medical evaluation.

Section 12. DOT Recurrent Examinations and Other Regular Physical Examinations. When the Company performs alcohol or drug testing in conjunction with a DOT or other regularly scheduled physical examination, the employee will be informed of the testing prior to administration of the examination. All tests must be analyzed pursuant to the methodology described in Sections 16 and 17. Testing performed in a DOT recurrent examination will be pursuant to DOT regulations. If a current non-DOT-covered employee is required to be tested under the DOT testing requirements, testing shall be subject to all provisions of this subsection.

Section 13. Random Testing. Employees may be subjected to random drug testing or as part of an employee's reinstatement after successfully completing an alcohol or drug rehabilitation program.

Section 14. Postaccident DOT Testing. "Postaccident testing" is defined as testing done because of an accident reportable to DOT when there is probable suspicion of alcohol or drug usage, or reasonable cause to believe a driver was operating a vehicle while under the influence of alcohol or drugs, or reasonable cause to believe the driver was at fault in the accident and alcohol or drug usage may have been a factor. Testing will be required after accidents under these conditions and employees are required to submit to testing within thirty-two (32) hours. An "accident reportable to DOT" is defined as an accident which results in:

a. The death of a human being; or

b. Bodily injury to a person who, as a result of the injury, immediately received medical treatment away from the accident; or

c. Total damage to all property of four thousand four hundred dollars ($4,400.00) or more, based upon actual costs or estimates.

The employee has the responsibility to make himself or herself available for testing within the thirty-two (32) hour period after the reportable accident.

Section 15. Chain of Possession Procedures. At the time specimens are collected for any testing, the employee shall be given a copy of the specimen collection procedures. The specimens must be immediately sealed, labeled, and initialed by the employee to ensure that the specimens tested by the laboratory are those of the employee. The required procedure is as follows:

a. **Probable Suspicion Testing.** Individual test tubes shall, in the presence of the employee, be sealed, labeled, and then initialed by the employee. The employee has an obligation to identify the specimen and initial it. The specimens shall be placed in the transportation container after being drawn. The container shall be sealed in the employee's presence and the employee given an opportunity to initial the container and witness his or her Social Security number placed on the container. The container shall be sent to the designated testing laboratory on that day or the soonest normal business day by air courier or other fastest available method.

b. **Urine Specimens.**

(1) At least sixty (60) milliliters (ml.) of specimen shall be collected and placed in one (1) self-sealing, screw-capped container. Urine specimen in excess of the first sixty (60) ml. shall be placed in a second container. They shall be sealed and labeled and initialed by the employee without the containers leaving the employee's presence. The employee has an obligation to identify each specimen and initial it. The specimens must be immediately sealed in a transportation container which is again initialed by the employee, and sent via air courier or other fastest available means to the designated testing laboratory.

(2) Urine shall be obtained directly in a wide-mouthed single-use specimen container which shall remain in full view of the employee until transferred to, and sealed and initialed in, the sixty (60) ml. tamper-resistant urine bottle in the kit, and the second "split-sample" bottle. At the employee's request he or she may void directly into the two (2) self-sealing tamper-resistant urine bottles in the kit.

(3) The Company has the right to request the clinic personnel administering a urine test to take such steps as checking the color and temperature of the urine specimen to detect tampering or substitution, provided that the employee's right of privacy is guaranteed and in no circumstances may observation take place while the employee is producing the urine specimens, unless required by DOT regulations. If it is established that the employee's specimen has been intentionally tampered with or substituted by the employee, the employee is subject to discipline up to and including termination as if the specimen tested positive.

(4) To deter adulteration of the urine specimen during the collection process, physiologic determinations such as creatinine, specific gravity, and/or chloride measurements may be performed by the laboratory.

(5) Any findings by the laboratory outside the normal ranges for creatinine, specific gravity, and/or chloride shall be immediately reported to the Company so that another specimen can be collected. The MRO shall also be advised in the case of a DOT-covered employee.

c. **Procedure's Integrity.** The key to chain-of-possession integrity is the immediate labeling and initialing of the specimen in the presence of the tested employee. If each container is received at the laboratory in an undamaged condition with properly sealed, labeled, and initialed specimens, as certified by that laboratory, the Company may take disciplinary action up to and including termination based upon properly obtained laboratory results.

Section 16. Drug Testing Kits.   For Company-required urine drug screens, the contents of the urine collection kit shall be as follows:

a. Two (2) screw-capped self-sealing tamper-resistant urine collection bottles, one of which must hold at least 60 ml.

b. Security seals for sealing and initialing the urine bottles.

c. Instructions for urine collection.

d. Chain-of-possession form.

e. Nylon-reinforced shipping seal or sealing flaps for securing the exterior of the urine kit.

f. A self-adhesive mailing label and a separate set of nylon-reinforced shipping seals for resealing the transportation container, for use in the event that the second part of the urine sample is to be shipped to a different lab.

The chain of possession form in the urine collection kit shall be completed by the clinic personnel before sealing the entire kit. The exterior of the urine collection kit shall then be secured (e.g., by placing the nylon-reinforced shipping seals over the outlined tab area or sealing the flaps if so provided). If possible, the employee should initial the nylon seal or sealing flaps.

Shrink-wrapped or similarly protected kits shall be used in all instances pertaining to (a) and (b) of this section. The employee to be tested shall be given a random choice of the available kits.

Section 17. DOT Laboratory Requirements.

a. **Urine Testing.** In testing urine samples, the testing laboratory shall test specifically for those drugs and classes of drugs listed in Section 18, employing the test methodologies and cutoff levels specified in Section 18.

b. **Specimen Retention.** All specimens deemed positive by the laboratory must be retained at the laboratory for a period of one (1) year.

c. **Split-Sample Procedure.** An optional split-sample procedure will be available to employees in DOT recurrent or other regularly scheduled physical examinations.

   (1) When a test kit is received by a laboratory, a 60-ml. sealed urine specimen bottle shall be removed immediately for testing. The shipping container with the remaining sealed bottle shall be immediately placed in secure refrigerated storage.

   (2) The employee will be given two (2) containers for the urine specimen. One (1) container must be filled with no less than 60 ml. of urine. Urine in excess of the first 60 ml. shall be placed in the second container. Both shall be sealed and then forwarded to an approved laboratory for testing. If an employee is told that the first sample tested positive, the employee may, within seventy-two (72) hours of receipt of actual notice, request that the second urine specimen be forwarded by the first laboratory to

another independent and unrelated, approved laboratory of the parties' choice for gas chromatography/mass spectrometry (GC/MC) confirmatory testing of the presence of the drug.

(3)   If the second test is positive, and the employee wishes to use this policy's rehabilitation procedures, the employee shall reimburse the employer for the cost of the second confirmation test before entering the rehabilitation program.

(4)   If an employee chooses to have the second sample analyzed, he or she shall at that time execute a special checkoff authorization form to ensure the split-sample procedure. Disciplinary action can only take place after the first laboratory confirms the presence of the drug. However, the employee may be taken out of service once the first laboratory reports a positive finding while the second test is being performed. If the second laboratory report is negative, the employee will be reimbursed for the cost of the second test.

d. **Laboratory Accreditation.** All laboratories used to perform DOT urine testing must be accredited by the National Institute on Drug Abuse (NIDA).

Section 18. DOT Laboratory Testing Methodology.

a. **Urine Testing.** Testing shall be by immunoassay which meets the requirements of the Food and Drug Administration for commercial distribution.

(1)   The initial cutoff levels used when screening urine specimens to determine whether they are negative or positive for various classes of drugs shall be those contained in the *Scientific and Technical Guidelines for Federal Drug Testing Programs,* subject to revision in accordance with subsequent amendments.

(2)   All specimens identified as positive on the initial test shall be confirmed using gas chromatography/mass spectrometry (GC/MS) techniques. Quantitative GC/MS confirmation procedures to determine whether the test is negative or positive for various classes of drugs shall be those contained in the *Scientific and Technical Guidelines for Federal Drug Testing Programs,* subject to revision in accordance with subsequent amendments.

(3)   All specimens that test negative on either the initial test or the GC/MS confirmation test shall be reported only as negative. Only specimens that test positive on both the initial test and the GC/MS confirmation test shall be reported as positive.

(4)   In reporting a positive test result in a drug test not subject to DOT regulations, the laboratory shall state the specific substance(s) for which the test is positive and shall provide the quantitative results of both the screening and the GC/MS confirmation test, in terms of nomograms per milliliter. All positive test results must be reviewed by the certifying scientist or laboratory director and certified as accurate.

b. **Blood Testing.** In testing blood specimens, the testing laboratory will analyze blood/serum by using gas chromatography/mass spectrometry as appropriate.

    (1)   In probable suspicion testing, a positive finding for cannabinoids will be forensically reported under any of the following results obtained after testing blood specimens by gas chromatography/mass spectrometry:

        (a)   The blood/serum contains at least two (2) and up to five (5) nomograms THC/ml. and at least ten (10) nomograms THC metabolites/ml.

        (b)   The blood/serum contains at least five (5) or more nomograms THC/ml., regardless of the THC metabolite concentration.

        (c)   The blood/serum contains twenty (20) or more nomograms THC metabolites/ml., regardless of the THC concentration.

If none of the above blood marijuana findings results are obtained, a negative finding shall be reported. If other Schedule I and II drugs in blood are detected, the laboratory is to report a positive test based on a forensically acceptable positive quantum of proof. All positive test results must be reviewed by the certifying scientist or laboratory director and certified as accurate.

c. **Prescription and Nonprescription Medications.** If an employee is taking a prescription or nonprescription medication in the appropriate described manner, he or she will not be disciplined. Medications prescribed for another individual, not the employee, shall be considered to be illegally used and subject the employee to discipline up to and including termination.

d. **Medical Review Officer (MRO).** The Medical Review Officer (MRO) shall be a licensed physician with knowledge of substance abuse disorders. The MRO shall review and interpret confirmed positive urine test results from the laboratory and shall examine alternate medical explanations for such positive tests. Prior to the final decision to verify a positive urine drug test result, the employee shall have the opportunity to discuss the results with the MRO. If the employee has not discussed the results of the positive urine drug test with the MRO within five (5) calendar days after being contacted, or refuses the opportunity to do so, the MRO shall proceed with the positive verification.

Section 19. Leave of Absence. An employee may be permitted to take a leave of absence for the purpose of undergoing treatment pursuant to an approved program of alcoholism or drug use. The leave of absence shall be granted on a one-time basis and shall be for a maximum of sixty (60) calendar days unless extended by the Company. Employees requesting to return to work from a leave of absence for alcoholism or drug use shall be required to submit to testing as provided for in Section 18. Failure to do so will subject the employee to discipline up to and including termination.

Section 20. Disciplinary Action Based on Positive Test Results. The Company may take disciplinary action up to and including termination based on the test results.

Section 21. Return to Employment after a Positive Test in a DOT Recurrent or Other Physical Examination.

a. Any employee testing positive for drugs in a DOT recurrent or other regularly scheduled physical examination, thereby subjecting the employee to discipline, may be granted reinstatement on a one-time basis if the employee successfully completes a rehabilitation program. Any cost of rehabilitation over and above that paid for by the applicable Company benefit plan must be paid by the employee.

b. Upon being reinstated, the employee will be subject to three (3) additional tests for drugs without prior notice, with two (2) tests to occur within six (6) months of the employee's return to employment, and the third test to occur within six (6) to twelve (12) months after the employee's return to employment. A positive test result or a refusal to submit to testing shall result in termination.

Section 22. Employee Assistance Program.   Any employee who desires assistance in dealing with an alcohol or drug dependency problem may seek help, voluntarily, in confidence, by contacting the Employee Assistance Program (EAP). These individuals must be capable of performing their assigned duties and must cease all involvement with alcohol and drugs that will impact their job with the Company. They must enroll in and complete a prescribed treatment program. Employees undergoing counseling or treatment will not be exempt from the Company's rules, policies, procedures, or disciplinary application.

Section 23. Rejection of Treatment or Failure of Rehabilitation.   Any employee who refuses to submit to testing or has a positive result from an alcohol or drug test will be referred to the Employee Assistance Program (EAP) to complete successfully a prescribed treatment program. Any employee who subsequently violates this policy, has a future positive test result, refuses to have alcohol or drug testing, or refuses to use the EAP as required by this policy, will be subject to discipline up to and including termination. An employee with a positive result from an alcohol or drug test may request an immediate confirmation test on the original specimen at his or her own expense. If the result of the confirmation test is negative, the Company will reimburse the employee.

Section 24. Confidentiality.   All information obtained in the course of testing, rehabilitation, and treatment of employees with alcohol and drug abuse problems shall be protected as confidential medical information and shall be kept separate from the employee's official personnel file. Only those who have a need to know shall be given access to this information. The importance of this confidentiality to the Company and its employees cannot be overemphasized.

Section 25. Effective Date and Notice to Employees.   The policies set forth herein are effective immediately upon notice of employees. Each present employee will be furnished a copy of this policy and will sign a receipt for it. Future employees will each be furnished a copy before hiring.

ALCOHOL AND DRUG ABUSE POLICY RECEIPT
AND ACKNOWLEDGMENT

I, (Name) , hereby acknowledge that I have received a copy of the (Employer's
Name) Alcohol and Drug Abuse Policy and understand that it is my obligation and
responsibility to read this policy and comply with its terms.

_____
(Signature)

_____
(Date)

§ 10.28 —The Supervisor's Responsibility: Alcoholism

The following may be considered in training supervisors regarding employee
alcoholism:[49]

THE SUPERVISOR'S RESPONSIBILITY: ALCOHOLISMm

Being Prepared to Act

As the alcoholic's supervisor, you have both a responsibility to act and an opportunity to help. Alcoholics place a very high value on their jobs, which gives supervisors a lot of leverage in getting them to enter a recovery program. You may be in a
pivotal position to cause a major turnaround in your alcoholic employee's life. But
the opportunity can be lost unless you are prepared.

Keep Your Company's Policies.   Before you take any action, study your company's
policies regarding alcoholism and chemical dependency, fitness for duty, and employee assistance. These policies will guide you in taking action, and assure that everyone's interests are protected. They'll also help keep you focused on the workplace
issues.

Document Safety and Performance.   If you suspect problems with an employee,
keep records of safety incidents and performance changes over time. The facts are
your most effective leverage with the alcoholic—your opportunity to intervene effectively. The facts also keep the attention focused where it belongs—on workplace
issues.

---

[49] Adapted from the booklet prepared and published by Krames Communications, *Alcoholism in
the Workplace: What You Can Do* 12–13 (1986). Krames Communications offers a variety of
booklets on alcohol and drug abuse for employers to use in educating their managers, supervisors, and employees. These booklets are practical and include attractive illustrations. Krames
Communications may be contacted at 312 90th Street, Daly City, California 94015-1898 or by
telephoning (415) 994-8800.

Know Your Network of Resources. You are not alone. There is plenty of help available to help you take action with an alcoholic employee. If your company has an employee assistance program (EAP), that is the place to start. If not, find out who in your company deals with alcoholism problems—the human resources department, or the company medical department. If you need additional advice and support, call your local office of the National Council on Alcoholism.

Taking Action

Dealing with an alcoholic employee can be difficult and painful, especially if he or she is your friend. Remember, though, this person is heading for self-destruction and that isn't good for anybody. Losing a valuable employee is a terrible waste, so you will be doing everyone a service by intervening before he or she gets fired. This can be done both sensitively and effectively.

Focus on Safety and Performance. Your responsibility is correcting the employee's work problems, not his or her alcoholism. Stay focused on the workplace issues.

Don't Diagnose. Leave diagnosis of alcoholism to the professionals. Many of the signs of alcoholism can be caused by other problems, and a misdiagnosis could be harmful.

Be Private. Talk to the employee face to face and in private. This avoids embarrassment, shows your respect, and encourages an open exchange of information and feelings.

Clarify Expectations. Be sure the employee knows what you expect and what the consequences will be if problems persist. This way the employee is responsible for his or her own future.

Show Your Concern. Let the employee know that you care—that you really want to see improvement, and that you are hoping for his or her continued service to the company.

Don't Be Manipulated. Remember, alcoholics sincerely believe they can control their drinking. Don't accept excuses or permit yourself to be talked out of your position.

§ 10.29 —Supervisor's Alcohol and Drug Abuse Manual

The following manual should be considered in training supervisors regarding alcohol and drug abuse:[50]

---

[50] *See* Edison Electric Institute, Policy Development at 47–68. The following information comes from a pamphlet which is based on the National Institute on Drug Abuse publication, *Let's Talk About Drug Abuse.* It was adapted for use by several electric companies by Peter Bensinger, consultant to the Edison Electric Institute Task Force and president of Bensinger, DuPont and Associates in Chicago, Illinois. This document may also be adapted for employee training.

FORM 10.29(1)
SUPERVISOR'S ALCOHOL AND DRUG ABUSE MANUAL

Section 1. Purpose.   This manual's purpose is to provide supervisory personnel with a uniform approach to their role in enforcing the Company's Alcohol and Drug Abuse Policy. There are certain points that should be remembered by all supervisors:

a. Alcohol or illegal drug use during off-duty hours which will adversely affect an employee's job performance, jeopardize other employees' safety, the public, or Company equipment, or generate other circumstances harmful to the Company's interest is subject to the same disciplinary action as job incidents.

b. The responsibility for reporting alcohol- or drug-related activities to the Human Resources Department lies with all employees and all supervisors.

c. Employees who have problems involving alcohol or drugs, or are suffering from emotional stress, should be encouraged to request assistance from the Employee Assistance Program. However, it is not intended that this request for assistance be used as a means for avoiding disciplinary action.

d. Supervisors are not expected to diagnose problem drinking, alcohol, drug, or emotional stress problems, or to prescribe treatment. Their role is to monitor job performance, including factors of work quality, attendance, dependability, and safety awareness, and call deficiencies to the attention of employees to be sure they understand satisfactory job performance standards.

e. Employees who are deemed incapacitated because of alcohol, drug, or emotional stress must be provided with transportation to ensure the individual's safety.

Section 2. Alcohol Guidelines.   When an employee's job performance does not improve following early warnings, it may be a sign of some personal problem involving alcohol dependency. The supervisor should arrange for a private meeting with the employee to discuss job performance, along with a union steward if the employee is in a bargaining unit, and indicate:

a. Job performance must improve to acceptable standards to avoid jeopardizing the employee's status with the Company.

b. If the employee has a personal problem that might be affecting job performance, counseling provided by the Employee Assistance Program or other sources of professional assistance might be helpful.

c. The Company will be supportive of efforts to improve job performance as long as there is an indication that the employee is taking positive action to remedy the problem. In cases where the abuse of alcohol has been confirmed, positive action must include a discontinuation of the abuse.

When an employee reports to work under the apparent influence of alcohol or is observed to be under this influence during the work day, the supervisor should:

a. Arrange, if practical, for at least one other supervisor to observe the employee's behavior and participate in the investigation.

b. Ask the employee involved to go to a location where he or she can be questioned privately about the incident. If requested of a bargaining unit employee, a union steward should be present.

c. Ask the employee to explain why he or she appears not to be in a condition to perform his or her work. Should discussions with the employee fail to explain his or her condition and it is still the determination that the employee is not in condition to work, the supervisor should accompany the employee to or arrange for him or her to be taken by another management employee to the Medical Department for a medical evaluation.

d. Following the incident, the supervisor should immediately make a detailed written record of all actions, statements, and other pertinent facts, along with reporting the facts to the Human Resources Department.

When a supervisor observes an employee drinking or with alcohol on Company property or on the job, the supervisor should:

a. Arrange, if practical, for at least one other supervisor to observe the employee's behavior.

b. Immediately contact Security to escort the employee to a location where he or she can be questioned privately about the incident. If requested of a bargaining unit employee, a union steward should be present.

c. Request the employee to place the substance in a secure location.

d. The supervisor should make a detailed written report of the incident. Report the facts to the next level of supervision and as soon as possible to the Human Resources Department.

Section 3. Drug Guidelines.   Each supervisor is responsible for taking appropriate action in any case where an employee who reports for work is not in a condition to perform his or her assignment. When there is suspicion that an employee may be under drug influence, the supervisor should:

a. Arrange, if practical, for at least one other supervisor to observe the employee's behavior and participate in the investigation.

b. Ask the employee involved to go to a location where he or she can be questioned privately about the incident. If requested of a bargaining unit employee, a union steward should be present.

c. Ask the employee to explain why he or she appears not to be in a condition to perform his or her work. Should discussions with the employee fail to explain his or her condition and it is still the supervisor's determination that the employee is not in a condition to work, the supervisor should accompany the employee to or arrange for him or her to be taken by another management employee to the Medical Department for medical evaluation.

When a supervisor observes employee drug use, sale, or possession on the job or on Company property, the supervisor should:

a. As soon as possible have another supervisor participate in the investigation.

b. Immediately request the employee to place the substance or paraphernalia in a secure location.

c. The supervisor should then prepare a list of this material.

d. Ask the employee involved to go to a location where he or she can be questioned privately about the incident. If requested of a bargaining unit employee, a union steward should be present.

e. Report the incident to the next level of supervision and, as soon as possible, to the Human Resources Department.

At this point, it may be necessary or appropriate to contact Security to conduct a search of the employee's locker or personal effects. Contact should also be made with the Human Resources Department if a bargaining employee is involved. However, supervisors should not conduct body searches.

Local law enforcement officials may be contacted by Security to confiscate any substances or paraphernalia turned over or found by supervisors. Following the incident, the supervisor should immediately make a detailed written report of all actions, statements, and other pertinent facts and forward these to the appropriate supervisor, department heads, and the Human Resources Department.

If a supervisor receives a report that an employee has violated the Company's policy, the supervisor should try to obtain as much detailed information as possible from the person reporting the violation. The next level of supervision and the Human Resources Department should then be notified. Human Resources will coordinate this report's investigation.

If the presence of illegal drugs is discovered in a medical examination of active employees, Human Resources and Security will coordinate an investigation.

If a supervisor observes drug use, sale, or possession on Company premises by people who are not Company employees, this should immediately be reported to the next level of supervision and to Security, who will be responsible for the investigation.

If drugs or drug paraphernalia are found on Company property and it is not obvious who the owner is, the incident should be to reported to Security and the Human Resources Department.

Section 4. Guidelines.   Many employees have temporary behavior changes that affect work performance which can be contributed to by marital problems, medical problems, financial problems, family problems, work problems, and so forth. These situations often put a strain on an employee's mental and physical abilities and may manifest themselves in lack of sleep, depression, quick temper, lack of interest in friends and outside activity, daydreaming, short attention span, and so forth.

Whenever a supervisor notes a behavior change in an employee that might be attributed to an emotional stress situation, the supervisor should:

a. Let the employee know that the supervisor is available to discuss the problem with the employee.

b. Arrange to discuss the problem with the employee in a location offering privacy.

c. If the case seems to be severe, make arrangements for Employee Assistance Counseling.

d. Contact the next level of supervision and the Human Resources Department if time off-the-job will be needed for counseling.

Section 5. General Drug Information.

What is a drug?

A drug is any chemical substance that produces physical, mental, emotional, or behavioral change in the user.

What is drug abuse?

Drug abuse is the use of a drug for other than medicinal purposes resulting in the impaired physical, mental, emotional, or social well-being of the user. Drug misuse is the unintentional or inappropriate use of prescription or over-the-counter drugs with similar results.

Which drugs are abused?

Narcotics, sedatives, alcohol, tobacco, stimulants, marijuana, inhalants, hallucinogens, and phencyclidine are the major drugs of abuse. All to one degree or another affect the user's feelings, perceptions, and behavior. Most of these drugs affect the user in physical ways as well, but they are abused because of their psychoactive mind-altering properties.

What is drug addiction?

Drug addiction has been used to describe a "physical" dependence on a drug.

What is tolerance?

Tolerance is a state which develops in users of certain drugs and requires them to take larger and larger drug amounts to produce the same effect. Tolerance often, but not always, occurs along with physical dependence.

Why do people abuse drugs?

There are many reasons, including the wish or belief that drugs can solve every problem, the pressure from friends to experiment, the enjoyment of drug effects, the easy access to socially acceptable drugs like alcohol and tobacco. Reasons for drug experimentation include curiosity or social pressure, enjoyment, availability, dependence, and fear of withdrawal.

What is drug dependence?

Drug dependence is the need for a drug which results from the continuous or periodic use of that drug. This need can be characterized by mental and/or physical changes in users making it difficult for them to control or stop their drug use. They believe that they must have the drug to feel good, normal, or just to get by. This mental aspect of drug dependence is often called psychological dependence.

Some drugs, like narcotics and barbiturates, change the body's physical system so that it becomes used to the drug and needs it to function. When a user stops taking the drug, he or she will experience withdrawal symptoms, like vomiting, tremors, sweating, insomnia, or even convulsions. To avoid withdrawal and to continue to function, the user takes the drug again. This aspect of drug dependence is often called physical dependence. Many people try to distinguish between psychological and physical dependence, believing that one type of dependence is worse than the other. However, heavy use of any psychoactive drug produces some type of dependence. This dependence interferes with the social, behavioral, and physical functioning of the individual.

Are drugs harmful?

Any drug can be harmful. Drug effects depend on many variables, including the amount of the drug taken, how often it is taken, the way it is taken, and other drugs used at the same time. Also, the user's weight, personality, mood, expectations, and environment help determine how a drug affects a person.

How can misuse of legally obtained drugs be controlled?

Drugs should be used only as prescribed and should be destroyed when they are no longer needed. All drugs, including nonprescription, over-the-counter drugs, should be kept away from children. Doctors and pharmacists should watch prescription renewals for drugs that can lead to dependence.

Are substances other than those commonly called drugs ever abused?

Yes. Substances like aerosols, gasoline, paint thinner, and model airplane glue contain volatile anesthetic-like chemicals that people sometimes sniff to get high. These inhalants should be bought and used with caution.

Do drug abusers ever take more than one drug?

Yes. Multiple drug abuse is common. People who abuse one drug are likely to abuse other drugs, either by taking a variety of them all at once or at different times. Multiple drug abuse means multiple risk. Mixing alcohol and sleeping pills, sedatives, or tranquilizers is especially dangerous.

Do drug experimenters become drug dependent?

No. Most people who experiment with drugs do not become dependent. In fact, most do not even become regular users.

What is the effect of drugs on sexual response?

No drug seems to be a true aphrodisiac in creating sexual desire rather than reducing inhibitions, although various substances have been considered aphrodisiacs throughout history. What users expect is probably more important than what drugs do. Alcohol and drugs may actually reduce sexual responsiveness. Small doses of certain drugs, however, may make a person feel less inhibited.

Is it unsafe to use drugs during pregnancy?

Pregnant women should be extremely cautious about taking any drug, even aspirin, without first consulting their physicians. Research has shown that heavy smoking and drinking can harm the developing fetus. Babies born of narcotic- and barbiturate-dependent mothers are often born drug dependent and require special care after birth.

What is drug overdose and what can I do about it?

An overdose of drugs is any amount which produces an acute and dangerous reaction. A severely low breathing rate, stupor, or coma are indicative of drug overdose. Get medical help immediately! In the meantime, make sure the overdosed person gets plenty of air. Artificial respiration may be necessary.

Sometimes hallucinogens, PCP, marijuana, or stimulants produce a panic reaction. The person may become frightened, suspicious, and may fear harm from others. It is crucial that everyone remain calm and reassure the person that these feelings are drug-related and will subside. Outside help is usually available from community hot lines, drug crisis centers, or hospital emergency rooms, and should be sought as soon as possible.

Is it possible to get medical help for drug problems without getting into trouble with the law?

Yes. There are important regulations to safeguard confidentiality for patients in treatment. Federal law requires doctors, psychologists, and drug treatment centers to keep confidential any information obtained from patients. However, under certain conditions, the law does allow disclosure. The information might be necessary so other doctors can treat the patient or so insurance carriers can provide benefits.

Can over-the-counter or nonprescription drugs be dangerous?

Yes. When these drugs are overused or misused in some other way, they too can cause serious problems. Drugs bought without prescription, including antihistamines, aspirin, cough medicines, diet pills, sleeping pills, and pep pills, can be helpful for minor, short-term discomforts. Although these preparations are relatively safe, users should always read labels carefully and check with their doctors if uncertain about the effect a particular over-the-counter drug may have.

What are controlled drugs?

Controlled drugs are those placed on a schedule or in special categories to prevent, curtail, or limit their distribution and manufacture. Under the Controlled Substances Act of 1970, the Attorney General of the United States, on the recommendation of the Secretary of Health, Education and Welfare, has the authority to place drugs into five schedules or categories based on their relative potential for abuse, scientific evidence of the drug's pharmacological effect, the state of current scientific knowledge about the drug, its history, and current abuse pattern.

What are the legal distinctions between possession, dealing, and trafficking in controlled substances?

"Possession" means: (1) having controlled legal drugs that are not obtained either directly from a doctor or from a pharmacist using a valid prescription; or (2) having controlled drugs which are illegal for use under any circumstance, like heroin or marijuana.

"Dealing" is illegally supplying or selling controlled drugs to users on a small scale.

"Trafficking" is the illegal manufacture, distribution, and sale of these drugs to dealers on a large scale.

Penalties for each offense vary from state to state.

What kind of treatment is available for the drug abuser?

In recent years, kinds of treatment programs have multiplied, since no single therapeutic approach seems to succeed for all people and all drugs. Treatment approaches for narcotics abusers principally include drug-free or methadone maintenance in residential or outpatient facilities. Approximately two-thirds of the treatment programs located across the country are drug-free. The remaining one-third utilize methadone maintenance. Rehabilitation services, including career development, counseling, and job skills training, are also available.

For alcohol-dependent people, treatment often includes drug therapy during the alcohol withdrawal phase, group or individual psychotherapy, and the particular kind of support provided by self-help groups similar to Alcoholics Anonymous.

Many other programs provide short-term counseling or drug crisis therapy through health agencies, schools, community mental health centers, and other organizations. The Company sponsors a confidential Employee Assistance Program to provide counseling on alcohol and drug abuse, along with other problems.

Section 6. Alcohol Information.

What is alcohol?

Alcohol is a drug. Like sedatives, it is a central nervous system depressant. The major psychoactive ingredient in wine, beer, and distilled liquor is alcohol, which is a natural substance formed by the reaction of fermenting sugar with yeast spores.

The kind of alcohol in alcoholic beverages is ethyl alcohol; i.e., a colorless, inflammable liquid. Technically, ethyl alcohol can also be classified as a food since it contains calories.

What effect does alcohol have?

In small doses, alcohol has a tranquilizing effect on most people, although it appears to stimulate others. Alcohol first acts on those parts of the brain that affect self-control and other learned behaviors. Lowered self-control may lead to the aggressive behavior associated with some people who drink.

In large doses, alcohol can dull sensation and impair muscular coordination, memory, and judgment. Taken in larger quantities over a long time period, alcohol can damage the liver and heart and cause permanent brain damage.

Can people become dependent on alcohol?

Yes. When drinkers see alcohol as an escape from the problems and stresses of everyday life, they may want to keep on drinking. They begin to depend on the drug for relief. Repeated drinking produces tolerance to the drug's effects and dependence. The drinker's body then needs more alcohol to function.

Once dependent, drinkers experience withdrawal symptoms when they stop drinking. Although considerable success has been reported in nonmedical withdrawal from alcohol, in some serious cases hospitalization may be required for a short time period.

Why does alcohol seem to affect different people differently?

Individual physical, mental, and environmental factors determine how people react to alcohol or any other psychoactive drug. How fast and how much they drink, whether they drink before or after eating, and factors of weight, personality, mood, and environment all interact to produce slightly different reactions in people.

How many Americans drink?

About two-thirds of all adults drink at least occasionally. Many younger people drink and evidence suggests that alcohol use among young people is spreading.

Why do people drink?

People drink for a variety of cultural, religious, medical, social, or personal reasons. Wine in particular has a long history of use among different ethnic groups. In certain religions, it is an element of sacrament or ceremony. Some people take a small glass of whiskey every now and then when they are ill because they believe it helps them feel better.

Most people probably think of themselves as social drinkers. Social drinking is usually defined as the light to moderate drinking people do for "social" reasons to help relax at get-togethers, to celebrate an occasion, or to "fit in" with others who are having a drink. There are probably as many reasons for social drinking as there are social situations. Other people use alcohol to forget their worries for the moment or to escape a distressing reality.

What dangers are associated with social drinking?

It is not definitely known if moderate amounts of alcohol are harmful to health. One problem is that "social drinking" means different amounts to different people. While research is being undertaken to find the answer, it is known that "social drinkers" can be a danger to themselves and others when they drive. Even one or two drinks can significantly impair a driver's judgment and reaction time. Of the deaths from car accidents each year in this country, about half are related to alcohol abuse.

What is alcoholism? And who is an alcoholic person?

Alcoholism is a condition characterized, among other things, by the drinker's consistent inability to choose whether to drink at all, or to stop drinking when he or she has had enough. But what is "enough"? It is certainly more than enough, for instance, when a person takes an overdose and becomes drunk, but one episode of intoxication does not make an alcoholic. In general, people have a problem with alcohol or are alcoholics if they cannot control their drinking, if they are dependent on the drug, and if their drinking has a negative impact on their families, friends, and jobs. The reasons people abuse alcohol and how seriously that abuse affects their lives may be more important in determining alcoholism than how long or how much they drink.

Can alcohol kill?

Yes. A large dose of alcohol, which can be as little as a pint or less of whiskey consumed at once, can interfere with the part of the brain that controls breathing. The resulting respiratory failure can bring death. On the average, heavy drinkers shorten their life span by about ten years.

Is alcohol mostly a man's problem?

No. It has been estimated that about half the alcoholic people in this country are women. However, women have historically been more reluctant than men to admit to alcohol dependence. One reason may be that society has looked upon female alcoholics as somehow "worse" than males.

What effect does alcohol have on the human fetus?

Recent studies show that women who drink heavily during pregnancy, more than three ounces of alcohol per day or equal to about two mixed drinks, run a higher risk than other women of delivering babies with physical, mental, and behavioral abnormalities.

A pregnant woman's occasional binge or light to moderate drinking may also affect her unborn child, but the evidence is not so clear as with heavy drinking. In addition, women who drink heavily are more likely to smoke heavily, eat poorly, and neglect their health in general. All of these factors can affect pregnancy.

Section 7. Specific Drug Information.

What are stimulants?

Stimulants, or "uppers," refer to several groups of drugs that tend to increase alertness and physical activity. Some people use stimulants to counteract the drowsiness or "down" feeling caused by sleeping pills or alcohol. This up/down cycle is extremely hard on the body and dangerous. Amphetamines, cocaine, and caffeine are all stimulants.

Amphetamines

What are amphetamines?

Amphetamines include three closely related drugs, namely amphetamine, dextroamphetamine, and methamphetamine. Their street names include: "speed," "white crosses," "uppers," "dexies," "bennies," and "crystal." In pure form, they are yellowish crystals that are manufactured in tablet or capsule form. Abusers also sniff the crystals or make a solution and inject it.

Are amphetamines used for medical purposes?

Amphetamines are used for treating narcolepsy, a rare disorder marked by uncontrolled sleep episodes and minimal brain dysfunction (MBD) in children. They are also prescribed for short-term obesity treatment.

What are the physical effects of amphetamines?

Amphetamines increase heart and breathing rates and blood pressure, dilate pupils, and decrease appetite. In addition, the user can experience a dry mouth, sweating, headache, blurred vision, dizziness, sleeplessness, and anxiety. Extremely high doses can cause people to flush or become pale. They can cause a rapid or irregular heartbeat, tremors, loss of coordination, and even physical collapse. An amphetamine injection creates a sudden increase in blood pressure that can cause death from stroke, very high fever, or heart failure.

How do amphetamine users feel?

In addition to the physical effects, users report feeling restless, anxious, and moody. Higher doses intensify the effects, and the user can become excited and talkative and have a false sense of self-confidence and power.

People who use large amounts of amphetamines over a long time period also can develop an amphetamine psychosis; i.e., seeing, hearing, and feeling things that do not exist (hallucinations), having irrational thoughts or beliefs (delusions), and feeling as though people are out to get them (paranoia). People in this extremely suspicious state frequently exhibit bizarre and sometimes violent behavior. These symptoms usually disappear when people stop using the drug.

What about long-term effects?

Long-term heavy use of amphetamines can lead to malnutrition, skin disorders, ulcers, and various diseases that come from vitamin deficiencies. Lack of sleep, weight loss, and depression also result from regular use. Frequent use of large amounts of amphetamines can produce brain damage that results in speech and thought disturbances. In addition, users who inject amphetamines intravenously can get serious and life-threatening infections from nonsterile equipment or self-prepared solutions that are contaminated. Injecting them can cause lung disease, heart disease, and other diseases of the blood vessels, which can be fatal. Kidney damage, stroke, or other tissue damage also may occur.

Can people become dependent on amphetamines?

Yes. Some people report a psychological dependence, a feeling that the drug is essential to their normal functioning. These users frequently continue to use amphetamines to avoid the "down" mood they get when the drug's effects wear off. In addition, people who use amphetamines regularly may develop tolerance; i.e., the need to take larger doses to get the same effect.

When people stop using amphetamines abruptly, they may experience fatigue, long periods of sleep, irritability, hunger, and depression. The length and severity of the depression seems to be related to how much and how often the amphetamines were used.

Look-Alikes

What are "look-alike" stimulants?

Look-alike stimulants are drugs manufactured to look like real amphetamines and mimic their effects. The drugs usually contain varying amounts of caffeine, ephedrine, and phenylpropanolamine. These three legal substances are weak stimulants and often are found in over-the-counter preparations, including diet pills and decongestants. More recently, new drugs called "act-alikes" have been manufactured to avoid new state statutes that prohibit look-alikes. The act-alikes contain the same ingredients as the look-alikes but do not physically resemble any prescription or over-the-counter drugs. These drugs are sold on the street as "speed" and "uppers" and are expensive, even though they are not as strong as amphetamines. They often are sold to young people who are told that the drugs are legal, safe, and harmless.

What are the effects of look-alikes?

Some negative effects of look-alikes, especially when taken in large quantities, are similar to the effects of amphetamines. These effects include anxiety, restlessness, weakness, throbbing headache, difficult breathing, and a rapid heartbeat. There have been several reports of severe high blood pressure leading to cerebral hemorrhaging and death. Often, in an emergency, look-alike drug overdose cases are misidentified by physicians and poison control centers. This can cause a problem in determining the proper treatment.

What are the dangers of look-alikes?

One of the greatest dangers is that these drugs are easily available and are being used by young people and others who do not normally abuse drugs. Once people start using these drugs, they may be at high risk for using other drugs.

Because look-alikes are not as strong as real amphetamines, they are extremely dangerous for people who deliberately or accidentally take the same amount of real amphetamines as they would take of the look-alikes. People who buy look-alikes on the street may, unknowingly, buy real amphetamines and take enough to cause an overdose. On the other hand, people who have abused amphetamines may underestimate the potency of the look-alike drugs and take excessive amounts that can result in a toxic reaction.

Cocaine

What is cocaine?

Cocaine is a drug extracted from the leaves of the coca plant, which grows in South America. Like the amphetamines, it is a central nervous system stimulant. Cocaine appears in several different forms. Cocaine hydrochloride is the most available form of the drug and is used medically as a local anesthetic. It is usually a fine white crystal-like powder, although at times it comes from larger pieces which on the street are called "rocks." Cocaine is usually sniffed or snorted into the nose, although some users inject it or smoke a form of the drug called free-base. It is also referred to as "crack."

Another form of the drug is coca paste, a crude product that is smoked in South America. It may be especially dangerous because it also consists of contaminants such as kerosene which can cause lung damage.

What are the immediate effects of cocaine?

When cocaine is "snorted," the effects begin within a few minutes, peak within 15 to 20 minutes, and disappear within an hour. These effects include dilated pupils and increases in blood pressure, heart rate, breathing rate, and body temperature. The user may have a sense of well-being and feel more energetic or alert and less hungry.

What is freebase?

Freebase is a cocaine form made by chemically converting "street" cocaine hydrochloride to a purified, altered substance that is then more suitable for smoking. Smoking freebase produces a shorter and more intense "high" than most other ways of using the drug because smoking is the most direct and rapid way to get the drug to the brain. Because larger amounts are getting to the brain more quickly, smoking also increases the risks associated with using the drug. These risks include confusion, slurred speech, anxiety, and serious psychological problems.

What are the dangers of cocaine use?

The dangers of cocaine use may vary, depending on how the drug is taken, the dose, and the individual. Some regular users report feelings of restlessness, irritability, anxiety, and sleeplessness. In some people, even low doses of cocaine may create psychological problems. People who use high doses of cocaine over a long time period may become paranoid or experience what is called a "cocaine psychosis." This may include hallucinations of touch, sight, taste, or smell.

What are some physical dangers of cocaine use?

Occasional use can cause a stuffy or runny nose, while chronic snorting can ulcerate the nose's mucous membrane. Injecting cocaine with unsterile equipment can cause hepatitis or other infections. Because freebase preparation involves using volatile solvents, deaths and serious injuries from fire or explosion can occur. Though few people realize it, overdose deaths can occur when the drug is injected, smoked, or even snorted. Death is a result of multiple seizures followed by respiratory and cardiac arrest.

Can people become dependent on cocaine?

Yes. It is a very dangerous, dependence-producing drug. People use cocaine repeatedly because they like its effects and can center their lives around seeking it and using the drug. Smoking freebase increases this dependence risk. Sometimes people who have been using the drug over some time continue to use it to avoid the depression and fatigue they would feel if they stopped using the drug.

Are there cocaine "look-alikes"?

Yes. The growing demand for cocaine, its high price, and limited supply have led to the widespread use of substitute drugs that resemble cocaine and may have stimulant effects. Cocaine look-alikes contain ingredients that are legal and that also appear as impurities in samples of street cocaine. Substances used to "cut," or dilute, cocaine include household items of flour, baking soda, talc, and sugar. Local anesthetics, caffeine, and other chemicals also are sold as substitutes.

Caffeine

Is caffeine a drug?

Yes. Caffeine may be the world's most popular drug. It is a white, bitter, crystal-like substance found in coffee, tea, cocoa, and cola. It also is found in some other products, including aspirin, nonprescription cough and cold remedies, soft drinks, diet pills, and some street drugs.

What are the effects of caffeine?

As with all drugs, the effects vary depending on the amount taken and the individual. When a person drinks two cups of coffee, the effects begin in 15–30 minutes. The person's metabolism, body temperature, and blood pressure may increase. Other effects include increased urine production, higher blood sugar levels, hand tremors, a loss of coordination, decreased appetite, and delayed sleep. Extremely high doses may cause nausea, diarrhea, sleeplessness, trembling, headache, and nervousness. Poisonous doses of caffeine have occurred occasionally and may result in convulsions, breathing failure, and death. Although it is almost impossible for death to occur from drinking coffee or tea, deaths have been reported through misuse of tablets containing caffeine.

Can a person become dependent on caffeine?

Tolerance to caffeine or the need for a larger dose to get the same effect may develop with the use of over 500–600 milligrams of caffeine per day, that found in five to six cups of coffee. A regular caffeine user who has developed a tolerance also may have a craving for the drug's effects, particularly to "get going" in the morning. Some researchers have found a withdrawal-like syndrome among people who suddenly stop using caffeine.

The symptoms include headache, irritability, and mood changes.

Hallucinogens

What are hallucinogens?

Hallucinogens or psychedelics are drugs that affect a person's perceptions, sensations, thinking, self-awareness, and emotions. Hallucinogens include LSD, mescaline, psilocybin, and DMT. Some hallucinogens come from natural sources, such as mescaline from the peyote cactus. Others, such as LSD, are synthetic or manufactured.

PCP is sometimes considered a hallucinogen because it has similar effects. However, it does not easily fit into any one drug category, because it also can relieve pain or act as a stimulant.

What is LSD?

Lysergic acid diethylamide, or LSD, is manufactured from lysergic acid, which is found in ergot, a fungus that grows on rye and other grains. LSD is one of the most potent mood-changing chemicals. It is odorless, colorless, and tasteless. LSD is sold on the street in tablets, capsules, or occasionally in liquid form. It is usually taken by mouth but sometimes is injected. Often it is added to absorbent paper, such as blotter paper, and divided into small decorated squares, with each square representing one dose.

What is mescaline?

Mescaline comes from the peyote cactus and, although it is not as strong as LSD, its effects are similar. Mescaline is usually smoked or swallowed in the form of capsules or tablets.

What are some other psychedelic drugs?

Psilocybin comes from certain mushrooms. It is sold in tablet or capsule form so people can swallow it. The mushrooms themselves, fresh or dried, may be eaten. DMT is another psychedelic drug that acts like LSD. Its effects begin almost immediately and last for 30–60 minutes.

What are the effects of psychedelics like LSD?

The effects of psychedelics are unpredictable. It depends on the amount taken, the user's personality, mood, and expectations, and the surroundings in which the drug is used. Usually, the user feels the first effects of the drug 30–90 minutes after taking it. The physical effects include dilated pupils, higher body temperature, increased heart rate and blood pressure, sweating, loss of appetite, sleeplessness, dry mouth, and tremors.

What are "bad trips"?

Having a bad psychological reaction to LSD and similar drugs is common. The scary sensations may last a few minutes or several hours and be mildly frightening or terrifying. The user may experience panic, confusion, suspiciousness, anxiety, feelings of helplessness, and loss of control. Sometimes taking a hallucinogen such as LSD can unmask mental or emotional problems that were previously unknown to the user. Flashbacks, in which the person experiences a drug's effects without having to take the drug again, can occur.

What are the effects of heavy use?

Research has shown some changes in the mental functions of heavy LSD users, but they are not present in all cases. Heavy users sometimes develop signs of organic brain damage, such as impaired memory and attention span, mental confusion, and difficulty with abstract thinking. These signs may be strong or they may be subtle. It is not known whether these mental changes are permanent or if they disappear when LSD use is stopped.

PCP

What is PCP?

Phencyclidine, or PCP, is most often called "angel dust." It was first developed as an anesthetic. However, it was taken off the market for human use because it sometimes caused hallucinations.

PCP is available in a number of forms. It can be a pure, white, crystal-like powder, a tablet, or capsule. It can be swallowed, smoked, sniffed, or injected. PCP is sometimes sprinkled on marijuana or parsley and smoked.

Although PCP is illegal, it is easily manufactured. It is often sold as mescaline, THC, or other drugs. Sometimes it may not even be PCP, but a lethal byproduct of the drug. Users can never be sure what they are buying since it is manufactured illegally.

What are the physical effects of PCP?

Effects depend on how much is taken, the way it is used, and the individual. Effects include increased heart rate and blood pressure, flushing, sweating, dizziness, and numbness. When large doses are taken, effects include drowsiness, convulsions, and coma.

Taking large amounts of PCP can also cause death from repeated convulsions, heart and lung failure, or ruptured blood vessels in the brain.

Why is PCP dangerous?

PCP can produce violent or bizarre behavior in people who are not normally that way. This behavior can lead to death from drownings, burns, falls, and automobile accidents. Regular PCP use affects memory, perception, concentration, and judgment. Users may show signs of paranoia, fearfulness, and anxiety. During these times, some users may become aggressive, while others may withdraw and have difficulty communicating. A temporary mental disturbance or a disturbance of the user's thought processes, i.e., a PCP psychosis, may last for days or weeks. Long-term PCP users report memory and speech difficulties, as well as hearing voices or sounds which do not exist.

How do PCP users feel?

Users find it difficult to describe and predict the drug's effects. For some users, PCP in small amounts acts as a stimulant speeding up body functions. For many users, PCP changes how users see their own bodies and things around them. Speech, muscle coordination, and vision are affected; senses of touch and pain are dulled; and body movements are slowed. Time seems to "space out."

Marijuana

What is marijuana?

Marijuana, or "grass," "pot," or "weed," is the common name for a crude drug made from the plant *Cannabis sativa.* The main mind-altering or psychoactive ingredient in marijuana is THC (delta-9-tetrahydrocannabinol), but more than 400 other chemicals are also in the plant. A marijuana "joint" or cigarette is made from the dried particles of the plant. The amount of THC in the marijuana determines how strong its effects will be.

The type of plant, the weather, the soil, the time of harvest, and other factors determine the marijuana's strength. The strength of today's marijuana is as much as ten times greater than the marijuana used in the early 1970s. The more potent marijuana increases physical and mental effects and the possibility of health problems for the user.

Hashish, or "hash," is made by taking the resin from the leaves and flowers of the marijuana plant and pressing it into cakes or slabs. Hash is usually stronger than crude marijuana and may contain five to ten times as much THC. Hash oil may contain up to 50 percent THC. Pure THC is almost never available, except for research. Substances sold as THC on the street often turn out to be something else, such as PCP.

What are some of the immediate effects of smoking marijuana?

Some immediate physical effects of marijuana include a faster heartbeat and pulse rate, bloodshot eyes, and a dry mouth and throat. No scientific evidence indicates that marijuana improves hearing, eyesight, and skin sensitivity.

Studies of marijuana's mental effects show that the drug can impair or reduce short-term memory, alter sense of time, and reduce ability to do things requiring concentration, swift reactions, and coordination, such as driving a car or operating machinery.

Are there any other adverse reactions to marijuana?

A common bad reaction to marijuana is the "acute panic anxiety reaction." People describe this reaction as an extreme fear of "losing control," which causes panic. The symptoms usually disappear in a few hours.

What about psychological dependence on marijuana?

Long-term regular users of marijuana may become psychologically dependent. They may have a hard time limiting their use, they may need more of the drug to get the same effect, and they may develop problems with their jobs and personal relationships. The drug can become the most important aspect of their lives.

What are the dangers for young people?

One major concern about marijuana is its possible effects on young people as they grow up. Research shows that the earlier people start using drugs, the more likely they are to go on to experiment with other drugs. In addition, when young people start using marijuana regularly, they often lose interest and are not motivated. The effects of marijuana can interfere with learning by impairing thinking, reading comprehension, and verbal and mathematical skills. Research shows that students do not remember what they have learned when they are "high."

How does marijuana affect driving ability?

Driving experiments show that marijuana affects a wide range of skills needed for safe driving. Thinking and reflexes are slowed, making it hard for drivers to respond to sudden, unexpected events. Also, a driver's ability to "track" or stay in the proper lane through curves, to brake quickly, to maintain speed, and the proper distance between cars is affected. Research shows that these skills are impaired for at least 4–6 hours after smoking a single marijuana cigarette, long after the "high" is gone. If a person drinks alcohol along with using marijuana, the risk of an accident greatly increases. Marijuana presents a definite danger on the road.

Does marijuana affect the human reproductive system?

Some research studies suggest that the use of marijuana during pregnancy may result in premature babies and in low birth weights. Studies of men and women who use marijuana have shown that marijuana may influence levels of some hormones relating to sexuality. Women may have irregular menstrual cycles. Men and women may have a temporary loss of fertility. These findings suggest that marijuana may be especially harmful during adolescence, a period of rapid physical and sexual development.

How does marijuana affect the lungs?

Scientists believe that marijuana can be especially harmful to the lungs because users often inhale the unfiltered smoke deeply and hold it in their lungs as long as possible. Therefore, the smoke is in contact with lung tissues for long time periods, which irritates the lungs and damages the way they work. Marijuana smoke contains some of the same ingredients in tobacco smoke that can cause emphysema and cancer. Many marijuana users also smoke cigarettes. The combined effects of smoking these two substances creates an increased health risk.

Can marijuana cause cancer?

Marijuana smoke has been found to contain more cancer-causing agents than are found in tobacco smoke. Examination of human lung tissue that had been exposed to marijuana smoke over a long time period in a laboratory showed cellular changes called metaplasia that are considered precancerous. In laboratory tests, the tars from marijuana smoke have produced tumors when applied to animal skin. These studies suggest that it is likely that marijuana may cause cancer if used for a number of years.

How are people usually introduced to marijuana?

Many young people are introduced to marijuana by their peers; i.e., usually acquaintances, friends, sisters, and brothers. People often try drugs like marijuana because they feel pressured by peers to be part of the group.

What is marijuana "burnout"?

"Burnout" is a term used to describe prolonged use effect. Young people who smoke marijuana heavily over long time periods can become dull, slow-moving, and inattentive. These "burned-out" users are sometimes so unaware of their surroundings that they do not respond when friends speak to them and they do not realize that they have a problem.

How long do chemicals from marijuana stay in the body after the drug is smoked?

When marijuana is smoked, THC, its active ingredient, is absorbed by most tissues and organs in the body; however, it is primarily found in fat tissues. The body, in its attempt to rid itself of the foreign chemical, chemically transfers the THC into metabolites.

Sedative-Hypnotics

What are sedative-hypnotics?

Sedative-hypnotics are drugs that depress or slow down the body's function. Often these drugs are referred to as tranquilizers and sleeping pills, or sometimes just as sedatives. Their effects range from calming down anxious people to promoting sleep. Tranquilizers and sleeping pills can have either effect, depending on how much is taken. At high doses, or when they are abused, many of these drugs can even cause unconsciousness and death.

What are some of the sedative-hypnotics?

Barbiturates and benzodiazepines are the two major categories of sedative-hypnotics. The drugs in each of these groups are similar in chemical structure. Some well-known barbiturates are secobarbital (Seconal) and phenobarbital (Nembutal). Diazepam (Valium), chlordiazepoxide (Librium), and chlorazepate (Tranzene) are examples of benzodiazepines.

A few sedative-hypnotics do not fit into either category. They include methaqualone (Quaalude), ethchlorvynol (Placidyl), chloral hydrate (Noctec), and meprobamate (Miltown).

All of these drugs can be dangerous when they are not taken according to a physician's instructions.

Can sedative-hypnotics cause dependence?

Yes. They can cause both physical and psychological dependence. Regular use over a long time period may result in tolerance, which means people have to take larger and larger doses to get the same effects.

When regular users stop using large doses of these drugs suddenly, they may develop physical withdrawal symptoms ranging from restlessness, insomnia, and anxiety to convulsions and death. When users become psychologically dependent, they feel as if they need the drug to function. Finding and using the drug becomes the focus in life.

Is it true that combining sedative-hypnotics with alcohol is especially dangerous?

Yes. Taken together, alcohol and sedative-hypnotics can kill. The use of barbiturates and other sedative-hypnotics with other drugs that slow down the body, like alcohol, multiplies their effects and greatly increases the risk of death. Overdose deaths can occur when barbiturates and alcohol are used together either deliberately or accidentally.

Can sedative-hypnotics affect an unborn fetus?

Yes. Babies born to mothers who abuse sedative during their pregnancy may be physically dependent on the drugs and show withdrawal symptoms shortly after they are born. Their symptoms may include breathing problems, feeding difficulties, disturbed sleep, sweating, irritability, and fever. Many sedative-hypnotics pass through the placenta easily and cause birth defects and behavioral problems in babies born to women who abused these drugs during their pregnancies.

What are barbiturates?

Barbiturates are often called "barbs" and "downers." Commonly abused barbiturates include amobarbital (Amytal), pentobarbital (Nembutal), and secobarbital (Seconal). These drugs are sold in capsules and tablets or sometimes liquid form or suppositories.

What are the effects of barbiturates when they are abused?

The effects of barbiturates are in many ways similar to alcohol effects. Small amounts produce calmness and relax muscles. Somewhat larger doses can cause slurred speech, staggering gait, poor judgment, and slow, uncertain reflexes. These effects make it dangerous to drive a car or operate machinery. Large doses can cause unconsciousness and death.

How dangerous are barbiturates?

Barbiturate overdose is a factor in nearly one-third of all reported drug-related deaths. These include suicides and accidental drug poisonings.

Accidental deaths sometimes occur when a user takes one does, becomes confused, and unintentionally takes additional or larger doses. With barbiturates there is less difference between the amount that produces sleep and the amount that kills. Barbiturate withdrawal can be more serious than heroin withdrawal.

What other sedative-hypnotics are abused?

All the other sedative-hypnotics can be abused, including the benzodiazepines. Diazepam (Valium), chlordiazepoxide (Librium), and chlorazepate (Tranxene) are examples of benzodiazepines. These drugs are sold on the street as downers. As with the barbiturates, tolerance and dependence can develop if benzodiazepines are taken regularly in high doses over prolonged periods of time.

Other sedative-hypnotics which are abused include glutethimide (Doriden), ethchlorvynol (Placidyl), and methaqualone (Sopor, Quaalude).

What is methaqualone?

Methaqualone ("Sopors," "Ludes") was originally prescribed to reduce anxiety during the day and as a sleeping aid. It is one of the most commonly abused drugs and can cause physical and psychological dependence. The dangers from abusing methaqualone include injury or death from car accidents caused by faulty judgment and drowsiness, and convulsions, coma, and death from overdose.

What are sedative-hypnotic "look-alikes"?

These are pills manufactured to look like real sedative-hypnotics and mimic their effects. Sometimes look-alikes contain over-the-counter drugs, including antihistamines and decongestants that tend to cause drowsiness. The negative effects can include nausea, stomach cramps, lack of coordination, temporary memory loss, becoming out of touch with the surroundings, and anxious behavior.

Opiates

What are opiates?

Opiates, sometimes referred to as narcotics, are a group of drugs used medically to relieve pain, but also have a high potential for abuse. Some opiates come from a resin taken from the seed pod of the Asian poppy. This group of drugs includes opium, morphine, heroin, and codeine. Other opiates, like meperidine or Demorol, are synthesized or manufactured.

Opium appears as dark brown chunks or as a powder, and is usually smoked or eaten. Heroin can be a white or brownish powder, which is usually dissolved in water and then injected. Most street preparations of heroin are diluted, or "cut," with other substances like sugar or quinine. Other opiates come in a variety of forms, including capsules, tablets, syrups, solutions, and suppositories.

Which opiates are abused?

Heroin ("junk" or "smack") accounts for 90 percent of the opiate abuse in the United States. Sometimes opiates with legal medicinal uses also are abused. They include morphine, meperidine, paregoric (which contains opium), and cough syrups that contain codeine.

What are the effects of opiates?

Opiates tend to relax the user. When opiates are injected, the user feels an immediate "rush." Other initial and unpleasant effects include restlessness, nausea, and vomiting. The user may go "on the nod," going back and forth from feeling alert to drowsy. With very large doses the user cannot be awakened, pupils become smaller, and the skin becomes cold, and bluish in color. Breathing slows down and death may occur.

Does using opiates cause dependence or addiction?

Yes. Dependence is likely, especially if a person uses a lot of the drug or even uses it occasionally over a long time period. When a person becomes dependent, finding and using the drug often becomes the main focus in life. As more and more of the drug is used over time, larger amounts are needed to get the same effects. This is called tolerance.

What are the physical dangers?

The physical dangers depend on the specific opiate used, its source, the dose, and the way it is used. Most of the dangers are caused by using too much of a drug, the use of unsterile needles, contamination of the drug itself, or combining the drug with other substances. Over time, opiate users may develop infections of the heart lining and valves, skin abscesses, and congested lungs. Infections from unsterile solutions, syringes, and needles can cause illnesses including liver disease, tetanus, and serum hepatitis.

What is opiate withdrawal?

When an opiate-dependent person stops taking the drug, withdrawal usually begins within four to six hours after the last dose. Withdrawal symptoms include uneasiness, diarrhea, abdominal cramps, chills, sweating, nausea, and runny nose and eyes. The intensity of these symptoms depends on how much was taken, how often, and for how long. Withdrawal symptoms for most opiates are stronger approximately 24 to 72 hours after they begin and subside within 7 to 10 days. Sometimes symptoms like sleeplessness and drug craving can last for months.

What are the dangers for opiate-dependent pregnant women?

Researchers estimate that nearly half of the women who are dependent on opiates suffer anemia, heart disease, diabetes, pneumonia, or hepatitis during pregnancy and childbirth. They have more spontaneous abortions, breech deliveries, caesarean sections, premature births, and stillbirths. Infants born to these women often have withdrawal symptoms that may last several weeks or months. Many of these babies die.

What treatment is available for opiate addiction?

The four basic approaches to drug abuse treatment are:

a. Detoxification or supervised withdrawal from drug dependence, either with or without medication, in a hospital or as an outpatient;

b. Therapeutic communities where patients live in a highly structured drug-free environment and are encouraged to help themselves;

c. Outpatient drug-free programs emphasizing various counseling forms as the main treatment; and

d. Methadone maintenance using methadone, a substitute for heroin, on a daily basis to help people lead productive lives while still in treatment.

How does methadone treatment work?

Methadone, a synthetic or manufactured drug, does not produce the same "high" as illegal drugs like heroin, but does prevent withdrawal and the craving to use other opiates. It often is a successful treatment for opiate dependence because it breaks the cycle of dependence on illegal drugs like heroin. When patients are receiving methadone in treatment they are not inclined to seek and buy illegal drugs on the street, activities which are often associated with crime. Patients in methadone maintenance programs also receive counseling, vocational training, and education to help them reach the ultimate goal of a drug-free normal life.

What are narcotic antagonists?

Narcotic antagonists are drugs that block the "high" and other effects of opiates without creating physical dependence or producing a "high" of their own. They are extremely useful in treating opiate overdoses and may prove useful in the treatment of opiate dependence.

Inhalants

What are inhalants?

Inhalants are breathable chemicals that produce psychoactive or mind-altering vapors. People do not usually think of inhalants as drugs because most of them were never meant to be used that way. They include solvents, aerosols, some anesthetics, and other chemicals. Examples are model airplane glue, nail polish remover, lighter and cleaning fluids, and gasoline. Aerosols that are used as inhalants include paints, cookware coating agents, hair sprays, and other spray products. Anesthetics include halothane and nitrous oxide ("laughing gas"). Amyl nitrite and butyl nitrite are also commonly abused inhalants.

What is butyl nitrite?

Butyl nitrite is packaged in small bottles and sold under a variety of names like "locker room" and "rush." It produces a "high" that lasts from a few seconds to several minutes. The immediate effects include decreased blood pressure followed by an increased heart rate, flushed face and neck, dizziness, and headache.

Who abuses inhalants?

Young people, especially between the ages of 7 and 17, are more likely to abuse inhalants, because they are readily available and inexpensive.

How do inhalants work?

Although different in composition, nearly all of the abused inhalants produce effects similar to anesthetics, in that they act to slow down the body's functions. At low doses, users may feel slightly stimulated; at higher amounts, they may feel less inhibited and less in control; at high doses, a user can lose consciousness.

What are the immediate negative effects of inhalants?

Initial effects include nausea, sneezing, coughing, nosebleeds, feeling and looking tired, bad breath, lack of coordination, and appetite loss. Solvents and aerosols also decrease the heart and breathing rate and affect judgment.

How strong these effects are depends on the user's experience and personality, how much is taken, the specific substance inhaled, and the user's surroundings. The "high" from inhalants tends to be short and can last several hours if used repeatedly.

What are the most serious short-term effects of inhalants?

Deep breathing of the vapors or using a lot over a short time period may result in losing touch with one's surroundings, a loss of self-control, violent behavior, unconsciousness, or death. Using inhalants can cause nausea and vomiting. If a person is unconscious when vomiting occurs, death can result from aspiration.

Sniffing highly concentrated amounts of solvents or aerosol sprays can produce heart failure and instant death. Sniffing can cause death the first time or any time. High concentrations of inhalants cause death from suffocation by displacing the oxygen in the lungs. Inhalants also can cause death by depressing the central nervous system so much that breathing stops.

Death from inhalants is usually caused by a very high concentration of inhalant fumes. Deliberately inhaling from a paper bag greatly increases the chance of suffocation. Even when using aerosol or volatile vaporous products for their legitimate purposes; i.e., painting, cleaning, and so forth, it is wise to do so in a well-ventilated room or outdoors.

What are the long-term dangers?

Long-term use can cause weight loss, fatigue, electrolyte or salt imbalance, and muscle fatigue. Repeated sniffing of concentrated vapors over a number of years can cause permanent damage to the nervous system, meaning greatly reduced physical and mental capabilities. Long-term sniffing of certain inhalants can damage the liver, kidneys, blood, and bone marrow. Tolerance, which means the sniffer needs more and more each time to get the same effect, is likely to develop from most inhalants when they are used regularly.

What happens when inhalants are used along with other drugs?

As in all drug use, taking more than one drug at a time multiplies the risks. Using inhalants while taking other drugs that slow down the body's functions, like tranquilizers, sleeping pills, or alcohol, increases the risk of death from overdose. Loss of consciousness, coma, or death can result.

§ 10.30 —Legal Guidelines

The following policy may be used to inform employees of their legal obligations regarding alcohol and drug abuse:

FORM 10.30(1)
LEGAL GUIDELINES REGARDING ALCOHOL
AND DRUG ABUSE

1. Employers do not have unlimited rights to discipline suspected alcohol or drug abusers. Privacy laws, along with federal and state FEP statutes, protect employees.

2. Alcohol and drug dependence has been recognized as a handicap under federal, state, and local FEP statutes. Employers have a responsibility to reasonably accommodate employees having this handicap. The duty of reasonable accommodation requires employers to give employees who are willing to

acknowledge an alcohol or drug dependence problem an opportunity to re-habilitate themselves through employee assistance programs or community resources, unless the granting of an opportunity would impose an undue hardship on the employer.

3. Certain statutes place restrictions on the employer's right to collect, use, maintain, and disclose employee information.

4. Privacy rights extend to employee expectations that information about their alcohol and drug use, including their participation in rehabilitation programs, will be maintained in confidence and not unnecessarily disclosed to any third person.

5. Employers have a right to investigate suspected violations of their legitimate rules and employees have a corresponding duty to cooperate in these investigations. In balancing employee privacy rights against the employer's legitimate needs to protect its property and maintain proper discipline, employers are permitted to conduct job-related investigations and searches of employees, their work stations, lockers, and lunch boxes where adequate prior notice of these workplace requirements has been given.

6. Regularly conducted exit-and-entry searches and other types of periodic or random searches are permissible when done for a legitimate job-related business purpose and according to a clearly established and well-defined policy that has been communicated to all employees.

§ 10.31 —Urine Drug Screen Collection Procedure

The following procedure should be used in collecting applicant/employee urine samples for alcohol or drug analysis:

FORM 10.31(1)
URINE DRUG SCREEN COLLECTION PROCEDURE

1. Before collecting:

   a. *Identification.* Positively identify the patient by checking a photograph identification.

      (i) This can be a driver's license, a photograph identification, a United States passport, or other official document that has a photograph.

      (ii) When the photograph identification has been presented and checked for authenticity, initial the appropriate space on the request form.

      (iii) If the patient cannot be positively identified, DO NOT COLLECT THE SAMPLE. Contact the Human Resources Department

b. *Medical-Legal Specimen Control Record.* Record correctly the patient's name, age, sex, and requesting physician, along with a chain of custody form.

c. *Company release form.* Have the employee read and sign this form, listing all over-the-counter and prescription medications by brand names. If the brand name is unknown, describe the medication and note: "Brand name unknown."

d. *Specimen labeling.* Label the specimen container cap with a Selex marker before handing it to the patient.

2. Collection:

a. Ask the applicant/employee to leave behind pocket books, bags, coats, extra sweaters, and so forth.

b. Accompany the applicant/employee to the restroom and do not leave the area during collection. Unless specifically instructed, do not go into the washroom with the applicant/employee.

3. After collection:

a. Take the specimen from the patient, be sure the cap is secure, then seal with the evidence security tape.

   (i)   When sealing, place the tape across the lid and down one side;

   (ii) Then put date, time and your initials on the tape with a Selex pen.

b. Record date collected on the request form.

c. Record date of collection, time, test requested, type of specimen, specimen collected by, and number of specimen(s) in the appropriate spaces on the Medical-Legal Specimen Control Record.

   (i)   Have the applicant/employee sign the first "Received From" line;

   (ii) Sign the "Received By" and "Sealed By" lines, and record the date and time.

d. Place the specimen in one zip-lock bag and the request form with the release form in a second zip-lock bag, and staple these together. Attach the Medical-Legal Specimen Control Record to this with a paper clip so that it may be removed when it needs to be signed.

§ 10.32   —Applicant/Employee Consent Form

The following forms should be considered in obtaining an applicant's/employee's consent to employer alcohol and drug testing:

FORM 10.32(1)
APPLICANT/EMPLOYEE CONSENT

I, __(Name)__ , understand and agree that the physical examination I am about to receive includes a:

( ) Blood test to detect the presence of alcohol/drugs in my system

( ) Urine test to detect the presence of alcohol/drugs in my system

I understand that if I decline to sign this consent and decline to take the test, the physical examination will not be completed. The Human Resources Department will be notified and my application for employment will be rejected and/or my employment may be terminated. I understand that the test results and other medical information will be released only to authorized Company personnel for appropriate consideration.

I have taken the following drugs, substances, or alcoholic beverages within the last 96 hours:

( ) Sleeping pills— _____

( ) Diet pills— _____

( ) Pain relief pills— _____

( ) Cold tablets— _____

( ) Anti-malarial drugs— _____

( ) Prescription drugs— _____

( ) Any other medication or substance— _____

( ) Alcoholic beverages— _____

I hereby   ( ) consent

            ( ) refuse to consent

to the physical examination including the test(s) to detect the presence of alcohol/drugs in my system.

Date: _____   Signed: _____

Date: _____   Witness: _____

FORM 10.32(2)
APPLICANT/EMPLOYEE CONSENT

I hereby voluntarily consent to allow the Company to collect urine and blood specimens from me for testing for alcohol, drugs, and controlled substances. Further, I give my consent for the release of the test results to the appropriate members of the Company's management. I understand that any positive result may preclude my employment.

_____   _____
Date   Signature

FORM 10.32(3)
APPLICANT/EMPLOYEE CONSENT

Step 1 (To be completed by the applicant/employee)

Employer name: _____

Employee I.D. #: _____
                 (Social Security number or employee number)

Step 2 (To be completed by employer or collector)

Reason for Test (Check One)

_____ Pre-employment   _____ Post Accident   _____ Random
_____ Periodic Medical   _____ Other (Specify Reason Below)

          _____
          _____

Step 3 (Collector must note that the temperature of the specimen has been read)

Record specimen temperature if not within the range of 32.5–37.7C/90.5–99.8F
_____.

Specimen temperature within range _____.

Step 4 (To be initiated by the person collecting the specimen and completed as necessary thereafter)

Received by: _____   Date: _____

            _____   _____

            _____   _____

            _____   _____

            _____   _____

            _____   _____

            _____   _____

            _____   _____

Step 5 (To be completed by the applicant/employee providing the specimen)

Name: _____

If you wish to have prescription or over-the-counter medications that you have taken or been administered within the past 30 days considered as your test results are reviewed, you may list them here or provide that information separately to your employer's Human Resources Department:

_____

_____

_____

_____

_____

_____

_____

I certify that the urine specimen identified on this form is my own; that it is fresh and has not been adulterated in any manner; and that the identification information provided on this form and on the collection bottle is correct. I consent to the submission of this specimen to the certified laboratory designated by my employer, to the analysis of the specimen for controlled substances as provided by federal requirements, and to the release of test results from that analysis to the Human Resources Department of my employer.

_____   _____
(Date)   (Signature)

Step 6 (To be completed by the person collecting the specimen)

Collector's name: _____

Collection date: _____

Collection site location: _____

Telephone: _____

Remarks concerning collection: _____

_____

_____

_____

I certify that the specimen identified on this form is the specimen presented to me by the applicant/employee providing the certification under Step 5 above, that I have certified that it bears the same identification number as that set forth above, and that it has been collected, labeled, and sealed as required.

_____
(Collector's Signature)

Step 7 (To be completed by the laboratory)

Accession No.: _____

I certify that the specimen identified by this accession number is the same specimen that bears the identification number set forth above, that the specimen has been examined upon receipt, handled, and analyzed in accordance with applicable federal requirements, and that the results attached are for that specimen.

_____   _____
(Printed Name)   (Signature)

_____
(Date)

§ 10.33   —Chain of Custody Form

The following form should be used to safeguard any urine, blood, hair, or other samples taken from an applicant/employee for alcohol or drug testing:

FORM 10.33(1)
CHAIN OF CUSTODY FORM

Name: _____

Date/Time: _____

Employer: _____

PART I

I certify that I personally obtained the specimens enclosed in this envelope. These specimens were either in my personal possession or personally secured by me until passed on to the person whose signature appears on the line below mine:

Signature: _____

Date/Time: _____

PART II

I certify that I received this sealed envelope from the person whose name appears above mine and that it was either in my personal possession or personally secured by me until given to the person whose signature follows mine:

Signature: _____ Time: _____ Date: _____

Signature: _____ Time: _____ Date: _____

Signature: _____ Time: _____ Date: _____

Signature: _____ Time: _____ Date: _____

PART III

I certify that I received this sealed envelope from the person whose name appears above mine and that the seal showed no signs of having been broken. I opened the envelope and personally performed or supervised the performance of testing for alcohol or drug content.

Signature: _____

Date/Time: _____

§ 10.34   —Employee Reinstatement Agreement for Alcohol or Drug Abuse

The following agreement should be considered where an employer desires to reinstate an employee who has been involved with alcohol or drug abuse:

FORM 10.34(1)
EMPLOYEE REINSTATEMENT AGREEMENT FOR
ALCOHOL OR DRUG ABUSE

It is hereby agreed as follows:

1.   (Employee's name)   recognizes that the Company will conditionally reinstate   (Him or her)   after he or she successfully completes a rehabilitation program and provides verification thereof along with release of any medical records involving his or her treatment at   (Name and location of rehabilitation program) ; provided the following conditions are met: _____   (List conditions)

_____

_____

2. If within the next   (Describe time) ,   (Employee's name)   is unable to perform job duties due to alcohol or drug abuse, fails to continue an alcohol or drug

rehabilitation program, or fails to meet the conditions set forth in "1" above, discipline up to and including termination may result.

3. I agree to cooperate in any additional alcohol or drug testing that the Company in its discretion deems appropriate during the __(Time period)__ immediately following my reinstatement, or discipline up to and including termination may result.

_____
(Date)

                                       _____
                                       (Employee)

                                       _____
                                       (Union Representative)

                                       _____
                                       (Employer)

§ 10.35   Acquired Immune Deficiency Syndrome (AIDS)

Acquired immune deficiency syndrome (AIDS) is a disease that affects the body's immune system, rendering it vulnerable to infections and viruses.[51] This disease has quickly become a significant employee privacy issue. It affects privacy interests present in association and lifestyle.

Constitutional employee privacy considerations that arise out of alcohol and drug testing are also applicable to AIDS testing.[52] Mandatory AIDS blood testing infringes on the employee's privacy interest in disclosing non-job-related personal matters. Significant psychological trauma might accompany an erroneous diagnosis, and disclosure to others could have serious results. The employee's most intimate personal relationships could be affected by a positive test. A positive reading might be construed falsely to perceive an employee as a homosexual or a drug user.[53] Through this, federal constitutional protections arising out of the first amendment's associational rights,[54] the fourth amendment's guarantee

---

[51] _See_ Decker, Privacy Law § 7.10.

[52] _See_ Decker, Privacy Law §§ 3.4–3.6, 3.9–3.11, 7.10.

[53] _See, e.g.,_ Little v. Bryce, 733 S.W.2d 937 (Tex. Ct. App. 1987) (employee's hasty termination for AIDS which employee did not have constituted defamation); _see also_ Decker, Privacy Law ch. 4.

[54] U.S. Const. amend. I; _see also_ Decker, Privacy Law § 3.4.

against unreasonable searches,[55] and the fifth amendment's protection against self-incrimination[56] are impacted. State constitutional relief may also exist.[57]

Federal[58] and state[59] FEP statutes may recognize AIDS as a protected handicap. While these statutes contain differences, their underlying intent is similar: i.e., employees capable of working, without endangering themselves or others, should be allowed to do so regardless of a physical or medical condition which is, or is perceived to be, disabling. Likewise, tort and contract litigation theories may safeguard employee privacy interests relating to AIDS.[60]

Knowledge of the diagnosis of AIDS is confidential medical information. Employers who use health questionnaires or prehire physical examinations should ensure that employment decisions are not predicated on anything other than the individual's present ability to perform the job. To exclude applicants presently able to perform the job because they have AIDS, have tested positive for HIV antibody, or are somehow at high risk of HIV infection is illegal, unless the decision can be justified as specifically job-related.

Should testing be used, it must apply to all employees to avoid liability for violation of FEP statutes. Perhaps the best advice in considering an AIDS testing program is not to do it unless absolutely necessary. Implementing an AIDS education and awareness program may be a better option.

Employers involved in AIDS testing are caught in a bind between duty to the employee in terms of privacy and confidentiality along with an overall duty to society, including what, if any, duty exists to inform spouses and other exposed individuals of potential risks. Most states recognize the tort of invasion of privacy that includes the unwarranted disclosure of private facts. It has been held to apply to personnel-related information and to the unwarranted disclosure within the employment context of medical information. An employer who learns that an employee has AIDS or AIDS-related complex (ARC) must be very sensitive not to unduly disclose or disseminate that information.[61] Employers face substantial liability in disclosing that an employee has AIDS to others, even when the basis for the disclosure is that other employees perceive a safety risk to themselves. However, disclosure to a supervisor who must deal with an AIDS-affected employee

---

[55] U.S. Const. amend. IV; *see also* Decker, Privacy Law § 3.5.

[56] U.S. Const. amend. V; *see also* Decker, Privacy Law § 3.6.

[57] *See, e.g.,* Calif. Const. art. I, § 1; *see also* Decker, Privacy Law §§ 3.9–3.11.

[58] *See, e.g.,* 42 U.S.C. §§ 2000e-1 to 2002-17 (1988) (Civil Rights Act of 1964); *see also* Decker, Privacy Law §§ 2.7–2.12.

[59] *See, e.g.,* Pa. Stat. Ann. tit. 43, §§ 951–963 (Purdon 1991) (Pennsylvania Human Relations Act); *see also* Decker, Privacy Law § 2.25.

[60] *See, e.g.,* Little v. Bryce, 733 S.W.2d 937 (Tex. Ct. App. 1987) (employee's hasty termination for AIDS which employee did not have constituted defamation); *see also* Decker, Privacy Law ch. 4.

[61] *See, e.g.,* Little v. Bryce, 733 S.W.2d 937 (Tex. Ct. App. 1987) (falsely accusing employee of having AIDS and terminating employee).

on a daily basis to accommodate health-related problems may be justified, provided the information is kept strictly confidential. Discussion of the disclosure issue in advance with the AIDS-affected employee may avoid trauma and reaction from an employee who suddenly discovers that word of his or her condition has spread throughout the workplace.

Out of this the following has emerged regarding AIDS:

1. AIDS is a new disease requiring behavioral changes and extensive educational efforts
2. AIDS is a worldwide epidemic
3. AIDS results from the human immunodeficiency virus (HIV)
4. AIDS transmission occurs through sexual contact, exchange of infected blood or blood products, or from mother-to-child *in utero* or at birth, but not through the air or by social or casual contact, saliva, tears, insects, or by eating food prepared by an AIDS-infected person
5. No vaccine or drug has proven effective in preventing or curing AIDS
6. AIDS has been concentrated among homosexual/bisexual males and intravenous drug users
7. AIDS has severe psychological, social, and economic consequences
8. The ELISA, or initial blood test for AIDS antibodies, can produce false positive results, requiring confirmation by a more specific test known as the Western Blot; in some instances, an AIDS-infected person may have a negative test result
9. Mandatory testing should be for blood, tissue, organ, and semen donors only and all other testing should be voluntary
10. Public disclosure of AIDS-related information constitutes a most serious personal privacy invasion
11. Discrimination should not be permitted against AIDS-infected persons
12. Except for the area of confidentiality, protective measures should be taken through regulations promulgated by the appropriate governmental agencies, rather than through statutory enactments.[62]

§ 10.36   —AIDS Policy Development Considerations

A possible approach in development of an AIDS policy might be as follows.

1. Form a task force of key personnel to develop, advise, and monitor policy development and educational efforts
2. Identify community medical/legal experts on AIDS for guidance/education

---

[62] *See* Pennsylvania Bar Association Task Force on Acquired Immune Deficiency Syndrome, AIDS: Law and Society 2-4 (May 11, 1988) [hereinafter PBA, AIDS].

3. Analyze employee demographics, workplace risks, and geographical location

4. Educate and gain senior management support

5. Collaborate with other employers, community public health departments and other medical experts and nonprofit organizations for technical guidance on policy and educational efforts

6. Develop and implement an employer educational approach on AIDS policy/philosophy and on disease

7. Evaluate education's impact on employees, customers, and the community.[63]

§ 10.37 —AIDS Policy Contents

In developing an AIDS policy, it should have the following characteristics.

1. It should be in compliance with all federal, state, and local laws as well as applicable collective bargaining agreements

2. Commitment to protect the health of all employees and provide a safe work environment

3. Commitment to treat AIDS like any other life-threatening disease

4. If medically fit and able to perform job duties, affected employees will be permitted to work

5. Provision of reasonable accommodation and job modification for AIDS victims when appropriate

6. Outlining the employer's position on AIDS testing, if any

7. Procedures for supervisors to fairly handle AIDS cases and encouragement to treat persons with AIDS with compassion and understanding

8. Commitment to maintain confidentiality of medical information

9. Commitment to keep policy medically updated and provide employee education on AIDS and policy

10. No special transfer request acceptable, unless medically indicated and substantiated

11. Overview of benefit plans for AIDS including provisions for case management, hospice/home health care and experimental treatment when applicable

12. Provision for referrals through the employer's Employee Assistance Program (EAP) or other departments to community resources/experts for consultation and treatment.[64]

---

[63] *See* Allstate Forum on Public Issues, AIDS: Corporate America Responds 6 (1988) [hereinafter Allstate Forum, AIDS].

[64] *Id.* at 6-7.

§ 10.38   —AIDS Human Resources Issues

The monitoring and management of workplace problems is generally the responsibility of the employer's human resources department. Regarding AIDS, key issues that should be addressed by this department include:

1.   Developing proper employment interviewing techniques to avoid discrimination
2.   Handling of medical information confidentiality
3.   Dealing with employee rumors/slanderous jokes, fears, and so forth
4.   Dealing with employee/supervisor concerns about death and dying
5.   Dealing with employee concerted action/work stoppage
6.   Dealing with transfer requests
7.   Managing fair discipline procedures for individuals with AIDS
8.   Providing guidance on AIDS testing and workplace safety concerns
9.   Providing recommendations to legislative representatives regarding AIDS issues/concerns.[65]

§ 10.39   —AIDS Training Program Issues

In developing a successful AIDS training program, the following issues will be relevant to the review.

AIDS Training Issues

1.   Medical issues
     a.   What is AIDS?
     b.   What is the AIDS-related complex?
     c.   What are the symptoms of AIDS?
     d.   Who is at high risk for developing AIDS?
     e.   How is AIDS transmitted from person to person?
     f.   What evidence is there that AIDS cannot be transmitted from person to person?
     g.   Is it dangerous to eat food that has been prepared by a person with the AIDS virus?
     h.   Is it possible to contract AIDS from donating blood?

---

[65] *Id.* at 7.

2. Spread of AIDS

    a. Will everyone who has been infected by the AIDS virus develop AIDS?

    b. Will everyone who develops AIDS die?

    c. How widespread is AIDS?

    d. How many people have died from AIDS?

    e. Where did AIDS originate?

    f. What is the Company's policy on AIDS' testing?

    g. How accurate is the screening test in determining whether or not an individual has been infected by the AIDS virus?

    h. Who, if anybody, should be tested for the AIDS virus?

    i. Is there an effective treatment for AIDS?

3. AIDS workplace risks

    a. Can an employee contract AIDS from another employee who has AIDS by using the same telephone or computer terminal?

    b. Can AIDS be spread at the workplace by drinking out of the same cup or using the same drinking fountain or using the same restroom facilities?

    c. Can AIDS be spread by kissing, a handshake, or a cough?

    d. If an employee is exposed to someone else's blood during a workplace accident should the employee be tested for AIDS?

    e. Can CPR be administered at the workplace?

    f. Who can employees contact in confidence to obtain information about AIDS?

4. Management and supervisor issues

    a. What should be done if someone in the workplace has AIDS?

    b. How should rumors regarding employees who allegedly have AIDS be handled?

    c. Can the Company insist or require that an employee take an AIDS screening test?

    d. What if there is pressure from other employees to terminate an employee who has AIDS or who is suspected of having AIDS?

    e. How is the issue of confidentiality and AIDS handled?

    f. What legal obligations exist in dealing with employees that have AIDS?

    g. What Company obligations exist to employees that must work with AIDS infected employees?

    h. What medical benefits are employees with AIDS entitled to?

    i. What response should be made to employees that refuse to work with an employee that is infected with AIDS?

    j. Is there confidential counseling available for employees with AIDS?[66]

---

[66] *Id.* at 10.

§ 10.40 　—AIDS Symptoms

AIDS cannot be diagnosed from symptoms alone. However, there are several symptoms that in combination for an extended time period may suggest a possibility of AIDS and are reason for consulting a physician. Among these are:

1. Unexplained, persistent fatigue
2. Unexplained fever, shaking chills, or drenching night sweats lasting longer than several weeks
3. Unexplained weight loss greater than ten pounds
4. Swollen glands; i.e., enlarged lymph nodes usually in the neck, armpits, or groin that are otherwise unexplained and last more than two months
5. Pink to purple flat or raised blotches or bumps occurring on or under the skin, inside the mouth, nose, eyelids, or rectum
6. Persistent white spots or unusual blemishes in the mouth
7. Persistent diarrhea
8. Persistent dry cough that has lasted too long to be caused by a common respiratory infection, especially if accompanied by shortness of breath.[67]

§ 10.41 　—AIDS Transmission

The methods by which the AIDS virus can be spread include:

1. Sexual intercourse with a person that is infected with the AIDS virus
2. Sharing drug needles with an infected person
3. Injection of a contaminated blood product through a blood transfusion or another method
4. A female infected with the AIDS virus who becomes pregnant or breast-feeds can pass the AIDS virus to the baby.[68]

§ 10.42 　—How AIDS Kills

The AIDS virus does not in itself damage organs; rather, by overwhelming the immune system, the virus permits a variety of infections, cancers, and other diseases the opportunity to spread throughout the body, eventually resulting in death. These opportunistic infections are the hallmark of the presence of AIDS and are listed in their frequency of occurrence:

---

[67] *Id.* at 20.

[68] *Id.*

1. **Pneumocystis carinii** is a lung infection caused by parasites. Under normal conditions this pneumonia occurs only in cancer or transplant patients taking drugs that suppress immunity

2. **Kaposi's sarcoma** is an especially virulent skin cancer. This normally rare cancer usually arises in the skin and produces characteristic purplish blotches or bumps before it spreads internally

3. **Candidiasis** is a fungal infection that commonly affects the mouth and esophagus of an AIDS victim

4. **Cryptococcosis** is a fungal infection that can cause meningitis (infection of the brain and spinal cord)

5. **Cytomegalovirus infections** can cause meningitis and colitis. They are usually detectable in AIDS victims' blood

6. **Atypical bacterial infections** can appear anywhere in the body. A frequently seen infection is one of the bone marrow and liver

7. **Herpes simplex** is a virus that can cause ulcerating anal and oral herpes sores. Any viral infection may attack AIDS patients, but herpes infections of the skin, mouth, or genitalia are common

8. **Cryptosporidiosis** is an organism that causes prolonged diarrhea

9. **Toxoplasmosis** is caused by protozoa that infect the brain and lungs.[69]

§ 10.43   —AIDS Procedures to Avoid Workplace Conflicts

The following procedures should be considered in avoiding workplace AIDS conflicts:[70]

1. Consider initial planning for dealing with AIDS

2. Do not feel compelled to announce an AIDS policy, absent genuine workplace concerns, because:

   a. Prematurely adopting an AIDS policy may lead employees to believe that the employer knows something that may create undue concern about an AIDS workplace risk

   b. Not knowing the circumstances of how the AIDS issue will arise, it is difficult to make a premature commitment to any particular course of action

   c. Unless some special risk of transmission exists, i.e., needle-stick injuries, the best policy is a case-by-case approach

---

[69] *See* W.R. Spence, *AIDS: What You Don't Know Can Kill You* 10-11 (1988).

[70] *See* Littler, Mendelson, Fastiff & Tichy, 1987 Employer at 0, 0–23 to 0–24.

3. Designate a small group of senior managers to deal with the AIDS issue, which should include people knowledgeable about the medical, human resource, and legal issues

4. Should the AIDS issue require action, institute employee AIDS education as the first step

5. Institute a reasonable AIDS policy that treats AIDS victims like those with any other degenerative, noninfectious disease, to minimize legal liability

6. Recognize that, given current technology, screening applicants or employees for AIDS may not be effective, because the most common blood serum AIDS antibody tests provide almost no useful information. In some states this testing is unlawful

7. Determine whether any federal, state, or local regulation would prohibit certain employee classes with infectious diseases from working in or near certain areas

8. Require an employee who is diagnosed with AIDS, or any other infectious or communicable disease:

    a. To provide a physician's certificate outlining whether the employee should work under any particular restrictions

    b. To provide a statement regarding whether the employee's being subject to exposure to common viruses carried by other workers might pose an imminent and substantial risk to his or her health

9. If the physician requires that work or exposure to others be restricted, make efforts to reasonably accommodate the AIDS-afflicted employee by:

    a. A job redefinition

    b. Transfer

    c. Consultation with the physician attending a pregnant employee might also be indicated

10. If the physician imposes no restrictions, and assuming that there are no other health or safety restrictions imposed by law with respect to the employee, permit the employee with AIDS to continue working in his or her job

11. Advise employees, based on the consensus of medical opinion, that there is no risk of contracting AIDS in a normal workplace environment

12. If an employee refuses to work with an AIDS victim, follow alternative courses, such as:

    a. The employee may be treated in accordance with counseling or progressive discipline procedures

    b. Reference may be made to employer policies regarding insubordination or harassment of employees who are members of a protected class

    c. The employer may wish to avail itself of the conciliation and remedial powers of a FEP agency to resolve the situation

13. Treat AIDS victims who, by virtue of their illness, no longer are able to work, the same as any employee who has a long-term, debilitating disease

14. Respect privacy rights and statutory rights to medical information confidentiality of AIDS-afflicted employees, in that disclosing that an employee has AIDS beyond those individuals with a need to know, can lead to:[71]

    a. Costly litigation

    b. Increased anxiety among co-employees

§ 10.44   —Sample Policies

The following examples should be considered in drafting AIDS policies:

POLICY 10.44(1)
AIDS POLICY

Section 1. Purpose.   The Company will deal with acquired immune deficiency syndrome (AIDS) in a humanitarian and nondiscriminatory fashion, while assuring the safety and health of all employees. All employees will be trained to understand AIDS.

Section 2. Nondiscrimination.   The Company is committed to a responsible policy of nondiscrimination regarding AIDS. An employee afflicted with AIDS wili be treated the same as any other employee suffering from a long-term disability.

Section 3. Confidentiality.   The Company will respect the confidentiality of all employees afflicted with AIDS.

Section 4. Employment.   The Company will employ applicants or employees who have AIDS or are suspected of having AIDS, so long as these persons remain qualified to perform their jobs. Some exceptions or deviations to this policy may be necessary for certain positions, but the Company will employ AIDS patients, while at the same time preserving the safety and morale of all its employees. According to the best medical evidence available to date, casual workplace contact with employees who have AIDS, or who have been exposed to the AIDS virus, will not result in the transmission of AIDS to others.

Section 5. Policy Updates.   The Company will remain current regarding the latest medical knowledge pertaining to this disease. Should it subsequently appear that this policy's implementation may present a danger to employees, the Company will make appropriate policy revisions.

---

[71] *See, e.g.,* Little v. Bryce, 733 S.W.2d 937 (Tex. Ct. App. 1987) (employee's hasty termination for AIDS which employee did not have constituted defamation); *see also* Decker, Privacy Law ch. 4.

POLICY 10.44(2)
INFECTIOUS DISEASE CONTROL POLICY

Section 1. Policy.   It is the Company's policy to establish procedures regarding infectious disease control and to present guidelines for the education, counseling, and management related to employees and program participants.

Section 2. Education and Training.   Education and training shall be provided to employees regarding infectious diseases and made available to all program participants. All employees will receive education and training pertaining to infectious diseases to implement and follow universal precautions in all Company programs and offices. Program participant training in areas involving personal hygiene, sexuality, and first aid will incorporate information on infectious diseases.

Initial training and yearly update trainings are mandatory for all employees. Employees will attend a basic education session on infectious diseases which will occur as needed but at least annually. This will be an orientation requirement. Additional training or counseling will be conducted to meet specific needs of employees and to disseminate updated information as necessary. All employees will receive training regarding death and dying. A health services specialist will be designated and trained to function as the trainer, and to be responsible for the continual dissemination of accurate and updated information on infectious diseases.

Section 3. Precautionary Guidelines.   The Company will implement precautionary guidelines in its programs and offices to prevent the transmission of infectious diseases in those work settings where program participant care, treatment, and services are provided.

Section 4. Discrimination and Confidentiality.   No employee or program participant shall be discriminated against in the provision of services or hiring because of the presence of an infectious disease. Likewise, his or her confidentiality shall not be breached as it pertains to or relates to an infectious disease, except as may be required under applicable legislative, regulatory, or court pronouncements.

Program participants and employees have the right to privacy and individual human dignity. Disciplinary action, up to and including termination, will be taken against any employee for disclosing confidential information relating to infectious diseases. Information regarding an individual's diagnosis and health will be communicated only when a clear "need to know" is established based on the program's needs.

Section 5. Infected Employees.   Infected employees will not routinely be relieved of assignments or restricted from work unless they have an illness for which a restriction would be warranted. Infected employees will be evaluated on an individual basis, considering the health status of the employee and the nature of the employee's responsibilities. As a normal practice, infected employees will maintain their assigned duties. However, based on individual circumstances associated with a given case, reassignment may be requested or recommended. These decisions are to be made in consultation with the affected employee and the employee's physician.

Section 6. Medical Services.   As long as community medical services are sufficient, available, and appropriate to meet the needs of the program participants with infectious diseases, the Company will continue to provide services.

Section 7. Infectious Disease Procedures.   The following procedures regarding infectious diseases will be followed:

a. Information on infectious diseases shall be made available to all employees and program participants

b. Education and training regarding infectious diseases shall be provided to employees and program participants in the following areas:

  1. What is an infectious disease?

  2. How infectious diseases affect the immune system

  3. Who is at risk?

  4. Methods of transmission

  5. How to prevent getting and transmitting infectious diseases

  6. General symptoms

  7. How to obtain additional information

  8. Issues of death and dying

  9. Confidentiality

c. All employees will receive a copy of this policy as part of their initial training

d. Universal precautions shall be instituted in every program and office of the Company in that persons can significantly reduce their risk of exposure to infectious diseases if hygiene recommendations are implemented. These include emphasis on a clean environment and careful personal hygiene. Due to the possibility of transmitting an infectious disease prenatally, pregnant and child-bearing age employees should be especially familiar with universal precautions. The following hygiene procedures shall be implemented in all Company programs and offices:

  1. Scrupulous personal hygiene must be followed by employees and program participants at all times, including frequent, careful handwashing using plenty of soap and water

  2. Personal toiletry items shall not be shared, including razors, towels, washcloths, toothbrushes, nail clippers, soap, and so forth

  3. Discourage all program participants from placing others' fingers in their months or their fingers into others' mouths

  4. Cover open breaks or lesions in the skin

5. Thoroughly clean with soap and water or discard items soiled by blood or body fluids

6. Disinfect blood contaminated objects if this can be done without damaging the contaminated surface

7. If the contaminated object cannot be cleaned without damaging the surface, the object should be discarded

8. The following protective wear is available and shall be utilized as necessary to minimize the risks of infection:

    (a) Gloves should be worn when handling urine specimens, blood soiled items, body fluids, excretions, and secretions, as well as surfaces, materials, and objects exposed to them

    (b) Gowns/aprons should be worn when clothing may be soiled with body fluids, blood, secretions, or excretions

    (c) Masks/protective eyewear/face shields should be worn when the face area may be splashed with body fluids, blood, secretions, or excretions, as in implementing some dental hygiene programs

9. Extraordinary care must be taken to avoid accidental wounds from sharp instruments and needles

10. To minimize the need for emergency direct mouth-to-mouth resuscitation, mouth pieces should be strategically located and available for use

11. Routine cleaning of dishes, eating utensils, and toilet facilities is adequate to eliminate the risk of disease transmission

12. Each program participant's clothing, towels, and bed linens should be laundered separately

13. Laundry items contaminated with blood or body fluids should be handled with gloves and stored and washed separately

14. Employees and program participants are encouraged to avoid high-risk behaviors which include the exchange of blood or body fluids.

§ 10.45 —Initial AIDS Position Statement

For the employer contemplating an AIDS policy, the following position statement may provide an initial reference point from which a more comprehensive AIDS policy can be later developed.

FORM 10.45(1)
AIDS POSITION STATEMENT

AIDS means Acquired Immune Deficiency Syndrome.

The Company understands that the generally known facts about this disease are as follows:

1. AIDS is not spread by casual contact

2. AIDS is spread by intimate sexual or anal intercourse or sharing of needles in the case of active drug abusers

3. The AIDS virus is most prevalent in blood and semen and much less prevalent in saliva

4. A person can be identified to be carrying the AIDS virus

5. AIDS cannot be contracted from unclean dishes, glasses, or utensils

6. AIDS cannot be contracted from a toilet seat

7. The only known way of contracting AIDS from another person is by intimate contact with the other person's body fluids who is infected with the AIDS virus.

Because AIDS cannot be transmitted by casual contact, and the Company's medical advisors have indicated that the presence of an AIDS-affected employee will not affect other employees, customers, or the Company's product, and AIDS-affected employee will be permitted to work as long as he or she is medically able.

The Company's medical advisors will alert it if there is a change in this information as it relates to the workplace.

The Company will consider AIDS in the same manner as it deals with any other nonoccupational illness.

Should any employee have questions or desire additional information regarding AIDS, they should contact the Human Resources Department.

The Company requests the cooperation of all employees in dealing with AIDS.

§ 10.46 Safety

Employers have certain legal requirements to maintain a safe working environment. Certain aspects of a safe work environment are regulated by federal[72] and state[73] statutes. Employers may not, however, use safety at all times to restrict employees from certain job opportunities even though workplace hazards may be present. For example, employers may not use a desire to protect the health or life

---

[72] 29 U.S.C. §§ 651–678 (1988) (Occupational Safety and Health Act of 1970); *see also* Decker, Privacy Law §§ 2.13, 7.6.

[73] Minn. Stat. §§ 181.950–.957 (West Supp. 1993) (employee drug testing); *see also* Decker, Privacy Law § 2.40A.

of unborn fetuses as a reason for barring fertile female employees from exposure to poisons or other job risks.[74]

An employee who reasonably believes there is a real danger or injury at the workplace and has no time to resort to administrative action to remedy the danger is statutorily protected and may refuse to do the dangerous work.[75] However, the employee risks termination should it subsequently be determined that the employee acted "unreasonably or in bad faith."[76]

§ 10.47 —Drafting

To drafting safety policies, the following should be considered:

1. Applicable federal[77] and state[78] statutes
2. Commitment to safety
3. Safety committee
4. Supervisors' responsibilities
5. Employee's responsibilities
6. Accident investigation and reporting procedures
7. Procedures for correcting or eliminating hazards
8. Safety training and education programs
9. Safety inspections
10. Protective equipment
11. Disciplinary action for safety rule violations.

§ 10.48 —Sample Policies

The following example should be considered in drafting safety policies:

---

[74] International Union, United Automobile, Aerospace & Agricultural Implement Workers of America, UAW v. Johnson Controls, Inc., 499 U.S. 187 (1991).

[75] Whirlpool Corp. v. Marshall, 455 U.S. 1 (1980).

[76] *Id.* at 21.; *see* Donovan v. Hahner, Foreman & Harness, Inc., 736 F.2d 1421 (10th Cir. 1984) (reasonable belief in imminent risk and insufficient time to seek OSHA action); Donovan v. Peter Zimmer America, Inc., 557 F. Supp. 642 (D.S.C. 1982) (employer liable for retaliatory OSHA termination).

[77] 29 U.S.C. §§ 651–678 (1988) (Occupational Safety and Health Act of 1970); *see also* Decker, Privacy Law §§ 2.13, 7.6.

[78] Minn. Stat. §§ 181.950–.957 (West Supp. 1993) (employee drug testing); *see also* Decker, Privacy Law § 2.40A.

CLAUSE 10.48(1)
SAFETY

If there is one thing that concerns the Company as much as quality of products, it is safety. The Company strives to ensure that all machinery is equipped with the best available safety devices. A Safety Committee helps to review conditions. The Safety Committee suggests that by following a few simple rules, employees can help to "play it safe" for themselves and their fellow employees:

1. Never reach into or clean a moving machine.

2. Use every piece of safety equipment required. Ask for any you do not have. Check to make sure guards are in place.

3. Walk, do not run.

4. Push, do not pull skids, carts, or handtrucks.

5. Do not wear jewelry, including earrings, or loose clothing that can get caught in machinery.

6. When driving equipment or moving material, especially around corners, observe a sensible speed limit, just as you do when driving a car and for the same reason: to avoid an accident.

7. When working around a piece of moving machinery, make sure that hair is properly protected.

8. When you lift something heavy, do it by lifting with your legs—they are stronger than your back. Also, if the item seems to be heavy, do not hesitate to ask for help; you have only one back.

9. If, despite every precaution, you do get hurt, obtain first aid immediately, even if the injury is nothing more than a tiny cut or scratch. A first aid representative is present on each shift.

CHAPTER 11

INFORMATION COLLECTION/DISTRIBUTION POLICIES

§ 11.1 Introduction to Workplace Information Collection and Distribution

Information collection continues at the workplace after an employee is hired.[1] Generally, employer workplace information collection involves updating, maintaining, and using information that has already been obtained, or procuring new information necessitated by workplace requirements.

At times, surreptitious methods may be used to collect workplace information that affects employee interests. Occasionally, employees or outside third parties may seek to solicit or distribute information at the workplace.[2] Depending upon the employer, various restrictions may be placed on these information solicitation and distribution activities. This chapter reviews workplace information collection and distribution procedures that arise out of searches,[3] monitoring,[4] surveillance,[5] and polygraphs,[6] along with literature solicitation and distribution.[7]

§ 11.2 Searches

Employer security problems have broadened from concerns over property and information theft to safeguarding the workplace from alcohol and drug abuse.[8] Searches or potential searches can create significant problems for employers by uncovering information that the employee has not voluntarily revealed and that may not be job-related. Employees who are stopped and searched may assert several claims against employers involving invasion of privacy,[9] defamation,[10] false

---

[1] Decker, Privacy Law §§ 7.12–7.20.

[2] *See* Decker, Privacy Law § 7.21.

[3] See §§ **11.2–11.10.**

[4] See §§ **11.11–11.16.**

[5] See §§ **11.17–11.20.**

[6] See §§ **11.21–11.23.**

[7] See §§ **11.24–11.26.**

[8] See ch. 10. *See also* Decker, Privacy Law §§ 7.9, 7.13.

[9] *See, e.g.,* Love v. Southern Bell Tel., 263 So. 2d 460 (La. Ct. App. 1972) (using a locksmith to force entry into employee's trailer home who failed to report to work); *see also* Decker, Privacy Law § 4.3.

[10] *See, e.g.,* Holloway v. K-Mart Corp., 113 Wis. 2d 143, 334 N.W.2d 570 (1983) (accusing employee of stealing candy); *see also* Decker, Privacy Law § 4.4.

imprisonment,[11] false arrest,[12] malicious prosecution,[13] intentional infliction of emotional distress,[14] and constitutional right infringement.[15]

False imprisonment arises when employers detain employees, even briefly, to search their bags, cases, purses, or person through a total restraint on the freedom to move that is against the employee's will.[16] Generally, the employee must be aware of the restraint. Merely stopping an employee is not a total restraint. The restraint, however, need not be lengthy or physically confining; namely, the employee need not be locked in a room.[17] Advising an employee not to leave may be a sufficient restraint.[18] Awareness is not necessary where substantial damages result from the confinement.[19] Where an employee remains free to leave despite being asked questions or being accompanied to or from work during an investigation, no false imprisonment occurs.[20]

Liability can be incurred through a false arrest for theft brought about by some employer affirmative direction, persuasion, request, or voluntary participation.[21] Generally, the employer does not incur potential false arrest liability until it causes an arrest.

The employer does not commit a false arrest by providing truthful information to law enforcement authorities and allowing them to make a determination.[22]

---

[11] See, e.g., Tocker v. Great Atl. & Pac. Tea Co., 190 A.2d 822 (D.C. Ct. App. 1963) (denying employee right to leave); see also Decker, Privacy Law § 4.5.

[12] See, e.g., Ramsden v. Western Union, 71 Cal. App. 3d 873, 138 Cal. Rptr. 426 (1977) (employer liability for false arrest may result where information disclosed to police is known to be incorrect).

[13] See, e.g., Wainauskis v. Howard Johnson Co., 339 Pa. Super. 266, 488 A.2d 1117 (1985) (malicious prosecution sustained against employer for alleged employee theft).

[14] See, e.g., Hall v. Macy Dep't Stores, 242 Or. 131, 637 P.2d 126 (1981) (security investigator's false statements during female clerk's interview regarding cash register shortages and threatening prosecution); see also Decker, Privacy Law § 4.6.

[15] See, e.g., O'Connor v. Ortega, 480 U.S. 709 (1987) (unauthorized search of public employee's desk); see also Decker, Privacy Law §§ 3.5, 3.9–3.11.

[16] See, e.g., Tocker v. Great Atl. & Pac. Tea Co., 190 A.2d 822 (D.C. Ct. App. 1963) (denying employee right to leave); see also Decker, Privacy Law § 4.5.

[17] See Schanafelt v. Seaboard Fin. Co., 108 Cal. App. 2d 420, 239 P.2d 42 (1951) (words not to depart sufficient for false imprisonment); Black v. Kroger Co., 527 S.W.2d 794 (Tex. Ct. App. 1975) (words of threat sufficient for false imprisonment).

[18] See Tocker v. Great Atl. & Pac. Tea Co., 190 A.2d 822 (D.C. Ct. App. 1963) (denying employee right to leave).

[19] Id.

[20] See Faniel v. Chesapeake & Potomac Tel. Co., 404 A.2d 147 (D.C. Ct. App. 1979) (detention time length insufficient to support false imprisonment); Delan v. CBS, Inc., 111 Misc. 2d 928, 445 N.Y.S.2d 898 (1981) (intent to confine not present to support false imprisonment).

[21] See Turner v. Mellon, 41 Cal. 2d 45, 257 P.2d 15 (1953) (employer must actively bring about employee's arrest to incur liability; merely giving information to police in good faith will not impose liability).

[22] Id.

Where information given to police is known to be false, and the employer insists on arrest, the employer may be liable for false arrest.[23] Probable cause for an arrest and detention is a valid defense to a false arrest or imprisonment claim.[24] *Probable cause* means having more evidence for than against the arrest; that is, a good faith, reasonable belief in the validity of the arrest and detention.[25] A signed, uncoerced statement admitting employee responsibility may protect an employer from liability.[26]

To establish malicious prosecution, an employee generally must show that a false accusation by the employer has been made, with knowledge of the statement's falsity or a reckless disregard for its truth that causes arrest, confinement, or other damages to the person accused.[27] This may arise in search situations when, for example, theft is alleged and the employer does more than discipline, causing a meritless criminal prosecution to be instituted.[28]

Defamation consists of libel or slander.[29] It requires a showing of accusation of a crime, or some other act that would bring disrepute to the employee, that is made falsely or with reckless disregard for its truth and is communicated to others orally or in writing.[30] Defamation liability may arise out of workplace search situations when the employer accuses an employee of theft and communicates this accusation to others not entitled to this information.[31] Should the employer's search lead to an accusation causing employee emotional upset with serious physical manifestations, a claim for intentional infliction of emotional distress may be made.[32]

---

[23] *See* Ramsden v. Western Union, 71 Cal. App. 3d 873, 138 Cal. Rptr. 426 (1977) (employer liability for false arrest may result where information disclosed to police is known to be incorrect).

[24] *See* Veras v. Truth Verification Corp., 87 A.D.2d 381, 451 N.Y.S.2d 761, *aff'd,* 57 N.Y.2d 947, 443 N.E.2d 489, 457 N.Y.S.2d 241 (1982) (good faith belief constitutes probable cause); Gabrou v. May Dep't Stores Co., 462 A.2d 1102 (D.C. Ct. App. 1983) (good faith, reasonable belief constitute probable cause).

[25] *See* Veras v. Truth Verification Corp., 87 A.D.2d 381, 451 N.Y.S.2d 761, *aff'd,* 57 N.Y.2d 947, 443 N.E.2d 489, 457 N.Y.S.2d 241 (1982) (good faith belief constitutes probable cause); Gabrou v. May Dep't Stores Co., 462 A.2d 1102 (D.C. Ct. App. 1983) (good faith, reasonable belief constitute probable cause).

[26] *See* Jacques v. Firestone Tire & Rubber Co., 183 Cal. App. 2d 632, 6 Cal. Rptr. 878 (1960).

[27] *See, e.g.,* Wainauskis v. Howard Johnson Co., 339 Pa. Super. 266, 488 A.2d 1117 (1985) (malicious prosecution sustained for alleged theft).

[28] *Id.*

[29] *See* Decker, Privacy Law § 4.4.

[30] *See* Decker, Privacy Law § 4.4.

[31] *See, e.g.,* Holloway v. K-Mart Corp., 113 Wis. 2d 143, 334 N.W.2d 570 (1983) (accusing employee of stealing candy); *see also* Decker, Privacy Law § 4.4; Perritt §§ 5.25, 6.11.

[32] *See, e.g.,* Hall v. Macy Dep't Stores, 242 Or. 131, 637 P.2d 126 (1981) (security investigator's false statements during female clerk's interview regarding cash shortages and threatening prosecution); *see also* Decker, Privacy Law § 4.6.

§ 11.3 —Problem Areas

The following problem areas may create the necessity to conduct workplace searches:[33]

1. Theft or misuse of property
2. Timecard discrepancies and mischarges
3. Procurement and purchasing irregularities
4. Conflict of interest
5. Fraudulent activities
6. Vendor gratuities
7. Travel pay fraud
8. Computer service unauthorized use
9. Information theft

§ 11.4 —Drafting

In drafting search policies, the following should be considered:

1. Applications should provide that employees agree to employer searches
2. The search procedure and policy should be communicated and explained to all employees
3. Employees should be informed that the purpose of the search is to deter theft and that the employee being searched is not under suspicion
4. Employees should not be selected for searches randomly, arbitrarily, capriciously, or discriminatorily
5. Publish a written statement outlining the workplace search policy and the circumstances under which a search will be conducted
6. Make clear to affected employees that assigned lockers, offices, desks, and so forth are subject to search; beware of permitting employees to provide their own locks, since it may create a privacy expectation
7. To avoid losing the right to conduct random searches, do so regularly
8. Make clear that all employees and designated areas are subject to search and that a search, in and of itself, does not imply or constitute an accusation of wrongdoing
9. Instruct management and security personnel not to touch an employee during a search absent compelling circumstances, for example, self-protection, or to prevent an employee from leaving the premises during a search

---

[33] *See* Murphy, *Investigating, Handling, and Protecting Against Employee Theft and Dishonesty,* in J. Kauff, Employment Problems in the Workplace 22 (1986) [hereinafter Murphy, Investigating].

10. Consider limiting the number, type, or size of bags or containers that an employee may bring into the facility, to obviate the need to search personal effects

11. The search measures adopted should be reasonably related to the search's objectives and the least intrusive effective method of carrying out the search should be used

12. Conduct searches professionally and limit dissemination of information obtained in searches to those who need to know

13. In unionized settings, seek explicit contractual authority to promulgate a comprehensive workplace search policy.[34]

§ 11.5   —Human Resource Considerations

In deciding whether to conduct workplace searches, the human resource staff should be involved with:[35]

1. Workplace theft problem management
2. Factfinding and investigation
3. Interaction with management
4. Interaction with legal counsel
5. Interaction with supervisors

§ 11.6   —Human Resource Staff Theft Investigations

In investigating alleged workplace thefts, the human resource staff should consider the following:[36]

1. Upon learning of theft allegations:
   a. Notify and consult with legal counsel
   b. Structure the theft investigation to maximize the likelihood that the attorney-client and the attorney work product privileges apply
   c. Consider whether legal counsel should participate in the investigation
2. Evaluate the need for special expertise in theft situations involving:
   a. Time mischarging, purchasing fraud, travel pay fraud, and so forth, where an accountant may need to be involved
   b. Theft of computer services, where a computer expert may be necessary

---

[34] See G. Henshaw & K. Youmans, *Employee Privacy in the Workplace and an Employer's Right to Conduct Workplace Searches and Surveillance,* Soc'y for Hum. Resource Mgmt. Legal Rep. 3 (Spring 1990).

[35] See Murphy, *Investigating* at 22–23.

[36] *Id.* at 23–24.

3. Establish the alleged theft's essentials regarding:

    a. By whom

    b. Against whom

    c. Persons involved

    d. Nature of the improper act

    e. When it occurred

4. Determine whether to inform the suspected employee of the investigation and suspend him or her pending the outcome, or leave the employee at the workplace to obtain additional evidence of any wrongdoing

5. Investigation procedures:

    a. Interview all potential witnesses, including employees and outside third parties

    b. Consider obtaining signed statements from persons who may later take a position adverse to the employer

    c. Examine all pertinent records and documents

    d. Avoid group interviews

    e. Be impartial and take care not to convey a prosecutorial image

    f. Take thorough, detailed, and exact notes by:

        (i) Using the witness's language

        (ii) Including proper names, job titles, salary grades, and reporting relationships for persons interviewed and mentioned

        (iii) Reviewing notes with the person interviewed to fill gaps or make necessary corrections

    g. Exhaust all pertinent lines of inquiry

6. Employee witness considerations[37]

    a. The Victim and Witness Protection Act of 1982 prohibits the following:

> (a) Whoever knowingly uses intimidation or physical force, or threatens another person, or attempts to do so, or engages in misleading conduct toward another person, with intent to—
>
>   (1) influence the testimony of any person in an official proceeding;
>
>   (2) cause or induce any person to—
>
>   (A) withhold testimony, or withhold a record, document, or other object, from an official proceeding;
>
>   (B) alter, destroy, mutilate, or conceal an object with intent to impair the object's integrity or availability for use in an official proceeding;

---

[37] *See* Altman, *Surveillance of the Workforce,* in J. Kauff, Employment Problems in the Workplace 105–08 (1986) [hereinafter Altman, Surveillance].

(C)   evade legal process summoning that person to appear as a witness, or to produce a record, document, or other object, in an official proceeding; or

(D)   be absent from an official proceeding to which such person has been summoned by legal process; or

(3)   hinder, delay, or prevent the communication to a law enforcement officer or judge of the United States of information relating to the commission or possible commission of a Federal offense or a violation of conditions of probation, parole, or release pending judicial proceedings . . .[38]

(i)   Penalty for violation is a fine of not more than $250,000 or imprisonment not more than ten years, or both[39]

(ii)   It forbids intentional harassment which hinders testimony or reports of possible federal offenses, for which punishment is a fine of not more than $25,000 or imprisonment for not more than one year, or both[40]

(iii) An official proceeding need not be pending or about to be instituted at the time of the offense[41]

(iv)   Misleading conduct includes:

(A)   Knowingly making a false statement

(B)   Intentionally omitting information from a statement causing a portion of the statement to be misleading

(C)   Intentionally concealing a material fact and creating a false impression by the statement

(D)   With intent to mislead, knowingly submitting or inviting reliance on a writing or recording that is false, forged, altered, or otherwise lacking in authenticity

(E)   With intent to mislead, knowingly submitting or inviting reliance on a sample, specimen, map, photograph, boundary mark, or other object that is misleading in a material respect

(F)   Knowingly using a trick, scheme, or device with intent to mislead[42]

(v)   Victims of an offense are allowed restitution in an amount equal to the property damage sustained or costs of physical injury, including lost income[43]

---

[38] 18 U.S.C. § 1512(a) (1988).

[39] *Id.*

[40] 18 U.S.C. § 1512(b) (1988).

[41] *Id.* § 1512(d)(1).

[42] *Id.* § 1515(3).

[43] *Id.* §§ 3579–3580.

b. The Act presents an additional employer constraint in dealing with withnesses, victims, and informants in that to avoid a prosecution for tampering with a witness, victim, or informant the following precautions should be taken:

(i) When appropriate, providing or advising of the need for separate legal counsel for an employee witness, victim, or informant at the earliest possible time

(ii) Two persons should be present when the employee is interviewed for witness purposes

(iii) Possibly obtaining a statement from the witness that:

(A) He or she agrees to the proposed interview, which he or she believes is reasonable and proper

(B) He or she will not disclose confidential employer trade secrets or other confidential material without allowing the employer to consider the need to protect it

(C) He or she has not removed employer files or information

(D) He or she has not made any files available to third parties

(E) He or she intends to cooperate fully with legal counsel

(iv) If the employee knows of the wrongdoing and refuses to cooperate with the employer to develop the facts, legitimate reason may exist to discipline or terminate the employee

§ 11.7   —Conducting Theft Investigations with Legal Counsel

In conducting workplace theft investigations with legal counsel, the following should be considered:[44]

1. Have a corporate officer or the human resource department specifically authorize the internal theft investigation by ensuring:

a. Authority to hire outside experts, if needed

b. That the investigation is being done in anticipation of litigation or because the civil or criminal proceedings possibility

2. Consider whether employees should be notified in writing that the investigation's purpose is to provide legal advice to the employer and that all employees should cooperate with legal counsel

3. Employees should be told of:

a. The importance of maintaining their communication confidentiality with legal counsel

---

[44] *See* Altman, *Surveillance* at 102–05.

     b.   Their right to personal counsel

     c.   The potential of a conflict of interest between the employee and employer

  4.   When interviewing employees, legal counsel should establish that:

     a.   He or she is representing the employer and not the employee

     b.   Any information learned will be passed on to the employer for use as it deems fit

  5.   At the outset of the interview, legal counsel should indicate that the employee has a right to his or her own personal counsel, especially where the person being interviewed may be a potential defendant or wrongdoer

  6.   Any reports prepared by legal counsel should recite that the facts are for the sole purpose of reaching opinions

  7.   Legal counsel's notes and memoranda should reflect mental impressions, conclusions, and legal theories or strategies, rather than a verbatim transcript of witness statements or findings

  8.   All notes and memoranda should be marked confidential, attorney work product, and attorney-client privileged material, along with being segregated from other employer documents

  9.   Maintain confidentiality of investigative results and materials[45] and restrict access to employer officials on a need-to-know basis

10.   Confidentiality could be waived by:

     a.   Voluntary disclosure to a government agency or third parties

     b.   Hiring nonlegal experts

     c.   Nonlegal experts should be:

        (i)   Retained by legal counsel

        (ii)   Directed solely by legal counsel

     d.   Any expert hired by legal counsel should be given a retention letter setting forth:

        (i)   Communication and information confidentiality

        (ii)   The expert's obligation

        (iii)   The need for the expert's advice to the legal counsel's rendering of advice

     e.   Advice sought to further crime or fraud is not subject to the attorney-client and/or work product privileges

     f.   Use of the attorney work product or other privileged data to refresh a witness's recollection, or as a basis for an expert to render an opinion, may waive the privilege

---

[45] *See* United States v. Upjohn, 449 U.S. 383 (1981) (attorney-client privilege exists to protect not only the giving of professional advice to those who can act on it, but also the giving of information to the attorney to enable sound and informed advice).

g.   Consider whether employee-signed statements should be obtained, in that Federal Rule of Civil Procedure 26(b)(3) requires that signed statements or transcripts be subject to discovery[46]

§ 11.8   —Adopting Search Policies

Specific steps should be undertaken to convey fairness and obtain or impute employee consent to employer workplace search procedures. Before actual policy implementation, the employer should:

1.   Announce that search procedures will be instituted
2.   Describe the policy
3.   If a union is involved, advise the union and offer to bargain; a search policy can be considered a term or condition of employment, in that disciplinary action can be imposed for its violation[47]

§ 11.9   —Sample Policies

POLICY 11.9(1)[48]
SEARCH POLICY

The Company reserves the right to question any person entering and leaving its property and to inspect any person, locker, vehicle, package, purse, handbag, briefcase, lunchbox, or other possessions carried to, on, and from its property. This includes all of the Company's employees.

POLICY 11.9(2)[49]
SEARCH POLICY

Effective ___(Date)___, the Company will implement procedures to improve security and to protect employees from unfair theft accusations. All persons entering and leaving the Company's premises, including employees, will be subject to questions

---

[46] Fed. R. Civ. P. 26(b)(3).

[47] *See, e.g.*, Amoco Chems., 211 N.L.R.B. 618 (1974), *enforced in pertinent part*, 529 F.2d 427 (5th Cir. 1976) (alteration of work and disciplinary rules is a mandatory collective bargaining subject).

[48] See K. McCulloch, Termination of Employment ¶ 41.107 (1993). This policy may also be included as a notice on the application or as a separate form to obtain the employee's written consent to the workplace search.

[49] *See* K. McCulloch, Termination of Employment ¶ 41.107 (1993). This policy may also be included as a notice on the application or as a separate form to obtain the employee's written consent to the workplace search.

and a search, at the Company's discretion. Lockers, vehicles, packages, purses, handbags, briefcases, lunchboxes, and other possessions will be subject to search.

§ 11.10 —Sample Forms

The following example should be considered in drafting a search consent form:

FORM 11.10(1)
SEARCH CONSENT FORM

As a condition of my employment, I understand that the Company has implemented procedures to improve security. To assist the Company in these security measures, I agree to cooperate and permit the Company to question me and to permit the Company to search workplace areas that I may be involved with, including my person and personal effects either at the workplace or when I am entering or leaving the Company's premises. I understand that searches include but not are not limited to lockers, vehicles, packages, purses, handbags, briefcases, lunch boxes, and other possessions.

_____
Employee's Name

_____
Witness's Name

_____
Date

§ 11.11   Monitoring

Monitoring involves using mechanical or electronic devices to obtain workplace employee information.[50] Computer, telephone, and video technology are the most common types of workplace monitoring.

Workplace monitoring's extent is unknown because it is done without employee awareness. Any time computers or telephones are used in the workplace, there is monitoring potential. Federal[51] and state[52] statutes regulate certain workplace monitoring. Employers may subject themselves to employee claims when

---

[50] _See_ Decker, Privacy Law § 7.14.

[51] _See, e.g.,_ 18 U.S.C. §§ 2510–2520 (1988) (Omnibus Crime Control and Safe Streets Act); _see also_ Decker, Privacy Law § 2.14.

[52] _See, e.g.,_ Cal. Penal Code §§ 630–637.3 (West 1970 & Supp. 1993) (California's statute restricting monitoring); _see also_ Decker, Privacy Law § 2.27.

monitoring devices are knowingly used to obtain non-job-related information. Invasion of privacy,[53] defamation,[54] or public policy[55] violations could be alleged.

§ 11.12   —Drafting

In drafting monitoring policies, the employer should consider:

1. Applicable federal[56] or state[57] statutes regulating the proposed monitoring
2. Ensure that the monitoring is job-related[58]
3. Clearly notify employees that job performance may be subject to monitoring
4. As a condition of employment, obtain the employee's written consent to monitoring job performance
5. Disclose to employees what mechanical or electronic devices may be used for monitoring job performance
6. Disclose to employees when, where, and how these mechanical or electronic devices may be used for monitoring job performance
7. Consider the fairness of work performance standards:
    a. Do they fairly reflect the particular work force's abilities?
    b. Will they create stress for many employees?
    c. Do they account for recurring system difficulties and other workplace problems?
    d. Do they include quality as well as quantity goals?
    e. Do they represent a fair day's pay for a fair day's work?
    f. Do employees share in productivity gains achieved through new technology?
8. Consider the fairness of the measurement process:
    a. Do employees know and understand how the measurements are being done?

---

[53] *See, e.g.,* Vernars v. Young, 539 F.2d 766 (3d Cir. 1976) (reading employee's mail); *see also* Decker, Privacy Law § 4.3.

[54] *See, e.g.,* Sias v. General Motors Corp., 372 Mich. 542, 127 N.W.2d 357 (1964) (informing employees not entitled to information regarding reasons for termination); *see also* Decker, Privacy Law § 4.4.

[55] *See, e.g.,* Novosel v. Nationwide Ins. Co., 721 F.2d 894 (3d Cir. 1983) (possibility of asserting a fourth amendment constitutional infringement as a public policy breach); *see also* Decker, Privacy Law § 4.10.

[56] *See, e.g.,* 18 U.S.C. §§ 2510–2520 (Omnibus Crime Control and Safe Streets Act); *see also* Decker, Privacy Law § 2.14.

[57] *See, e.g.,* Cal. Penal Code §§ 630–637.3 (West 1970 & Supp. 1993) (California's statute restricting monitoring); *see also* Decker, Privacy Law § 2.27.

[58] Office of Technology Assessment, The Electronic Supervisor: New Technology, New Tensions 87 (1987).

    b. Can the measurement system be defeated, impairing morale of those willing to follow the rules?

    c. Do employees receive statistics on performance directly and in time to affect their work rate?

    d. Is the relationship between quality and quantity communicated by supervisors when discussing problems with performance?

    e. Do supervisors communicate clearly that they are taking system/workplace problems into account?

    f. Are group rather than individual rates used when this approach is more equitable?

    g. Is there a formal complaint process for contesting how work date is used?

9. Consider the fairness in applying the measurements to performance evaluations:

    a. Are there meaningful recognition programs for superior performance?

    b. Is work quantity only one of a well-rounded and objective set of evaluation criteria?

    c. Does the employee see and participate in the performance evaluation?

    d. Is there an appeal process from the supervisor's performance evaluation?

    e. Is there a performance-planning system to identify and help performance problems?

§ 11.13 —Monitoring Uses

Workplace monitoring may be used to measure and document employee transactions involving:

1. Planning and scheduling personnel and equipment

2. Evaluating employee performance and personnel decisions concerning promotion, retraining, termination, and so forth

3. Increasing productivity by providing feedback on speed, work pacing, and so forth

4. Providing security for employer property, including intellectual property and personnel records

5. Investigating incidents of misconduct, crime, or human error

6. Increasing employer control, discouraging union organizing activities, identifying dissidents, and so forth

Some workplace activities that are currently subject to monitoring include:[59]

---

[59] *Id.* at 29, 38.

Job	What Is Measured	How Obtained
Word processors	Speed, errors, time working	Keystrokes counted by computer
Data-entry clerks	Speed, errors, time working	Keystrokes counted by computer
Telephone operators	Average time per call	Each call timed by call distribution system
Customer service workers	Time per customer number and type of transaction	Each call timed by call distribution system; transactions counted by computer
Telemarketing/other sales	Time per customer; sales volume	Each call or transaction timed; sales tabulated by computer
Insurance claims clerks	Number of cases per unit of time	Time spent on each form tabulated by computer
Mail clerks	Letters or packages per unit of time	Collected by letter- or package-sorting machines
Bank proof clerks	Checks processed per unit of time	Collected by proof machine

Workplace privacy issues that relate to monitoring include:

	Privacy and Access Related	Labor Relations or "Fairness"	Health/ Quality of Life
Is monitoring constant or intermittent?	X		X
Can employees see their own records?	X		
Can the employee challenge, explain, or correct records?	X	X	
Does the employee or the machine pace the work?		X	X
Do employees understand performance criteria and use of information?		X	X
Are quotas set on an individual or group basis?		X	
Are quotas fair, allowing work at a reasonable pace?		X	X
Is pay standard or based on performance?		X	
What happens to employees falling short of quota?		X	X

§ 11.14   —Factors Affecting Monitoring

The following factors may affect monitoring regarding:[60]

1.   Its increase due to:
     a.   Economics and increasing technology sophistication
     b.   Labor market trends
     c.   Macroeconomic trends
     d.   Employer liability
     e.   Vendor equipment promotions
     f.   Technological imperatives
2.   Its limiting due to:
     a.   Employee backlash, morale, and turnover
     b.   Diminishing returns
     c.   Job deskilling or upgrading
     d.   Information overload
     e.   Management priorities

§ 11.15   —Sample Policies

The following example should be considered in drafting monitoring policies:

POLICY 11.15(1)
WORK PERFORMANCE MONITORING

The Company may periodically monitor or review employee work performance through the use of mechanical or electronic devices. Among the mechanical or electronic devices that the Company may use are telephone monitoring, transponders, beepers, pen registers, touch-tone decoders, diodes, and so forth. These may be used to limit personal calls at the workplace, review driver routes, investigate workplace problems, and so forth.

§ 11.6   —Work Performance Monitoring:
Employee Authorization Form

Where workplace monitoring is used, the following employee authorization should be considered:

---

[60] *Id.* at 97.

FORM 11.16(1)
WORK PERFORMANCE MONITORING:
EMPLOYEE AUTHORIZATION

As an employment condition, I understand that the Company may periodically monitor or review my work performance by using mechanical or electronic devices. Among the devices that the Company may use are telephone monitoring, transponders, beepers, pen registers, touch-tone decoders, and diodes. To this work performance monitoring, I expressly consent.

_____
Employee Signature

_____
Date

§ 11.17 Surveillance

Unlike monitoring, surveillance generally involves physical observation of employees without their knowledge.[61] Surveillance may be done by observation, extraction, or reproduction. Observational surveillance involves viewing the employee at the workplace, although the employee may not be aware of this. Surveillance by extraction generally involves employee information collection through questionable testing; i.e., by a polygraph examination,[62] honesty testing,[63] and so forth. Reproduction surveillance generally involves employee information collection through photographic, recording, or other similar devices.

Employers use surveillance for various purposes. These purposes may include:

1. Determining union organization activity extent[64]

2. General workplace surveillance for job performance purposes[65]

3. Manipulating employees[66]

---

[61] _See_ Decker, Privacy Law §§ 7.15–7.21.

[62] _See, e.g.,_ Southwire Co., 282 N.L.R.B. No. 117 (1987) (use of a polygraph to discover union sympathies); 29 U.S.C. §§ 2001–2009 (1988) (Employee Polygraph Protection Act of 1988); _see also_ Decker, Privacy Law §§ 2.20B, 2.35, 6.19.

[63] _See, e.g.,_ Minnesota v. Century Camera, Inc., 309 N.W.2d 735 (Minn. 1981) (use of a test to measure employee honesty); _see also_ Decker, Privacy Law § 6.20.

[64] _See, e.g.,_ Custom Coating & Laminating Corp., 249 N.L.R.B. 765 (1980); _see also_ Decker, Privacy Law §§ 2.6, 2.24, 3.4, 7.16, 8.6.

[65] _See, e.g.,_ Nader v. General Motors Corp., 25 N.Y.2d 560, 255 N.E.2d 765, 307 N.Y.S.2d 647 (1970) (privacy invaded only if information sought is of a confidential nature and conduct was unreasonably intrusive); _see also_ Decker, Privacy Law § 7.17.

[66] _See, e.g.,_ Rossmore House, 269 N.L.R.B. 1176 (1984), _enforced as_ Hotel & Restaurant Employees, Local 11 v. NLRB, 760 F.2d 1006 (9th Cir. 1985) (employee interrogation); _see also_ Decker, Privacy Law §§ 2.6, 2.24, 7.18.

4.   Photographing employees[67]

5.   Electronic surveillance.[68]

§ 11.18 —Drafting

In drafting surveillance policies, the following should be considered:

1.   Applicable federal[69] and state[70] statutes regulating the proposed surveillance

2.   Ensure that the surveillance is job-related

3.   Clearly notify employees that their job performance may be subject to surveillance

4.   As a condition of employment, obtain the employee's written consent to job performance surveillance

5.   Disclose to employees what mechanical, electronic, or other devices may be used for job performance surveillance

6.   Disclose to employees when, where, and how these mechanical, electronic, or other devices may be used for job performance surveillance

§ 11.19 —Sample Policies

The following example should be considered in drafting surveillance policies:

POLICY 11.19(1)
WORK PERFORMANCE SURVEILLANCE POLICY

The Company may periodically monitor, survey, or review employee work performance through the use of mechanical, electronic, or other methods, which may include photographing, observation, telephone monitoring, transponders, beepers, pen registers, touch-tone decoder, diodes, and so forth.

---

[67] *See, e.g.,* School Bd. of Escambia County v. Public Employee Relations Comm'n, 350 So. 2d 819 (Fla. Dist. Ct. App. 1977) (photographing picketing employees coercive); *see also* Decker, Privacy Law §§ 2.6, 2.24, 7.19.

[68] *See, e.g.,* NLRB v. J.P. Stevens & Co., 563 F.2d 8 (2d Cir. 1977) (union organizer's motel room illegally placed under electronic surveillance by employer); *see also* Decker, Privacy Law §§ 2.6, 2.24, 7.20.

[69] *See, e.g.,* 29 U.S.C. §§ 2001–2009 (1988) (Employee Polygraph Protection Act of 1988); *see also* Decker, Privacy Law §§ 2.20B, 2.35, 6.19.

[70] *See, e.g.,* Pa. Cons. Stat. Ann. tit. 18 § 7321 (Purdon 1983) (Pennsylvania's polygraph protection act); *see* Decker, Privacy Law § 2.35.

§ 11.20   —Work Performance Surveillance: Employee Authorization Form

Where workplace surveillance is used, the following employee authorization should be considered:

FORM 11.20(1)
WORK PERFORMANCE SURVEILLANCE: EMPLOYEE AUTHORIZATION

As an employment condition, I understand that the Company may periodically survey, monitor, or review my work performance by using mechanical, electronic, or other methods. To this work performance surveillance, I expressly consent.

_____

Employee Signature

_____

Date

§ 11.21   Employee Polygraph Protection Act of 1988

The Employee Polygraph Protection Act of 1988 (EPPA) prohibits most private employers from using any polygraph examinations either for pre-employment screening or during the course of employment.[71] Exempted from EPPA's provisions are federal, state, and local government employers. There are also exemptions covering national defense and federal government security contractors. For example, Department of Defense contractors and their employees may have polygraph examinations administered to them by the federal government in the performance of intelligence functions.

Private sector employers may still request that employees take polygraph examinations during an ongoing investigation of economic loss or injury involving a theft or embezzlement. However, the examination's result or the employee's refusal to take the examination must be accompanied by additional supporting evidence before an employer can commence an adverse employment action against the employee. EPPA also contains similar exemptions for security and pharmaceutical employers. Employers are required to post notices of EPPA's protections at the workplace and violations will subject employers to fines of up to $10,000.

In dealing with EPPA, questions regarding preemption and comparable state polygraph examination legislation may arise. It may have to be determined whether state statutory provisions that impose stricter standards over a polygraph examination's administration or use control over a conflicting federal provision,

---

[71] 29 U.S.C. §§ 2001–2009 (1988) (Employee Polygraph Protection Act of 1988); *see also* Decker, Privacy Law §§ 2.20B, 2.35, 6.19.

even though EPPA specifically provides that it shall not preempt any state statute, local law, or any negotiated collective bargaining agreement's provision that prohibits polygraph examinations or that is more restrictive in its provisions than EPPA.

§ 11.22   —Employee Polygraph Protection Act Procedures

Incident specific use of polygraph examinations by private employers is permitted provided that the following requirements are *all* met.[72]

1.   The polygraph examination may be employed only as part of an ongoing investigation of an incident involving economic loss or injury to the employer

2.   The employee requested to take the polygraph examination must have had access to the matter under investigation

3.   The employer must be able to articulate some basis, in addition to access, to support a reasonable suspicion of the employee's involvement in the matter under investigation and

4.   The employer must follow all procedures for the pre-examination, examination-phase, and post-examination administration of the polygraph examination.

§ 11.23   —Employee Polygraph Protection Act Forms

The Employee Polygraph Protection Act (EPPA) requires the employer to obtain a statement from the examinee before the polygraph examination is administered.[73] The statement must be given to the examinee at least 48 hours prior to the examination to provide the examinee with adequate pre-examination notice of the specific incident or activity that is being investigated. It also affords the employee with sufficient time prior to the examination to obtain and consult with an attorney or an employee representative. The following form should be considered by the employer for this use:

---

[72] *Id.*

[73] *Id.*

FORM 11.23(1)
EMPLOYEE POLYGRAPH PROTECTION ACT

Company's name: _____

To: _____
(Examinee's name)

   The Company is investigating an incident or activity that has resulted in economic loss or injury to the Company. An investigation indicates that you had access to the property that is the subject of this investigation and that there is a reasonable basis for the Company's suspecting your involvement because of this. The company, therefore, requests that you submit to a polygraph examination pursuant to the detailed statement that is required by the Employee Polygraph Protection Act of 1988.

1.   The specific incident or activity being investigated by the Company involves the following: _____

_____

_____

_____

_____

2.   As a result of the incident or activity now under investigation by the Company, the Company suffered the following economic loss or injury: _____

_____

_____

_____

_____

3.   The specific basis for the Company's suspicion that you may have been involved in the incident or activity under investigation is as follows: _____

_____

_____

_____

_____

                              _____
                              (Examinee signature)

_____
(Date)

Before being examined, the individual must be given a statement of his or her rights under the Employee Polygraph Protection Act of 1988 (EPPA) and must have the statement read aloud to him or her. Set forth below is the format of what must be given to the examinee and read aloud.

FORM 11.23(2)
EMPLOYEE POLYGRAPH PROTECTION ACT

Your rights under the Employee Polygraph Protection Act of 1988 (EPPA) are as follows:

Section 8(b) of EPPA, and the Department of Labor's regulations require that you be given the following information before taking a polygraph examination:

1. The polygraph examination area [does] [does not] contain a two-way mirror, a camera, or other device through which you may be observed

2. Another device, such as those used in conversation or recording [will] [will not] be used during the polygraph examination

3. Both you and the employer have the right, with the other's knowledge, to record electronically the entire polygraph examination

4. You have the right to terminate the polygraph examination at any time

5. You have the right and will be given the opportunity to review all questions to be asked during the polygraph examination

6. You may not be asked questions in a manner that degrades or needlessly intrudes your personal privacy

7. You may not be asked any questions concerning:

    a. Religious beliefs or opinions

    b. Beliefs regarding racial matters

    c. Political beliefs or affiliations

    d. Matters relating to sexual behavior, beliefs, affiliations, opinions, or lawful activities regarding unions or labor organizations

8. The polygraph examination may not be conducted if there is sufficient written evidence by a physician that you are suffering from a medical or psychological condition or undergoing treatment that might cause abnormal responses during the examination

9. The polygraph examination is not and cannot be required as an employment condition

10. The employer may not terminate, discipline, deny employment or promotion, or otherwise discriminate against you based on the analysis of a polygraph examination or based on your refusal to take the examination without additional evidence that would support the employer's adverse action

11. In connection with an ongoing investigation, the additional evidence required for an employer to take adverse action against you, including termination, may be:

    a. Evidence that you had access to the property that is subject of the investigation, together with

    b. The evidence supporting the employer's reasonable suspicion that you were involved in the incident or activity under investigation

12. Any statement made by you before or during the polygraph examination may serve as additional supporting evidence for an adverse employment action and any admission of criminal conduct by you may be transmitted to an appropriate government law enforcement agency

13. Information acquired from a polygraph examination may be disclosed by the examiner or by the employer only:

    a. To you or any other person specifically designated in writing by you to receive this information

    b. To the employer that requested the polygraph examination

    c. To a court, government agency, arbitrator, or mediator that obtains a court order

    d. To a U.S. Department of Labor official when specifically designated in writing by you to receive this information

14. Information acquired from a polygraph examination may be disclosed by the employer to an appropriate governmental agency without a court order where, and only insofar as, the information disclosed is an admission of criminal conduct

15. If any of your rights or protections under the law are violated, you have the right to file a complaint with the Wage and Hour Division of the U.S. Department of Labor, or to take action in court against the employer

16. Employers who violate this law are liable to the affected examinee who may recover legal or equitable relief as may be appropriate, including employment reinstatement, promotion, payment of lost wages and benefits, and reasonable costs, including attorney's fees

17. The Secretary of Labor may also bring action to restrain violations of EPPA or may assess civil money penalties against the employer

18. Your rights under EPPA may not be waived either voluntarily or involuntarily by contract or otherwise, except as part of a written statement to a pending action or complaint under EPPA and agreed to and signed by parties.

   I acknowledge that I have received a copy of the above notice and that it has been read to me by the Company.

_____
(Signature)

_____
(Date)

Set forth below is a written notice that must be provided to an examinee before administering a polygraph examination under the Employee Polygraph Protection Act of 1988 (EPPA).

FORM 11.23(3)
EMPLOYEE POLYGRAPH PROTECTION ACT

Notice of Polygraph Examination

Company's name: _____

To: _____
(Examinee's name)

   You are hereby notified that you have been scheduled to take a polygraph examination at the following time and location:

   Date and Time: _____

   Location: _____

   _____

   You have the right to obtain and consult with an attorney or an employee representative before each phase of the examination process, although you do not have the right to bring your representative with you into the examination room.

   You have the right to refuse to be examined or to terminate the examination at any time, although failure to take the examination may itself be considered by the Company in the resolution of the matter under investigation by it.

   The nature and the characteristics of the examination that you will undergo and the instruments involved are as follows: _____

   _____

   _____

Accompanying this notice of the polygraph examination are several other statements, including a statement of your rights, a statement of the basis for the Company's request that you be tested, and a list of the questions to be used in the examination itself. You and your attorney or representative should carefully review and study these documents.

_____
(Signature)

_____
(Date)

Under the Employee Polygraph Protection Act of 1988 (EPPA), the polygraph examiner cannot ask any question that was not presented to the examinee in advance of the examination. The questions must be provided to the examinee 48 hours or more before the examination is administered. Set forth below is a form that should be considered for this use.

FORM 11.23(4)
EMPLOYEE POLYGRAPH PROTECTION ACT

Notice of Questions To Be Asked
During Your Polygraph Examination

Company's name: _____

To: _____
(Examinee's name)

The attached list of questions includes every question or inquiry that you will be asked in your upcoming polygraph examination. You will not be asked in your upcoming polygraph examination any question that is not on the attached list. These questions are furnished to you for your review before the examination in accordance with the Employee Polygraph Protection Act of 1988 (EPPA).

I certify that I received this document along with its attachment of the list of questions referred to above at:

Time: _____

Date: _____

_____
(Signature)

§ 11.24   Literature Solicitation and Distribution

Employee interests are affected through an employer's regulation of workplace literature solicitation and distribution.[74] This regulation or restriction curtails certain aspects of employee constitutional speech, association, and right to information. Regulation may cause employees to refrain from exercising union organizational rights under federal[75] and state[76] labor relations statutes.

These employee interests normally arise when literature is brought into or distributed at the workplace by employees or third parties. This may extend to prohibiting the reading of "adult" literature, soliciting donations for a charitable organization during lunch periods, and so forth.

§ 11.25   —Drafting

Federal and state labor relations boards have set certain presumptions regarding employer rules regulating union solicitation and distribution.[77] Employer literature solicitation and distribution rules are generally valid absent a showing of the employer's antiunion animus or discrimination. It is presumptively valid for an employer to promulgate a rule prohibiting:

1.   Union solicitation by employees in work areas during working time[78]
2.   Solicitation by employees during nonworking time, even if on employer property[79]
3.   Literature distribution by employees in work areas at any time[80]
4.   Literature distribution by employees in nonwork areas during nonwork time[81]

---

[74] *See* Decker, Privacy Law § 7.21.

[75] *See, e.g.,* 29 U.S.C. §§ 151–169 (1988) (National Labor Relations Act); *see also* Decker, Privacy Law § 2.6.

[76] *See, e.g.,* Pa. Stat. Ann. tit. 43, §§ 211.1–211.11 (Purdon 1991) (Pennsylvania Labor Relations Act); *see also* Decker, Privacy Law § 2.24.

[77] *See generally* J. Feerick, H. Baer & J. Arfa, NLRB Representation Elections—Law, Practice & Procedure § 3.3 (2d ed. 1985); *see also* Decker, Privacy Law § 7.21.

[78] *See* Veeder-Root Co., 192 N.L.R.B. 973 (1971).

[79] *See* Peyton Packing Co., 49 N.L.R.B. 828 (1943), *enforced,* 142 F.2d 1009 (5th Cir. 1944); *but see* House of Mosaics, Inc., 215 N.L.R.B. 704 (1974) (where a no-solicitation rule in the building at any time was held lawful, since evidence showing that it was nondiscriminatory and promulgated for disciplinary reasons overcame the invalidity presumption).

[80] *See* Rockingham Sleepwear, Inc., 188 N.L.R.B. 698 (1971), *enforced,* 80 L.R.R.M. (BNA) 180 (4th Cir. 1972).

[81] *See* Republic Aviation Corp. v. NLRB, 324 U.S. 793 (1945); Stoddard-Quirk Mfg. Co., 138 N.L.R.B. 615 (1962).

§ 11.26   —Sample Policies

The following examples should be considered in drafting literature solicitation and distribution policies:

POLICY 11.26(1)
LITERATURE SOLICITATION AND DISTRIBUTION POLICY

Solicitation, distribution of literature, or trespassing by nonemployees on these premises are prohibited.[82]

POLICY 11.26(2)
LITERATURE SOLICITATION AND DISTRIBUTION POLICY

Distribution of advertising material, handbills, or other literature in working areas[83] of this plant is prohibited at any time.

POLICY 11.26(3)
LITERATURE SOLICITATION AND DISTRIBUTION POLICY

Solicitation by an employee of another employee is prohibited while either the person doing the soliciting or the person being solicited is on working time. Working time is the period when an employee is required to perform his or her job duties.[84]

---

[82] *See* Erie Marine, Inc., 192 N.L.R.B. 793 (1971), *enforced,* 465 F.2d 104 (3d Cir. 1972); Stoddard-Quirk Mfg. Co., 138 N.L.R.B. 615 (1962).

[83] *See* Eastex, Inc., 215 N.L.R.B. 271 (1974), *enforced,* 550 F.2d 198 (5th Cir.), *petition for reh'g denied,* 556 F.2d 1280 (5th Cir. 1977), *aff'd,* 437 U.S. 1045 (1978) (term "working areas" is that portion of a facility where production is actually performed).

[84] *See* Essex Int'l, Inc., 211 N.L.R.B. 749, 750 (1974).